HIGH COURT
CASE SUMMARIES

BUSINESS ASSOCIATIONS

Keyed to Klein, Ramseyer and Bainbridge's
Casebook on Business Associations,
5th Edition

THOMSON

WEST

Mat #40371016

© 2005 Thomson/West
      610 Opperman Drive
      P.O. Box 64526
      St. Paul, MN 55164–0526
      1–800–328–9352

Printed in the United States of America

ISBN 0–314–16149–X

TEXT IS PRINTED ON 10% POST CONSUMER RECYCLED PAPER

Table of Contents

*

Alphabetical Table of Cases

CHAPTER ONE

Agency

Gorton v. Doty

Instant Facts: Gorton (P) was injured in an automobile accident after Doty (D) loaned her vehicle to Garst to transport Gorton (P) and others to a football game.

Black Letter Rule: An agency relationship results from one person's consent that another will act on his behalf and subject to his control, and the other person's consent so to act.

A. Gay Jenson Farms Co. v. Cargill, Inc.

Instant Facts: The plaintiffs entered into grain contracts with Warren Grain & Seed Co., which was financed and controlled by Cargill, Inc. (D), a separate entity.

Black Letter Rule: A creditor that assumes control of its debtor's business may become liable as principal for the debtor's acts in connection with the business.

Mill Street Church of Christ v. Hogan

Instant Facts: Hogan (P) was injured after he was hired by a church employee to paint the inside of the church.

Black Letter Rule: Implied authority is actual authority that the principal intended the agent to possess and includes such powers as are practically necessary to carry out the delegated duties.

Lind v. Schenley Industries, Inc.

Instant Facts: Lind (P) sued for commissions owed to him under an agreement made with the defendant's sales manager.

Black Letter Rule: Apparent authority need not be authority actually given to an agent as long as the principal's manifestations lead third parties to reasonably believe that the agent possesses authority to act on the principal's behalf.

Three-Seventy Leasing Corp. v. Ampex Corp.

Instant Facts: Three–Seventy Leasing Corp. (P) executed a document provided by an Ampex Corp. (D) representative for the purchase of computer leasing equipment, but Ampex (D) never executed the document.

Black Letter Rule: An agent has apparent authority sufficient to bind the principal when the principal's acts would lead a reasonably prudent person to suppose that the agent had the authority he purports to exercise.

Watteau v. Fenwick

Instant Facts: Humble operated Fenwick's (D) tavern under Humble's name and credit and purchased goods from Watteau (P) without Fenwick's (D) express authority.

Black Letter Rule: When a principal is undisclosed to third parties, the actions taken by an agent in furtherance of the principal's usual and ordinary business binds the principal.

Kidd v. Thomas A. Edison, Inc.

Instant Facts: Kidd (P) entered into a singing contract with Fuller, as was typical in the industry, although Fuller had no actual authority to bind his principal.

Black Letter Rule: If a conduct custom is established in an industry, an agent acting within that industry possesses inherent authority to act on all such matters.

Nogales Serv. Ctr. v. Atlantic Richfield Co.

Instant Facts: Atlantic Richfield Co. (D) refused to extend a per-gallon fuel discount to NSC (D), even though the defendant's truck-stop financing manager orally agreed to it.

Black Letter Rule: Inherent authority exists if a general agent, as one authorized to conduct a series of transactions involving a continuity of service, does something similar to what he is authorized to do, even if he was not actually authorized to do it.

Botticello v. Stefanovicz

Instant Facts: Botticello (P) agreed with Walter Stefanovicz (D) to lease property that he owned as tenants in common with his wife, and the lease contained an option to purchase.

Black Letter Rule: Ratification requires affirmance by a person with full knowledge of the material terms of a prior act which did not bind him but which was done or professedly done on his account.

Hoddeson v. Koos Bros.

Instant Facts: Hoddeson (P) paid money for the purchase of furniture to an impostor salesperson in Koos Bros. (D) furniture store.

Black Letter Rule: If a business proprietor by his dereliction of duty enables one who is not his agent to act conspicuously as such and to transact the proprietor's business with a patron in the establishment, estoppel prevents the proprietor from defensively availing himself of the impostor's lack of authority in order to escape liability for the customer's consequential loss.

Atlantic Salmon A/S v. Curran

Instant Facts: Curran (D) purchased imported salmon from the plaintiffs, and the plaintiffs sought to recover unpaid money from Curran (D) individually.

Black Letter Rule: An agent is personally liable for his principal's debts if he fails to disclose to a third party that he is acting as an agent and his principal's identity.

Humble Oil & Refining Co. v. Martin

Instant Facts: Martin (P) was injured by a vehicle that rolled away from the service station owned by Humble Oil & Refining Co. (D), but operated by another person under contract.

Black Letter Rule: One who maintains control over a business enterprise's operation, even if it entrusts the operation to one acting without meaningful discretion, is liable as a principal for the negligence of those entrusted with his business.

Hoover v. Sun Oil Co.

Instant Facts: Hoover (P) was injured when his car caught fire while a service station employee was fueling it.

Black Letter Rule: Agency arises if a principal retains the right to control the details of the day-to-day operation of the agent's business.

Murphy v. Holiday Inns, Inc.

Instant Facts: Murphy (P) slipped and fell in a motel owned and operated by a franchisee under a license agreement.

Black Letter Rule: If a franchise contract so regulates the activities of the franchisee as to vest the franchiser with control within the definition of agency, the agency relationship arises even if the parties expressly deny it.

Billops v. Magness Constr. Co.

Instant Facts: Billops (P) was wrongfully treated by a ballroom employee at a facility franchised by Hilton (D).

Black Letter Rule: A franchise agreement establishes an agency relationship if the franchisor maintains the right to control the franchisee's business operations or manifests to a third person that the franchisee has authority to bind the franchisor.

Ira S. Bushey & Sons, Inc. v. United States

Instant Facts: A drunken sailor employed by the U.S. Coast Guard caused damage to the plaintiff's drydock while returning to the ship from leave.

Black Letter Rule: Respondeat superior imposes liability on an employer for an employee's conduct if the employer created the risk that the conduct would occur.

Manning v. Grimsley

Instant Facts: Grimsley (D) threw a baseball at Manning (P) in response to Manning's (P) heckling at a baseball game.

Black Letter Rule: To recover from an employer for an assault committed by its employee, the plaintiff must show that the employee's assault was in response to the plaintiff's conduct which was presently interfering with the employee's ability to perform his duties successfully.

Arguello v. Conoco, Inc.

Instant Facts: Several Hispanic plaintiffs were treated improperly in stores owned or branded by Conoco, Inc. (D).

Black Letter Rule: A master is not liable for his servants' intentional acts if they occurred beyond the servants' scope of employment.

Majestic Realty Assoc., Inc. v. Toti Contracting Co.

Instant Facts: Majestic Realty Associates, Inc. (P) suffered property damage to its building caused by the negligent demolition of an adjacent building.

Black Letter Rule: Ordinarily, if a person engages a contractor, who conducts an independent business by means of his own employees, to do work not itself a nuisance, the person is not liable for the contractor's negligent acts in performing the contract.

Reading v. Regem

Instant Facts: Reading (P) obtained payments for accompanying unlawful contraband past civilian police checkpoints while employed by the British army.

Black Letter Rule: A servant is accountable to his master for profits he obtains because of his position, if the servant takes advantage of his position and violates his duty of good faith and honesty to make the profit for himself.

Gen. Auto. Mfg. Co. v. Singer

Instant Facts: Singer (D), while employed by General Automotive Manufacturing Co. (P), secretly concealed profits earned by accepting personal orders from the plaintiff's customers.

Black Letter Rule: An agent owes his principal the duty of good faith and loyalty not to act adversely to his principal's business interests in the furtherance of his own.

Town & Country House & Home Serv., Inc. v. Newbery

Instant Facts: Newbery (D) and other defendants established a competing housekeeping business using methods and techniques similar to those the plaintiff had developed.

Black Letter Rule: A business proprietor may not solicit his former employer's customers who are not openly engaged in business in advertised locations or whose availability as patrons cannot readily be ascertained, but whose trade and patronage have been secured by years of business effort, advertising, and the expenditure of time and money.

Gorton v. Doty

(Injured Passenger) v. *(Vehicle Owner)*

69 P.2d 136 (Idaho 1937)

PERMISSION TO DRIVE ONE'S VEHICLE CREATES AN AGENCY RELATIONSHIP

■ **INSTANT FACTS** Gorton (P) was injured in an automobile accident after Doty (D) loaned her vehicle to Garst to transport Gorton (P) and others to a football game.

■ **BLACK LETTER RULE** An agency relationship results from one person's consent that another will act on his behalf and subject to his control, and the other person's consent so to act.

■ **PROCEDURAL BASIS**

On appeal to review a judgment for the plaintiff.

■ **FACTS**

Gorton (P), a high school football player, was transported to a game at another school in a private vehicle owned by Doty (D) but driven by Garst, Gorton's (P) football coach. The day before the game, Doty (D) asked Garst if he had enough vehicles to transport the players and offered the use of her vehicle provided the coach drove it. She received no compensation for the use of her vehicle, but the school district paid the gasoline expenses. Doty (D) did not employ or compensate Garst while he used her vehicle. On the way to the game, the vehicle was involved in an accident, and Gorton (P) was injured. Gorton (P) sued Doty (D) to recover for his personal injuries and medical expenses. The jury entered a verdict awarding Gorton (P) damages, and the court denied the defendant's motion for a new trial. Doty (D) appealed.

■ **ISSUE**

Is an agency relationship created when one loans her vehicle to another on the condition that the other drive the vehicle?

■ **DECISION AND RATIONALE**

(Judge Undisclosed) Yes. Agency "is the relationship which results from the manifestation of consent by one person to another that the other shall act on his behalf and subject to his control, and consent by the other so to act." Agency takes on three separate forms—a principal-agent relationship, a master-servant relationship, and an employer-employee or independent contractor relationship. Because Doty (D) and Garst exchanged no compensation, the latter two forms are not at issue. A principal-agent relationship arises not only when one transacts business for another, but also when one is generally authorized to "manage some affair for another." Here, Doty (D) volunteered the use of her vehicle upon the express condition that Garst drive it. Although she could have driven the vehicle herself, she specifically and exclusively authorized Garst to drive it in order to supply the transportation needed for the football team. Doty (D) manifested her consent to permit Garst to act on her behalf, and Garst consented to do so. Regardless of whether the parties executed a contract or paid compensation, Garst acted as Doty's (D) agent. Further, when a driver exercises control over another's vehicle, whether the owner is present or not, the driver's permissive use of the vehicle establishes a prima facie case of agency. The jury's conclusion that Garst acted as Doty's (D) agent was reasonable. Affirmed.

■ DISSENT

(Budge, J.). The evidence does not establish an agency relationship between Doty (D) and Garst. Agency requires a specific undertaking on behalf of another and passive permission is not sufficient. Doty (D) merely loaned her vehicle to Garst as a kind gesture to provide the necessary transportation for the football team. That Doty (D) conditioned the vehicle's use on Garst's agreement to drive merely ensured that none of the players would drive her vehicle. Although no contractual relationship existed, holding Garst to be Doty's (D) agent imposes liability on her for each act committed by Garst as if Doty (D) had committed it herself. Garst was a mere gratuitous bailee, not Doty's (D) agent.

Analysis:

Many states provide by statute that a driver of another's vehicle is presumed to be acting as the owner's agent. The owner may rebut this presumption only with sufficient evidence that the driver was not his agent, such as through evidence that the driver acted without the owner's express or implied permission or that the vehicle was stolen. Thus, if a person is injured in an automobile accident, the burden of proving the owner's liability shifts away from the injured plaintiff to the vehicle owner.

■ CASE VOCADULARY

AGENCY: A fiduciary relationship created by express or implied contract or by law, in which one party (the agent) may act on behalf of another party (the principal) and bind that other party by words or actions.

AGENT: One who is authorized to act for or in place of another; a representative.

BAILEE: A person who receives personal property from another as a bailment.

BAILMENT: A delivery of personal property by one person (the bailor) to another (the bailee) for a certain purpose under an express or implied-in-fact contract.

PRINCIPAL: One who authorizes another to act on his or her behalf as an agent.

A. Gay Jenson Farms Co. v. Cargill, Inc.

(*Local Farmer*) v. (*Grain Company*)
309 N.W.2d 285 (Minn. 1981)

A CREDITOR WHO CONTROLS ITS DEBTOR'S BUSINESS OPERATIONS IS LIABLE FOR THE DEBTOR'S DEBTS

■ **INSTANT FACTS** The plaintiffs entered into grain contracts with Warren Grain & Seed Co., which was financed and controlled by Cargill, Inc. (D), a separate entity.

■ **BLACK LETTER RULE** A creditor that assumes control of its debtor's business may become liable as principal for the debtor's acts in connection with the business.

■ **PROCEDURAL BASIS**

On appeal to review a judgment for the plaintiffs.

■ **FACTS**

Warren Grain & Seed Co. operated a grain elevator whereby it purchased and stored grain from A. Gay Jenson Farms Co. (P) and other local farmers for resale on the Minneapolis Grain Exchange. Seeking financial assistance, Warren entered into a financing agreement with Cargill, Inc. (D) to loan Warren money for its operations. Pursuant to the agreement, Warren paid its operating expenses with checks drawn from Cargill's (D) bank account, but in both Warren's and Cargill's (D) names. In return, proceeds from Warren's grain sales would be deposited in Cargill's bank account. Cargill (D) was also appointed Warren's agent for transacting with the Commodity Credit Corp., and Cargill (D) had a right of first refusal to purchase the grain Warren sold on the grain market. The contract was later renegotiated to require Warren to provide Cargill (D) annual financing statements so that Cargill (D) could audit Warren's accounts. Warren was also precluded from making capital improvements, extending mortgages or other security interests on its capital assets, declaring dividends, or buying or selling stock without Cargill's (D) permission. Shortly after the parties executed the renegotiated contract, Cargill (D) executives visited Warren's facility to examine its annual statement, accounts receivable, inventory, and other financial data, informing Warren that Cargill (D) would give it periodic recommendations concerning expected improvements. Three years later, Cargill (D) entered into a separate contract with Warren, whereby Warren would serve as Cargill's (D) agent for developing a new type of wheat. Warren entered into contracts on Cargill's (D) behalf with farmers who would agree to grow the wheat and would be paid directly by Cargill (D). A year later, Warren arranged a similar contract for sunflower seeds. Over the next few years, the parties modified the agreement to increase the loan from Cargill (D) to Warren. At that time, Warren was selling approximately ninety percent of its grain exclusively to Cargill (D). Nonetheless, Warren's debts continued to exceed its Cargill (D) credit line. Cargill (D) notified Warren that because it was using Cargill's (D) funds, Cargill (D) was exercising its right to make drastic changes in Warren's operations. Cargill (D) assigned a regional manager to work with Warren on a daily basis and opened a separate checking account in Warren's name with funds drawn from Cargill's (D) bank account. When Warren began experiencing severe financial problems, several farmers who had sold Warren grain were assured by Cargill (D) that Warren's checks would be honored. Eventually, Warren's operations succumbed to financial problems, with Warren owing the plaintiffs $2 million for past grain sales. Unable to collect from Warren, the plaintiffs sued Cargill (D) as the principal. At trial, the jury awarded judgment to the plaintiffs.

■ ISSUE

Is a creditor that assumes control of its debtor's business a principal that is liable on the debtor's contracts?

■ DECISION AND RATIONALE

(Judge Undisclosed) Yes. "Agency is the fiduciary relationship that results from the manifestation of consent by one person to another that the other shall act on his behalf and subject to his control, and consent by the other so to act." Agency need not arise from a formal contract between the principal and agent and need not be understood as an agency at the time both parties give their consent. Instead, once one party gives its consent to another to permit control over one's activities, an agency is created and the principal is liable for the agent's debts. Cargill (D) indicated its consent to Warren when it insisted that Warren implement its recommendations for Warren's operations and internal affairs, establishing Cargill's (D) control. "A creditor who assumes control of his debtor's business may become liable as principal for the acts of the debtor in connection with the business." However, control over a business's purchases and sales is not sufficient to establish agency. De facto control over the management is determinative. Here, Cargill's (D) consistent recommendations to Warren, its rights of first refusal, its power to inspect and audit Warren's financial statements, and its prohibition of mortgages, stock purchases, or dividend declarations indicate Cargill's (D) control over Warren's operations. Warren sold nearly all of its incoming grain to Cargill (D), indicating that the two were not separate enterprises. If Cargill (D) was merely a financier rather than an active participant in Warren's business operations, Cargill (D) would not be liable as a principal. However, because Cargill (D) exercised control over Warren's business decisions, the relationship transcends that of a debtor and creditor. Cargill (D) is liable as Warren's principal. Affirmed.

Analysis:

As indicated by the court's holding, a lender may be liable for a borrower's debts if the lender exhibits control over the borrower's business. While banks and other creditors often engage in lending practices that direct a certain sum of money be used a particular manner, lender liability does not automatically arise. Generally, the lender is liable if its control affects the borrower's management decisions beyond those necessary merely to protect the lender's investment.

■ CASE VOCABULARY

CREDITOR: One to whom a debt is owed; one who gives credit for money of goods.

DEBTOR: One who owes an obligation to another, especially an obligation to pay money.

DE FACTO: Actual; existing in fact; having effect even though not formally or legally recognized.

RIGHT OF FIRST REFUSAL: A potential buyer's contractual right to meet the terms of a third party's offer if the seller intends to accept that offer.

Mill Street Church of Christ v. Hogan

(*Church*) v. (*Painter*)
785 S.W.2d 263 (Ky. Ct. App. 1990)

CONTINUOUS PAST AUTHORIZED ACTS SUFFICIENTLY CONFER IMPLIED AUTHORITY ON AN AGENT

■ **INSTANT FACTS** Hogan (P) was injured after he was hired by a church employee to paint the inside of the church.

■ **BLACK LETTER RULE** Implied authority is actual authority that the principal intended the agent to possess and includes such powers as are practically necessary to carry out the delegated duties.

■ **PROCEDURAL BASIS**

On appeal to review the New Workers' Compensation Board's decision, reversing the Old Workers' Compensation Board's decision denying the plaintiff's benefits.

■ **FACTS**

Mill Street Church of Christ (D) hired the plaintiff's brother, Bill Hogan, to paint the church building. In the past, the Church (D) had hired Bill Hogan to do similar jobs, and had allowed his brother, Sam Hogan (P), to assist him. No longer a member of the Church (D), Sam (P) was not authorized to assist Bill on the present job, and the Church (D) hired a second painter to assist Bill. The Church (D) failed to inform Bill that it had hired a second painter, and Bill painted the majority of the church himself. As he reached a high point on the church, Bill asked a Church (D) Elder about obtaining assistance. The Elder and Bill discussed hiring the Church's (D) recommended helper, but the Elder told Bill that the recommended helper was difficult to reach and that he should hire whomever he chose. Without first consulting the Church (D) Elders, Bill asked Sam (P) to help him paint the remainder of the church. The leg of Sam's (P) ladder broke, and Sam (P) broke his arm. Bill informed a Church (D) Elder of the accident, and the Elder indicated that the church had insurance. The Church (D) paid Bill for the time he spent painting the church, including Sam's (P) time. The Church provided all tools and supplies Bill needed for the job. Sam (P) sought workers' compensation benefits for his injuries. The Old Workers' Compensation Board determined that Sam (P) was not a Church (D) employee and denied his claim. On appeal, the New Workers' Compensation Board reversed, and awarded Sam (P) benefits.

■ **ISSUE**

Does an agent who is told to hire whomever he chooses have implied or apparent authority to hire any person to assist him?

■ **DECISION AND RATIONALE**

(Judge Undisclosed). Yes. Apparent authority is "not actual authority but is the authority the agent is held out by the principal as possessing." Implied authority, however, is "actual authority . . . which the principal actually intended the agent to possess and includes such powers as are practically necessary to carry out the duties actually delegated." In order to establish implied authority, the agent must establish through circumstantial evidence, including the parties' acts and conduct and especially the continuous past conduct between the parties, that the agent reasonably believed the principal wished him to act in a certain manner because he had been similarly authorized in the past. Here, Bill Hogan possessed implied authority to hire Sam (P) to assist him. The Church (D) had authorized Bill to hire Sam (P) when he needed assistance in the past, and the Church (D) informed neither Bill nor Sam (P) that it expected Bill to hire a different person. The Church Elder with whom Bill spoke about gaining assistance informed Bill that he could hire whomever he wished. Because the Church (D) had an interest in ensuring the church was painted well and one person could not adequately paint the structure, Bill needed to hire another person to complete the job. Sam (P) believed that Bill possessed the authority to hire him based on past practices. Sam's (P) hire was further ratified when the Church (D) paid Bill for the time Sam (P) spent on the job. Because Bill possessed implied authority, Sam (P) was a Church (D) employee at the time of his injury. Affirmed.

Analysis:

The distinctions between actual authority, apparent authority, and implied authority can be confusing. The crucial facts distinguishing the three are the knowledge of the parties involved. If an agent knows he has a principal's authority, *actual* authority exists. If actual authority does not exist, but a third party reasonably believes from the principal's actions that authority exists, *apparent* authority is created. Finally, *implied* authority is actual authority that the principal never formally conferred, but that can be inferred based on the authority granted and past conduct between the principal and the agent. If the third party knows that the authority does not in fact exist, any inference of authority is destroyed.

■ CASE VOCABULARY

ACTUAL AUTHORITY: Authority that a principal intentionally confers on an agent, including the authority that the agent reasonably believes he or she has as a result of the agent's dealings with the principal.

APPARENT AUTHORITY: Authority that a third party reasonably believes an agent has, based on the third party's dealings with the principal. Apparent authority can be created by law even when no actual authority has been conferred.

AUTHORITY: The right or permission to act legally on another's behalf; the power delegated by a principal to an agent.

EXPRESS AUTHORITY: Authority given to the agent by explicit agreement, either orally or in writing.

IMPLIED AUTHORITY: Authority given to the agent as a result of the principal's conduct, such as the principal's earlier acquiescence to the agent's actions.

Lind v. Schenley Industries, Inc.

(Sales Manager) v. *(Employer)*

278 F.2d 79 (3d Cir. 1960)

SALES MANAGER HAS APPARENT AUTHORITY TO OFFER PAY INCREASES WHEN CHARGED WITH TRANSFERING INFORMATION AMONG EXECUTIVES

■ **INSTANT FACTS** Lind (P) sued for commissions owed to him under an agreement made with the defendant's sales manager.

■ **BLACK LETTER RULE** Apparent authority need not be authority actually given to an agent as long as the principal's manifestations lead third parties to reasonably believe that the agent possesses authority to act on the principal's behalf.

■ **PROCEDURAL BASIS**

On appeal to review the trial court's entry of a judgment notwithstanding the verdict in favor of the defendant.

■ **FACTS**

Lind (P) sued Park & Tilford Distiller's Corp., which merged into Schenley Industries, Inc. (D), for breach of contract. Lind (P) had worked for Park for many years when Herrfeldt, Park's vice-president, appointed him as an assistant to the metropolitan New York sales manager. After consulting with the New York sales manager upon the vice-president's direction, Lind (P) received a written memorandum informing him that he had been provided the title "District Manager" and that his responsibilities and salary would materially reflect that of a "State Manager." The sales manager orally informed Lind (P) that, in addition to his salary, he would receive a one-percent commission on all sales made by the employees working under his direction. A year later, Lind (P) was transferred from New York to New Jersey to become the defendant's state manager, during which time he received a raise. Finally, five years later, Park transferred Lind (P) back to New York when it terminated his New Jersey position. At no time before the transfer did Lind (P) receive his commission, nor did he request it. Lind (P) sued for breach of contract to recover money allegedly owed to him. At trial, the jury concluded that the sales manager offered to pay Lind (P) one percent of the gross sales of the employees under his direction, that Park caused Lind (P) to believe that the sales manager was authorized to offer the commission, and that Lind (P) was justified in believing the sales manager had such authority. The judge entered a judgment notwithstanding the verdict in favor of the defendant, reasoning that Lind (P) had not demonstrated that the sales manager possessed apparent authority and, even if apparent authority could be found, the contract was not sufficiently definite to entitle Lind (P) to a judgment. In the event of a reversal on appeal, the trial court ordered a new trial.

■ **ISSUE**

Does a sales manager charged with exchanging information between higher executives and lower executives have inherent authority to offer compensation increases?

■ **DECISION AND RATIONALE**

(Biggs, C.J.) Yes. Actual authority is the authority that a principal expressly confers on his agent. Apparent authority, on the other hand, need not be actually given to an agent as long as the manifestations to third parties lead them to reasonably believe that the agent possesses authority to act on the principal's behalf. Additionally, implied authority (also called "inherent authority"), is defined as that authority implicitly conferred by a principal or the authority that an agent under the circumstances would ordinarily possess. Here, the evidence demonstrates that the sales manager had inherent authority to offer Lind (P) a one-percent commission. The sales manager had been charged with relaying information from the higher executives to the lower executives. Furthermore, the vice president directed Lind (P) to discuss his responsibilities and compensation directly with the sales manager, who thereafter offered the commission rate. While the law is not clear on whether Lind (P) was required to change his position in reliance on the promise in order to establish apparent authority, the element was nonetheless established once Lind (P) changed his job position and accepted increased responsibilities. Although it appears the sales manager had no authority to establish salaries or compensation, the sales manager's actual authority has no bearing on apparent authority. The evidence supported the jury's conclusion that Lind (P) reasonably believed the sales manager was authorized to offer him the commission based on the added responsibilities he assumed and his projected annual income, even though the compensation would nearly quadruple his base salary. Reversed and remanded to reinstate the verdict.

■ DISSENT

(Hastie, J.) While the jury's verdict should not have been set aside, the court ignores the trial court's alternative order requiring a new trial because the evidence did not support the verdict. On the evidence, Lind (P) could not have reasonably believed the sales manager was authorized to quadruple his compensation to a level exceeding the compensation paid to the defendant's managers and supervisors. The unreasonableness of Lind's (P) belief is underscored by the fact that although the sales manager had promised him the commission, the company did not pay him the commission for several years and Lind (P) never demanded it. The case should be remanded for a new trial.

Analysis:

The difference between apparent authority and implied authority is often conceptual. Under apparent authority, a principal becomes liable because it has made representations to a third party to suggest that an agent possesses authority to act on the principal's behalf. Apparent authority is also created when an agent's actions are an ordinary and proper extension of the actual authority bestowed on him by his principal. This latter scenario encompasses the rule of implied authority, leaving the line between the two very thin.

■ CASE VOCABULARY

INHERENT AUTHORITY: Authority of an agent arising from the agency relationship.

JUDGMENT NOTWITHSTANDING THE VERDICT: A judgment entered for one party even though a jury verdict has been rendered for the opposing party.

Three-Seventy Leasing Corp. v. Ampex Corp.

(*Leasing Company*) v. (*Computer Manufacturer*)

528 F.2d 993 (5th Cir. 1976)

ABSENT CONTRARY KNOWLEDGE, A SALESPERSON HAS APPARENT AUTHORITY TO BIND HIS PRINCIPAL TO SELL ITS PRODUCTS

■ **INSTANT FACTS** Three–Seventy Leasing Corp. (P) executed a document provided by an Ampex Corp. (D) representative for the purchase of computer leasing equipment, but Ampex (D) never executed the document.

■ **BLACK LETTER RULE** An agent has apparent authority sufficient to bind the principal when the principal's acts would lead a reasonably prudent person to suppose that the agent had the authority he purports to exercise.

■ **PROCEDURAL BASIS**

On appeal to review the district court's judgment for the plaintiff.

■ **FACTS**

Joyce formed Three–Seventy Leasing Corp. (P) to purchase computer software from manufacturers for lease to its customers. Joyce, on behalf of Three–Seventy Leasing (P), engaged in discussions with Kays, on behalf of Ampex Corp. (D), to purchase computer equipment from the defendant. At a meeting involving Joyce, Kays, and Kays' superior at Ampex (D), Joyce was informed that Ampex (D) could sell Three–Seventy Leasing (P) computer equipment only if Three–Seventy Leasing (P) passed the defendant's credit requirements. At approximately the same time, Joyce secured a verbal commitment from a customer to lease six Ampex (D) computer core memories. Thereafter, Kays' superior directed Kays to extend a written contract offer to Joyce providing for the sale of six computer core memories at $100,000 each, with a down payment of $150,000 and the understanding that the equipment would be leased to Joyce's customer. The contract included space for the signature of representatives of Three–Seventy Leasing (P) and Ampex (D). Although Joyce executed the document on behalf of Three–Seventy Leasing (P), no Ampex (D) representative ever signed the contract. The plaintiff sued Ampex (D) for breach of contract, arguing that the contract was an offer to sell that was accepted upon Joyce's signature. Ampex (D) argues that the document was merely a solicitation and that the signed document constituted an offer to purchase that Ampex (D) did not accept. The district court concluded that the document was an enforceable contract without determining whether it was an offer to sell or a solicitation.

■ **ISSUE**

Does an agent have apparent authority sufficient to bind a principal if the principal's acts would lead a reasonably prudent person to suppose that the agent had the authority he purports to exercise?

■ **DECISION AND RATIONALE**

(Judge Undisclosed). Yes. To form a contract, there must be a meeting of the minds expressing agreement to the contract's terms. On its face, the document demonstrates no intention by Ampex (D) to consent to its terms. Similarly, no written or oral evidence demonstrates that Ampex (D) intended to consent to the document at the time Joyce signed it. Without evidence of intent, Ampex (D) cannot be

---

deemed to have consented to the document's terms so that Joyce created an enforceable contract when he signed it. However, after Ampex (D) received Joyce's signed document, Kays' supervisor distributed an inter-office memorandum announcing the agreement between Ampex (D) and Three-Seventy Leasing (P) and directing that Kays was the primary contact through which all Three-Seventy Leasing (P) correspondence should flow. Kays later sent Joyce a letter confirming the delivery dates of the core memories that were the subject of the document. Because Kays had apparent authority to act on behalf of Ampex (D) and the letter to Joyce reasonably constitutes an acceptance of Joyce's signed offer, an enforceable contract was created. "An agent has apparent authority sufficient to bind the principal when the principal acts in such a manner as would lead a reasonably prudent person to suppose that the agent had the authority he purports to exercise." Apparent authority exists when a third party has no reason to believe actual authority does not exist and the authority is exercised in the furtherance of the usual and proper business duties he was employed to perform. Here, Kays was employed as a salesperson, which can reasonably be believed to have authority to sell Ampex's (D) products. None of Ampex's (D) actions would reasonably suggest to Joyce that Kays had no authority. At the direction of Kays' supervisor, he submitted the document to Joyce containing a signature block for Ampex (D) to sign. No corporate officer or director was individually designated on the document and Joyce could reasonably assume Kays was authorized to execute the contract. Also, Joyce understood that all correspondence would be directed through Kays, without any express limitation on his authority to enter into contracts on Ampex's (D) behalf. Without knowledge that only Ampex (D) managers or supervisors could bind the company, Joyce was reasonable in his belief that Kays spoke for the defendant. Under this belief, Kays' letter constituted a valid acceptance of Joyce's signed offer to purchase, creating an enforceable contract. Affirmed.

Analysis:

Generally, an agent's representations cannot create apparent authority. Although Joyce's belief that Kays was authorized to act came primarily from Kays' statements, Kays had apparent authority because Joyce had been informed by Kays' supervisor that all communication with Ampex (D) would go through Kays. Without the supervisor's participation, apparent authority may not have existed.

■ CASE VOCABULARY

ACCEPTANCE: An agreement, either by express act or by implication from conduct, to the terms of an offer so that a binding contract is formed.

CONTRACT: An agreement between two or more parties creating obligations that are enforceable or otherwise recognizable at law.

MEETING OF THE MINDS: Actual assent by both parties to the formation of a contract.

OFFER: A promise to do or refrain from doing some specified thing in the future; a display of willingness to enter into a contract on specified terms, made in a way that would lead a reasonable person to understand that an acceptance, having been sought, will result in a binding contract.

Watteau v. Fenwick

(Cigar Vendor) v. *(Undisclosed Principal)*
1 Q.B. 346 (1892)

UNDISCLOSED TAVERN OWNER IS LIABLE FOR HIS AGENT'S DEBTS OWED TO AN UNKNOWING CIGAR VENDOR

■ **INSTANT FACTS** Humble operated Fenwick's (D) tavern under Humble's name and credit and purchased goods from Watteau (P) without Fenwick's (D) express authority.

■ **BLACK LETTER RULE** When a principal is undisclosed to third parties, the actions taken by an agent in furtherance of the principal's usual and ordinary business binds the principal.

■ **PROCEDURAL BASIS** On appeal to review a judgment entered for the plaintiff.

■ **FACTS**

For years, Watteau (P) had sold cigars and other products on credit to Humble, who operated a tavern. After Humble sold his tavern to Fenwick (D), Humble remained as the manager and operated the tavern in his name, but was not authorized to purchase Watteau's (P) goods on behalf of Fenwick (D). Unaware that Fenwick (D) had purchased the tavern, Watteau (P) continued to sell his goods to Humble on credit. Watteau (P) sued Fenwick (D) to recover the outstanding balance on goods sold to the tavern. The court awarded judgment to Watteau (P).

■ **ISSUE**

Is a principal bound by the acts of an agent who conducts the principal's business under the agent's name and credit, unbeknownst to third parties?

■ **DECISION AND RATIONALE**

(Wills, J.) Yes. A principal is generally liable for his agent's acts when authority to act is usually conferred upon an agent in the course of the principal's business. Generally, such authority, though not actually conferred by the principal, must arise from the principal's actions holding the agent out as his agent. However, if the principal is undisclosed to a third party and the third party is unaware that the person with whom he is dealing is actually an agent serving a principal's interests, apparent authority could not be established. Therefore, only those acts specifically authorized by the principal could bind the principal to a third party. Just as a secret partner in a partnership cannot escape liability for the actions and debts of his active partners, an undisclosed principal may not avoid liability for the actions of an agent who incurs usual and ordinary debts necessary to conduct the principal's business. If the third party knows that he is dealing with an agent, the agent may bind the principal only if he acts with actual authority or the principal otherwise holds the agent out as having authority. Affirmed.

Analysis:

The undisclosed-principal rule appears to contradict traditional notions of contract law. Although a third party freely contracted with an agent, not knowing he was an agent, the principal becomes liable on the contract, even though he was never a party to the contract. In essence, the third party gains a windfall from his contract because, upon breach, he discovers that two parties are liable rather than the one for which he reasonably bargained. Nonetheless, the principal's liability is justified because the third party often relies on the principal's resources, such as physical assets and creditworthiness, which were entrusted to the agent without the third party's knowledge.

■ **CASE VOCABULARY**

SECRET PARTNER: A partner whose connection with the firm is concealed from the public.

SILENT PARTNER: A partner who shares in the profits but who has no active voice in management of the firm and whose existence is often not publicly disclosed.

Kidd v. Thomas A. Edison, Inc.

(Singer) v. *(Recording Equipment Manufacturer)*

239 F. 405 (S.D.N.Y. 1917)

ENTERTAINMENT RECITAL CUSTOMS APPLY TO ADVERTISING RECITALS, ABSENT KNOWLEDGE OF THE DISTINCTIONS

■ **INSTANT FACTS** Kidd (P) entered into a singing contract with Fuller, as was typical in the industry, although Fuller had no actual authority to bind his principal.

■ **BLACK LETTER RULE** If a conduct custom is established in an industry, an agent acting within that industry possesses inherent authority to act on all such matters.

■ PROCEDURAL BASIS

Motion to set aside a verdict for the plaintiff.

■ FACTS

Kidd (P) agreed with Fuller, a Thomas A. Edison, Inc. (D) employee, to perform in touring singing recitals so that the defendant could demonstrate the accuracy and clarity of reproductions created by its recording equipment. Maxwell, an Edison (D) supervisor, entrusted Fuller to locate singing artists, negotiate compensation, arrange travel plans, and prepare a contract to engage the singers. However, Maxwell informed Fuller that Fuller was not to execute the contracts himself, but that Maxwell would review them and their compensation demands and accept the contracts by written letter. Kidd (P) sued Edison (D) for breach of contract, and the judge entered a verdict for the plaintiff. Edison (D) moved to set aside the verdict.

■ ISSUE

Is a principal bound by an agent's minor deviations from his actual authority if third parties were unaware that the agent exceeded his authority in entering into contracts on the principal's behalf?

■ DECISION AND RATIONALE

(Learned Hand, J.) Yes. The extent of one's authority is measured not merely by the words expressed, but also under the circumstances in which the authority was made, including past customs. While the recitals at issue were the first of their kind and differed from touring recitals intended for entertainment purposes, the customary practices of hiring touring singers apply because the distinctions between the two types of recitals were not sufficient to alert the singers that different customs should be followed. Just as with entertainment recitals, the singers were hired to further the promoter's business interests at the promoter's expense. Therefore, the natural understanding is that when Fuller was authorized to engage the singers, he possessed the full authority to do so. However, apparent authority does not necessarily involve estoppel principles. Unlike in torts, where an agent's actions are binding on his principal if committed within the scope of his employment even if they are outside the scope of his actual authority, estoppel does not bind a principal in contract if the agent disregards the principal's specific instructions. It would be unfair to hold the principal liable for misleading the public if his agent deliberately exceeds his actual authority. However, because the defendant here specifically trusted Fuller to exercise his discretion, minor deviations from the actual authority conferred bind the principal once a third party reasonably determines the apparent scope of the agent's authority. Fuller was trusted to organize the recital arrangements without involving Maxwell or others. Because Fuller was the defendant's chosen representative, the defendants reasonably understood him to have the authority to bind the defendant. Motion denied.

Analysis:

The court's opinion is difficult to follow because the court discusses principles of apparent authority, inherent agency, and estoppel. Ultimately holding that apparent authority and estoppel do not apply, the court rested its opinion on inherent agency. Although the Restatement of Agency defines the subtle differences between apparent authority and inherent agency, many courts have interchanged the two principles, as well as estoppel, to reach the same conclusion.

■ CASE VOCABULARY

ESTOPPEL: A bar that prevents one from asserting a claim or right that contradicts what one has said or done before or what has been legally established as true.

INHERENT AUTHORITY: Authority of an agent arising from the agency relationship.

Nogales Serv. Ctr. v. Atlantic Richfield Co.

(Truck Stop Owner) v. *(Fuel Provider)*
126 Ariz. 133, 613 P.2d 293 (1980)

A AGENT WITH ACTUAL AUTHORITY TO EXTEND VARIOUS DISCOUNTS HAS INHERENT AUTHORITY TO OFFER PER–GALLON DISCOUNTS

■ **INSTANT FACTS** Atlantic Richfield Co. (D) refused to extend a per-gallon fuel discount to NSC (D), even though the defendant's truck-stop financing manager orally agreed to it.

■ **BLACK LETTER RULE** Inherent authority exists if a general agent, as one authorized to conduct a series of transactions involving a continuity of service, does something similar to what he is authorized to do, even if he was not actually authorized to do it.

■ **PROCEDURAL BASIS**

On appeal to review a judgment for the defendant.

■ **FACTS**

Cafone and McKenzie were produce brokers in Nogales, Arizona. Realizing that a seasonal facility providing fuel to produce trucks passing through the city would make a profitable business, they approached Atlantic Richfield Co. (ARCO) (D) to finance the construction of a fuel facility and equipment necessary to its operation. Looking to establish a truck stop in the area, ARCO (D) agreed with Cafone's and McKenzie's newly established corporation, Nogales Service Center (NSC) (P), to loan NSC (P) part of the funds it needed to finance the facility. The facility was constructed, but no motel or restaurant was built. The parties also entered into a product agreement whereby NSC (P) agreed to purchase at least fifty percent of its fuel from ARCO (D) and to sell the fuel at a fixed price established by ARCO (D). Because the price that ARCO (D) established was not competitive with other truck stops elsewhere in the state, NSC's (P) truck stop struggled financially. Cafone subsequently agreed to sell his interest in the truck stop to Terpenning. Cafone and Terpenning met with the ARCO (D) manager of truck stop financing to discuss the fixed price problem. At this meeting, the manager allegedly insisted on the construction of a motel at the truck stop and orally agreed on behalf of ARCO (D) to loan NSC (P) the funds to finance the motel in part and to give NSC (P) a one-cent per-gallon discount on all fuel purchased from ARCO (D). With this understanding, Terpenning bought Cafone's interest in NSC (P) and used his personal funds to complete the motel construction. ARCO (D) failed to extend the fuel discount, but it did extend the loan to offset the motel construction expenses. NSC (P) and Terpenning thereafter defaulted on ARCO's (D) loans, and ARCO (D) successfully foreclosed on the truck stop. A counterclaim for breach of contract brought by NSC (P) during the foreclosure action was tried separately. At trial, ARCO (D) argued that its manager never promised to extend the fuel discount and that, if he did, he exceeded his authority. The court instructed the jury that ARCO (D) could be liable for breach of contract only if it concluded that ARCO's (D) officers or authorized agents actually or impliedly represented to NSC (P) that the manager had authority to bind the defendant. Representations from the manager himself were insufficient if he possessed no actual authority from ARCO (D). NSC (P) did not object to this instruction. The court refused, however, to grant NSC's (P) request to instruct the jury that ARCO (D) was liable for the manager's oral representations if the substance of the representations were of a kind "that usually accompany or are incidental to transactions which the agent is authorized to conduct ... if Nogales Service Center reasonably believed that ARCO's employees were authorized to make them, and has no notice that ARCO's employees were not so authorized." The jury returned a verdict for ARCO (D).

■ ISSUE

Does a court err if it refuses to instruct the jury on the distinctions between actual authority, apparent authority, and inherent authority?

■ DECISION AND RATIONALE

(Judge Undisclosed) Yes. The court's instructions covered only the law on actual authority and apparent authority, while the plaintiff's proposed instruction addressed the law of inherent authority. Unlike actual authority or apparent authority, inherent authority exists without actual consent by the principal or manifestations to a third person. Under inherent authority, a principal is liable for the actions of an employee or servant in three situations. First, if a general agent "authorized to conduct a series of transactions involving a continuity of service" does something similar to what he is authorized to do, the principal is liable even if the agent was not authorized. Second, if a general agent is not authorized to act because of the agent's improper motive, but would be authorized to act with proper motives, the principal is liable. Finally, if an agent is authorized to sell or otherwise dispose of a principal's goods, but deviates from the manner in which they are to be disposed, the principal is liable. These situations impose liability on a principal not because he has represented an agent's authority to a third person, but because the agent's actions are generally in furtherance of the principal's business interests and subject to the principal's control. Under such circumstances, the principal is better suited to bear the risk of loss arising from the agent's actions. Here, ARCO's (D) manager was generally authorized to handle problems related to investments and discounts with ARCO's (D) truck stops. He had been authorized to extend a number of discounts on ARCO's (D) behalf, though not of the kind extended to NSC (P). Since NSC (P) had no reason to believe the manager was not so authorized and the per-gallon discount falls within the general scope of the manager's duties and powers, the manager possessed inherent authority. However, because NSC (P) failed to object to the trial court's instruction with specificity, the court committed no error in refusing NSC's (D) inherent authority instruction. Affirmed.

Analysis: Holding a principal liable for the unauthorized actions of its agent, even though it made no representations to a third party, has been justified primarily on two grounds. First, the principal is generally in a better position to bear the risk of loss from the agent's actions, in terms of both financial responsibility and deterrence. Second, inherent agency ensures a free flow of commerce by refusing to burden third parties with the task of ensuring that the person with whom they deal possesses the authority he reasonably claims to possess.

■ CASE VOCABULARY

GENERAL AGENT: An agent authorized to transact all the principal's business of a particular kind or in a particular place.

Botticello v. Stefanovicz

(Land Purchaser) v. *(Landowner)*
177 Conn. 22, 411 A.2d 16 (1979)

RECEIPT OF RENT MONEY UNDER A LEASE WITH AN OPTION TO PURCHASE DOES NOT CONSTITUTE RATIFICATION OF THE LEASE

■ **INSTANT FACTS** Botticello (P) agreed with Walter Stefanovicz (D) to lease property that he owned as tenants in common with his wife, and the lease contained an option to purchase.

■ **BLACK LETTER RULE** Ratification requires affirmance by a person with full knowledge of the material terms of a prior act which did not bind him but which was done or professedly done on his account.

■ **PROCEDURAL BASIS**

On appeal to review a judgment for the plaintiff.

■ **FACTS**

Mary (D) and Walter (D) Stefanovicz owned property as tenants in common. Botticello (P) desired to purchase the property and approached Walter (D) about his asking price. Walter informed him that he would sell the property for $100,000. Several months later, Botticello (P) counteroffered $75,000. Mary (D) indicated that she would not sell the property at that price. Thereafter, Botticello (P) and Walter (D) agreed to lease the property for $85,000, which Mary (D) stated was her lowest selling price. The lease agreement contained a purchase option. With counsels' assistance, Walter (D) and Botticello (P) executed a lease contract, but neither attorney was aware of Mary's (D) interest as a tenant in common. Botticello (P) took possession of the property, made improvements on it, and sought to exercise his purchase option. When the defendants refused to sell him the property, Botticello (P) sued for breach of contract, seeking specific performance and damages. The trial court ordered specific performance on the option, finding that although Mary (D) was not a party to the contract, Walter (D) acted as her agent at all times relating to the contract.

■ **ISSUE**

Is a party bound by an agreement that a third party alleges the other party ratified, even if the other party did not have full knowledge of the material terms?

■ **DECISION AND RATIONALE**

(Judge Undisclosed) No. Agency requires "a manifestation from a principal that an agent will act for him, acceptance by the agent of the undertaking, and an undertaking between the parties that the principal will be in control of the undertaking." Neither marital status nor joint property ownership alone establish agency. Here, the evidence does not establish agency. Although Mary (D) indicated she would not sell the property for less than $85,000, no evidence suggests that Mary (D) actually agreed to sell the property to the plaintiff. Also, although Walter (D) tended to most of the family's business affairs, he never executed any documents as Mary's (D) agent. Whenever deeds, mortgages, or other legal documents required a signature, Mary (D) signed them on her own behalf. Walter (D) was not Mary's (D) agent. Mary (D) did not ratify the contract by her subsequent conduct in accepting payments from the plaintiff and permitting him to make improvements on the property. Ratification requires "the affirmance by a person" with full knowledge of the material terms "of a prior act which did not bind him but which was done or professedly done on his account." The evidence fails to demonstrate that Mary (D) intended to ratify the contract or that she was aware of its material terms. At most, the evidence shows that Mary (D) was aware that the plaintiff possessed the property, that she was receiving rental payments for the plaintiff's use and possession, and that she had an interest in the property. This evidence does not show that Mary (D) intended to subject her property interest to the purchase option. Further, the receipt of rent money from Botticello (P) does not constitute a ratification of the agreement, because Walter (D) never contended he was acting on Mary's (D) behalf. Because Walter (D) was a proper party to the contract, his property interest may be subject to specific performance or damages, but Mary's (D) interest remains unaffected. Reversed and remanded.

Analysis:

Receipt of a contract's benefits is generally sufficient to establish ratification, even if the party receiving the benefits was not a party to the contract. However, if agency is not established and the evidence supports an interpretation of the contract that does not support ratification, ratification will not be established. Thus, if the contract had been a purchase agreement for the property, rather than a lease with an option to purchase, Mary (D) would likely have been bound by the purchase agreement if she accepted the payments with the understanding that Botticello (P) intended to purchase the property.

■ CASE VOCABULARY

RATIFICATION: A person's binding adoption of an act already completed but either not done in a way that originally produced a legal obligation or done by a third party having at the time no authority to act as the person's agent.

SPECIFIC PERFORMANCE: A court-ordered remedy that requires precise fulfillment of a legal or contractual obligation when monetary damages are inappropriate or inadequate, as when the sale of real estate or a rare article is involved.

TENANTS IN COMMON: A tenancy by two or more persons, in equal or unequal undivided shares, each person having an equal right to possess the whole property but no right of survivorship.

Hoddeson v. Koos Bros.

(Shopper) v. *(Furniture Store)*

47 N.J.Super. 224, 135 A.2d 702 (N.J. Super. Ct. App. Div. 1957)

PROPRIETOR IS ESTOPPED FROM CLAIMING LACK OF AUTHORITY IF REASONABLE DILIGENCE COULD HAVE PREVENTED THE ACTIONS

■ **INSTANT FACTS** Hoddeson (P) paid money for the purchase of furniture to an impostor salesperson in Koos Bros. (D) furniture store.

■ **BLACK LETTER RULE** If a business proprietor by his dereliction of duty enables one who is not his agent to act conspicuously as such and to transact the proprietor's business with a patron in the establishment, estoppel prevents the proprietor from defensively availing himself of the impostor's lack of authority in order to escape liability for the customer's consequential loss.

■ **PROCEDURAL BASIS**

On appeal to review a judgment for the plaintiff.

■ **FACTS**

Hoddeson (P) found bedroom furniture she wished to purchase while she was shopping at Koos Bros. (D). Hoddeson's (P) mother-in-law gave her the money to buy the furniture. Returning to the defendant's store to purchase the furniture, Hoddeson (P) was greeted by a Koos Bros. (D) employee, who guided her to the specific bedroom furniture she wished to purchase. After paying for the furniture, the employee informed Hoddeson (P) that the items were not in stock and that the items would be delivered to her when the store received them. Hoddeson (P) left the store without a receipt. The defendant never delivered the furniture and claimed no record of receiving payment. At trial, neither Hoddeson (P) nor any other witnesses were able to identify the salesperson to whom the money was paid. The defendant argued that the plaintiff had paid the money to an imposter in the store without the defendant's knowledge.

■ **ISSUE**

Does an imposter in a defendant's store possess sufficient apparent authority to bind the defendant?

■ **DECISION AND RATIONALE**

(Judge Undisclosed) No. Apparent authority requires a manifestation of a principal as to the authority conferred upon its agent and cannot arise out of the agent's manifestations. Here, the evidence demonstrates no affirmative manifestation as to the imposter's authority sufficient to establish apparent authority. Yet, principles of estoppel may apply to bar the defendant from denying the authority of a person posing as a salesperson in its store. A storeowner owes its customers not merely a duty to keep its premises free of objects that may result in injury, but also to monitor its business carefully to ensure the safety and security of its customers from all hazards that an ordinarily prudent customer would not recognize. "Where a proprietor of a place of business by his dereliction of duty enables one who is not his agent conspicuously to act as such and ostensibly to transact the proprietor's business with a patron in the establishment . . . , the law will not permit the proprietor defensively to avail himself of the impostor's lack of authority" and thus escape liability for the customer's consequential loss. Evidence at trial was not viewed with respect to the defendant's duty. Reversed and remanded for a new trial.

Analysis:

Apparent authority possesses some elements of estoppel, although the two legal concepts are distinct. A principal's liability under apparent authority is justified because the principal's actions reasonably lead a third person to believe that an agent has authority that he does not. However, under a strict estoppel theory, the principal need not make affirmative representations to a third party if the equities at play justify holding the principal liable to an innocent third party.

■ **CASE VOCABULARY**

CONSEQUENTIAL LOSS: A loss arising from the results of damage rather than from the damage itself.

Atlantic Salmon A/S v. Curran

(*Salmon Exporter*) v. (*Salmon Importer*)

32 Mass. App. Ct. 488, 591 N.E.2d 206 (1992)

AN AGENT IS LIABLE FOR DEBTS INCURRED BY HIS PRINCIPAL IF A THIRD PARTY DOES NOT KNOW THE PRINCIPAL'S IDENTITY

■ **INSTANT FACTS** Curran (D) purchased imported salmon from the plaintiffs, and the plaintiffs sought to recover unpaid money from Curran (D) individually.

■ **BLACK LETTER RULE** An agent is personally liable for his principal's debts if he fails to disclose to a third party that he is acting as an agent and his principal's identity.

■ **PROCEDURAL BASIS**

On appeal to review a judgment for the defendant.

■ **FACTS**

Over several years, Curran (D) purchased imported salmon from Atlantic Salmon A/S (P) and Salmoner A/S (P) as a representative for Boston Seafood Exchange, Inc., which sold the imported salmon to other wholesalers. As payment for the salmon, Curran (D) issued a check with the "Boston Seafood Exchange, Inc." printed on it and signed his name as "Treas." to indicate his capacity as Treasurer. Wire transfers were also made directly from Boston Seafood's bank account, and the defendant's business cards indicated Curran (D) was Boston Seafood's marketing director. All Curran's advertising was solely in Boston Seafood's name. Curran (D) did not separately incorporate at any time during his relationship with the plaintiffs. Ten years earlier, however, Curran (D) served as the president, treasurer, clerk, director, and sole shareholder of Marketing Designs, Inc., which was engaged in motor vehicle sales. Marketing Designs had been dissolved before the defendant's dealings with the plaintiffs, but a certificate filed with the Boston city clerk after the transactions indicated Marketing Designs was doing business under the name of "Boston Seafood Exchange." Curran (D) never informed the plaintiffs that Marketing Designs ever existed, and the plaintiffs were unaware of its existence until after it brought suit against Curran (D) individually to recover money. After the suit was filed, Curran (D) revived Marketing Designs. At trial, Curran (D) testified that he chose to call the corporation "Boston Seafood Exchange, Inc." because the name indicated where it was located, the nature of its business, and its status as a corporation. However, he argued that at the time he accrued the debt to the plaintiffs, he was acting on behalf of Marketing Designs. Curran (D) also argued that it did not matter whether the plaintiffs knew he was acting for Marketing Designs, because the plaintiffs were put on notice that Curran (D) was acting on behalf of a corporation, relieving him of individual liability. The lower court agreed.

■ **ISSUE**

Is an individual personally liable for the debts owed to the plaintiffs if the debts were incurred on behalf of a partially undisclosed or unidentified principal?

■ **DECISION AND RATIONALE**

(Judge Undisclosed) Yes. Restatement (Second) of Agency § 4(2) provides that "[i]f the other party [to a transaction] has notice that the agent is or may be acting for a principal but has no notice of the

---

principal's identity, the principal for whom the agent is acting is a partially undisclosed principal.'' Under such circumstances, the agent is a party to the transaction, because it is the agent's duty to disclose his status as an agent as well as the identity of his principal in order to escape personal liability. To avoid personal liability, the other party must actually know the agent's principal's identity, even if the means of discovery were readily available through public records. Here, Curran (D) clearly informed the plaintiffs that he was acting as an agent, but failed to disclose that his principal was Marketing Designs. The plaintiffs had dealt with Curran (D) on occasion before the debts accrued and after Marketing Designs had been revived. His failure to disclose Marketing Designs, together with the continued use of the ''Boston Seafood Exchange'' trade name, does not inform the plaintiffs of the principal's identity. Reversed.

Analysis:

Equity requires that an agent acting on behalf of an undisclosed or partially undisclosed principal remains liable on a contract with a third party. When entering into the contract, the third party's bargaining position is considerably limited by the agent's lack of candor. The decision to enter into a contract is often based upon the creditworthiness of the other party. Without disclosing that the agent is acting on behalf of a principal, a third party is unable to evaluate fully the situation to make an informed decision to enter into the contract.

■ CASE VOCABULARY

ACTUAL KNOWLEDGE: Direct and clear knowledge, as distinguished from constructive knowledge.

DISCLOSURE: The act or process of making known something that was previously unknown; a revelation of facts.

PERSONAL LIABILITY: Liability for which one is personally accountable and for which a wronged party can seek satisfaction out of the wrongdoer's personal assets.

Humble Oil & Refining Co. v. Martin

(*Service Station Owner*) v. (*Injured Bystander*)
148 Tex. 175, 222 S.W.2d 995 (1949)

OWNER IS LIABLE FOR AN OPERATOR'S NEGLIGENCE IF THE OWNER DIRECTS THE MANNER UNDER WHICH THE STATION IS OPERATED

■ **INSTANT FACTS** Martin (P) was injured by a vehicle that rolled away from the service station owned by Humble Oil & Refining Co. (D), but operated by another person under contract.

■ **BLACK LETTER RULE** One who maintains control over a business enterprise's operation, even if it entrusts the operation to one acting without meaningful discretion, is liable as a principal for the negligence of those entrusted with his business.

■ PROCEDURAL BASIS

On appeal to review a decision of the Texas Court of Civil Appeals, affirming the trial court's judgment for the plaintiffs.

■ FACTS

Mr. and Mrs. Love (D) left their vehicle at the Humble Oil & Refining Co. (D) service station for repairs. Humble (D) owned the service station and its products, but Schneider operated the station under contract and hired and paid all station employees. Shortly after the Loves' (D) vehicle was left at the station, it rolled off the service station premises and struck Martin (P) and his two daughters while they were walking in their yard. Martin (P) sued the Loves (D) and Humble (D) for personal injury. The trial court found the Loves (D) and Humble (D) jointly and severally liable, but awarded the Loves (D) a judgment for contribution against Humble (D). On appeal, the judgments against the defendants were affirmed, but the appellate court reversed the judgment for contribution. The defendants appealed, challenging the judgment in favor of the Martins (P) and each seeking indemnity against the other. Specifically, Humble (D) claims that an independent contractor, for whom Humble (D) cannot be held liable, committed the negligent act.

■ ISSUE

Is a principal liable for the negligence of one who contractually operates its business?

■ DECISION AND RATIONALE

(Judge Undisclosed) Yes. The terms of the contract and extrinsic evidence indicate that Humble (D) and Schneider had a master-servant relationship. Although the contract gave Schneider the power to hire, compensate, manage, and discharge employees, the remaining operations of the service station were under Humble's (D) control. The contract provided that Schneider would perform certain duties and obligations as Humble (D) required. Humble (D) retained title to the service station and the products sold, paying Schneider a commission on profits. Humble (D) also paid all advertising costs, purchased the products, and paid a substantial portion of the operating expenses. Schneider was no different in practical effect than a store clerk hired by Humble (D) and paid on commission. Schneider was Humble's (D) servant, and Humble (D) is liable for his negligence. Affirmed.

Analysis:

A franchisor's degree of control over the franchise operations is a question of fact. There is no bright line distinguishing between the control that amounts to a master-servant relationship and the control that establishes an independent contractor relationship. Instead, the fact finder must weigh all evidence to determine whether the franchisor displays a sufficient measure of control over the business operations to hold him liable for the franchisee's actions.

■ CASE VOCABULARY

JOINT AND SEVERAL LIABILITY: Liability that may be apportioned either among two or more parties or to only one or a few select members of the group, at the adversary's discretion.

CONTRIBUTION: The right that gives one of several persons who are liable on a common debt the ability to recover ratably from each of the others when that one person discharges the debt for the benefit of all; the right to demand that another who is jointly responsible for a third party's injury supply part of what is required to compensate the injured party.

INDEMNITY: Reimbursement or compensation for loss, damage, or liability in tort; especially the right of a party who is secondarily liable to recover from the party who is primarily liable for reimbursement of expenditures paid to a third party for injuries resulting from a violation of a common-law duty.

MASTER AND SERVANT: The relation between two persons, one of whom (the master) has authority over the other (the servant), with the power to direct the time, manner, and place of the services. This relationship is similar to that of principal and agent, but that terminology applies to employments in which the employee has some discretion, while the servant is almost completely under the control of the master. Also, an agent usually acts for the principal in business relations with third parties, while a servant does not.

Hoover v. Sun Oil Co.

(Injured Customer) v. *(Petroleum Dealer)*
58 Del. 553, 212 A.2d 214 (1965)

NO AGENCY EXISTS IF AN OIL COMPANY DOES NOT CONTROL A SERVICE STATION'S OPERATIONS

■ **INSTANT FACTS** Hoover (P) was injured when his car caught fire while a service station employee was fueling it.

■ **BLACK LETTER RULE** Agency arises if a principal retains the right to control the details of the day-to-day operation of the agent's business.

■ **PROCEDURAL BASIS**

Consideration of the defendant's motion for summary judgment.

■ **FACTS**

Hoover (P) suffered injuries when his car caught fire due to an employee's negligence during fueling at a service station owned by Sun Oil Company (D) and operated by Barone (D). Barone (D) had entered into a lease with Sun Oil (D) that allowed Barone (D) to use the station and its equipment for his business purposes. Payment on the lease varied, depending upon the volume of gasoline sold on a monthly basis. Along with the lease, Barone (D) and Sun Oil (D) entered into a dealer's agreement whereby Barone (D) agreed to purchase Sun Oil's (D) petroleum products and Sun Oil (D) agreed to loan the equipment and advertising necessary for the petroleum's retail sale. Pursuant to the agreement, Barone (D) was permitted to sell competitors' petroleum products, but was required to sell Sun Oil's (D) products under its label and without combining them with other products. Barone (D) displayed a large Sunoco sign, advertised under the "Sunoco" trade name, and required his employees to wear Sunoco uniforms. Barone (D) also attended a Sun Oil (D) training course to familiarize himself with Sun Oil (D) products, station maintenance guidelines, and other policies and techniques. Also, a Sun Oil (D) sales representative visited Barone's station weekly to take Barone's (D) gasoline orders, inspect the bathrooms, and discuss customer service issues. However, Barone (D) bore the risk of profit and loss from the business, determined his own business hours, managed his workforce, and posted his name as the proprietor on the premises. The plaintiff sued both Barone (D) and Sun Oil (D) for the employee's negligence. Sun Oil (D) moved for summary judgment, arguing that Barone (D) was an independent contractor and that Sun Oil (D) is not liable for the negligence of an independent contractor's employee.

■ **ISSUE**

Is a business operator who bore the risk of profit and loss, determined his own business hours, managed his workforce, and posted his name as the proprietor an independent contractor so that the principal is not liable for the operator's employee's negligence?

■ **DECISION AND RATIONALE**

(Judge Undisclosed). Yes. While legal definitions of master and servant are often difficult to apply to oil companies' unique distribution systems, the facts clearly support that Barone (D) is an independent contractor. Although Barone (D) sells primarily Sun Oil's (D) products under the Sunoco name and advertises Sunoco's reputation for quality products and quality service, neither the terms of the contract

---

nor the parties' conduct supports an agency relationship. "The test to be applied is that of whether the oil company has retained the right to control the details of the day-to-day operation of the service station; control or influence over results alone being viewed as insufficient." Sun Oil (D) and Barone (D) remained in close contact because they have a mutual interest in Barone's (D) success, but Sun Oil (D) has not retained any control over the day-to-day operations and cannot be held liable for Barone's (D) employee's negligence. Summary judgment granted.

Analysis:

The extent of control is generally a question of fact for the fact finder. Therefore, summary judgment is usually inappropriate in cases concerning the agency relationship. However, if the evidence clearly shows that the franchisor did not retain control over the day-to-day operations, as opposed to providing the means to conduct the franchise business, the court may grant summary judgment.

■ CASE VOCABULARY

INDEPENDENT CONTRACTOR: One who is hired to undertake a specific project but who is left free to do the assigned work and to choose the method for accomplishing it. Unlike an employee, an independent contractor who commits a wrong while carrying out the work does not create liability for the one who did the hiring.

RESPONDEAT SUPERIOR: The doctrine holding an employer or principal liable for the employee's or agent's wrongful acts committed within the scope of the employment or agency.

SCOPE OF EMPLOYMENT: The range of reasonable and foreseeable activities that an employee engages in while carrying out the employer's business.

VICARIOUS LIABILITY: Liability that a supervisory party (such as an employer) bears for the actionable conduct of a subordinate or associate (such as an employee) because of the relationship between the two parties.

Murphy v. Holiday Inns, Inc.

(Injured Guest) v. *(Franchiser)*

216 Va. 490, 219 S.E.2d 874 (1975)

A FRANCHISE AGREEMENT THAT PROVIDES AN OPERATION SYSTEM FOR A FRANCHISEE DOES NOT ESTABLISH A PRINCIPAL–AGENT RELATIONSHIP

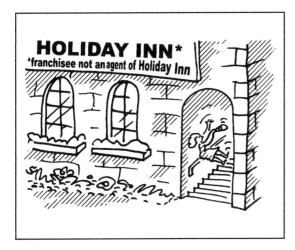

HOLIDAY INN*
*franchisee not an agent of Holiday Inn

■ **INSTANT FACTS** Murphy (P) slipped and fell in a motel owned and operated by a franchisee under a license agreement.

■ **BLACK LETTER RULE** If a franchise contract so regulates the activities of the franchisee as to vest the franchiser with control within the definition of agency, the agency relationship arises even if the parties expressly deny it.

■ **PROCEDURAL BASIS**

On appeal to review a judgment for the defendant.

■ **FACTS**

Murphy (P) slipped and fell on water that had accumulated on a motel floor. Holiday Inns, Inc. (D), licensed the motel to the operator, who operated it under the defendant's franchise name, subject to the terms of a license agreement. The defendant filed a motion for summary judgment, arguing it had no principal-agent or master-servant relationship with the operator such that the defendant should be liable for Murphy's (P) injuries. The lower court agreed and entered judgment for the defendant.

■ **ISSUE**

Does a franchise agreement whereby the franchisor provides the trade name and trademark under which a franchisee does business establish a principal-agent relationship if the franchisor retains no power to control daily operations?

■ **DECISION AND RATIONALE**

(Judge Undisclosed). No. Although the license agreement contains a disclaimer requiring the operator to hold itself out as the owner and operator of the premises, if the license agreement itself supports an agency relationship, the disclaimer does not relieve the defendant of liability for the operator's negligence. In determining whether the agreement establishes an agency relationship, the nature and extent of the defendant's control over the premises is crucial. Here, the license agreement affords the operator access to a system the defendant developed for operating its motel under the defendant's trade name, trademarks, advertising style, and methods of operation. In exchange for the use of the defendant's system, the operator paid a monthly fee and a portion of its profits to be designated for advertising expenditures. The operator also agreed to conduct its motel according to the defendant's operating rules, which generally required the operator to operate its motel in a location approved by the defendant, to use the defendant's trade name and trade marks, to refrain from competitive businesses and to subject its managers and housekeepers to training provided by the defendant. In all material respects, the license agreement is a franchise contract whereby the defendant supplied the standardized means and methods, but the franchisee bears the risk of loss and the reward of profits. If a franchise contract "so regulates the activities of the franchisee as to vest the franchiser with control within the definition of agency, the agency relationship arises even though the parties expressly deny it." Here, the license contract gave the defendant no managerial control over the motel's daily operations. The defendant did not have the power to maintain the premises, establish customer rates, hire or fire employees, or establish work rates or conditions. Absent such powers, the license contract did not establish a principal-agent relationship. Affirmed.

Analysis:

Although the court determined that there was no genuine issue of material fact concerning Holiday Inn's control over the motel, in the same year the Fifth Circuit Court of Appeals held that, under a similar Holiday Inn franchise agreement, a question of fact did exist. In that case, Holiday Inn had reserved the right to deny credit to a customer, and a motel clerk wrongfully denied the customer credit. In that respect, the court held that a jury should determine whether Holiday Inn maintained sufficient control under its franchise agreement.

■ CASE VOCABULARY

FRANCHISE: The sole right granted by the owner of a trademark or trade name to engage in business or to sell a good or service in a certain area.

FRANCHISE AGREEMENT: The contract between a franchisor and a franchisee establishing the terms and conditions of the franchise relationship. State and federal laws regulate franchise agreements.

Billops v. Magness Constr. Co.

(Customer) v. *(Undisclosed Defendant)*

391 A.2d 196 (Del. 1978)

EVIDENCE OF A FRANCHISOR'S RIGHT TO CONTROL AND AGENCY MANIFESTATIONS WITHSTANDS SUMMARY JUDGMENT

■ **INSTANT FACTS** Billops (P) was wrongfully treated by a ballroom employee at a facility franchised by Hilton (D).

■ **BLACK LETTER RULE** A franchise agreement establishes an agency relationship if the franchisor maintains the right to control the franchisee's business operations or manifests to a third person that the franchisee has authority to bind the franchisor.

■ **PROCEDURAL BASIS**

On appeal to review a judgment for the defendants.

■ **FACTS**

Billops (P), who paid an advance rental fee for a ballroom operated under the Hilton (D) name and trademark, intended to use the ballroom for an art exhibit, fashion show, and dance. The hotel was operated by a franchisee pursuant to a franchise agreement that required the franchisee to comply with regulations governing advertising, front office procedures, cleaning services, room standards, food preparation, staff procedures and standards, and other daily operations. On the day of the exhibit, the banquet director demanded payment from Billops (P). When Billops (P) refused to pay, the director harassed Billops (P) and his guests by loudly demanding payment, refusing to heat the ballroom, failing to provide adequate dance room, impounding the art exhibit, and calling the police. Billops (P) sued the franchisee, the franchiser, and others for false imprisonment, invasion of privacy, intentional and negligent infliction of emotional distress, battery, assault, and defamation. The Superior Court granted the franchisor's motion for summary judgment after it concluded that no actual or apparent authority existed to hold them liable for the director's actions.

■ **ISSUE**

Is evidence of the right to control a franchisee's operations and the outward manifestations of agency sufficient to create a genuine issue of material fact as to the existence of actual or apparent authority?

■ **DECISION AND RATIONALE**

(Judge Undisclosed) Yes. "Actual authority is that authority which a principal expressly or implicitly grants to an agent" and may be established when a franchisor has the right to control the franchisee's business. Here, the franchise agreement's detailed provisions require franchisee compliance subject to the franchisor's inspections and approval and demonstrate a question of fact as to the franchisor's control over the franchisee's business operations. Similarly, material issues of genuine fact exist as to the franchisee's apparent authority. "Manifestations by the alleged principal which create a reasonable belief in a third party that the alleged agent is authorized to bind the principal create an apparent agency from which spring the same legal consequences as those which result from an actual agency." In order for apparent agency to bind the principal, however, a third party must demonstrate reasonable reliance on the principal's manifestations. Here, the franchisee was required to display the Hilton logo and trademark to the exclusion of all others, to identify itself completely with Hilton, and to hold itself out as a Hilton facility. In reliance on these requirements, Billops (P) chose the ballroom because of his expectation of quality service associated with Hilton. On the evidence presented, genuine issues of material fact exist so as to withstand summary judgment on the issue of actual and apparent authority. Reversed and remanded.

Analysis:

The Restatement of Agency defines an agent as one who acts "on behalf" of another. If a franchisee retains the risks and rewards of the franchise operation, it is difficult to understand how a franchisee who receives only a franchisor's trade name, logo, and operating procedures is the franchisor's agent. The only benefit seemingly received by the franchisor, other than a franchise fee, is the good reputation associated with its franchisee's good customer service. Yet, if the franchisor operates no franchisor-owned business of its own, that benefit furthers only its future business relationship with prospective franchisees, not the general public.

■ CASE VOCABULARY

FRANCHISE: The sole right granted by the owner of a trademark or trade name to engage in business or to sell a good or service in a certain area.

FRANCHISE AGREEMENT: The contract between a franchisor and a franchisee establishing the terms and conditions of the franchise relationship. State and federal laws regulate franchise agreements.

SUMMARY JUDGMENT: A judgment granted on a claim about which there is no genuine issue of material fact and upon which the movant is entitled to prevail as a matter of law.

Ira S. Bushey & Sons, Inc. v. United States

(Drydock Owner) v. *(Federal Government)*
398 F.2d 167 (2d Cir. 1968)

GOVERNMENT IS LIABLE FOR DAMAGE CAUSED BY DRUNKEN SAILOR RETURNING TO A DOCKED SHIP

■ **INSTANT FACTS** A drunken sailor employed by the U.S. Coast Guard caused damage to the plaintiff's drydock while returning to the ship from leave.

■ **BLACK LETTER RULE** Respondeat superior imposes liability on an employer for an employee's conduct if the employer created the risk that the conduct would occur.

■ **PROCEDURAL BASIS**

Appeal from a district court judgment for the plaintiff.

■ **FACTS**

While a U.S. Coast Guard ship was being overhauled overnight in a floating drydock in Brooklyn, a drunken sailor returned to the ship and opened valves that flooded one side of the drydock, shifting the balance of the drydock and causing the ship to fall against the drydock wall. Parts of the drydock and part of the ship sank into the water. Ira S. Bushey & Sons, Inc. (P), the owner of the drydock, sued the U.S. Government (D) in federal district court for the damage caused by its employee. The district court granted judgment for the plaintiff. The Government (D) appealed.

■ **ISSUE**

Is the Government vicariously liable for damages to a drydock on which its ship was docked that were caused by a drunken sailor who was returning to the ship?

■ **DECISION AND RATIONALE**

(Friendly, J.) Yes. Under the doctrine of respondeat superior, the government is liable for the actions of an employee only if it is within the scope of his employment. Section 228(1) of the Restatement (Second) of Agency holds an employee is acting within the scope of his employment "if, but only if . . . (c) it is actuated, at least in part by a purpose to serve the master." The Second Circuit has previously adhered to this principle in enforcing the doctrine of respondeat superior. Applying this principle, it cannot be concluded that the sailor's act in opening the drydock valves served the Government's (D) purpose, even if his return to the ship does. However, the trial court enforced respondeat superior based not on this test, but on the purposes that the doctrine is intended to serve. The trial court's belief that the efficient allocation of resources requires the Government (D) to bear liability for the sailor's actions because the government is in a better position to screen its employees to deter future conduct does not justify extending the respondeat superior doctrine. The focus of respondeat superior must be not on the employee's motive for acting in a certain manner, but on the necessary conduct characteristic of the employer's enterprise. Here, the sailor's conduct was not so unforeseeable to relieve the Government (D) of liability for his actions. Sailors on leave commonly engage in drinking and other behavior before returning to the ship. The fact that the Government (D) could not foresee the sailor's precise conduct is immaterial as long as the Government (D) created the risk that the conduct could

---

occur. Unlike conduct related to a sailor's personal life, the risk that seamen coming and going may have an opportunity to damage the dry dock is sufficient to impose liability on the Government (D). Affirmed.

Analysis:

Vicarious liability, including respondeat superior, places liability on a master for the actions of another, even if the master did not actually cause the damage suffered. The doctrine has been justified on primarily two grounds. First, the master, who has the right of control over his servant's actions, is in a better position to prevent the damage from occurring. Second, the master generally has the financial means to cover the damages suffered by the innocent third party. However, upon assuming the responsibility to the third party, the master generally maintains a right of indemnification against its guilty servant.

■ CASE VOCABULARY

RESPONDEAT SUPERIOR: The doctrine holding an employer or principal liable for the employee's or agent's wrongful acts committed within the scope of the employment or agency.

SCOPE OF EMPLOYMENT: The range of reasonable and foreseeable activities that an employee engages in while carrying out the employer's business.

VICARIOUS LIABILITY: Liability that a supervisory party (such as an employer) bears for the actionable conduct of a subordinate or associate (such as an employee) because of the relationship between the two parties.

Manning v. Grimsley

(Spectator) v. *(Pitcher)*
643 F.2d 20 (1st Cir. 1981)

HECKLING INTERFERES WITH A BASEBALL PLAYER'S ABILITY TO FULFILL HIS EMPLOYMENT DUTIES

■ **INSTANT FACTS** Grimsley (D) threw a baseball at Manning (P) in response to Manning's (P) heckling at a baseball game.

■ **BLACK LETTER RULE** To recover from an employer for an assault committed by its employee, the plaintiff must show that the employee's assault was in response to the plaintiff's conduct which was presently interfering with the employee's ability to perform his duties successfully.

■ **PROCEDURAL BASIS**

On appeal to review a trial court decision directing a verdict for the defendant.

■ **FACTS**

Manning (P) was a spectator in the right field bleachers at Fenway Park in Boston. Sitting behind a wire mesh fence, Manning (P) and others began heckling Grimsley (D), who was warming up in the bullpen for a possible appearance in the game. During the course of the heckling, Grimsley (D) deliberately looked at the hecklers, acknowledging their antics. Upon completing his warm-up pitches, Grimsley (D) threw a final pitch after the catcher had left his stance, firing the baseball at a ninety-degree angle from the plate. The ball traveled through the wire mesh fence, striking the plaintiff. Manning (P) sued Grimsley (D) and his employer, the Baltimore Baseball Club, Inc. (D), for negligence and battery. The judge directed a verdict for the defendant on the battery count, and the jury returned a verdict for the defendants on negligence.

■ **ISSUE**

Is an employer liable for a battery committed by its employee in response to conduct interfering with his employment duties?

■ **DECISION AND RATIONALE**

(Judge Undisclosed) Yes. Evidence shows that Grimsley (D) is an expert pitcher who deliberately noticed the plaintiff and threw a baseball at a high-rate of speed at an unusual angle. Therefore, the jury could reasonably conclude that Grimsley (D) intentionally threw the baseball to cause the plaintiff a reasonable apprehension of contact, which actually occurred. Accordingly, the court erred in directing a verdict in favor of Grimsley (D) on the battery count. Similarly, the court erred in directing a verdict in favor of the Baltimore Baseball Club, Inc. (D), Grimsley's (D) employer. To recover from an employer for an assault committed by its employee, the plaintiff must show "that the employee's assault was in response to the plaintiff's conduct which was presently interfering with the employee's ability to perform his duties successfully." While mere insulting remarks that may annoy or harass an employee are not normally sufficient conduct by a plaintiff to interfere with the employee's duties, Manning's (P) heckling arises to such level. The jury could reasonably conclude that the plaintiff heckled in order to disrupt or interfere with Grimsley's (D) ability to warm-up adequately. Unlike a mere annoyance, the plaintiff's

---

remarks rise to conduct that was presently interfering with Grimsley's (D) ability to perform his duties. The lower court should have submitted the battery count to the jury. Vacated and remanded.

Analysis:

It seems illogical to presume that a principal specifically authorized its agent to commit intentional torts. However, in some instances, the purpose for which the principal engages the agent is to commit acts that may reasonably rise to intentional torts. Thus, one who employs a security guard to remove trespassers from his property forcibly may be held liable for torts committed in the scope of the employment.

■ CASE VOCABULARY

BATTERY: An intentional and offensive touching by another without lawful justification.

Arguello v. Conoco, Inc.

(Hispanic Plaintiff) v. *(Petroleum Provider)*
207 F.3d 803 (5th Cir. 2000)

RACIAL EPITHETS MADE DURING AN EMPLOYEE'S NORMAL, AUTHORIZED EMPLOYMENT DUTIES ARE WITHIN THE SCOPE OF EMPLOYMENT

■ **INSTANT FACTS** Several Hispanic plaintiffs were treated improperly in stores owned or branded by Conoco, Inc. (D).

■ **BLACK LETTER RULE** A master is not liable for his servants' intentional acts if they occurred beyond the servants' scope of employment.

■ **PROCEDURAL BASIS**

On appeal to review the trial court's dismissal of the plaintiffs' claims and grant of summary judgment to the defendant.

■ **FACTS**

Arguello (P), an Hispanic, went into a store owned by Conoco, Inc. (D), to pay for gasoline with her credit card. When Arguello (P) presented an out-of-state driver's license as identification, the store clerk refused to accept the card and began using racial epithets and making obscene gestures toward Arguello (P). Arguello (P) left the store and used a payphone to call Conoco (D) customer service to complain. Arguello's (P) father, Govea, attempted to reenter the store, but the clerk had locked the doors. Conoco's (D) district manager, upon reviewing the videotape of the incident, determined that the clerk had acted inappropriately. The district manager confronted the clerk and admonished her, but did not suspend or terminate her. In a separate incident, three Hispanic men entered a store branded by Conoco (D), but the clerk refused to serve them allegedly because of their ethnicity. On a third occasion Escobedo (P) entered a different store branded by Conoco (D) in which the clerk refused to provide toilet paper for his wife and made racial comments. Upon complaining to a Conoco (D) customer service representative, Escobedo (P) was told that nothing could be done because Conoco (D) did not own the store. At separate Conoco-branded stores, Escobedo (P) was otherwise treated differently than Caucasian customers. The plaintiffs sued Conoco (D) for racial discrimination in violation of state and federal statutes. The trial court dismissed the plaintiffs' disparate impact claims and their claims brought under state law. The court later granted Conoco (D) summary judgment on the plaintiffs' remaining claims.

■ **ISSUE**

Is a petroleum provider liable for the actions of its employees or its independent contractors' employees that occur outside the scope of employment?

■ **DECISION AND RATIONALE**

(Judge Undisclosed) No. The district court concluded that because Conoco (D) maintained no control over the daily operations of the two stores branded by Conoco (D), Conoco (D) could not be held liable for the employees' actions. In order to hold Conoco (D) liable for the employees' discriminatory actions, the plaintiffs must prove that an agency relationship had been established through Conoco's (D) manifestation of consent that the store operators act on Conoco's (D) behalf and subject to its control.

Conoco's (D) petroleum marketing agreements clearly provide that branded-store operators are independent proprietors and separate entities. They are not business partners, employees, or agents. Although the agreements require the operators to conduct their business operations consistent with Conoco (D) standards, they do not direct the manner in which operations are to be conducted and do not give Conoco (D) control over the daily operations. Absent such control, no agency relationship exists. As to the employee's actions at the store owned by Conoco (D), the district court found that Conoco (D) could not be held liable because the employee's actions were beyond the scope of her employment. A master is not liable for the unlawful actions committed by his servants if the actions occur outside the scope of employment. In determining whether actions are within the scope of employment, a court must consider the action's time, place, and purpose, their similarity to actions the servant is authorized to perform, whether the servant commonly performs the actions, the extent the servant's actions departed from normal methods of acting, and whether the master would reasonably expect that the servant would perform such an act. Here, the request for identification occurred in Conoco's (D) store during normal work hours for the purpose of verifying Arguello's (P) creditworthiness. The clerk acted in a manner in which she was authorized to perform, including the sale of gasoline and a request for identification. Furthermore, the use of racial epithets was a departure from Conoco's (D) normal methods for carrying out the clerk's acts. However, although Conoco (D) could not anticipate that the clerk would behave in such a manner, the behavior occurred at a time and place within the scope of her employment and while she performed authorized acts. Finally, there is no evidence that Conoco (D) could have reasonably expected the clerk to use racial epithets. The jury should consider any evidence that Conoco (D) could not reasonably expect the clerk to act out of racial animosity, and Arguello's (D) evidence creates a genuine issue of material fact as to whether the clerk acted within the scope of employment. Summary judgment should have been denied in this respect. If the jury determines that the clerk acted outside the scope of her employment, Conoco (D) cannot be held liable. Conoco's (D) disciplinary action demonstrates that Conoco (D) did not ratify the clerk's actions. Finally, the plaintiffs failed to demonstrate that the various employees' actions were a result of a company-wide policy of discrimination necessary to establish a disparate impact claim. The court was correct in granting summary judgment on this point. Affirmed in part, reversed in part.

Analysis:

The court's decision places a heavy burden on employers when selecting their agents. Because many businesses require their employees and agents to have customer contact, seemingly any inappropriate conduct directed toward a customer will be seen as coming within the scope of employment. Pre-employment screening and on-the-job training may relieve the employer of liability, but such efforts may be insufficient to avoid a genuine issue of material fact on the issue.

■ CASE VOCABULARY

DISCRIMINATION: The effect of a law or established practice that confers privileges on a certain class or that denies privileges to a certain class because of race, age, sex, nationality, religion, or handicap.

DISPARATE IMPACT: The adverse effect of a facially neutral practice (especially an employment practice) that nonetheless discriminates against persons because of their race, sex, national origin, age, or disability and that is not justified by business necessity.

Majestic Realty Assoc., Inc. v. Toti Contracting Co.

(Building Owner) v. *(Demolition Company)*

30 N.J. 425, 153 A.2d 321 (1959)

BUILDING OWNER MAY NOT BE LIABLE FOR A DEMOLITION CONTRACTOR'S NEGLIGENCE

■ **INSTANT FACTS** Majestic Realty Associates, Inc. (P) suffered property damage to its building caused by the negligent demolition of an adjacent building.

■ **BLACK LETTER RULE** Ordinarily, if a person engages a contractor, who conducts an independent business by means of his own employees, to do work not itself a nuisance, the person is not liable for the contractor's negligent acts in performing the contract.

■ **PROCEDURAL BASIS**

On appeal to review a decision of the New Jersey Appellate Division reversing a trial court's judgment for the defendant.

■ **FACTS**

Majestic Realty Associates, Inc. (P), leased a portion of its building to Bohen's (P) for Bohen's dry goods business. The Parking Authority of Paterson (D) acquired adjacent properties with the intention of constructing a parking area in the center of the municipality. In order to establish the parking area, the Authority (D) contracted with Toti Contracting Co. (D) to demolish the existing buildings, including one adjacent to the plaintiff's building. While demolishing the adjacent building, Toti (D) used a wrecking ball to topple the building wall next to the plaintiffs' building, causing a large segment of the wall to fall on the plaintiffs' roof, causing damage. Expert testimony established that the wall should have been demolished in small segments to reduce the risk of damage to adjoining buildings. The plaintiffs sued the Authority (D) and Toti (D) for damages. At trial, the court concluded that, although testimony established demolition was an inherently dangerous activity, it was not a nuisance per se. Accordingly, the Authority (D) was not liable for its contractor's negligence because the Authority (D) exercised no control over the demolition operations. On appeal, the New Jersey Appellate Division reversed.

■ **ISSUE**

Is a property owner who hires a demolition contractor liable for damages caused by the contractor's negligence if the activity is not inherently dangerous?

■ **DECISION AND RATIONALE**

(Judge Undisclosed) No. "Ordinarily where a person engages a contractor, who conducts an independent business by means of his own employees, to do work not itself a nuisance, he is not liable for the negligent acts of the contractor in the performance of the contract." However, if the person retains control over the contractor's operations or hires an incompetent contractor or if the work constitutes a nuisance per se, the person may be responsible for his contractor's negligence. A contractor's competency refers not to the contractor's financial capabilities, but rather to the skill and experience expected of the contractor. Liability insurance is readily available to contractors and must be presumed to exist as an ordinary business expense. The plaintiffs argue that the demolition activities constituted nuisance per se, which leaves the Authority (D) liable for the damages. An activity is "inherently dangerous" when it "can be carried on safely only by the exercise of special skill and care, and ... involves grave risk of danger to persons or property if negligently done." Inherently dangerous, however, must be distinguished from "ultra-hazardous," in which an activity "necessarily involves a serious risk of harm to the person, land or chattels of others which cannot be eliminated by the exercise of the utmost care, and is not a matter of common usage." Where damage arises from an ultra-hazardous activity, liability is absolute. Where reasonable minds may differ concerning whether an activity, such as demolition, is inherently dangerous, the question must be left to the discretion of the jury. Affirmed and remanded.

Analysis:

Typically, if a person engages a contractor to do work that does not in itself constitute a nuisance, the person is not liable for the contractor's negligent acts. However, this court recognizes that a property owner is under a non-delegable duty to maintain its property in a manner that safeguards innocent third parties from injury or damage. This duty extends beyond those third parties actually on the property owner's premises to adjoining landowners, passersby, and others in the general vicinity.

■ CASE VOCABULARY

INHERENTLY DANGEROUS: Requiring special precautions at all times to avoid injury; dangerous per se.

NUISANCE PER SE: Interference so severe that it would constitute a nuisance under any circumstances; a nuisance regardless of location or circumstances of use, such as a leaky nuclear-waste storage facility.

Reading v. Regem

(Sergeant) v. (Government Official)

2 K.B. 268, 2 All Eng. Rep. 27 (1948)

A SERGEANT MUST SURRENDER ILLEGAL BRIBES RECEIVED BECAUSE OF HIS EMPLOYMENT POSITION

■ **INSTANT FACTS** Reading (P) obtained payments for accompanying unlawful contraband past civilian police checkpoints while employed by the British army.

■ **BLACK LETTER RULE** A servant is accountable to his master for profits he obtains because of his position, if the servant takes advantage of his position and violates his duty of good faith and honesty to make the profit for himself.

■ **PROCEDURAL BASIS**

Before the trial court on the Crown's motion to dismiss.

■ **FACTS**

Reading (P) was a sergeant in the British army with little means of earning substantial income. While stationed in Egypt, Reading (P) accompanied a truck loaded with cases across town in full uniform so as to avoid inspection by the civilian police. At the truck's destination, the cases were unloaded and reloaded onto another truck. Reading (P) received substantial payments for performing this act on several occasions. Upon discovering the money in Reading's (P) bank account and apartment, military authorities seized the funds as a violation of Reading's (P) duty to his employer. Reading (P) sued to recover the money.

■ **ISSUE**

Does a military employee violate his duty to his employer when he accepts payment from a third party for military protection from the civilian police?

■ **DECISION AND RATIONALE**

(Judge Undisclosed) Yes. If a servant takes advantage of the position he occupies on behalf of a master, violating the duty of good faith and honesty to make a profit for himself, and if he obtains a profit because of his position, the servant is accountable to his master. It is not relevant whether the master lost profits by the servant's actions or whether the master could not have performed the acts himself. If the servant is unjustly enriched solely based on his service to his master without the master's permission, the servant must surrender his profit to his master. Here, Reading (P) earned a profit solely because of the uniform and position bestowed by his master. Although he acted outside the scope of his employment, Reading's (P) uniform and military position did not merely offer him the opportunity to earn a profit. For example, the location of Reading's (P) service did not present the opportunity to earn his profit, because the location would have been immaterial if he did not have a position of authority. Accordingly, unlike instances when one's employment causes the profitable opportunity, Reading's (P) profit derived solely from his service to his master, and he must surrender the money. Petition dismissed.

Analysis:

Although a principal may suffer no financial injury in a breach of loyalty case, the court infers damages. A principal who places an agent in a certain position of prestige or authority maintains an interest in using that position. For example, if all soldiers were permitted to engage in illegal conduct based on their authority, the authority's credibility would be undermined and lose its value. As a result, the master could potentially experience monetary damages in the future.

■ **CASE VOCABULARY**

GOOD FAITH: A state of mind consisting in (1) honesty in belief or purpose, (2) faithfulness to one's duty or obligation, (3) observance of reasonable commercial standards of fair dealing in a given trade or business, or (4) absence of intent to defraud or to seek unconscionable advantage.

General Auto. Mfg. Co. v. Singer

(Principal) v. *(Agent)*

19 Wis.2d 528, 120 N.W.2d 659 (1963)

DEFENDANT IS LIABLE TO HIS EMPLOYER FOR PROFITS DERIVED FROM AN UNDISCLOSED COMPETING BUSINESS

■ **INSTANT FACTS** Singer (D), while employed by General Automotive Manufacturing Co. (P), secretly concealed profits earned by accepting personal orders from the plaintiff's customers.

■ **BLACK LETTER RULE** An agent owes his principal the duty of good faith and loyalty not to act adversely to his principal's business interests in the furtherance of his own.

■ PROCEDURAL BASIS

On appeal to review a judgment for the plaintiff.

■ FACTS

General Automotive Manufacturing Co. (P) hired Singer (D) as the general manager of its machine shop jobbing business. Singer's (D) employment contract's terms required Singer (D) to devote his "entire time, skill, labor, and attention" to the plaintiff's business, including the solicitation of machine shop work for the plaintiff. Singer maintained a good reputation as a highly skilled machinist, which resulted in general business growth for the plaintiff. When business was slow, Singer (D) often personally financed the plaintiff's operations to enable it to continue in business. However, while working for the plaintiff, Singer (D) received potential orders that he knew General Automotive Manufacturing Co. (P) could not fulfill due to insufficient equipment or inability to meet a competitive price. Rather than turn the orders away, Singer (D) quoted the customers a price and brokered the orders out to a suitable machine shop, keeping any difference between the quoted price and his agreed-upon price with the machine shop. Eventually, Singer (D) established his own broker business dealing in the same products as the plaintiff manufactured and sold. General Automotive (P) sued Singer (D) for breach of contract to recover the secret profits. The trial court determined that Singer (D) breached his contract and entered judgment for the plaintiff.

■ ISSUE

Does an agent violate his fiduciary duties to his principal when the agent endeavors in a competing business while employed by the principal?

■ DECISION AND RATIONALE

(Judge Undisclosed) Yes. As the plaintiff's agent, Singer (D) owed the plaintiff the duty of good faith and loyalty not to act adversely to his principal's business interests in the furtherance of his own. To determine whether an agent's business interests are adverse to his principal's, the court must examine the nature of the competing businesses. Here, Singer (D) was hired to solicit orders from customers and fill them as inexpensively as possible. By soliciting orders but placing them with competing manufacturers for profit, Singer (D) advanced his personal interests above those of his principal. Further, Singer (D) violated his duty of good faith by not disclosing the orders Singer (D) believed the plaintiff could not handle. The plaintiff should have been the party to decide whether to accept, decline, or subcontract the orders generated by Singer (D), and the plaintiff is entitled to any profit resulting from the orders. Because Singer (D) violated his duty of good faith and loyalty to his principal, General Automotive (P) is entitled to recover all profits earned, less Singer's (D) contractual commission. Affirmed.

Analysis:

Generally, an agent violates his fiduciary duties to his principal if the agent endeavors in a competing business while employed by the principal. However, the crucial element of this case is Singer's (D) failure to disclose the potential sales to his principal. If Singer (D) had presented General Automotive (P) with the opportunity to complete the orders or broker the sale to another manufacturer for a profit, Singer (D) would have fulfilled his duty of loyalty. By depriving his employer of such an opportunity and thereafter generating a profit for himself, Singer (D) breached his duties.

■ CASE VOCABULARY

FIDUCIARY: One who owes to another the duties of good faith, trust, confidence, and candor.

Town & Country House & Home Serv., Inc. v. Newbery

(*Former Employer*) v. (*Former Employee*)

3 N.Y.2d 554, 170 N.Y.S.2d 328, 147 N.E.2d 724 (1958)

FORMER EMPLOYEES MAY NOT TARGET A COMPETING BUSINESS EXCLUSIVELY AT THEIR FORMER EMPLOYER'S ESTABLISHED CUSTOMERS

■ **INSTANT FACTS** Newbery (D) and other defendants established a competing housekeeping business using methods and techniques similar to those the plaintiff had developed.

■ **BLACK LETTER RULE** A business proprietor may not solicit his former employer's customers who are not openly engaged in business in advertised locations or whose availability as patrons cannot readily be ascertained, but whose trade and patronage have been secured by years of business effort, advertising, and the expenditure of time and money.

■ PROCEDURAL BASIS

On appeal to review a decision of the New York Appellate Division, reversing a trial court order that dismissed the plaintiff's complaint.

■ FACTS

Town & Country House & Home Service, Inc. (P), employed Newbery (D) and other defendants for approximately three years as housekeepers. Town & Country (P) developed an assembly-line system, in which housekeepers were sent at different intervals to clean different parts of the homes while others attended to other customers. After the defendants left the plaintiff's employ, they formed a competing business implementing a similar cleaning system. Town & Country (P) sued for an injunction and damages, seeking to restrain the defendants from continuing their business and soliciting the plaintiff's customers. Town & Country (P) alleged that the defendant usurped personal and confidential information from the plaintiff's business. The trial court dismissed the complaint upon finding that the defendants' housekeeping methods and techniques are not confidential and that the defendants did not obtain their customers through a confidential relationship between the plaintiff and the defendants. The New York Appellate Division reversed, ruling that while employed by the plaintiff, the defendants conspired to create their own business in violation of their fiduciary duties.

■ ISSUE

Does a former employee breach his fiduciary duties to his former employer if the former employee engages in a competing business exclusively with the former employer's present customers?

■ DECISION AND RATIONALE

(Judge Undisclosed) Yes. A business proprietor may not solicit his former employer's customers "who are not openly engaged in business in advertised locations or whose availability as patrons cannot readily be ascertained but whose trade and patronage have been secured by years of business effort and advertising, and the expenditure of time and money, constituting a part of the good will of the business." Here, the plaintiff's customers could not be obtained from advertised locations or readily ascertained through the telephone directory or elsewhere. Town & Country (P) had invested considerable time and effort in locating those homeowners who desired to entrust their housecleaning chores to an outside agency. Town & Country (P) obtained its customers by selecting a geographic area in which it calculated its services would be desired, telephoning residents in the area, and separating those customers who were interested from those who were not. After three years, the plaintiff collected a sizeable customer base and expanded its cleaning crew to accommodate the increased business. The defendants did not expend similar effort. They specifically targeted selected customers on the plaintiff's list without attempting to obtain customers who had not previously engaged the plaintiff's services. Although the defendants did not misappropriate the plaintiff's customers while employed by the plaintiff, the defendants nonetheless breached their duties to Town & Country (P). Affirmed.

Analysis:

Common law generally provides that a former employee breaches his fiduciary duties to his former employer if he engages in a competing business exclusively with the former employer's present customers. However, the problems that arose in this case are often avoided by a non-compete agreement in the employment contract. Under a non-compete agreement, an employee is generally precluded from engaging in a competing business in a specified geographic area within a specified time after the termination of the employment agreement. If the parties here had entered into a non-compete agreement, the court likely would have decided the case under contract law rather than relying on the breach of a duty.

■ CASE VOCABULARY

FIDUCIARY: One who owes to another the duties of good faith, trust, confidence, and candor.

TRADE SECRET: A formula, process, device, or other business information that is kept confidential to maintain an advantage over competitors; information—including a formula, pattern, compilation, program, device, method, technique, or process—that (1) derives independent economic value, actual or potential, from not being generally known or readily ascertainable by others who can obtain economic value from its disclosure or use, and (2) is the subject of reasonable efforts, under the circumstances, to maintain its secrecy.

CHAPTER TWO

Partnerships

Fenwick v. Unemployment Compensation Comm'n

Instant Facts: Cheshire and Fenwick (D) entered into a partnership agreement, pursuant to which Fenwick contributed all capital investments, possessed exclusive control over the management of the business, and bore the risk of all business losses.

Black Letter Rule: A partnership is an association of two or more persons to carry on as co-owners of a business for profit.

Martin v. Peyton

Instant Facts: Martin (P) sued Peyton (D), Perkins (D), and Freeman (D), as alleged partners of a firm that owned Martin (P) money, when the defendants entered into an elaborate loan agreement with the firm.

Black Letter Rule: A partnership is created by an express or implied contract between two persons with the intention to form a partnership.

Southex Exhibitions, Inc. v. Rhode Island Builders Assoc., Inc.

Instant Facts: Rhode Island Builders Association, Inc. (D), replaced Southex Exhibitions, Inc. (P), as the promoter of its home show after terminating a contract it had entered into with the plaintiff's predecessor.

Black Letter Rule: Sharing profits is prima facie evidence of a partnership, which can be rebutted by evidence sufficiently demonstrating that the parties did not intend to create a partnership.

Young v. Jones

Instant Facts: Young (P) and others invested money in reliance upon a fraudulent audit statement prepared by Price Waterhouse–Bahamas.

Black Letter Rule: A person who represents himself, or permits another to represent him, as a partner in an existing partnership or with others not actual partners, is liable to any person to whom such a representation is made who has, in reliance on the representation, given credit to the actual or apparent partnership.

Meinhard v. Salmon

Instant Facts: Salmon (D) terminated a lease belonging to his joint venture with Meinhard (P) to enter into a new lease on behalf of his solely owned business.

Black Letter Rule: Like partners, joint adventurers owe one another the duty of loyalty.

Bane v. Ferguson

Instant Facts: Bane's (P) pension payments were terminated when his former firm's management council decided to merge with another law firm, ultimately resulting in dissolution.

Black Letter Rule: The fiduciary duties owed by one partner to another terminate when the partnership is dissolved.

Meehan v. Shaughnessy

Instant Facts: Meehan (P), Boyle (P), and Cohen (P) separated from Parker Coulter (D), their former law partnership, to form a new law firm with cases removed from Parker Coulter (D).

Black Letter Rule: A partner must render on demand true and full information of all things affecting the partnership to any partner.

Lawlis v. Kightlinger & Gray

Instant Facts: Lawlis (P) was expelled from the law partnership of Kightlinger & Gray (D) despite complying with all conditions for his continued relationship.

Black Letter Rule: When a partner is involuntarily expelled from a business, his expulsion must be in good faith for a dissolution to occur without violating the partnership agreement.

Putnam v. Shoaf

Instant Facts: Putnam (P) sold all her interest in her partnership to Shoaf (D) in exchange for Shoaf's (D) assumption of personal liability on a bank note.

Black Letter Rule: A partner's property rights include rights in specific partnership property, interests in the partnership, and the right to participate in the partnership's management.

National Biscuit Co. v. Stroud

Instant Facts: Freeman purchased bread from National Biscuit Co. (P), although his partner, Stroud (D), had informed Freeman and the plaintiff that he would no longer be responsible for additional bread purchases.

Black Letter Rule: Every partner is an agent of the partnership for the purpose of its business, and every partner's acts for apparently carrying on in the usual way the partnership's business binds the partnership, unless the acting partner has in fact no authority to act for the partnership and the person with whom he is dealing knows that he has no such authority.

Summers v. Dooley

Instant Facts: Summers (P) incurred expenses when he hired a partnership employee despite Dooley's (D) objection.

Black Letter Rule: Absent a contrary agreement, each partner possesses equal rights to manage the partnership's affairs, and no partner is responsible for expenses incurred without majority approval.

Day v. Sidley & Austin

Instant Facts: Day (P) sued Sidley & Austin (D) for breach of contract, fraud, and breach of fiduciary duty after he resigned due to the defendant's decision to merge with another law partnership.

Black Letter Rule: Managing partners have no fiduciary duty to disclose changes in the partnership's internal structure if the changes do not generate a profit or loss for the partnership.

Owen v. Cohen

Instant Facts: The court dissolved Cohen's (P) and Owen's (D) partnership upon finding that the parties could not practicably continue in business together.

Black Letter Rule: Courts of equity may order the dissolution of a partnership if the partners' quarrels and disagreements are of such a nature and to such an extent that all confidence and cooperation between the parties has been destroyed or if a partner's misbehavior materially hinders the proper conduct of the partnership's business.

Collins v. Lewis

Instant Facts: Collins (P) and Lewis (D) entered into a partnership to operate a cafeteria, with Collins (P) providing the financial backing and Lewis (D) devoting his experience and management ability.

Black Letter Rule: A partner may not obtain a judicial dissolution of the partnership if his own interference causes the partnership to be unprofitable.

Page v. Page

Instant Facts: The plaintiff seeks to dissolve his unprofitable partnership with the defendant.

Black Letter Rule: A partnership may be dissolved by the express will of any partner if the partnership agreement specifies no definite term or particular undertaking.

Prentiss v. Sheffel

Instant Facts: Upon dissolution of a partnership, the former partners purchased the partnership assets at a judicial sale.

Black Letter Rule: Upon dissolution of a partnership, a former partner may bid on the partnership assets at a judicial sale.

Monin v. Monin

Instant Facts: After the plaintiff assumed ownership of all partnership assets, the defendant acquired a milk-hauling contract that had previously belonged to the partnership.

Black Letter Rule: Partners owe the utmost duty of good faith and fairness to former partners after the partnership is dissolved and until the partnership affairs are wound up.

Pav-Saver Corp. v. Vasso Corp.

Instant Facts: Vasso Corporation (D) alleged Pav–Saver Corporation (P) wrongfully dissolved the partnership, seeking to continue the partnership business.

Black Letter Rule: Upon a wrongful dissolution of a partnership in violation of the partnership agreement, each partner who has not wrongfully dissolved the partnership is entitled to damages for breach of contract and may continue the partnership business for the term required under the partnership agreement with the right to possess the partnership property upon posting a bond.

Kovacik v. Reed

Instant Facts: Kovacik (P) sought recovery from Reed (P) of one-half of the money capital he invested in a losing business venture.

Black Letter Rule: If one partner or joint adventurer contributes the money capital and the other contributes the skill and labor necessary for the venture, neither party is entitled to contribution from the other.

G & S Inv. v. Belman

Instant Facts: G & S Investments' (P) partner died while suit for dissolution was pending, triggering the partnership agreement's buy-out provisions.

Black Letter Rule: Under the Uniform Partnership Act, a court may dissolve a partnership when a partner becomes incapable of performing under the partnership agreement, when a partner's conduct tends to affect the business prejudicially, or when a partner willfully breaches the partnership agreement's terms.

Jewel v. Boxer

Instant Facts: After dissolution of a law firm partnership, the former partners sought to recover their respective partnership shares in the legal fees generated after dissolution on cases that originated with the former partnership.

Black Letter Rule: In the absence of a partnership agreement, the Uniform Partnership Act requires that attorneys' fees received on cases in progress upon dissolution of a law partnership are to be shared by the former partners according to their right to fees in the former partnership, regardless of which former partner provides legal services in the case after the dissolution.

Meehan v. Shaughnessy

Instant Facts: Meehan (P), Boyle (P), and Cohen (P) separated from Parker Coulter (D), their former law partnership, to form a new law firm with cases removed from Parker Coulter (D).

Black Letter Rule: Every partner must account to the partnership and hold as trustee for the partnership any profits he derives, without the other partners' consent, from any transaction connected with the partnership's formation, conduct or liquidation.

Holzman v. De Escamilla

Instant Facts: Holzman (P), as bankruptcy trustee, sued the limited partners of a bankrupt partnership to establish them as general partners liable for their creditors' debts.

Black Letter Rule: A limited partner is not liable as a general partner unless, in addition to exercising his rights and powers as a limited partner, he takes part in the control of the business.

Fenwick v. Unemployment Compensation Comm'n

(Employer) v. *(Government Agency)*

133 N.J.L. 295, 44 A.2d 172 (1945)

A PARTNERSHIP IS NOT FORMED BY MERELY AGREEING TO SHARE BUSINESS PROFITS

■ **INSTANT FACTS** Cheshire and Fenwick (D) entered into a partnership agreement, pursuant to which Fenwick contributed all capital investments, possessed exclusive control over the management of the business, and bore the risk of all business losses.

■ **BLACK LETTER RULE** A partnership is an association of two or more persons to carry on as co-owners of a business for profit.

■ PROCEDURAL BASIS

On appeal to review a decision of the New Jersey Supreme Court reversing a determination of the Unemployment Compensation Commission.

■ FACTS

Fenwick (D) operated a beauty shop. He hired Cheshire as a cashier and a reception clerk to receive customers, take orders, and collect payments. Cheshire was paid a weekly salary. Approximately a year later, Cheshire asked for a raise. Fenwick (D) agreed, and they entered into a contract stating that the parties agreed to "associate themselves into a partnership" for the operation of the beauty shop, but Cheshire was not required to make a capital contribution, nor did she receive any right to control or manage the business. Similarly, Cheshire bore no risk of the shop's losses. She was paid a weekly salary, with a year-end bonus equal to a percentage of the annual profits. Cheshire terminated the arrangement three years later, and she sought unemployment compensation. The Unemployment Compensation Commission (P) determined that the arrangement only set Cheshire's compensation as an employee and awarded her benefits. On appeal, the New Jersey Supreme Court reversed, finding that the parties entered into a partnership agreement, called themselves partners, and did not act inconsistently with a partnership agreement.

■ ISSUE

Does an agreement providing a person a potential share in the profits of a business, without conferring a right to control the business or bear a share of the losses, establish a partnership?

■ DECISION AND RATIONALE

(Judge Undisclosed) No. A partnership is an association "of two or more persons to carry on as co-owners a business for profit." To determine whether a partnership exists, a court must consider several factors. First, the court must determine the parties' intent. Here, Fenwick (D) testifies that the agreement came about because Cheshire requested more money and Fenwick (D) wished to avoid the obligation of compensating her if the business failed to earn a profit. Thus, the agreement allows Fenwick (D) to retain his employee with a conditional pay raise subject to the business' annual profits. Therefore, despite the agreement's language, the parties' intent was not to form a partnership. Second, a partnership involves the partners' rights to share in the profits. That element is established by the agreement, but that factor alone is not conclusive of a partnership. Third, a partnership involves an obligation to share the partnership's losses. Here, the agreement specifically states that Cheshire does not share in the losses. Fourth, partners share ownership and control over the partnership property and business. Again, the agreement provides that Cheshire has no such rights. Fifth, partners maintain the power to administer business affairs. By withholding the right of control and management from Cheshire, the agreement does not authorize her to tend to any business matters. Sixth, the court must consider the agreement's language. Here, the agreement's express terms withhold many of the rights generally afforded to a partner. Seventh, the parties' conduct toward third parties may indicate a partnership. Although Fenwick (D) represents his income as partnership income and asserts to the Unemployment Compensation Commission (P) that a partnership was formed, the parties represented to no other third parties that they acted as a partnership. Finally, the parties' rights upon dissolution are instructive. Here, Cheshire gains no interest in the partnership income or assets upon dissolution, but rather the partnership continues as if it has merely lost an employee. On the balance of these factors, it is clear that despite the written agreement's language to the contrary, the failure to confer upon Cheshire the normal rights associated with a partnership interest indicates the agreement's intent is to provide her, as an employee, a means of earning additional wages. No partnership is formed. Reversed.

Analysis:

Because it is presumed that partnerships are formed to earn a profit, the sharing of profits between two or more persons is necessary to establish a partnership. The mere sharing of profits, however, does not conclusively establish a partnership absent other factors, such as sharing the losses or control of business operations. Thus, a salesperson or employee who earns a commission or a percentage of profits as compensation is generally not a partner.

■ CASE VOCABULARY

PARTNER: One of two or more persons who jointly own and carry on a business for profit.

PARTNERSHIP: A voluntary association of two or more persons who jointly own and carry on a business for profit.

PARTNERSHIP AGREEMENT: A contract defining the partners' rights and duties toward one another—not the partners' relationship with third parties.

Martin v. Peyton

(Creditor) v. *(Lender)*

246 N.Y. 213, 158 N.E. 77 (1927)

A LOAN AGREEMENT THAT ALLOWS FOR SHARING OF PROFITS AS REPAYMENT DOES NOT ESTABLISH A PARTNERSHIP ABSENT INTENT

■ **INSTANT FACTS** Martin (P) sued Peyton (D), Perkins (D), and Freeman (D), as alleged partners of a firm that owned Martin (P) money, when the defendants entered into an elaborate loan agreement with the firm.

■ **BLACK LETTER RULE** A partnership is created by an express or implied contract between two persons with the intention to form a partnership.

■ **PROCEDURAL BASIS**

On appeal to review a judgment for the defendants.

■ **FACTS**

The banking firm of Knauth, Nacod & Kuhne was in financial trouble. It turned to Peyton (D), a friend of one of the firm's partners, for a loan that the firm could use as collateral to secure bank advances. That loan was not sufficient to cover the firm's liabilities, so it sought an additional loan from Perkins (D) and Freeman (D). While discussing the second loan, it was proposed that Peyton (D), Perkins (D), and Freeman (D) should become partners of the firm. The firm rejected the proposal, but the parties agreed that in exchange for a loan of securities, Peyton (D), Perkins (D), and Freeman (D) would receive as collateral speculative securities owned by the firm, and forty percent of the firm's profits until the loan was repaid. The agreement also contained an option for Peyton (D), Perkins (D), or Freeman (D) to join the firm if they so chose. Martin (P), a creditor, sought payment from Peyton (D), Perkins (D), and Freeman (D) of the debt owed to him by the firm, arguing that the defendants had became partners of the firm. The trial court entered a judgment for the defendants, finding that no partnership existed.

■ **ISSUE**

Does the loan of money in exchange for securities owned by the debtor and a percentage of the debtor's income create a partnership?

■ **DECISION AND RATIONALE**

(Andrews, J.) No. A partnership is created by an express or implied contract between two persons with the intent to form a partnership. By receiving the firm's speculative securities as collateral for a loan, the defendants are mere trustees. As trustees, they have the right to be informed of all transactions affecting the securities and the power to veto any decisions that are detrimental to their value. They do not, however, have the power to initiate any transaction or to bind the firm by their own actions. Their power of control is limited to those transactions that directly affect their collateral's value. Similarly, the provision entitling the defendants to a percentage of the firm's profit pending repayment of the loan does not demonstrate an intention to form a partnership. The profit-sharing provision is merely protection for the defendants' loan. In order to establish the firm's profit, each member is required to assign a portion of his interest in the firm to the defendants to enable a calculation of the firm's profits.

However, the agreement does not compel the firm to continue in business. Finally, the option to join the firm demonstrates at most a future intent between the firm and the defendants to create a partnership, but it does not form a partnership as of the date of the agreement. No partnership is formed. Affirmed.

Analysis:

The court emphasizes that a partnership is created by an express or implied contract between two persons only if they intend to form a partnership. While a partnership cannot be formed without the parties' intent to do so, the focus is on the intended consequences of the parties' agreement, not the label attached to their relationship. Thus, if parties agree to share profits, losses, and control over a business venture, a partnership is formed even though the parties have chosen not to call their relationship a partnership.

■ CASE VOCABULARY

COLLATERAL: Property that is pledged as security against a debt; the property subject to a security interest.

CREDITOR: One to whom a debt is owed; one who gives credit for money or goods.

Southex Exhibitions, Inc. v. Rhode Island Builders Assoc., Inc.

(*Home Show Promoter*) v. (*Home Show Sponsor*)

279 F.3d 94 (1st Cir. 2002)

TWO PROMOTERS' MUTUAL SHARING OF PROFITS AND INTELLECTUAL PROPERTY DOES NOT ESTABLISH A PARTNERSHIP

■ **INSTANT FACTS** Rhode Island Builders Association, Inc. (D), replaced Southex Exhibitions, Inc. (P), as the promoter of its home show after terminating a contract it had entered into with the plaintiff's predecessor.

■ **BLACK LETTER RULE** Sharing profits is prima facie evidence of a partnership, which can be rebutted by evidence sufficiently demonstrating that the parties did not intend to create a partnership.

■ **PROCEDURAL BASIS**

On appeal to review a judgment for the defendant.

■ **FACTS**

In 1974, Rhode Island Builders Association, Inc. (RIBA) (D), entered into a five-year renewable agreement with Sherman Exposition Management, Inc. (SEM), to act as "sponsors and partners" in the production of home shows at the Providence Civic Center. Under the agreement, RIBA (D) agreed to produce only shows sponsored by SEM, to persuade RIBA (D) members to exhibit at SEM shows, and to allow SEM to use RIBA's (D) name for promotional uses. SEM agreed to secure all leases, licenses, and permits necessary for the shows, to indemnify RIBA (D) for any losses, to allow RIBA (D) the right to select the shows' exhibitors, to monitor the shows' profits, and to provide the capital needed to finance the shows. All profits earned from the shows were to be divided unequally, with fifty-five percent distributed to SEM and forty-five percent to RIBA (D). SEM's president clearly indicated that he wanted no ownership in the home show because of the uncertainty of the shows' financial prospects. SEM routinely referred to itself as the producer of the RIBA (D) show. Twenty years later, Southex Exhibitions, Inc. (P), acquired SEM and determined that the 1974 agreement needed modification to maintain the shows' financial prosperity. RIBA (D) was unhappy with the new arrangement and entered into a contract with another producer to sponsor its show. Southex (P) sued RIBA (D) in federal court claiming it had entered into a partnership with SEM. Based on the partnership, Southex (P) sought to enjoin a RIBA (D) home show produced by the new producer, claiming RIBA (D) wrongfully dissolved the partnership and breached its fiduciary duties to Southex (P). The federal trial court entered judgment for RIBA (D), finding that no partnership had been created.

■ **ISSUE**

Did RIBA (D) and SEM enter into a partnership by agreeing to share profits earned from sponsored home shows and mutually contributing time, skill, and intellectual property to the shows?

■ **DECISION AND RATIONALE**

(Judge Undisclosed) No. A partnership is "an association of two (2) or more persons to carry on as co-owners a business for profit." In determining whether a partnership is formed, mutual ownership of property does not establish a partnership, regardless of whether the co-owners share profits earned from the property. To the contrary, sharing profits is prima facie evidence of a partnership, which can be rebutted with a showing that the profits were received in payment of a debt, employee wages, rent, interest on a loan, or the sale of goodwill. Southex (P) asserts that the 1974 agreement established a partnership because the parties each shared in the profits earned from the shows, maintained control over the business operations, and contributed valuable property to the business. Such evidence, even if accepted as true, does not demonstrate that the trial court erred in concluding that no partnership exists. The agreement between RIBA (D) and SEM was not titled a partnership agreement and was not for an indefinite duration. Similarly, SEM undertook to contribute all the operating costs necessary to produce the shows and indemnify RIBA (D) for any losses realized. SEM made the majority of the management decisions, and Southex (P) entered into contracts with third parties in its own name rather than the name of the alleged partnership. There is no evidence that the intellectual property contributed by RIBA (D) and SEM was intended to convey a property interest upon the other, especially since the agreement covered only an annual event of a fixed duration. Finally, SEM's president testified that he considered SEM to be the producer of the RIBA (D) shows and that SEM had disclaimed any ownership interest in the shows in 1974. Although the parties referred to themselves as "partners" in the 1974 agreement, the court may not enforce a label alleged by the parties if the substance of their relationship indicates otherwise. On the evidence presented, the trial court rationally concluded that no partnership exists. Affirmed.

Analysis:

In this case, the court found that although the parties referred to themselves as "partners" in their agreement, it would not enforce the label if the substance of the parties' relationship indicated otherwise. However, although the parties' reference to themselves as partners in their agreement does not conclusively establish a partnership between them, the parties' reference may establish a partnership by estoppel. Under partnership by estoppel, a partnership is established, even if the intended relationship does not amount to a partnership, if the parties manifest to others that a partnership exists and third persons rely upon those manifestations.

■ CASE VOCABULARY

DISSOLUTION: The termination of a previously existing partnership upon the occurrence of an event specified in the partnership agreement, such as a partner's withdrawal from the partnership.

INTELLECTUAL PROPERTY: A category of intangible rights protecting commercially valuable products of the human intellect. The category comprises primarily trademark, copyright, and patent rights, but also includes trade-secret rights, publicity rights, moral rights, and rights against unfair competition.

PROFIT: The excess of revenues over expenditures in a business transaction.

Young v. Jones

(Investor) v. *(Accounting Firm Representative)*
816 F.Supp. 1070 (D.S.C. 1992)

PRICE WATERHOUSE–US IS NOT A PARTNER BY ESTOPPEL WITH PRICE WATERHOUSE–BAHAMAS

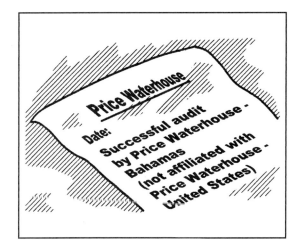

■ **INSTANT FACTS** Young (P) and others invested money in reliance upon a fraudulent audit statement prepared by Price Waterhouse–Bahamas.

■ **BLACK LETTER RULE** A person who represents himself, or permits another to represent him, as a partner in an existing partnership or with others not actual partners, is liable to any person to whom such a representation is made who has, in reliance on the representation, given credit to the actual or apparent partnership.

■ **PROCEDURAL BASIS**

Consideration of the defendant's motion for summary judgment.

■ **FACTS**

In reliance upon an unqualified audit statement concerning Swiss American Fidelity and Insurance Guaranty (SAFIG) prepared by Price Waterhouse–Bahamas, the plaintiffs deposited $550,000 in a South Carolina bank. The audit was prepared on Price Waterhouse letterhead and was signed by "Price Waterhouse." The plaintiff later learned that the audit statement was fraudulent, and the plaintiffs lost their investment. The plaintiffs sued Price Waterhouse–Bahamas, Price Waterhouse–US, and others as business partners jointly liable for their damages. Price Waterhouse–Bahamas and Price Waterhouse–US provided certified documents establishing that the two entities operated independently and had no control over one another. Price Waterhouse–US filed for summary judgment. The plaintiffs responded that even if the two entities were not actual partners, they operated as partners by estoppel.

■ **ISSUE**

Are Price Waterhouse–US and Price Waterhouse–Bahamas partners by estoppel?

■ **DECISION AND RATIONALE**

(Judge Undisclosed) No. Although not partners in fact, "a person who represents himself, or permits another to represent him, to anyone as a partner in an existing partnership or with others not actual partners, is liable to any such person to whom such a representation is made who has, on the faith of the representation, given credit to the actual or apparent partnership." The plaintiffs provide no evidence that Price Waterhouse–US has represented itself as a partner with Price Waterhouse–Bahamas. The plaintiffs contend that brochures indicating that Price Waterhouse–US is part of a global conglomerate of accounting professionals represents to third parties that Price Waterhouse–US has joined with Price Waterhouse–Bahamas and others to gain public confidence in the quality of their accounting services. The brochure, however, gives no indication that Price Waterhouse–US is liable for the debts of Price Waterhouse–Bahamas or any other Price Waterhouse affiliate. Further, the plaintiffs do not contend that they actually relied on the brochure in making their investment. Also, no licensing agreements between Price Waterhouse–US and Price Waterhouse–Bahamas address the use of trademarks or trade names so as to provide a connection between the two entities. Under state law, partnership by estoppel arises only when a third party has "given credit" in reliance upon a partnership representation. There is no evidence that the plaintiffs have extended any credit to Price Waterhouse–Bahamas or Price Waterhouse–US. Finally, no evidence demonstrates that Price Waterhouse–US had anything to do with the preparation or dissemination of the fraudulent audit statement. Absent some involvement or representation from Price Waterhouse–US, it cannot be held liable for the actions of Price Waterhouse–Bahamas. Motion granted.

Analysis:

Partnership by estoppel confers upon third parties rights against alleged partners that the alleged partners do not possess against one another. A third party who deals with a business in reasonable reliance upon representations that a partnership exists may hold each individual partner liable for any debts incurred, even if a partnership does not exist. The individual parties, however, may not hold each other liable as partners because no partnership exists.

■ CASE VOCABULARY

ESTOPPEL: A bar that prevents one from asserting a claim or right that contradicts what one has said or done before or what has been legally established as true.

PARTNERSHIP BY ESTOPPEL: A partnership implied by law when one or more persons represent themselves as partners to a third party who relies on that representation. A person who is deemed a partner by estoppel becomes liable for any credit extended to the partnership by the third party.

Meinhard v. Salmon

(Joint Adventurer) v. *(Joint Adventurer)*
249 N.Y. 458, 164 N.E. 545 (1928)

A JOINT ADVENTURER'S SEIZURE OF A JOINT VENTURE'S OPPORTUNITY BREACHES HIS DUTY OF LOYALTY TO THE OTHER JOINT ADVENTURERS

Not honesty alone, but the punctilio of an honor the most sensitive, is then the standard of behavior

■ **INSTANT FACTS** Salmon (D) terminated a lease belonging to his joint venture with Meinhard (P) to enter into a new lease on behalf of his solely owned business.

■ **BLACK LETTER RULE** Like partners, joint adventurers owe one another the duty of loyalty.

■ **PROCEDURAL BASIS**

On appeal to review a judgment for the plaintiff.

■ **FACTS**

Salmon (D) leased a hotel building from Louisa Gerry to convert it into a shopping and office building. At the same time, Salmon (D) entered into a joint venture with Meinhard (P) to finance one-half of the conversion expenses in exchange for a share of the profits. Each party bore equally any or the business' losses, but Salmon (D) possessed all management rights. When the lease approached termination, Elbridge Gerry, who had acquired the lease rights, planned to lease the property, along with other adjoining property he owned, to a developer intending to demolish the building and build a new building on the property. Unable to secure the necessary financing for his construction plans, the developer approached Salmon (D) about joining his project. Salmon (D) allowed his original lease with Louisa to terminate and executed a new lease between Elbridge and Salmon's (D) realty company. Salmon (D) never informed Meinhard (P) of the arrangement. Upon learning of the new lease, Meinhard (P) demanded that the lease was the joint venture's property. When Salmon (D) refused to hold the lease in trust, Meinhard (P) sued. A referee declared the new lease to be the property of the joint venture, and awarded Meinhard (P) a one-fourth interest. On appeal, the New York Appellate Division modified the award to grant Meinhard (P) his one-half interest.

■ **ISSUE**

Does a joint adventurer breach his or her duty of loyalty by seizing an opportunity for the joint venture for his or her own personal gain?

■ **DECISION AND RATIONALE**

(Cardozo, C.J.) Yes. Like partners, joint adventurers owe one another the duty of loyalty. Here, Salmon (D) held the original lease not as an individual, but as a fiduciary to Meinhard (P), his joint adventurer. Not only did Salmon (D) fail to disclose his secret negotiations to Meinhard (P), but he appeared to Elbridge to be acting on his own behalf. If Salmon (D) had informed Elbridge of his joint venture, he likely would have presented the lease to both Salmon (D) and Meinhard (P) as a joint venture rather than to Salmon (D) individually. By all appearances, Salmon (P), the manager of the property under the lease, controlled the decision to renew the prior lease or terminate it in favor of a new one. By failing to disclose his joint venture and failing to inform Meinhard (P) of the opportunity presented, Salmon (D) deprived Meinhard (P) of the chance to compete for the new lease. Though Meinhard's (P) chance may have been slim given Salmon's (D) position as a real estate merchant, Meinhard (P) may have forged a new joint venture with better qualified allies or may have persuaded Elbridge to continue to contract with the original partnership. Whatever the outcome may have been, Salmon's (D) duty of loyalty to Meinhard (P) requires a good faith disclosure of the joint venture to preserve Meinhard's (P) opportunity. Salmon's (D) actual motive is irrelevant. While Salmon (D) likely acted in good faith considering the impending end to the original lease and the need to take action for the future, his actions may not place his personal interests before those of the joint venture. By failing to disclose the new opportunity to Meinhard (P) and taking advantage of it himself, Salmon (D) breached his duty of loyalty. However, although Salmon (D) breached his duty, the lease should not be held in trust for the joint venture's benefit. To do so would restrict Salmon's (D) right to assign the lease should he choose to do so with Elbridge's consent. Instead, Meinhard (P) should be compensated by an apportionment of the stock held in the joint venture. However, because an equal division of the stock would deprive Salmon (D) of control and management of the venture, Meinhard (P) should be awarded one share short of half of those issued, but Meinhard's (P) interest must equal one-half of the value of the lease. The judgment is modified to afford Salmon (D) the option to substitute Meinhard's (D) interest in the lease for his share of the venture's stock. Affirmed as modified.

■ DISSENT

(Andrews, J.) Had the parties entered into a partnership, the court's holding would be correct. The parties, however, entered into a joint venture, so much more lenient principles apply. The parties' business venture had a limited purpose with a definite duration. It was formed to take advantage of a favorable lease during the lease period to generate a profit. There was no expectation that the venture would extend beyond the lease period or its stated purpose. Meinhard (P) has an interest in the venture, but that interest ended with the venture. Salmon (D) has done no act that he promised not to do. Since the new lease was formed after the end of the joint venture, Meinhard (P) has no interest in it.

Analysis:

Courts often apply partnership law to joint ventures, although the two business relationships are distinct. A partnership is generally a longstanding relationship with general undertakings designed to generate profit. A joint venture, on the other hand, is more limited in duration and generally for a specific undertaking. For example, two lawyers may join together to form a partnership to share the profits and losses from their practice. On the other hand, if two attorneys collaborate as co-counsel to defend a particular client, the attorneys may establish a joint venture with each contributing time, money and labor.

■ CASE VOCABULARY

FIDUCIARY RELATIONSHIP: A relationship in which one person is under a duty to act for the benefit of the other on matters within the scope of the relationship.

JOINT VENTURE: A business undertaking by two or more persons engaged in a single defined project. The necessary elements are: (1) an express or implied agreement; (2) a common purpose that the group intends to carry out; (3) shared profits and losses; and (4) each member's equal voice in controlling the project.

Bane v. Ferguson

(Former Partner) v. *(Management Council Member)*

890 F.2d 11 (7th Cir. 1989)

FORMER PARTNER IS NOT OWED A FIDUCIARY DUTY TO MAINTAIN A PENSION PLAN UPON TERMINATION OF THE PARTNERSHIP

■ **INSTANT FACTS** Bane's (P) pension payments were terminated when his former firm's management council decided to merge with another law firm, ultimately resulting in dissolution.

■ **BLACK LETTER RULE** The fiduciary duties owed by one partner to another terminate when the partnership is dissolved.

■ **PROCEDURAL BASIS**

On appeal to review a judgment for the defendants.

■ **FACTS**

Bane (P) was a partner in a prestigious Chicago law firm. During his employment, the firm established a retirement plan that entitled partners to a pension upon retirement. The plan was to terminate in the event that the firm dissolved without forming a successor entity. Four months after the plan was established, Bane (P) retired and began drawing his pension. Several months later, the firm merged with another firm, but dissolved several years later without forming a new entity. The firm's retirement plan and Bane's (P) pension payments ceased. Bane (P) sued the firm's management council for negligent management in deciding to merge, for purchasing computers and other office equipment before the dissolution, and for leaving the firm for better jobs before the dissolution.

■ **ISSUE**

Does a retired partner in a law firm have either a common law or a statutory claim against the firm's managing council for acts of negligence that, by causing the firm to dissolve, terminate his retirement benefits?

■ **DECISION AND RATIONALE**

(Posner, C.J.) No. Bane (P) argues that by mismanaging the firm's business, the management council members violated the Uniform Partnership Act by engaging in actions that "would make it impossible to carry on the ordinary business of the partnership." This provision of the Uniform Partnership Act, however, protects partners from liability for their partners' negligence. Upon his retirement, Bane (P) ceased being a partner and cannot claim protection as a partner. Similarly, his former partners owed Bane (P) no fiduciary duty upon his retirement. Fiduciary duties run only between partners, and the termination of the partnership relationship also terminates any fiduciary duties owed. Neither does the pension plan create a trust, through which the management council owes a fiduciary duty to its beneficiaries. Even if a fiduciary duty exists, the management council's good-faith decision to merge the firm is protected by the business-judgment rule. Affirmed.

Analysis:

The fiduciary duties one partner owes to another terminate when the partnership is dissolved. Therefore, when a partnership relationship ends, it becomes crucial to preserve the exiting partner's legal rights in the termination agreement or some other contract. Because the law generally relieves the remaining partners of all fiduciary duties to the exiting partner, the partnership need not act in the exiting partner's best interests. Thus, the remaining partners may only be held in breach of contract if the termination agreement fully defines the former partners' rights and obligations.

■ CASE VOCABULARY

BUSINESS–JUDGMENT RULE: The presumption that in making business decisions not involving direct self-interest or self-dealing, corporate directors act on an informed basis, in good faith, and in the honest belief that their actions are in the corporation's best interest.

Meehan v. Shaughnessy

(*Former Law Partner*) v. (*Law Partnership Representative*)
404 Mass. 419, 535 N.E.2d 1255 (1989)

ONE-SIDED SOLICITATIONS TO A PARTNERSHIP'S CLIENTS BREACH THE DUTY OF GOOD FAITH AND FAIR DEALING

■ **INSTANT FACTS** Meehan (P), Boyle (P), and Cohen (P) separated from Parker Coulter (D), their former law partnership, to form a new law firm with cases removed from Parker Coulter (D).

■ **BLACK LETTER RULE** A partner must render on demand true and full information of all things affecting the partnership to any partner.

■ PROCEDURAL BASIS

On appeal to review a judgment for the plaintiffs.

■ FACTS

Meehan (P) and Boyle (P) were partners in the law partnership of Parker Coulter (D). Growing dissatisfied with the firm, Meehan (P) and Boyle (P) decided to leave the partnership to form their own law firm. They arranged a meeting with Cohen (P), a Parker Coulter (D) junior partner, to ask her to join them at their new firm. In preparation for the meeting, Boyle (P) prepared lists of his current cases, including their settlement value and value to the new firm, and asked Cohen (P) to review the lists before the scheduled meeting, but to hold them confidential until they formally notified Parker Coulter (D) of their separation. At the meeting, Cohen (P) indicated she would consider the offer to join the new firm and that she would hold the lists in confidence. After a month, Cohen (P) agreed to join the new firm because she enjoyed working with the new firm's plaintiffs. Earlier, Boyle (P) had also offered Schafer, an associate, an associate position with the new firm. Boyle (P) asked Schafer to prepare a list of his cases to take to the new firm and to withhold the resolution of cases until after the new firm was established, if possible. Two other Parker Coulter (D) associates were recruited to the new firm after receiving assurances that their primary clients would follow. With the associates in place, Meehan (P), Boyle (P), and Cohen (P) began arranging the formation of the new firm, including leasing office space and consulting an attorney to plan the formation. Approximately one month before their expected separation from Parker Coulter (D), the plaintiffs prepared form letters for their Parker Coulter (D) clients notifying them of the changes and requesting authorization to remove their cases to the new firm. Before they sent the letters and gave a separation notice to Parker Coulter (D), the plaintiffs were confronted by several partners concerning rumors that they were leaving the firm. The plaintiffs assured the partners that they were not planning to leave. On one occasion, Shaughnessy (D) confronted Boyle (P) on the rumors, to which Boyle (P) gave an evasive response. Meehan (P) and Boyle (P) then decided to distributed notices to each partner indicating their separation effective one month from the date of the letter. Shortly thereafter, Parker Coulter (D) requested that Boyle (P) provide a list of his cases, indicating which he intended to take to the new firm. Boyle (P), meanwhile, had been contacting referring attorneys for their continued referrals and mailed his form letters to his clients. Boyle (P) did not provide his list of cases to Parker Coulter (D) for two weeks. During that time, Boyle (P) continued to ensure the removal of his cases. When the new firm commenced, the plaintiffs had successfully removed approximately two-thirds of the contingent fee cases pending at Parker Coulter (D), although several large cases and prominent clients remained at Parker Coulter (D). The Parker Coulter (D) partnership agreement allowed a voluntarily retiring partner to remove those cases he or she brought to the firm out of his or her personal efforts or that arose out of the retiring partner's connections for a "fair charge," subject to the clients' choice to remain with the firm. Of the cases removed to the new firm, thirty-five had come to Parker Coulter (D) by the efforts or connections of other Parker Coulter (D) attorneys, but the plaintiffs had spoken with each client and obtained a written authorization for the cases' removal. At all times during the planning and formation of the new firm, the plaintiffs had worked full-time for Parker Coulter (D) and handled their cases appropriately, resolving cases consistent with the clients' best interests and maintaining their general job standards. The plaintiffs sued Parker Coulter (D) for amounts allegedly due under the partnership agreement and for a ruling on the amount owed to Parker Coulter (D) for profit earned on the removed cases. Parker Coulter (D) counterclaimed for breach of fiduciary duty and breach of the partnership agreement resulting from the plaintiffs removing the cases improperly from Parker Coulter (D) and inducing employees to leave Parker Coulter (D) for the new firm. The court denied relief under the counterclaim, finding that the plaintiffs did not manipulate or mishandle cases before they were removed, and awarded the plaintiffs relief under the partnership agreement. However, the court ruled that Parker Coulter (D) was entitled to a share of fees earned on the removed cases equal to the time billed and the expenses incurred while the cases were handled at Parker Coulter (D). Parker Coulter (D) appealed the court's decision that the plaintiffs did not breach their fiduciary duties.

■ ISSUE

Does a partner breach his fiduciary duty of good faith and loyalty to his partners by inducing the partnership's clients to withdraw their business from the partnership without ample time for the partnership to compete to retain the business?

■ DECISION AND RATIONALE

(Judge Undisclosed) Yes. Parker Coulter (D) contends that the plaintiffs breached their fiduciary duties by mishandling cases for their own benefit, competing with the partnership, and unfairly inducing Parker Coulter (D) clients and referring attorneys to transfer their business from Parker Coulter (D) to the new firm. As a partner, each person owes his partners the duty of good faith and loyalty and must refrain from self-dealing. The court's factual determination that Meehan (P) and Boyle (P) did not mishandle cases for their own benefit is supported by the evidence and must not be disturbed. Evidence that Boyle (P) instructed Schafer to withhold the resolution of cases until they were removed to the new firm does not establish that the cases were in fact mishandled. Meehan (P) and Boyle (P) did not secretly compete with the partnership. A partner may plan to compete with his partnership as long as he does not otherwise breach a fiduciary duty owed to the partnership. Meehan (P) and Boyle (P) did nothing more than make logistical arrangements for the physical location of its new firm while carrying out their normal duties to Parker Coulter (D). However, Meehan (P) and Boyle (P) did breach their fiduciary duties to the partnership by secretly selecting those clients they sought to remove to their new firm and failing to disclose their method of obtaining the clients' consent to Parker Coulter (D). A partner must "render on demand true and full information of all things affecting the partnership to any partner." On several occasions, Meehan (P) and Boyle (P) failed to disclose their plans to partners demanding such information. Meanwhile, the plaintiffs were communicating with clients and referring attorneys to obtain consent to remove their cases. After the plaintiffs gave their separation notice, they continued to use their position of trust to place the partnership at a competitive disadvantage. They delayed the partnership's request for a list of cases to be removed until the plaintiffs could obtain consents from all clients on the list. Additionally, the form letters they sent to their clients failed to inform the clients that they had a right to choose between Parker Coulter (D) and the new firm. By sending the letters so soon after giving their separation notice, the plaintiffs deprived Parker Coulter (D) from effectively presenting the quality of its services to those clients. The plaintiffs breached their fiduciary duty to the defendant. Reversed and remanded.

Analysis:

Disputes often arise concerning the status of partnership clients following the dissolution of a law partnership. While partnership law generally prohibits a departing partner from grabbing the partnership's customers and taking them to a new business venture, the court here relaxed that requirement because of the partnership agreement's specific terms. If the partnership agreement provides the manner in which partnership business can be removed from the partnership, the court will enforce the agreement. Of course, the departing partner must follow the terms of the partnership agreement without violating any fiduciary duties owed to the partnership.

■ **CASE VOCABULARY**

SELF–DEALING: Participation in a transaction that benefits oneself instead of another who is owed a fiduciary duty.

Lawlis v. Kightlinger & Gray

(*Expelled Partner*) v. (*Law Partnership*)

562 N.E.2d 435 (Ind. Ct. App. 1990)

INVOLUNTARY EXPULSION FROM A PARTNERSHIP WITHOUT BAD FAITH DOES NOT GIVE RISE TO DAMAGES FOR WRONGFUL DISSOLUTION

■ **INSTANT FACTS** Lawlis (P) was expelled from the law partnership of Kightlinger & Gray (D) despite complying with all conditions for his continued relationship.

■ **BLACK LETTER RULE** When a partner is involuntarily expelled from a business, his expulsion must be in good faith for a dissolution to occur without violating the partnership agreement.

■ **PROCEDURAL BASIS**

On appeal to review a decision granting the defendants' motion for summary judgment.

■ **FACTS**

Lawlis (P) joined the law partnership of Kightlinger & Gray (D) as a general partner. The partnership agreement compensated Lawlis (P) according to units assigned to him annually by the partnership. Twelve years later, Lawlis (P) underwent treatment for alcohol abuse, but did not disclose his treatment to the partnership. When he finally did disclose the treatment, the partnership met with a physician and amended the partnership agreement to condition Lawlis' (P) continued relationship with the partnership upon meetings with alcohol specialists, continued treatment and therapy, and physician reports indicating favorable progress. Lawlis (P) complied with all conditions. Nonetheless, Lawlis' (P) annual units were reduced following the amendment. Lawlis (P) believed he had met all conditions and demanded his units be increased. Less than a month later, Lawlis (P) was informed that the partnership proposed to expel him from the partnership, and all files were removed from his office. The partnership presented its plan to Lawlis (P) for signature, but he refused to sign it. Lawlis (P) was involuntarily expelled nevertheless upon a vote exceeding the two-thirds required by the partnership agreement, with Lawlis (P) casting the only dissenting vote. The agreement allowed Lawlis (P) to remain on as a partner for six months, drawing a salary and benefits, to facilitate a smooth transition to another job. Lawlis (P) sued for breach of contract, and the court granted the defendants' motion for summary judgment.

■ **ISSUE**

When a partnership agreement provides for involuntary expulsion of a partner without cause, may the expelled partner recover damages for wrongful expulsion absent a showing of bad faith?

■ **DECISION AND RATIONALE**

(Judge Undisclosed) No. Lawlis (P) argues that the defendant wrongfully dissolved the partnership upon notice to him that it intended to expel him. Because that dissolution plan was not approved by two-thirds of the partners, as the partnership agreement requires, Lawlis (P) claims damages for breach of contract. The partnership's intention to dissolve merely informed Lawlis (P) of its future plans. He continued as a senior partner, drawing compensation and exercising voting power over partnership affairs until the final vote. Lawlis (P) considered himself a partner during this time, as indicated by his refusal to sign the expulsion proposal and to cast the dissenting vote. Pursuant to the partnership agreement, only partners have those powers. Lawlis (P) has no claim for damages for breach of contract. Similarly, Lawlis (P) cannot recover for a breach of fiduciary duty. "When a partner is involuntarily expelled from a business, his expulsion must have been ... in good faith for a dissolution to occur without violation of the partnership agreement." Lawlis (P) claims the partnership acted in bad faith by eliminating his position in order to increase the other partners' profits by dividing his interest in the partnership income. The partnership, however, demonstrated a concern over Lawlis' (P) personal well-being during his treatment period even though his work had become unproductive. Rather than expelling him at that time and claiming his income interest for themselves, the partners worked to solve Lawlis' (P) personal problems to enable him to return to his position as a senior partner with the firm. Furthermore, upon voting to expel Lawlis (P), the partnership allowed him to remain a partner for six months and paid him a salary, even though it expected his productivity to decrease dramatically. On these facts, there is no genuine issue of material fact concerning the defendant's bad faith. The parties involved knowingly intended that the involuntary expulsion procedure contained in the partnership agreement was in the partnership's best interests. Where the agreement is freely negotiated and defines the partners' rights and responsibilities, the court will enforce the parties' intent. Affirmed.

Analysis:

Partnership expulsion is virtually always guided by the terms of the partnership agreement. Most well-drafted partnership agreements provide the manner in which a partner can be expelled and the rights to be afforded the partner upon expulsion. In the absence of an agreement, however, the law generally requires only that the partnership act in good faith. No notice or cause is generally required, although proof of bad faith by the partnership can create a cause of action for damages.

■ CASE VOCABULARY

BAD FAITH: Dishonesty of belief or purpose.

DISSOLUTION: The termination of a previously existing partnership upon the occurrence of an event specified in the partnership agreement, such as a partner's withdrawal from the partnership.

EXPULSION: An ejectment or banishment, either through depriving a person of a benefit or by forcibly evicting a person.

Putnam v. Shoaf

(*Transferor*) v. (*Transferee*)

620 S.W.2d 510 (Tenn. Ct. App. 1981)

A PARTNER HAS NO INTEREST IN THE UNKNOWN CHOSES OF ACTION BELONGING TO THE PARTNERSHIP

■ **INSTANT FACTS** Putnam (P) sold all her interest in her partnership to Shoaf (D) in exchange for Shoaf's (D) assumption of personal liability on a bank note.

■ **BLACK LETTER RULE** A partner's property rights include rights in specific partnership property, interests in the partnership, and the right to participate in the partnership's management.

■ **PROCEDURAL BASIS**

Undisclosed.

■ **FACTS**

The Frog Jump Gin Company was organized as a partnership among Carolyn Putnam (P), her husband, and two others. When Putnam's (P) husband passed away in 1974, his interest passed to Putnam (P), who then held a one-half interest in the partnership. By early 1976, the company was operating at a loss, and Putnam (P) sought to withdraw from the partnership. The partnership was heavily indebted to a local bank. Nonetheless, Shoaf (D) and his wife expressed an interest in purchasing Putnam's (P) partnership share. After reviewing the partnership's financial records, Shoaf (D) agreed to purchase Putnam's (P) interest and to assume personal liability for the partnership's debts if she and the other remaining two partners each made equal payments totaling approximately two-thirds of the partnership's debt to the bank. The partners made the payments, Shoaf (D) assumed the remainder of the debt, and Putnam (P) sold Shoaf (D) her partnership interest. Putnam (P) executed a quitclaim deed providing that in exchange for Shoaf's (D) assumption of personal liability on the bank notes, she conveyed to Shoaf (D) her one-half interest in the real property owned by the partnership and "all of the personal property and machinery" used by the business. At the same time, Putnam (P) and Shoaf (D) entered into an agreement that mutually released them from "any and all claims and demands on account of, connected with, or growing out of the said partnership, or the division of assets thereof." Putnam (D) also obtained a release of her personal liability from the bank. Thereafter, Shoaf (D) hired a new bookkeeper, who recognized that the partnership's previous bookkeeper had embezzled from the partnership. Litigation commenced against the bookkeeper and the banks that honored the fraudulent checks, and Putnam (P) intervened claiming a one-half interest in the judgment obtained against the banks.

■ **ISSUE**

May a former partner recover an interest in a judgment obtained by the partnership after transferring his or her interest in the partnership without knowledge of the chose in action's existence?

■ **DECISION AND RATIONALE**

(Judge Undisclosed) No. Under the Uniform Partnership Act, a partner's property rights include rights in specific partnership property, an interest in the partnership, and the right to participate in the partnership's management. A partner's rights in the specific partnership property, however, are not an "interest" in the partnership, for those rights reflect a mere possessory right to the equal use of the partnership's property. A partner's possessory rights do not exist without the partnership. The partner's real interest in the partnership is the right to share in the partnership's profits and surplus, which constitute personal property. However, because the partnership owns all partnership property, the partner's interest is merely a pro rata share of the property's value, not the property itself. Accordingly, a sale of partnership property must be made in the partnership's name and not in an individual partner's name. Therefore, Putnam (P) had no specific interest in the choses of action against the bookkeeper or the banks, which she unknowingly transferred to Shoaf (D) by quitclaim deed. Putnam (P) clearly intended to dissolve the partnership by transferring her partnership interest to Shoaf (D). Although she was unaware of her full interest in the partnership at the time of the transfer, she may not reform her transfer agreement to reflect the value of the later-discovered interests. At the time of the agreement, Putnam's (P) only interest in the partnership was a share of the profits and losses, which she intended to sell to Shoaf (D). Putnam (P) is not entitled to a portion of the judgment.

Analysis:

The general rule is that a partner's property rights include only rights in specific partnership property, an interest in the partnership, and the right to participate in the partnership's management. The partner's rights in the specific partnership property are only possessory rights that do not exist without the partnership. Therefore, generally, partnership property belongs to the partnership, and individual partners maintain only a pro rata interest in the property. Accordingly, if property is acquired in the name of the partnership, rather than an individual partner, or if the property is acquired with other clearly defined partnership property, the property is partnership property.

■ CASE VOCABULARY

CHOSE IN ACTION: The right to bring an action to recover a debt, sum of money, or thing.

INTEREST: A legal share of something; all or part of a legal or equitable claim to or right in property.

REFORMATION: An equitable remedy by which a court will modify a written agreement to reflect the actual intent of the parties, usually to correct fraud or mutual mistake, such as an incomplete property description in a deed.

National Biscuit Co. v. Stroud

(Bread Wholesaler) v. *(Grocery Store Partner)*

249 N.C. 467, 106 S.E.2d 692 (1959)

AN OBJECTING PARTNER IS RESPONSIBLE FOR THE DEBT RESULTING FROM HIS PARTNER'S BREAD PURCHASE

■ **INSTANT FACTS** Freeman purchased bread from National Biscuit Co. (P), although his partner, Stroud (D), had informed Freeman and the plaintiff that he would no longer be responsible for additional bread purchases.

■ **BLACK LETTER RULE** Every partner is an agent of the partnership for the purpose of its business, and every partner's acts for apparently carrying on in the usual way the partnership's business binds the partnership, unless the acting partner has in fact no authority to act for the partnership and the person with whom he is dealing knows that he has no such authority.

■ **PROCEDURAL BASIS**

On appeal to review a judgment for the defendant.

■ **FACTS**

Stroud (D) and Freeman entered into a partnership to operate a grocery store. Nothing in the partnership agreement indicated that Freeman had less control over the daily business operations than Stroud (D). Nonetheless, Stroud (D) informed Freeman that he would no longer be held financially responsible for any bread purchased from National Biscuit Co. (Nabisco) (P). Although Nabisco (P) was informed of Stroud's (D) proclamation, it delivered bread to the partnership at Freeman's request. Nabisco (P) sued Stroud (D) to recover payment for the bread after Stroud (D) and Freeman dissolved the partnership and all partnership assets and debts were assigned to Stroud (D) for liquidation. The trial court held that the debt was a partnership liability, holding Stroud (D) liable to Nabisco (P).

■ **ISSUE**

Is a partner bound to a third party if the partner disagrees with the other partner's business decision and expresses to a third party his or her intention not to be bound by the other partner's decision?

■ **DECISION AND RATIONALE**

(Judge Undisclosed) Yes. Under North Carolina law, "every partner is an agent of the partnership for the purpose of its business, and the act of every partner . . . for apparently carrying on in the usual way the business of the partnership . . . binds the partnership, unless the partner so acting has in fact no authority to act for the partnership . . . and the person with whom he is dealing has knowledge of the fact that he has no such authority." Generally, all partners have equal power to bind the partnership and any difference of business opinion must be resolved by a majority vote. Here, Freeman was a general partner with equal powers as Stroud (D), and Stroud (D) could not restrict Freeman's power to act on behalf of the partnership because the bread purchase was an ordinary business transaction and Stroud (D) did not constitute a majority of the partners. When a disagreement arises between an even division of partners, actions related to the partnership's ordinary business are not restricted. Because Freeman had authority to purchase the plaintiff's bread as an ordinary business transaction, the partnership is liable for the debt. Affirmed.

Analysis:

Small partnerships of only two partners may create considerable problems. Because each partner possesses the power to make ordinary business decisions that bind the partnership, neither partner requires the other's consent to act. Therefore, unilateral actions bind the other partner, and unanimous consent is required to revoke the action. As long as both parties act in good faith without violating any fiduciary duties, a disagreeing partner is powerless to veto his or her partner's ordinary business decisions.

■ CASE VOCABULARY

GENERAL PARTNERSHIP: A partnership in which all partners participate fully in running the business and share equally in profits and losses (though the partners' monetary contributions may vary).

MAJORITY: A number that is more than half of a total; a group of more than 50 percent.

Summers v. Dooley

(Hiring Partner) v. *(Objecting Partner)*
94 Idaho 87, 481 P.2d 318 (1971)

A PARTNER IS NOT LIABLE FOR EXPENSES INCURRED BY ANOTHER PARTNER'S UNILATERAL DECISION TO HIRE AN ADDITIONAL EMPLOYEE

■ **INSTANT FACTS** Summers (P) incurred expenses when he hired a partnership employee despite Dooley's (D) objection.

■ **BLACK LETTER RULE** Absent a contrary agreement, each partner possesses equal rights to manage the partnership's affairs, and no partner is responsible for expenses incurred without majority approval.

■ **PROCEDURAL BASIS**

On appeal to review a partial judgment for the defendant.

■ **FACTS**

Summers (P) and Dooley (D) formed a partnership to operate a trash collection business. The two men ran the business, and when one was unavailable for work, a replacement was found at the unavailable partner's expense. Several years after the business began, Summers (P) approached Dooley (D) about hiring an additional employee. When Dooley (D) refused, Summers (P) hired the employee and paid him out of his personal funds. When Dooley (D) learned of the additional employee, he objected. A year later, Summers (P) sued Dooley (D) to recover one-half of the expenses of hiring the additional employee. Summers (P) argued that although Dooley (D) objected to the hiring, he retained a portion of the profits generated from the employee's labor, ratifying the hiring. The trial court awarded Summers (P) a portion of his claim, and he appealed.

■ **ISSUE**

Is a partner liable for a portion of the expenses arising out of another partner's decision made despite the other partner's knowledge of his or her objection?

■ **DECISION AND RATIONALE**

(Judge Undisclosed) No. Each partner shares equal rights to manage business affairs absent an agreement to the contrary. Further, "any difference arising as to ordinary matters connected with the partnership business may be decided by a majority of the partners." Here, one partner voiced his objections to other's business decision, and a majority did not concur with the decision. Dooley (D) did not ratify Summers' (P) decision, and it would be unjust to hold Dooley (D) responsible for expenses incurred solely from Summers' (P) decision. Affirmed.

Analysis:

Whether a partner is bound by an employment contract entered into by another partner depends on the facts of the situation. If the hiring is an ordinary business matter in the partnership's operation, the employment contract will bind the partnership in the absence of an objection by the majority. If the

---

hiring is not an ordinary business matter, such as when the partnership has not previously hired employees, the employment contract is considered to be with the individual partner, not the partnership.

■ **CASE VOCABULARY**

RATIFICATION: Confirmation and acceptance of a previous act, thereby making the act valid from the moment it was done.

Day v. Sidley & Austin

(*Law Partner*) v. (*Law Partnership*)
394 F.Supp. 986 (D.D.C. 1975)

MANAGING PARTNERS NEED NOT DISCLOSE MANAGEMENT DECISIONS TO PARTNERS WITH NO RIGHT TO CONTROL BUSINESS OPERATIONS

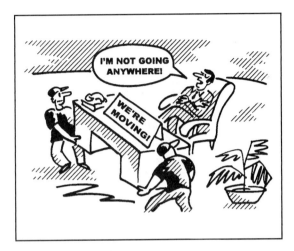

■ **INSTANT FACTS** Day (P) sued Sidley & Austin (D) for breach of contract, fraud, and breach of fiduciary duty after he resigned due to the defendant's decision to merge with another law partnership.

■ **BLACK LETTER RULE** Managing partners have no fiduciary duty to disclose changes in the partnership's internal structure if the changes do not generate a profit or loss for the partnership.

■ **PROCEDURAL BASIS**

Consideration of the defendant's motion for summary judgment.

■ **FACTS**

Day (P), a senior partner at the law firm of Sidley & Austin (D), played an integral role in establishing the firm's office in Washington, D.C. Although Day (P) shared in the partnership's profits and was entitled to vote on certain matters, he did not serve on the executive committee that controlled the firm's day-to-day operations. At a special partner meeting, the executive committee informed the partners that it was considering merging the firm with Liebman, Williams, Bennett, Baird and Minow (the Liebman firm). Day (P) and the other partners approved the proposed merger with the understanding that any formal merger would be subject to a vote by all partners. Once the merger was finalized, a memorandum of understanding and amended partnership agreement were submitted to all partners, including Day (P), who approved the merger. After the merger, the merged firm's executive committee decided to join their two Washington offices and office committees. Shortly thereafter, the Washington office committee recommended that the office be moved from the former Sidley & Austin (D) office building to a new location. Over Day's (P) protests, the office was moved. Two months later, Day (P) resigned from Sidley & Austin (D) because he was unable to work under the new environment. Day (P) sued Sidley & Austin (D) for fraud, breach of contract, conspiracy, wrongful dissolution, and breach of fiduciary duty, claiming his right under the original partnership agreement to remain as sole chairman of the Washington office. Day (P) alleged that Sidley & Austin (D) had decided before the merger to consolidate the two Washington offices and committees, but withheld that information from the other partners. Day (P) further alleged that Sidley & Austin (D) misrepresented that after the merger, "no Sidley partner would be worse off in any way." According to Day (P), this misrepresentation and others voided the merger's approval. Day (P) claimed that the events following the merger were designed to humiliate him into resigning from the firm. In its motion for summary judgment, Sidley & Austin (D) countered that, even if true, Day's (P) arguments did not create genuine issues of material fact because only a majority vote was required to adopt the merger. Further, Sidley & Austin (D) argued that under the partnership agreement, Day (P) had no vested contractual right to remain in his position and the executive committee had complete control over all office committees' composition.

■ **ISSUE**

Does a non-managing partner possess legal rights in a firm's management, entitling him or her to relief?

■ DECISION AND RATIONALE

(Judge Undisclosed) No. Day's (P) fraud claim centers on the alleged misrepresentation that his status would be no worse off than before the merger. This claim fails because Day (P) has no legal right to remain in his position on the Washington office committee. The original partnership agreement does not provide that Day (P) would be the Washington office chairman, although similar provisions establish similar arrangements for other partners. If an unwritten understanding existed to that effect, Day (P) bears the burden of proving the understanding in order to overcome the partnership agreement's language. Having failed to do so, his fraud claim fails. Similarly, Day (P) could not have reasonably believed that no change would come from the merger. Because Day (P) possesses no legal right to his committee position under the partnership agreement, he likewise cannot maintain a cause of action for breach of contract or conspiracy. As for wrongful dissolution, the partnership agreement calls for merely a majority vote to dissolve the partnership and form a new one. Because Day's (P) vote was not the deciding vote in favor of the merger, the partnership could act whether or not he approved the merger. Although fundamental changes in the nature of the partnership's business and the partners' rights generally require unanimous consent, parties are free to abandon that requirement in their partnership agreement. Finally, Day (P) alleges that Sidley & Austin (D) breached their fiduciary duties by negotiating its merger with the Liebman firm without informing the other partners and by concealing major operational changes that would result from the merger. Partners owe one another the duties to account for any profit acquired against the partnership's interests, not to acquire or misappropriate a partnership asset for his or her own use, and not to compete with the partnership business. "The essence of a breach of fiduciary duty between partners is that one partner has advantaged himself at the expense of the firm." There is no fiduciary duty to reveal changes in the partnership's internal structure that do not generate a profit or loss for the partnership. By withholding such information, the executive committee members gained no additional profit for themselves and derived no additional power. Summary judgment granted.

Analysis:

While the Uniform Partnership Act generally requires complete disclosure of all information material to the partnership's business operations, the partnership agreement may temper this requirement. If a partner relinquishes his or her management rights in certain areas by executing the partnership agreement, the managing partners need not disclose information that does not affect that partner's interests. Under such circumstances, some partnership decisions are on a need-to-know basis.

■ CASE VOCABULARY

MERGER: The joining of a company that ceases to exist into another that retains its own name and identity and acquires the assets and liabilities of the former.

Owen v. Cohen

(Partner) v. *(Misbehaving Partner)*

19 Cal.2d 147, 119 P.2d 713 (1941)

MUTUAL DISHARMONY AND DISRESPECT ARE BASES FOR A JUDICIAL DISSOLUTION OF A PARTNERSHIP

■ **INSTANT FACTS** The court dissolved Cohen's (P) and Owen's (D) partnership upon finding that the parties could not practicably continue in business together.

■ **BLACK LETTER RULE** Courts of equity may order the dissolution of a partnership if the partners' quarrels and disagreements are of such a nature and to such an extent that all confidence and cooperation between the parties has been destroyed or if a partner's misbehavior materially hinders the proper conduct of the partnership's business.

■ **PROCEDURAL BASIS**

On appeal to review a judgment of dissolution.

■ **FACTS**

Cohen (P) and Owen (D) entered into an oral partnership agreement to operate a bowling alley for an indefinite term. Cohen (P) supplied the upfront capital with the understanding that the money was a loan to be repaid out of profits. For over three months, the bowling alley operated at a profit, each partner earned an income, and part of the business debt was repaid. Nonetheless, the parties engaged in a dispute over the decline in monthly profits and the repayment of the remaining debt. The defendant frequently humiliated the plaintiff in front of employees and customers, refused to do a substantial amount of the work, and dominated the partnership. Owen (D) also withdrew money from partnership funds for his personal use when he grew dissatisfied with his weekly salary. At Cohen's (P) request, the court appointed a receiver to conduct the partnership's business. The court thereafter determined that the partners fundamentally disagreed with the management of the business, that Owen (D) had breached the partnership agreement, and that the partnership could not carry on. The court entered judgment dissolving the partnership and ordering the receiver to sell the partnership assets, to pay the partnership's liabilities, and to distribute the remaining proceeds between the parties.

■ **ISSUE**

Is a court-ordered dissolution justified if the partners' quarrels and disagreements are of such a nature and to such an extent that all confidence and cooperation between the parties has been destroyed or if a partner's misbehavior materially hinders the proper conduct of the partnership's business.?

■ **DECISION AND RATIONALE**

(Judge Undisclosed) Yes. The totality of the evidence demonstrates that the parties continually disagreed on decisions as to monetary matters. While minor differences of opinion are not a basis for dissolving a partnership, "courts of equity may order the dissolution of a partnership where there are quarrels and disagreements of such a nature and to such extent that all confidence and cooperation between the parties has been destroyed or where one of the parties by his misbehavior materially hinders a proper conduct of the partnership business." The trial court correctly determined that the defendant's treatment of the plaintiff undermines the equality necessary for a partnership to flourish. With such treatment, neither party can reasonably be expected to honor his duties of cooperation, coordination and harmony to the other. If a partner demonstrates conduct that affects the business negatively or willfully breaches the partnership agreement, the court is justified in ordering dissolution. The trial court correctly ordered the dissolution. Upon dissolution, the defendant may not rest on the contract's terms requiring repayment of the plaintiff's loan solely from partnership profits, because the defendant's actions created the need for the dissolution. Affirmed.

Analysis:

Partners must be able to agree to a certain extent on partnership decisions. Generally, the partners may dissolve a partnership by unanimous consent. In absence of unanimity, a partner may seek judicial dissolution for a number of reasons, including a partner's mental unfitness, inability to carry out the partnership agreement, misconduct, and willful breach of the partnership agreement.

■ CASE VOCABULARY

EQUITY: Fairness; impartiality; evenhanded dealing.

Collins v. Lewis

(Financing Partner) v. *(Managing Partner)*

283 S.W.2d 258 (Tex. Civ. App. 1955)

A PARTNER'S INTERFERENCE IN A PARTNERSHIP'S PROPER MANAGEMENT MAY NOT CREATE A RIGHT TO DISSOLUTION

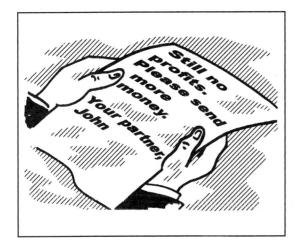

■ **INSTANT FACTS** Collins (P) and Lewis (D) entered into a partnership to operate a cafeteria, with Collins (P) providing the financial backing and Lewis (D) devoting his experience and management ability.

■ **BLACK LETTER RULE** A partner may not obtain a judicial dissolution of the partnership if his own interference causes the partnership to be unprofitable.

■ **PROCEDURAL BASIS**

On appeal to review a judgment for the defendant.

■ **FACTS**

Lewis (D) received a commitment to lease space to operate a cafeteria. Lewis (D) approached Collins (P) for financial support. Under the parties' proposed plan, Lewis (D) would provide the lease, experience and management ability, and Collins (P) would pledge the financial means to operate the business. Profits from the business would first be apportioned to Lewis' (D) established salary, and then to repay Collins' (P) investment. Collins (P) and Lewis (D) executed a written partnership agreement for a term equal to the lease's thirty-year term. Collins (P) agreed to provide the funds for the construction, equipment, and opening of the cafeteria, and Lewis (D) would repay Collins (D) specified minimum annual payments over the term of the partnership. Lewis (D) agreed that if he failed to meet the minimum repayment obligations, he would forfeit his partnership interest to Collins (P). Each party obtained a fifty-percent interest in the partnership. Collins (P) secured the financing on a note from a Dallas bank and requested that Lewis (D) execute a note to the bank for repayment of a portion of the loan upon demand. Fearful of being unable to meet this obligation, Lewis (D) was reluctant to execute the note, but Collins (P) assured Lewis (D) that the notes would be "renewed as often as necessary to protect [him]." Lewis (D) executed the notes and delivered to Collins (P) a mortgage for his share of the partnership. After the parties executed the lease agreement, Lewis (D) immediately prepared plans for the construction and operation of the cafeteria, and estimated to Collins (P) that the start-up costs would be $300,000. However, the start of business was delayed for two-and-a-half years by unforeseen circumstances involving construction and procuring equipment. The parties resolved most of their disagreements regarding the delay, but the actual start-up costs significantly exceeded those quoted by Lewis (D). Collins (P) alleged that the increase was because of Lewis' (D) mismanagement, while Lewis (D) claimed it was due to inflation and unanticipated expenses. Nonetheless, Collins (P) paid the additional start-up costs. After the cafeteria opened, it operated at a significant loss. Still believing the loss was due to Lewis' (D) mismanagement, Collins (P) informed Lewis (D) that he would advance no additional funds until the cafeteria became profitable. When the business failed to become profitable, Collins (P) sued to have a receiver appointed and to obtain a judicial dissolution. Collins (P) also sought foreclosure on the mortgage securing Lewis' (D) interest in the partnership after the bank demanded repayment, thus maturing Collins' (P) obligation on the notes. After the court denied Collins' (P) request for a receivership, a jury entered a verdict for the defendant after concluding that Lewis (D) was

---

competent to manage the business, that the business could not be reasonably expected to generate a profit under Lewis' (D) management, that Collins' (P) interference in the management left the business unprofitable, and that Collins' (P) interference was unreasonable.

■ ISSUE

Is a partner entitled to dissolve the partnership when his or her actions created a lack of reasonable expectation of profit and the other partner met his or her obligations?

■ DECISION AND RATIONALE

(Judge Undisclosed) No. Every partnership is subject to dissolution in the sense that the power to dissolve always exists, but there may be no right to dissolution. Here, Collins (P) has no right to dissolve the partnership based on the jury's findings. The jury concluded that Lewis (D) is capable of managing the cafeteria, but that Collins' (P) actions prevented him from properly doing so. A partner may not obtain a dissolution of the partnership when his own interference causes the partnership to be unprofitable. Also, Collins (P) is not entitled to foreclose the mortgage on Lewis' (D) partnership interest. Collins (P) seeks foreclosure because the bank demanded repayment of the note, but pursuant to the partnership agreement, Collins (P) was obligated to secure the financing for the construction, equipment, and opening of the business. The right to foreclose the mortgage arises only upon Lewis' (D) failure to repay Collins (P) the annual minimum amount required by the partnership agreement. Accordingly, Collins (P) may not seek foreclosure based on the bank's demand, but only upon evidence that Lewis (D) defaulted on his obligation to repay Collins (P). It was Collins' (P) duty to protect Lewis (D) on the bank notes as long as Lewis (D) met his repayment obligations to Collins (P). Lewis (D) has met this obligation. Although Lewis (D) never paid Collins (P) directly during the first year of the business, the business' actual costs during that year exceeded Collins' (P) investment by more than his required minimum repayment. Collins' (P) refusal to contribute additional funds forced Lewis (D) to pay the overage out of the partnership's first-year profits. Since the agreement charged Collins (P) with providing the financial means to open the business, Lewis's (D) payment of the additional expenses satisfied his obligation to Collins (P). Affirmed.

Analysis:

A partner is entitled to dissolve the partnership pursuant to the partnership agreement's terms, but he or she may not force a dissolution when his or her actions interfered with management and created a lack of reasonable expectation of profit. Partnership dissolution in contravention to a partnership agreement constitutes a wrongful dissolution. A wrongful dissolution does not necessarily require a partner to act in bad faith, but merely arises from a dissolution on grounds not permitted by the partnership agreement or the Uniform Partnership Act.

■ CASE VOCABULARY

MORTGAGE: A conveyance of title to property that is given as security for the payment of a debt or the performance of a duty and that will become void upon payment or performance according to the stipulated terms.

Page v. Page

(*Partner*) v. (*Partner*)
55 Cal.2d 192, 10 Cal.Rptr. 643, 359 P.2d 41 (1961)

ABSENT BAD FAITH OR A BREACH OF FIDUCIARY DUTY, A PARTNER MAY DISSOLVE A PARTNER-SHIP AT WILL BY EXPRESS NOTICE TO HIS PARTNER

■ **INSTANT FACTS** The plaintiff seeks to dissolve his unprofitable partnership with the defendant.

■ **BLACK LETTER RULE** A partnership may be dissolved by the express will of any partner if the partnership agreement specifies no definite term or particular undertaking.

■ **PROCEDURAL BASIS**

On appeal to review a judgment for the defendant.

■ **FACTS**

The plaintiff and the defendant entered into an oral partnership to operate a linen supply business, with each partner contributing an equal amount of money and assets to the partnership. The business was unprofitable for eight years and owed a debt to a corporation wholly owned by the plaintiff. After eight years, the partnership's business began to improve, but the plaintiff sought to terminate the partnership. The trial court determined that the parties had agreed that the partnership would continue until such a time as the business generated profits sufficient to recoup the parties' initial contributions and all indebtedness was paid.

■ **ISSUE**

May a partner dissolve the partnership even though the partnership has not generated sufficient profits to cover the parties' initial investment and acquired debt?

■ **DECISION AND RATIONALE**

(Traynor, J.) Yes. "A partnership may be dissolved by the express will of any partner when no definite term or particular undertaking is specified." At best, the evidence shows that the parties expected the business to cover all initial investments and partnership debt incurred during the course of business. While partnerships may be implied to continue for such term as is necessary to recover the initial investment, the evidence here does not support such an implication. The defendant's testimony establishes merely a common hope that the business would be profitable. All partnerships are created with such hope, and, absent additional evidence that the parties established a specified term, the partnership is terminable at will. Further, no evidence indicates that the plaintiff is acting in bad faith in seeking to terminate the partnership. Although the plaintiff may receive some financial benefit from terminating the partnership, no evidence shows that any benefit is more than temporary. The defendant is protected against abuse by the plaintiff's fiduciary duties to his partner. Although a partner is not bound to remain in an unprofitable partnership at will, he must not use outside pressures to appropriate the partnership's business for his own use. Because the partners established no term for their partnership, the plaintiff is free to dissolve it by express notice to the defendant. Reversed.

Analysis:

A partnership at will can arise if the original partnership agreement contains no specified duration or undertaking. Also, upon the expiration of a specified duration or undertaking in a partnership agreement, the partners may choose to continue the partnership consistent with the agreement. In either circumstance, any partner may choose to dissolve the partnership at any time and for any reason, absent contractual restrictions.

■ **CASE VOCABULARY**

BAD FAITH: Dishonesty of belief or purpose.

PARTNERSHIP AT WILL: A partnership that any partner may dissolve at any time without thereby incurring liability.

Prentiss v. Sheffel

(Partner) v. *(Complaining Partner)*
20 Ariz.App. 411, 513 P.2d 949 (1973)

FORMER PARTNERS MAY PURCHASE THE PARTNERSHIP ASSETS

■ **INSTANT FACTS** Upon dissolution of a partnership, the former partners purchased the partnership assets at a judicial sale.

■ **BLACK LETTER RULE** Upon dissolution of a partnership, a former partner may bid on the partnership assets at a judicial sale.

■ **PROCEDURAL BASIS**

On appeal to review a dissolution order in which the plaintiffs were permitted to bid at the judicial sale.

■ **FACTS**

Three partners formed a partnership to acquire and operate a shopping center. The plaintiffs filed suit, seeking dissolution of the partnership because the defendant failed to contribute his proportionate share of the business's operating losses. Rather than liquidating the dissolved partnership, the plaintiffs requested that they be permitted to continue the business without the defendant and asked the court to determine the defendant's partnership interest. The defendant counterclaimed, asking for a winding up of the partnership and the appointment of a receiver because he had been wrongfully excluded as a partner. The court concluded that the defendant owned a fifteen-percent interest in the partnership. It also found that no partnership agreement addressed the manner in which the partners were to manage the business or established the partnership's duration, that the relationship among the partners had deteriorated, that the defendant had been granted full physical access to the business, that the defendant failed to contribute his pro-rata share of the operating losses, and that the plaintiffs had committed no waste. The court also concluded that the plaintiffs had frozen the defendant out from partnership management decisions. Based on these findings, the court held that the parties were in an at-will partnership that was dissolved when the plaintiffs' froze out the defendant. The court appointed a receiver pending the sale of the partnership assets, and the plaintiffs were permitted to bid on the assets at the judicial sale. The plaintiffs were the highest bidders, purchased the assets, and continued to carry on the partnership's business.

■ **ISSUE**

May two partners in a three-man partnership-at-will, who have excluded the third partner from partnership management, purchase the partnership assets at a judicially supervised dissolution sale?

■ **DECISION AND RATIONALE**

(Judge Undisclosed) Yes. A partner is not precluded from bidding on the partnership assets at a judicial sale upon dissolution. Here, although some general disharmony existed among the parties, the evidence fails to show that the plaintiffs wrongfully excluded the defendant from the partnership's management. Further, the defendant has not been prejudiced by the plaintiffs' participation in the judicial sale. If the plaintiffs had not participated, the sale price would have been substantially less, decreasing the defendant's pro-rata share of the sale proceeds. Also, the defendant was not wrongfully excluded from participation in the sale, because he, too, could have bid for the assets. Affirmed.

Analysis:

Any partner may bid on the partnership assets at a judicial sale upon dissolution. Unlike instances when partners freeze out another partner and seize partnership assets or opportunities without the other's knowledge, all parties have equal purchasing power in a judicial sale. If one partner had been deprived of an opportunity to compete for the business assets, the other partners would have breached their fiduciary duties.

■ CASE VOCABULARY

WINDING UP: The process of settling accounts and liquidating assets in anticipation of a partnership's or a corporation's dissolution.

Monin v. Monin

(Partner) v. *(Partner)*

785 S.W.2d 499 (Ky. Ct. App. 1989)

A FORMER PARTNER BREACHED HIS FIDUCIARY DUTY BY ASSUMING A PARTNERSHIP CONTRACT AFTER DISSOLUTION

■ **INSTANT FACTS** After the plaintiff assumed ownership of all partnership assets, the defendant acquired a milk-hauling contract that had previously belonged to the partnership.

■ **BLACK LETTER RULE** Partners owe the utmost duty of good faith and fairness to former partners after the partnership is dissolved and until the partnership affairs are wound up.

■ **PROCEDURAL BASIS**

On appeal to review a judgment for the defendant.

■ **FACTS**

Charles Monin (P) and Sonny Monin (D) entered into a partnership for a milk-hauling business. After their relationship deteriorated, Sonny (D) informed Charles (P) that he wanted to terminate the partnership. Sonny (D) also informed a client, Dairymen Incorporated (DI), that he was canceling the partnership's DI contract at its renewal time and asked to apply for the right to haul DI's milk personally after the partnership's contract had expired. The DI contract required DI approval before any sale or transfer of the contract. Charles (P) and Sonny (D) entered into a formal partnership termination agreement calling for a private auction of all partnership assets and routes, establishing a covenant not to compete, and declaring that if DI refused to consent to the transfer of its contract to the high bidder, the DI contract would be null and void. At the auction, Charles (P) was the high bidder and took over the business. The same day, DI voted not to use Charles (P) as its hauler and awarded its contract to Sonny (D). As a result, Sonny (D) assumed a principal asset of the former partnership at no cost. Charles (P) sued Sonny (D) for breach of fiduciary duty and tortious interference with contract. The trial court entered a judgment for Sonny (D) reasoning that once DI decided to terminate its contract with the partnership, the contract was no longer partnership property and Sonny (D) breached no fiduciary duty by accepting the later contract.

■ **ISSUE**

Did a partner breach his fiduciary duty to the other partner by acquiring the former partnership's customer contract?

■ **DECISION AND RATIONALE**

(McDonald, J.) Yes. Partners owe the utmost duty of good faith and fairness to former partners after the partnership is dissolved and until the partnership affairs are wound up. These duties are particularly applicable when one partner pays the other to continue the partnership business. Here, Sonny (D) breached his fiduciary duty to Charles (P) when he failed to withdraw his application for the DI contract after Charles (P) was the high bidder. By usurping the DI contract from the partnership, Sonny (D) reduced the partnership's value significantly, while placing himself in a no-lose situation. If DI awarded the contract to Charles (P), the value of Sonny's (D) partnership interest increased; if DI awarded the contract to Sonny (D), he benefited from the profits arising out of the hauling contract. Sonny (D) may not benefit at the expense of the partnership. Reversed and remanded.

■ DISSENT

(Emberton, J.) The evidence fails to show that Sonny (D) breached his fiduciary duty to Charles (P). Instead, it demonstrates that most of Charles' (P) producers expressed their intention not to work with Charles (P), and his drivers indicated that they would quit their employment before working for Charles (P). DI specifically indicated that it could not work with Charles (P), and no evidence shows that this decision was a result of Sonny's (D) influence.

Analysis:

The key fact in this case is that the partnership had not been wound up, even though dissolution had occurred. Fiduciary duties run between partners while the partnership is in force, as well as after dissolution. However, these duties cease to exist once the partnership is wound up. Thus, after a partnership winds up, the partners are free to compete with their former partnership in the absence of a covenant not to compete or other restriction in the former partnership agreement. If such covenants exist, damages arise not from the breach of fiduciary duty, but from the breach of the partnership agreement.

■ CASE VOCABULARY

GOOD FAITH: A state of mind consisting in (1) honesty in belief or purpose, (2) faithfulness to one's duty or obligation, (3) observance of reasonable commercial standards of fair dealing in a given trade or business, or (4) absence of intent to defraud or seek unconscionable advantage.

WINDING UP: The process of settling accounts and liquidating assets in anticipation of a partnership's or a corporation's dissolution.

Pav-Saver Corp. v. Vasso Corp.

(Patent–Holding Partner) v. *(Partner Continuing in Business)*

143 Ill.App.3d 1013, 97 Ill.Dec. 760, 493 N.E.2d 423 (1986)

UPON WRONGFUL DISSOLUTION, A PARTNER RETAINS THE USE OF A FORMER PARTNER'S TRADEMARKS AND PATENTS

■ **INSTANT FACTS** Vasso Corporation (D) alleged Pav–Saver Corporation (P) wrongfully dissolved the partnership, seeking to continue the partnership business.

■ **BLACK LETTER RULE** Upon a wrongful dissolution of a partnership in violation of the partnership agreement, each partner who has not wrongfully dissolved the partnership is entitled to damages for breach of contract and may continue the partnership business for the term required under the partnership agreement with the right to possess the partnership property upon posting a bond.

■ **PROCEDURAL BASIS**

On appeal to review a judgment for the defendant.

■ **FACTS**

Harry Dale was the inventor of the Pav–Saver "slip-form" paver and the majority shareholder of Pav–Saver Corporation (P), which owned the trademark and patents for various pavers. Meersman was the sole shareholder of Vasso Corporation (D). Dale, Pav–Saver Corporation (P), and Meersman formed a partnership called Pav–Saver Manufacturing Company to manufacture and sell paver machines. Dale contributed his services, Pav–Saver Corporation (P) contributed the necessary patents and trademarks, and Meersman provided the financing. The partnership agreement provided that Pav–Saver Corporation (P) would grant the partnership the exclusive right to use its "Pav–Saver" trademark on all machines sold, and the plaintiff would have the right to inspect the quality of all machines manufactured from time to time. The agreement also gave the partnership the exclusive license for the patent on Dale's invention, which remained the plaintiff's property. Further, the agreement provided that the partnership was permanent and incapable of dissolution without all partners' mutual agreement. If one party sought to dissolve the partnership without mutual approval, it would owe liquidated damages. Two years later, the partners dissolved the partnership by mutual agreement, and it was replaced with a new partnership formed by Pav–Saver Corporation (P) and Vasso (D), without involving the individual partners. The new partnership prospered for several years until a slumping economy hindered the business. Pav–Saver Corporation (P) then sent a letter to Meersman, as the owner and sole shareholder of Vasso (D), dissolving the partnership. In response, Meersman moved his office into the partnership business premises and replaced Dale as business manager. Pav–Saver Corporation (P) sought a court-ordered dissolution, the return of its patents and trademarks, and an accounting. Vasso (D) counterclaimed for wrongful dissolution and the right to continue the partnership. The trial court concluded that the plaintiff had wrongfully dissolved the partnership and that the defendant was entitled to carry on the partnership business and to receive liquidated damages under the partnership agreement. The plaintiff appealed, alleging that the court erred in not directing the return of its trademarks and patents or, alternatively, assigning them a value as a partnership asset.

■ ISSUE

Is a partner entitled to retain a former partner's trademarks and patents used in the partnership business upon the former partner's wrongful dissolution of the partnership?

■ DECISION AND RATIONALE

(Judge Undisclosed) Yes. Upon a wrongful dissolution of a partnership in violation of the partnership agreement, each partner who has not wrongfully dissolved the partnership is entitled to damages for breach of contract and may continue the partnership business for the term required under the partnership agreement, with the right to possess the partnership property upon posting a bond. Here, the partnership agreement required a permanent partnership until all parties agreed to dissolution. Therefore, upon Pav–Saver Corporation's (P) wrongful dissolution, Vasso (D) had the right to continue the partnership business with possession of all partnership assets, including the plaintiff's trademarks and patents. These trademarks and patents are instrumental in the partnership business, as the paver machines cannot be manufactured without them. Thus, in order for Vasso (D) to receive its statutory right to continue the partnership business, the plaintiffs' trademarks and patents must remain in the partnership's possession. Similarly, no value should be assigned to the trademarks and patents, as they constitute the good will of the business, which is statutorily exempt from valuation upon a wrongful dissolution. Affirmed.

DISSENT IN PART

(Stouder, J.) While the plaintiff wrongfully dissolved the partnership, the defendant should not retain the trademarks and patents. If a partner wrongfully dissolves the partnership, the remaining partners have the right to continue the partnership business, provided they pay the dissolving partner his interest in the dissolved partnership. But if the partnership agreement highlights the consequences of a wrongful dissolution, the remedies available to the remaining partners are confined to the agreement's terms. Here, the partnership agreement states that the patents remain the plaintiff's property and must be returned upon the partnership's expiration. Further, liquidated damages are due when the partnership is terminated or dissolved. Because the partnership agreement limits the remedies available upon dissolution to liquidated damages, the plaintiff should pay such damages and is entitled to the return of its patents. While the patents may be necessary for the defendant to conduct a profitable business, nothing in the partnership agreement assures the defendant of a profitable business. The defendant may continue the partnership without the use of the plaintiff's trademarks and patents, though likely at a lesser profit. The contract's liquidated damages provision contemplates the return of the plaintiff's patents upon dissolution, because liquidated damages are unnecessary if the partnership retains the patents.

Analysis:

There is considerable controversy over the court's interpretation of the partnership agreement. While the agreement states that Pav–Saver Corporation (P) maintains ownership of the patents and that upon the termination of the partnership the patents are to be returned, it also provides that upon termination, liquidated damages would be due. The difficulty is that permanent partnerships are rare, and the law of dissolution does not fit neatly into such situations. However, critics find it hard to believe that although the partnership was permanent, Pav–Saver Corporation (P) agreed to surrender its patents indefinitely for as long as the defendant desired to use them. The liquidated damages provision appears to declare Vasso's (D) remedy should Pav–Saver Corporation (P) seek the patents' return.

■ CASE VOCABULARY

LIQUIDATED DAMAGES: An amount contractually stipulated as a reasonable estimation of actual damages to be recovered by one party if the other party breaches. If the parties to a contract have agreed on liquidated damages, the sum fixed is the measure of damages for a breach, whether it exceeds or falls short of actual damages.

Kovacik v. Reed

(Capital Contributor) v. *(Labor Contributor)*

49 Cal.2d 166, 315 P.2d 314 (1957)

INVESTOR IS NOT ENTITLED TO RECOVER LOST CAPITAL FROM A JOINT ADVENTURER WHO HAD INVESTED ONLY HIS LABOR

■ **INSTANT FACTS** Kovacik (P) sought recovery from Reed (P) of one-half of the money capital he invested in a losing business venture.

■ **BLACK LETTER RULE** If one partner or joint adventurer contributes the money capital and the other contributes the skill and labor necessary for the venture, neither party is entitled to contribution from the other.

■ **PROCEDURAL BASIS**

On appeal to review a judgment for the plaintiff.

■ **FACTS**

Kovacik (P) agreed with Reed (D) to act as the plaintiff's superintendent and estimator on kitchen remodeling jobs. Kovacik (P) informed Reed (D) that he would invest the money necessary for the jobs and that they would split the profits equally. There was no discussion regarding who would bear any losses. For nearly a year, the two parties completed remodeling jobs, but operated at a loss. Kovacik (P) thereafter demanded Reed (D) contribute money to the venture to offset the losses, and Reed (D) refused. Kovacik (P) sued Reed (D) for an accounting and Reed's (D) proportionate share of the losses. The court concluded that Kovacik (P) and Reed (D) had agreed to share equally in the profits and losses of the venture, and awarded judgment to the plaintiff.

■ **ISSUE**

Is a capital contributor to a joint adventure entitled to recover one-half of the business losses from a joint adventurer who contributed his labor?

■ **DECISION AND RATIONALE**

(Judge Undisclosed) No. Generally, in the absence of a contrary agreement, each partner or joint adventurer shares equally in the profits and losses of the business venture. However, if one partner or joint adventurer contributes the money capital and the other contributes the necessary skill and labor, neither party is entitled to contribution from the other. In the event of a loss, each party loses the value of his contribution. The party contributing money loses his monetary investment and the party contributing his services loses his time and labor. Here, Kovacik (P) is not entitled to contribution for his lost capital. Reversed.

Analysis:

The Uniform Partnership Act (UPA) fashions a default rule that differs from the rule established in *Kovacik*. Under the UPA's approach, each partner shares losses in proportion to their share of the profits. Section 401 of the UPA does not base the burden of losses on the type of contribution made by

---

each partner, but rather on the share of profits to which each partner is entitled. However, elsewhere in the UPA, losses realized upon dissolution are treated differently. In a comment to § 807, the UPA provides that the parties may agree to share operating losses differently than capital losses in the event of dissolution. From this language, a court could determine an implied agreement that a partner contributing only his services would not bear liability for capital losses.

■ **CASE VOCABULARY**

CONTRIBUTION: The right that gives one of several persons who are liable on a common debt the ability to recover ratably from each of the others when that one person discharges the debt for the benefit of all; the right to demand that another who is jointly responsible for a third party's injury supply part of what is required to compensate the third party.

JOINT VENTURE: A business undertaking by two or more persons engaged in a single defined project. The necessary elements are: (1) an express or implied agreement; (2) a common purpose that the group intends to carry out; (3) shared profits and losses; and (4) each member's equal voice in controlling the project.

G & S Inv. v. Belman

(*Partner*) v. (*Representative of Former Partner's Estate*)

145 Ariz. 258, 700 P.2d 1358 (Ct. App. 1984)

THE COURT MUST HONOR A PARTNERSHIP AGREEMENT'S TERM PROVIDING FOR THE BUY–OUT OF A PARTNER UPON DEATH

I think it's time we bought him out

■ **INSTANT FACTS** G & S Investments' (P) partner died while suit for dissolution was pending, triggering the partnership agreement's buy-out provisions.

■ **BLACK LETTER RULE** Under the Uniform Partnership Act, a court may dissolve a partnership when a partner becomes incapable of performing under the partnership agreement, when a partner's conduct tends to affect the business prejudicially, or when a partner willfully breaches the partnership agreement's terms.

■ **PROCEDURAL BASIS**

On appeal to review a judgment for the plaintiff.

■ **FACTS**

G & S Investments (P), Nordale, and others entered into a partnership to own and operate a multi-unit apartment complex. As a result of drug abuse, Nordale became easily agitated and suspicious of others. He stopped going to work and began threatening his partners for acts he alleged they committed. During his divorce, Nordale was permitted to live temporarily in the apartment complex. He disrupted the tenants and refused to pay rent or vacate the apartment. Nordale also repeatedly insisted on unreasonable business decisions that the other partners did not support. As a result, G & S Investments (P) filed suit under the Uniform Partnership Act (UPA) to seek dissolution of the partnership to allow it to buy out Nordale's interest and carry on the partnership business. While the suit was pending, Nordale died. G & S Investments (P) filed a supplemental complaint seeking relief through the partnership agreement rather than the UPA. The trial court concluded that upon Nordale's death, G & S Investments (P) was entitled to continue the partnership upon payment of Nordale's interest to Belman (D), a representative of Nordale's estate.

■ **ISSUE**

May a surviving partner continue the partnership business upon the death of a partner with payment of the deceased partner's interest to his estate as determined by the partnership agreement?

■ **DECISION AND RATIONALE**

(Judge Undisclosed) Yes. Filing a suit for dissolution does not dissolve a partnership. Under the UPA, a court may dissolve a partnership when a partner becomes incapable of performing under the partnership agreement, when a partner's conduct tends to affect the business prejudicially, or when a partner willfully breaches the partnership agreement's terms. However, dissolution occurs only when decreed by the court. The partnership agreement stipulates that upon a partner's death, the remaining partners may carry on the partnership business upon payment of the deceased partner's capital account plus other specified amounts. While the agreement does not define "capital account," generally acceptable accounting principles require a capital account to be calculated on a cost basis, leaving the term unambiguous. Furthermore, a G & S Investments (P) partner testified that the agreement's intent was to use the cost basis. The difference is significant, for on a cost basis, Nordale's capital account would be negative, while he would have substantial sums in his capital account at fair market value. Because a partnership is formed by contract, the court must honor the contract's terms when resolving disputes among partners. Here, the parties intended to measure a capital account using the value of the assets on the partnership's books, and the court may not rewrite the partnership agreement. Affirmed.

Analysis:

This case demonstrates the importance of careful drafting of partnership agreements. All material terms, including definitions and clarifications, should be clearly set forth in the agreement. Courts will strictly enforce the agreement's terms as indicative of the partners' intent. Careful drafting can minimize disputes over the meaning of otherwise ambiguous provisions.

■ CASE VOCABULARY

BUYOUT: The purchase of all or a controlling percentage of the assets or shares of a business.

Jewel v. Boxer

(*Former Partner*) v. (*Former Partner*)

156 Cal.App.3d 171, 203 Cal.Rptr. 13 (1984)

POST–DISSOLUTION INCOME ON UNFINISHED BUSINESS MUST BE ALLOCATED TO EACH FORMER PARTNER

...IF WE DIVIDE OUR FEES ACCORDING TO OUR RESPECTIVE INTERESTS...

■ **INSTANT FACTS** After dissolution of a law firm partnership, the former partners sought to recover their respective partnership shares in the legal fees generated after dissolution on cases that originated with the former partnership.

■ **BLACK LETTER RULE** In the absence of a partnership agreement, the Uniform Partnership Act requires that attorneys' fees received on cases in progress upon dissolution of a law partnership are to be shared by the former partners according to their right to fees in the former partnership, regardless of which former partner provides legal services in the case after the dissolution.

■ **PROCEDURAL BASIS**

On appeal to review a judgment for the plaintiffs.

■ **FACTS**

Jewel (P), Leary (P), and Boxer (D) were partners in a law firm that was formed without a written partnership agreement. Upon mutual agreement, the partnership was dissolved, and the former partners created two new firms. However, their agreement failed to allocate legal fees earned after the dissolution on cases in progress while the old partnership existed. Shortly after the dissolution, Boxer (D) sent a letter to his active clients announcing the dissolution and asking them to sign a substitution of counsel. Jewel (P) and Leary (P), who had joined to form one of the new firms, did the same with their active clients. The fee agreements for each client remained in force as they were under the old partnership. Thereafter, Jewel (P) and Leary (P) filed suit for an accounting, claiming their interests in fees as members of the former partnership. The court allocated the fees based on quantum meruit, considering the time each subsequent firm spent handling each case, the source of each case, and the result achieved by each firm. Assigning percentage values to the factors, the court determined the amount of legal fees each former partner should paid to the old partnership and allocated the fees according to each attorney's interest in the old partnership.

■ **ISSUE**

Should post-dissolution legal fees generated from cases originating with a former partnership be allocated to all former partners based on their respective interests in the former partnership?

■ **DECISION AND RATIONALE**

(Judge Undisclosed) Yes. "In the absence of a partnership agreement, the Uniform Partnership Act requires that attorneys' fees received on cases in progress upon dissolution of a law partnership are to be shared by the former partners according to their right to fees in the former partnership, regardless of which former partner provides legal services in the case after the dissolution." The Uniform Partnership Act (UPA) also provides that a partnership continues until the winding up of all unfinished business, and any income generated from unfinished business is shared among the former partners. Although legal fees occurring after a partnership dissolves are the exclusive product of a former partner's time, skill, and labor, the former partner is not entitled to receive extra compensation for services rendered to complete unfinished business. A substitution of counsel does not convert the former partnership's unfinished business into new business for a new partnership. Courts in other states have held that legal fees generated on cases originating with the old partnership should be distributed according to the former partners' interests in the partnership and not as quantum meruit. While clients have the right to select the counsel of their choice, they are not free to alter the partnership agreement's terms or the distribution of partnership assets as contemplated by the UPA. The rule against extra compensation "prevents partners from competing for the most remunerative cases during the life of the partnership in anticipation that they might retain those cases should the partnership dissolve." Further, the rule lessens the risk of a former partner seizing a client's legal file in order to solicit that client upon dissolution, but creates little additional risk of undue hardship upon the former partners because, although other partners will benefit from one partner's post-dissolution efforts, he or she will benefit from their efforts as well. The partners, through a written partnership agreement, can resolve the risk of a disproportionate assignment of unfinished business to one former partner over another. Here, the parties executed no such agreement, and they must bear the consequences of their failure to do so. The post-dissolution legal fees generated from cases originating with the old partnership must be divided according to the former partners' partnership interests. Reversed and remanded.

Analysis:

The court's insistence that the rule minimizes the undue hardship on the partners because each benefits from the post-dissolution efforts of the others may apply in this case, but not necessarily in others. If a partner leaves his firm for another established firm without taking any cases that originated with the old firm, the departing partner would receive a windfall from the post-dissolution work performed by his former partners. Of course, the departing partner may have performed substantial pre-dissolution work for which he had not yet been compensated because the cases had not been resolved at the time of dissolution.

■ CASE VOCABULARY

ACCOUNTING: A legal action to compel a defendant to account for and pay over money owed to the plaintiff but held by the defendant.

QUANTUM MERUIT: The reasonable value of services; damages awarded in an amount considered reasonable to compensate a person who has rendered services in a quasi-contractual relationship.

WINDING UP: The process of settling accounts and liquidating assets in anticipation of a partnership's or a corporation's dissolution.

Meehan v. Shaughnessy

(*Former Law Partner*) v. (*Law Partnership Representative*)
404 Mass. 419, 535 N.E.2d 1255 (1989)

WRONGFULLY RETAINED PROFITS ARE PLACED IN A CONSTRUCTIVE TRUST FOR THE PARTNER-SHIP'S BENEFIT

■ **INSTANT FACTS** Meehan (P), Boyle (P), and Cohen (P) separated from Parker Coulter (D), their former law partnership, to form a new law firm with cases removed from Parker Coulter (D).

■ **BLACK LETTER RULE** Every partner must account to the partnership and hold as trustee for the partnership any profits he derives, without the other partners' consent, from any transaction connected with the partnership's formation, conduct or liquidation.

■ **PROCEDURAL BASIS**

On appeal to review a judgment for the plaintiffs.

■ **FACTS**

Meehan (P) and Boyle (P) were partners in the law partnership of Parker Coulter (D). Growing dissatisfied with the firm, Meehan (P) and Boyle (P) decided to leave the partnership to form their own law firm. They arranged a meeting with Cohen (P), a Parker Coulter (D) junior partner, to ask her to join them at their new firm. In preparation for the meeting, Boyle (P) prepared lists of his current cases, including their settlement value and value to the new firm, and asked Cohen (P) to review the lists before the scheduled meeting, but to hold them confidential until they formally notified Parker Coulter (D) of their separation. At the meeting, Cohen (P) indicated she would consider the offer to join the new firm and that she would hold the lists in confidence. After a month, Cohen (P) agreed to join the new firm because she enjoyed working with the new firm's plaintiffs. Earlier, Boyle (P) had also offered Schafer, an associate, an associate position with the new firm. Boyle (P) asked Schafer to prepare a list of his cases to take to the new firm and to withhold the resolution of cases until after the new firm was established, if possible. Two other Parker Coulter (D) associates were recruited to the new firm after receiving assurances that their primary clients would follow. With the associates in place, Meehan (P), Boyle (P), and Cohen (P) began arranging the formation of the new firm, including leasing office space and consulting an attorney to plan the formation. Approximately one month before their expected separation from Parker Coulter (D), the plaintiffs prepared form letters for their Parker Coulter (D) clients notifying them of the changes and requesting authorization to remove their cases to the new firm. Before they sent the letters and gave a separation notice to Parker Coulter (D), the plaintiffs were confronted by several partners concerning rumors that they were leaving the firm. The plaintiffs assured the partners that they were not planning to leave. On one occasion, Shaughnessy (D) confronted Boyle (P) on the rumors, to which Boyle (P) gave an evasive response. Meehan (P) and Boyle (P) then decided to distributed notices to each partner indicating their separation effective one month from the date of the letter. Shortly thereafter, Parker Coulter (D) requested that Boyle (P) provide a list of his cases, indicating which he intended to take to the new firm. Boyle (P), meanwhile, had been contacting referring attorneys for their continued referrals and mailed his form letters to his clients. Boyle (P) did not provide his list of cases to Parker Coulter (D) for two weeks. During that time, Boyle (P) continued to ensure the removal of his cases. When the new firm commenced, the plaintiffs had successfully

---

removed approximately two-thirds of the contingent fee cases pending at Parker Coulter (D), although several large cases and prominent clients remained at Parker Coulter (D). The Parker Coulter (D) partnership agreement allowed a voluntarily retiring partner to remove those cases he or she brought to the firm out of his or her personal efforts or that arose out of the retiring partner's connections for a "fair charge," subject to the clients' choice to remain with the firm. Once the cases were removed, all future fees were to be retained by the departing partner. The agreement does not address the disposition of removed cases not brought to the partnership because of the departing partner's personal efforts or contacts. Of the cases removed to the new firm, thirty-five had come to Parker Coulter (D) by the efforts or connections of other Parker Coulter (D) attorneys, but the plaintiffs had spoken with each client and obtained a written authorization for the cases' removal. The partnership agreement similarly provided that upon the voluntary dissolution of the partnership by a partner, the departing partner would receive a share of the firm's current net income and reimbursement of his capital contributions. At all times during the planning and formation of the new firm, the plaintiffs had worked full-time for Parker Coulter (D) and handled their cases appropriately, resolving cases consistent with the clients' best interests and maintaining their general job standards. The plaintiffs sued Parker Coulter (D) for amounts allegedly due under the partnership agreement and for a ruling on the amount owed to Parker Coulter (D) for profit earned on the removed cases. Parker Coulter (D) counterclaimed for breach of fiduciary duty and breach of the partnership agreement resulting from the plaintiffs removing the cases improperly from Parker Coulter (D) and inducing employees to leave Parker Coulter (D) for the new firm. The court denied relief under the counterclaim, finding that the plaintiffs did not manipulate or mishandle cases before they were removed, and awarded the plaintiffs relief under the partnership agreement. However, the court ruled that Parker Coulter (D) was entitled to a share of fees earned on the removed cases equal to the time billed and the expenses incurred while the cases were handled at Parker Coulter (D). Parker Coulter (D) appealed the court's decision that the plaintiffs did not breach their fiduciary duties.

■ ISSUE

Must a partner who breaches a fiduciary duty resulting in a personal benefit hold the wrongfully obtained profits in a constructive trust for the benefit of his former partners?

■ DECISION AND RATIONALE

(Judge Undisclosed) Yes. Although the partnership agreement does not address the disposition of removed cases not brought to the partnership because of the plaintiffs' personal efforts or contacts, the agreement's intent is to treat them similarly. The rules of ethics forbid an attorney from entering into an arrangement that deprives a client of the freedom to select the attorney of his or her choice. Similarly, because the partnership agreement departs from the winding up method of the Uniform Partnership Act (UPA) as it relates to cases generated from personal effort, the partners' intent was to depart from the UPA on all dissolution matters. Accordingly, pursuant to the agreement, a departing partner may remove any case upon payment of a fair charge to the partnership, subject to the client's choice of counsel. In effect, the agreement eliminates unfinished business upon the dissolution of the partnership, because the removed cases become the new business of the new firm, and those retained by Parker Coulter (D) become new business for it. Neither party has an interest in the future profits generated from the other's new business. However, since the dissolution resulted from breaches of the fiduciary duties Meehan (P) and Boyle (P) owed to Parker Coulter (D), the plaintiffs are liable to the defendant for damages unless they prove that the clients in the removed cases would have consented to the removal in the absence of the breaches. If the plaintiffs meet their burden, damages are measured pursuant to the terms of the partnership agreement. However, if they do not meet their burden, damages are determined as provided by the UPA. "Every partner must account to the partnership for any benefit, and hold as trustee for it any profits derived by him without the consent of the other partners from any transaction connected with the formation, conduct or liquidation of the partnership." To determine the profit earned on the cases wrongfully removed from Parker Coulter (D), the fees received on the cases must be reduced by the reasonable overhead expended by the new firm and the fair charge called for by the partnership agreement. While this profit must be treated as earned by the new firm, not Parker Coulter (D), to avoid a windfall to the defendant, the defendant is entitled to its percentage share of the fair charge owed by the plaintiffs for each removed case plus the same percentage of the profit earned by the new firm. Holding these profits in a constructive trust for Parker Coulter (D) ensures that Meehan

(P) and Boyle (P) enjoy the fruit of their labor even though the cases were wrongfully removed and provides the court a means to punish their breach of fiduciary duty. Reversed and remanded.

Analysis:

Generally, the damages available for a misappropriation of a partnership's customer list are the lost profits the partnership would have enjoyed had the partnership continued with the misappropriated business. In a law partnership, ethics rules and public policy form a different basis for damages than that applicable to other partnerships. Because clients always have the right to the attorney of their choice, a partnership is generally not entitled to a share of the lost profits unless it proves that the clients would have remained with the partnership but for a departing partner's wrongful conduct.

■ CASE VOCABULARY

CONSTRUCTIVE TRUST: A trust imposed by a court on equitable grounds against one who has obtained property by wrongdoing, thereby preventing the wrongful holder from being unjustly enriched.

Holzman v. De Escamilla

(*Bankruptcy Trustee*) v. (*General Partner*)
86 Cal.App.2d 858, 195 P.2d 833 (1948)

CONTROL OVER LIMITED PARTNERSHIP'S CROP SELECTION AND BANK TRANSACTIONS ESTAB-
LISHES LIMITED PARTNERS AS GENERAL PARTNERS

You two are only limited partners... I'm planting what I want to plant

■ **INSTANT FACTS** Holzman (P), as bankruptcy trustee, sued the limited partners of a bankrupt partnership to establish them as general partners liable for their creditors' debts.

■ **BLACK LETTER RULE** A limited partner is not liable as a general partner unless, in addition to exercising his rights and powers as a limited partner, he takes part in the control of the business.

■ **PROCEDURAL BASIS**

On appeal to review a judgment for the plaintiff.

■ **FACTS**

Russell and Andrews entered into a limited partnership with De Escamilla (D) to operate Hacienda Farms, Limited. Pursuant to the agreement, De Escamilla (D) was the acting general partner, and Russell and Andrews were limited partners. De Escamilla (D) had originally harvested beans, but he conferred with Russell and Andrews concerning decisions to plant and harvest other crops. Through the course of operations, Russell and Andrews frequently visited the crop fields and decided, with De Escamilla (D), which crops to plant. Some time later, Russell and Andrews called for De Escamilla's resignation as manager, and he was replaced by another man. Bank transactions for the business required signatures of two of the three partners, and De Escamilla (D) was powerless to withdraw money on his own initiative. After Hacienda Farms filed for bankruptcy, Holzman (P), as bankruptcy trustee, sued to declare Russell and Andrews liable as general partners. Finding that Russell and Andrews had taken part in the control of the business, the lower court entered a judgment that Russell and Andrews were liable as general partners.

■ **ISSUE**

Do limited partners who give business advice and dictate business transactions have sufficient control of the limited partnership's business to convert them into general partners?

■ **DECISION AND RATIONALE**

(Judge Undisclosed) Yes. "A limited partner shall not become liable as a general partner, unless in addition to the exercise of his rights and powers as a limited partner, he takes part in the control of the business." Here, Russell and Andrews clearly took control of the business. They were free to dictate business transactions through their own initiative and could veto any business transaction by refusing to sign checks. They actively chose the crops to be planted and replaced De Escamilla (D) with a suitable successor. Because they took control of the business, they are liable as general partners for the partnership's debts. Affirmed.

Analysis:

A limited partner is liable as a general partner only if, in addition to exercising his rights and powers as a limited partner, he participates in the control of the business. Therefore, to hold a limited partner liable for the partnership's debts, a court must draw a line between activities in control of the business and those in control of the limited partner's investment. Actions such as consulting with general partners, acting as a general partner's agent, voting or conferring on business decisions that relate to financing or dissolution, or deciding on a change in the business do not establish control over the business sufficient to hold the limited partner liable as a general partner.

■ CASE VOCABULARY

GENERAL PARTNER: A partner who ordinarily takes part in the daily operations of the business, shares in the profits and losses, and is personally responsible for the partnership's debts and obligations.

LIMITED PARTNER: A partner who receives profits from the business but does not take part in managing the business and is not liable for any amount greater than his or her original investment.

LIMITED PARTNERSHIP: A partnership composed of one or more persons who control the business and are personally liable for the partnership's debts (called general partners), and one or more persons who contribute capital and share profits but who cannot manage the business and are liable only for the amount of their contribution (called limited partners).

CHAPTER THREE

The Nature of the Corporation

Southern-Gulf Marine Co. No. 9, Inc. v. Camcraft, Inc.

Instant Facts: Southern–Gulf Marine Co. (P) signed an agreement as a corporation to purchase a 156–foot supply vessel from Camcraft (D), but it did not incorporate until later.

Black Letter Rule: A defendant may not interpose as a defense to a breach of contract that a plaintiff corporation lacked the capacity to contract because it was not incorporated at the time it executed the contract, unless the failure to incorporate actually harmed the defendant.

Walkovszky v. Carlton

Instant Facts: A pedestrian struck by a taxicab sued the corporation in whose name the taxi was registered, the cabdriver, nine corporations in whose names other taxicabs were registered, two additional corporations, and three individuals.

Black Letter Rule: Absent an allegation that the defendant was conducting business in his individual capacity, a complaint charging that an individual defendant organized a fleet of taxicabs in a fragmented manner solely to limit his liability for personal injury claims is insufficient to hold the individual liable for the claim.

Sea-Land Services, Inc. v. Pepper Source

Instant Facts: Pepper Source (D) owed Sea–Land Services, Inc. (Sea–Land) (P) for the cost of shipping peppers; however, Pepper Source (D) was dissolved before Sea–Land (P) could enforce a judgment against it.

Black Letter Rule: In order to pierce the corporation veil and impose individual liability, a creditor must show (1) that there was such a unity of interest between the individual and the corporate entity that separate identities no longer existed, and (2) that a failure to do so would promote "injustice" in some way beyond simply leaving a creditor unable to satisfy its judgment.

Kinney Shoe Corp. v. Polan

Instant Facts: Kinney Shoe Corp. (P) sublet property to Industrial Realty Co., after negotiating with Lincoln M. Polan (D), the company's sole shareholder, and Industrial Realty defaulted on the lease.

Black Letter Rule: If a corporation's shareholder took no stock in the corporation, undercapitalized it, kept no minutes, elected no officers and attempted to protect assets by placing them in another corporation, a party may pierce the corporate veil.

In re Silicone Gel Breast Implants Products Liability Litigation

Instant Facts: Breast implant recipients brought a products liability action against Bristol–Myers Squibb Co. (D), which was the sole shareholder of Medical Engineering Corporation (D), a major supplier of breast implants.

Black Letter Rule: If a parent corporation uses a subsidiary as its alter ego, as demonstrated by shared common directors or business departments, consolidated financial statements and tax returns, and an inadequately capitalized subsidiary, a plaintiff may assert its claims against the parent.

Frigidaire Sales Corp. v. Union Prop., Inc.

Instant Facts: Frigidaire Sales Corp. (P), a creditor of Commercial Investors, a limited partnership, brought an action against the corporate general partner and its limited partners individually when the partnership failed to pay installments due on contract.

Black Letter Rule: Limited partners are not liable for the debts of a limited partnership simply by their status as officers, directors, or stockholders of the corporate general partner as long as they conscientiously keep the corporate matters separate from their personal business and no fraud or manifest injustice results.

Cohen v. Beneficial Indus. Loan Corp.

Instant Facts: David E. Cohen brought a shareholder's derivative suit against Beneficial Industrial Loan Corp. (Beneficial) (D) and others, and Beneficial brought a motion seeking to have Hannah Cohen (P), David's executrix, post security for the expenses associated with prosecuting the lawsuit.

Black Letter Rule: A New Jersey statute that requires a holder of less than five per cent of a corporation's outstanding shares who brings a derivative suit to pay for all expenses of defending the suit and that requires security for the payment of these expenses should be enforced in cases prosecuted under federal diversity jurisdiction.

Eisenberg v. Flying Tiger Line, Inc.

Instant Facts: A stockholder in a corporation that ceased to exist post-merger, brought an action on behalf of himself and all other stockholders of the dissolved corporation, to enjoin the plan of reorganization and merger.

Black Letter Rule: An action seeking to overturn a reorganization and merger that deprived an acquired corporation's shareholders from having a voice in the surviving corporation's business operations is a personal action rather than a derivative action under the New York statute requiring the posting of security for the corporation's costs.

Grimes v. Donald

Instant Facts: Grimes (P), who learned of the extremely generous compensation package DSC Communications (DSC) (D) had extended to Donald (D), demanded DSC cancel Donald's (D) contract.

Black Letter Rule: A shareholder need not make a demand that a company's board institute a lawsuit before bringing a derivative suit on behalf of the corporation on a showing the demand would be futile, and if a demand is made and rejected, a shareholder may still proceed by establishing that the board's refusal was wrongful.

Marx v. Akers

Instant Facts: A shareholder brought a derivative action charging breach of fiduciary duty and corporate waste by International Business Machines' (IBM) board of directors for excessive compensation of IBM's executives and outside directors.

Black Letter Rule: A plaintiff establishing that a demand on a company's board would have been futile must show either that the measure furthered the board's self-interest, that the directors did not fully inform themselves about the challenged transaction, or that the challenged transaction was so egregious on its face that it could not have been the product of the directors' sound business judgment.

Auerbach v. Bennett

Instant Facts: A corporation appointed a special committee to investigate the basis of a shareholders' derivative suit charging mismanagement of corporate funds, and the committee determined the suit should be terminated.

Black Letter Rule: A special litigation committee's determination forecloses further inquiry into a matter, provided the committee's investigation is bona fide.

Zapata Corp. v. Maldonado

Instant Facts: Maldonado (P), a Zapata Corp. (D) shareholder, sued Zapata's officers and directors for breach of fiduciary duty, but Maldonado (P) did not ask Zapata's board to bring the action, considering the request to be futile.

Black Letter Rule: While a majority of a board may lack the independence to evaluate a derivative claim, the taint of self-interest is not necessarily sufficient to prevent the board from delegating the evaluation to an independent committee comprised of disinterested board members who may recommend dismissal of a shareholder's action.

A.P. Smith Mfg. Co. v. Barlow

Instant Facts: Barlow (P), an A.P. Smith Manufacturing (D) shareholder, brought an action seeking to find that a charitable donation made by the corporation was invalid.

Black Letter Rule: A corporation may make reasonable charitable contributions, even in the absence of express statutory provisions.

Dodge v. Ford Motor Co.

Instant Facts: Ford Motor Company (D) made extraordinary profits and its founder, Henry Ford (D), intended to use those profits to lower the price of its cars and expand its factories' capabilities by adding a steel plant, but Ford Motor's shareholders (P) objected to these policies claiming that the company's first obligation was to make profits for its shareholders.

Black Letter Rule: Although a corporation's directors have discretion in the means they choose to make products and earn a profit, the directors may not reduce profits or withhold dividends from the corporation's shareholders in order to benefit the public.

Shlensky v. Wrigley

Instant Facts: Shlensky, a Chicago Cubs' shareholder, brought a derivative suit against the Chicago Cubs and its directors for negligence and mismanagement and for an order that the defendant install lights for night baseball games.

Black Letter Rule: A shareholder fails to state a cause of action unless it alleges that a corporation's directors' conduct was causing financial loss to the shareholder and was based upon fraud, illegality or conflict of interest.

Southern-Gulf Marine Co. No. 9, Inc. v. Camcraft, Inc.

(Ship Buyer) v. (Supply Vessel Builder)
410 So.2d 1181 (La. Ct. App. 1982)

LACK OF FORMAL CORPORATE STATUS DOES NOT EXCUSE NONPERFORMANCE

■ **INSTANT FACTS** Southern–Gulf Marine Co. (P) signed an agreement as a corporation to purchase a 156–foot supply vessel from Camcraft (D), but it did not incorporate until later.

■ **BLACK LETTER RULE** A defendant may not interpose as a defense to a breach of contract that a plaintiff corporation lacked the capacity to contract because it was not incorporated at the time it executed the contract, unless the failure to incorporate actually harmed the defendant.

■ PROCEDURAL BASIS

On appeal from the trial court's decision in favor of the defendant.

■ FACTS

Southern–Gulf Marine Co. (Southern–Gulf) (P), designated as "a company to be formed," executed a "Letter of Agreement" to purchase a 156–foot supply vessel from Camcraft, Inc. (D) for $1.35 million. The agreement, which set a delivery date and authorized Camcraft (D) to start purchasing parts for the vessel, was signed by Dudley Bowman, the president of Camcraft (D), and D.W. Barrett, as president of Southern–Gulf (P). Both men also signed in their individual capacities. Both companies later signed a Vessel Construction Contract, in which Barrett was again designated as president of Southern–Gulf (P), which was described as a Texas corporation. One of the contract terms provided, in accordance with the Shipping Act of 1916 (the Act), that the plaintiff warranted being a United States citizen and agreed to be subject to the Act's prohibitions on ownership transfers. Barrett wrote Camcraft (D), informing him that the company had decided to incorporate in Cayman, British West Indies, due to financial concerns. He assured Camcraft (D) that the resulting Cayman company had ratified and adopted the agreement the parties had negotiated. Barrett signed the letter in both his individual capacity and in his capacity as president of Southern–Gulf (P). Bowman replied to Southern–Gulf's (P) letter, accepting and agreeing to Barrett's letter. Southern–Gulf (P) sued for breach of contract after Camcraft (D) failed to deliver the vessel on time. Camcraft's (D) response claimed that the plaintiff did not exist at the time the contract was formed, and that although the plaintiff later became incorporated, it was under the laws of a different sovereign than was stated in the agreement. At trial, the judge noted that a contract requires two parties, and because Southern–Gulf (P) was not incorporated at the time the parties signed the contract, there was no contract. The lower court also held that although Southern–Gulf's (P) ratification of the contract was evidence of its own recognition of the contract's invalidity at that point, the ratification was not effective because the company was not a Texas corporation and the parties were not substituted. The trial judge also prohibited Barrett from enforcing the contract in his individual capacity.

■ ISSUE

Does a party's failure to have incorporated before signing a contract with the defendant render the contract unenforceable?

■ DECISION AND RATIONALE

(Doucet, J.) No. Once the defendant agreed to build the vessel, it should not be permitted to escape its obligations by arguing the buyer's failure to have previously incorporated, unless the lack of the plaintiff's organization affects the defendant's rights. Nothing in the record shows that the lack of the plaintiff's corporate status affected the defendant's rights. If the plaintiff had been in default, the defendant would have had no trouble arguing that both the corporation and Barrett were liable on the contract. The contract grants the parties the right to assign their contractual rights and obligations without violating the Shipping Act. Nonetheless, when Camcraft (D) first had the opportunity to object to the Cayman incorporation, it did not; rather, it accepted the notification and agreed to it. The likely reason for the Camcraft's (D) objection now is that it can resell the vessel for more money. The plaintiff's legal status is not relevant and cannot be used to avoid the obligations under the contract. The court made no decision as to whether Barrett could pursue the contract as an individual because the issue was not raised on appeal. Reversed and remanded.

Analysis:

Frequently, a corporation is formed for a single purpose, such as to purchase property, to consult for a business, or, as here, to own and operate a cargo vessel. Corporate formation may be one of the last pieces of the puzzle to come together for many reasons, including the fact that smaller entrepreneurs do not consult with an attorney until fairly late in the process. Southern–Gulf's (P) organizers assumed they would form a corporation under Texas law, probably because it was where they lived. They did not contact an attorney or accountant to discuss the legal liabilities and tax ramifications, and hence did not learn of the advantages of a Cayman corporation, until after they signed the contract with Camcraft (D).

■ CASE VOCABULARY

EXECUTORY CONTRACT: A contract that remains wholly unperformed or for which there remains something still to be done on both sides, often as a component of a larger transaction and sometimes memorialized by an informal letter agreement, by a memorandum, or by oral agreement.

PEREMPTORY EXCEPTION: A defensive pleading asserting that no legal remedy exists for the plaintiff's alleged injury, that res judicata or prescription bars the claim, or that an indispensable party has not been included in the litigation.

RATIFICATION: Confirmation and acceptance of a previous act, thereby making the act valid from the moment it was done. In contracts, a person's binding adoption of an act already completed but either not done in a way that originally produced a legal obligation or done by a third party having at the time no authority to act as the person's agent.

Walkovszky v. Carlton

(Personal Injury Victim) v. *(Taxicab Owner)*

18 N.Y.2d 414, 276 N.Y.S.2d 585, 223 N.E.2d 6 (1966)

A COURT MAY DISREGARD CORPORATE FORM TO PREVENT FRAUD OR ACHIEVE EQUITY

■ **INSTANT FACTS** A pedestrian struck by a taxicab sued the corporation in whose name the taxi was registered, the cabdriver, nine corporations in whose names other taxicabs were registered, two additional corporations, and three individuals.

■ **BLACK LETTER RULE** Absent an allegation that the defendant was conducting business in his individual capacity, a complaint charging that an individual defendant organized a fleet of taxicabs in a fragmented manner solely to limit his liability for personal injury claims is insufficient to hold the individual liable for the claim.

■ **PROCEDURAL BASIS**

The plaintiff appeals a lower court's dismissal of his complaint against the individual defendant for failure to state a cause of action.

■ **FACTS**

Walkovszky (P) was severely injured when he was struck by a taxicab owned by Seon Cab Corp. (D) and driven by Marchese (D). Carlton (D) is a stockholder in ten taxicab corporations, including Seon Cab (D). Each company owns only two cabs and maintains the minimum required amount of insurance on the vehicles. The ten companies share the same financing, supplies, repairs, employees and garages. Walkovszky (P) named each of the ten companies as defendants. Carlton (D) successfully moved to dismiss the action for failure to state a claim. The Appellate Division reversed, and the defendants appeal.

■ **ISSUE**

May a plaintiff recover against individual stockholders if a corporate structure limits the corporations' liability for personal injuries, even if there is no showing that the stockholders used the companies for personal, rather than corporate, gain?

■ **DECISION AND RATIONALE**

(Fuld, J.) No. Although the law permits individuals to incorporate solely to avoid personal liability, courts disregard the corporate form as needed to prevent fraud and ensure equity. In deciding whether to pierce the corporate veil and reach an individual's assets, courts are guided by general agency rules. If an individual controls a corporation for personal gain rather than the corporation's gain, the individual is responsible under respondeat superior for the corporation's acts in commercial dealings and in tort claims. Here, the plaintiff alleged that none of the defendant corporations existed separately and that the defendants organized a fragmented corporate structure. However, the plaintiff does not allege that the individual defendants were acting in their individual capacities. Even if only one corporation owned the taxi fleet, the plaintiff would have an uphill battle trying to establish the stockholders' personal liability. A court may not overlook corporate formalities to provide a plaintiff with resources for his or her injuries. The cab owner carried the required insurance. If that amount is inadequate, the problem must

---

be brought to the legislature. There are no allegations here that the individual stockholders commingled funds, that the companies are undercapitalized, or that the stockholders are operating the businesses without regard to corporate formalities. The plaintiff is alleging only fraud, and the corporations' activities are not fraudulent. Reversed; trial court's order reinstated with leave to allow the plaintiff to file an amended complaint.

■ DISSENT

(Keating, J.) Carlton (D) organized the ten corporations so that each company owned only two vehicles and carried the minimum amount of required insurance. The companies are undercapitalized and have been since they were formed. The reason they were structured in this way was to ensure a minimum amount of assets would be available to satisfy their liability for negligent acts. The legislature has responded to concerns about victims of motor vehicle accidents by passing the law requiring minimum insurance coverage. That the defendants here had the minimum insurance demanded by statute does not end the discussion. The insurance laws were not designed to protect those who abused the corporate structure and would otherwise have income necessary to purchase additional coverage. The fact that the legislature has not acted to increase those minimum levels is not evidence that it considers the current requirements sufficient. The defendants here manipulated the law to the owner's benefit to eliminate reserves that could support higher premiums.

Analysis:

While the court here found no illegal motives behind the fragmented ownership of the multiple taxicab companies, the court reached a different result in *Goldberg v. Lee Express Cab Corp.*, 166 Misc. 2d 668, 634 N.Y.S.2d 337 (N.Y. Sup. Ct. 1995). In *Goldberg*, the plaintiff's complaint alleged a myriad of abuses the owner engaged in while running multiple cab companies. In contrast to the *Walkovszky* complaint, *Goldberg* alleged that the same individual operated all of the companies, commingled the financial records, purchased supplies through one source, and had one pool of dispatchers to assign drivers to all of the taxicabs, among other things. The *Goldberg* court found the multiple corporations were nothing more than shams without their own existence, serving only to enable the defendant to defraud the public.

■ CASE VOCABULARY

ALTER EGO: A corporation used by an individual in conducting personal business, the result being that a court may impose liability on the individual by piercing the corporate veil when fraud has been perpetrated on someone dealing with the corporation.

ALTER EGO RULE: The doctrine that stockholders will be treated as the owners of a corporation's property, or as the real parties in interest, whenever it is necessary to do so to prevent fraud or to do justice.

CORPORATE VEIL: The legal assumption that the acts of a corporation are not the actions of its stockholders, so that the stockholders are exempt from liability for the corporation's actions.

PIERCING THE CORPORATE VEIL: The judicial act of imposing personal liability on otherwise immune corporate officers, directors, and stockholders for the corporation's wrongful acts.

Sea-Land Services, Inc. v. Pepper Source

(Ocean Carrier) v. (Cargo Shipper)

941 F.2d 519 (7th Cir. 1991)

INABILITY TO SATISFY A JUDGMENT IS INSUFFICIENT TO PIERCE THE CORPORATE VEIL

■ **INSTANT FACTS** Pepper Source (D) owed Sea–Land Services, Inc. (Sea–Land) (P) for the cost of shipping peppers; however, Pepper Source (D) was dissolved before Sea–Land (P) could enforce a judgment against it.

■ **BLACK LETTER RULE** In order to pierce the corporation veil and impose individual liability, a creditor must show (1) that there was such a unity of interest between the individual and the corporate entity that separate identities no longer existed, and (2) that a failure to do so would promote "injustice" in some way beyond simply leaving a creditor unable to satisfy its judgment.

■ **PROCEDURAL BASIS**

On appeal from a grant of summary judgment in favor of the plaintiff.

■ **FACTS**

Sea–Land Services, Inc. (P) shipped Jamaican sweet peppers for its customer, Pepper Source (D). Pepper Source (D) then refused to pay Sea–Land (P) for the cost of shipping. Although the lower court awarded Sea–Land (P) $86,767.70 in damages, Sea–Land (P) was unable to find Pepper Source (D) to collect that amount. It appeared that Pepper Source (D) had dissolved for failure to pay its franchise taxes prior to the court's entry of judgment and had no remaining assets. Sea Land (P) then brought suit against Marchese (D), a former shareholder of Pepper Source (D) and five business entities owned by him in an effort to pierce the corporate veil and obtain payment, arguing that they were all alter egos of each other. Pepper Source (D) then filed with the Illinois Secretary of State to revive its charter. Sea Land (P) later amended its complaint to add a sixth company of Marchese's (D), which he owned jointly with another individual, George Andre, who had no previous ties to Pepper Source (D). After substantial discovery, Sea–Land (P) moved for and was granted summary judgment based on *Van Dorn Co. v. Future Chemical and Oil Corp.*, 753 F.2d 565 (7th Cir. 1985).

■ **ISSUE**

Should the corporate veil be pierced simply to prevent the injustice that would result from a substantial debt going unpaid?

■ **DECISION AND RATIONALE**

(Bauer, C.J.) No. In order to pierce the corporation veil, a creditor must show (1) that there was such a unity of interest between the individual and the corporate entity that separate identities no longer existed, and (2) that a failure to do so would promote "injustice" in some way beyond simply leaving a creditor unable to satisfy its judgment. Based on a review of the record, it is apparent that the companies listed as defendants by Sea–Land (P) are simply Marchese's (D) "playthings." Only one of the multiple companies has ever held board meetings, adopted articles and bylaws, or adhered to other corporate formalities. All companies operate from the same physical office and share expense accounts, which are used to provide loans to Marchese (D), interest free, and pay his personal expenses. Thus, clearly the first prong of *Van Dorn* has been satisfied—there is "shared control/unity of interest and ownership." The second prong of the *Van Dorn* test is more problematic. In order to pierce the corporate veil, a plaintiff must show that "honoring the separate corporate existences . . . 'would sanction a fraud or promote injustice.' " Rather than face the difficult burden of proving fraud, Sea Land (P) has chosen to expound on the injustice that would result from allowing Marchese (D) to avoid responsibility for Pepper Source's (D) debt. While the level of proof necessary to establish an injustice is less than that required to establish fraud, injustice does not occur simply because the plaintiff says it will. The promotion of an injustice requires more than simply a showing of an unsatisfied debt. Other cases have interpreted the term "promotion of injustice" and have held that something akin to fraud must be present in order to disregard the corporate veil. The cases have all found that something beyond an inability to collect on a debt must be shown, such as an unjust enrichment or an intentional scheme to defraud creditors. In this case, Sea Land (P) must establish this element against Marchese (D) and the other defendants—which it did not do in the summary judgment motion. Reversed and remanded.

Analysis:

On remand, the court found that "a corporate owner who used his several corporations to avoid responsibilities to creditors was unjustly enriched and that the corporate veil was properly pierced." *Sea-Land Servs., Inc. v. Pepper Source,* 993 F.2d 1309, 1312 (7th Cir.1993). It would seem that the court could have reached this conclusion without the need for remand. The court was truly amazed at the lack of apparent separation between Marchese's personal financial affairs and the financial affairs of the business, and found it noteworthy that Marchese did not even maintain a personal checking account. Aside from sloppy bookkeeping, though, most corporations do exist for the financial benefit of their owners, so the fact that Marchese took business assets for his own use was not, without more, evidence of injustice.

■ CASE VOCABULARY

INJUSTICE: 1. An unjust state of affairs; unfairness. 2. An unjust act.

Kinney Shoe Corp. v. Polan

(Sublessor) v. (Sublessee's Sole Shareholder)

939 F.2d 209 (4th Cir. 1991)

CORPORATIONS DO NOT SHIELD SHAREHOLDERS FROM PERSONAL LIABILITY IF NO CORPORATE FORMALITIES WERE OBSERVED

■ **INSTANT FACTS** Kinney Shoe Corp. (P) sublet property to Industrial Realty Co., after negotiating with Lincoln M. Polan (D), the company's sole shareholder, and Industrial Realty defaulted on the lease.

■ **BLACK LETTER RULE** If a corporation's shareholder took no stock in the corporation, undercapitalized it, kept no minutes, elected no officers and attempted to protect assets by placing them in another corporation, a party may pierce the corporate veil.

■ **PROCEDURAL BASIS**

On appeal to the Fourth Circuit Court of Appeals following judgment in favor of the defendant.

■ **FACTS**

Lincoln M. Polan (D) formed two companies, Industrial Realty Co. and Polan Industries. Each company played a part in Polan's manufacturing business. Polan (D) owned both companies, but neither entity obtained certificates of incorporation, elected officers or held organizational meetings. Polan (D) negotiated with Kinney Shoe Corp. (P) to sublease one of its buildings. Industrial Realty occupied the premises under the lease and leased a portion of the premises to Polan Industries. The Kinney Shoe (P) sublease was Industrial Realty's sole asset. The first and only rental payment to Kinney Shoe (P) came from Polan's personal funds. Kinney Shoe (P) sued Polan (D) individually for unpaid rent from the sublease between Kinney Shoe (P) and Industrial Realty. At trial, the court determined that Polan (D) was not personally liable for the debt. On appeal, Kinney Shoe argued that the court should have pierced Industrial Realty's corporate veil.

■ **ISSUE**

Is a company's owner personally liable for a corporation's obligations if the company failed to observe even the most minimal corporate formalities?

■ **DECISION AND RATIONALE**

(Chapman, J.) Yes. Corporations have long been recognized as entities separate from their officers and stockholders, but this legal fiction may be disregarded to avoid injustice. The party seeking to pierce the corporate veil bears the burden of proof. Whether a situation merits the court's disregard of the corporate entity is determined using a two-prong test, as set forth in *Laya v. Erin Homes, Inc.*, 352 S.E.2d 93 (W.Va. 1986). Under that test, the court examines first whether a unity of interest and ownership exists so as to eliminate a distinction between the corporation and its stockholders. Second, the court determines whether by treating the acts as corporate actions, the result would still be equitable. The district court found these two questions were adequately answered to the plaintiff's benefit and no evidence has been presented to contradict that result. The law demands that those who

---

receive the benefit of protection from personal liability observe the few formalities the law requires. Polan (D) observed none of the corporate formalities. Industrial Realty was inadequately capitalized and had no paid-in capital. Polan (D) bought no stock, elected no officers, paid no capital and kept no minutes, yet he protected his assets by placing them in Polan Industries. These facts satisfy the *Laya* test. In some cases, the court may consider a third prong under which a financial institution is held to have assumed the risk that a company was undercapitalized if the institution's investigation should have uncovered that fact. Based on this "third prong," the district court concluded that Kinney Shoe (P), like a financial institution, had assumed the risk of Industrial Realty's uncreditworthiness. However, the third prong is not mandatory and need not be considered to reach an equitable result. The law allows a stockholder to limit his risk in a venture to the amount invested; but, here, Polan (D) invested nothing. Absent a legitimate investment, the corporation provides its owner with no protection. Reversed and remanded with instructions.

Analysis:

The result here differs from that in *Walkovszky v. Carlton*, 18 N.Y.2d 414, 276 N.Y.S.2d 585, 223 N.E.2d 6 (1966). In *Walkovszky*, the taxicab owners, who did nothing that was not required, at least observed the law, purchased the required insurance and kept corporate records. In *Southern-Gulf Marine Co. No. 9, Inc. v. Camcraft, Inc.*, 410 So. 2d 1181 (La. Ct. App. 1982), the corporation disclosed in the contract that the corporation had yet to be formed and made a full disclosure of the formation once it was completed. Here, Polan did not even bother to create a paper trail for the corporation other than making sure the lease was in the name of the company without assets.

■ CASE VOCABULARY

PAID-IN CAPITAL: The money paid for the capital stock of a corporation.

UNDERCAPITALIZATION: The financial condition of a firm that does not have enough capital to carry on its business.

In re Silicone Gel Breast Implants Products Liability Litigation

(Defendant Implant Manufacturers) v. (Breast Implant Recipients)

887 F.Supp. 1447 (N.D. Ala. 1995)

A PARENT CORPORATION IS LIABLE FOR ITS SUBSIDIARY'S TORTS IF THE PARENT CONTROLLED THE SUBSIDIARY AS ITS ALTER EGO

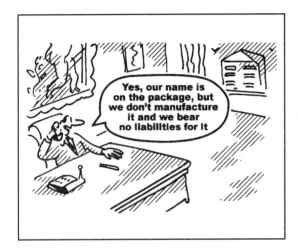

■ **INSTANT FACTS** Breast implant recipients brought a products liability action against Bristol–Myers Squibb Co. (D), which was the sole shareholder of Medical Engineering Corporation (D), a major supplier of breast implants.

■ **BLACK LETTER RULE** If a parent corporation uses a subsidiary as its alter ego, as demonstrated by shared common directors or business departments, consolidated financial statements and tax returns, and an inadequately capitalized subsidiary, a plaintiff may assert its claims against the parent.

■ **PROCEDURAL BASIS**

On a motion for summary judgment by the parent company.

■ **FACTS**

Bristol–Myers Squibb Co. (Bristol–Myers) (D) is the sole shareholder of Medical Engineering Corporation (MEC) (D), a major breast implant supplier. Bristol–Myers (D) purchased MEC's (D) stock after conducting a study of problems associated with MEC's breast implants. Bristol–Myers (D) subsequently purchased two other companies engaged in the same business and merged them into MEC (D). As part of its due diligence, Bristol–Myers again reviewed documents concerning possible hazards associated with the implants. MEC's (D) three-person board of directors included a Bristol–Myers vice president, another Bristol (D) executive and MEC's president. The former MEC (D) presidents did not even know MEC (D) had a board, and Bristol–Myers' officials prepared MEC's few board resolutions. MEC (D) prepared reports for Bristol–Myers (D) that included information on testing, production problems and budgeting, and provided full financial information to Bristol–Myers (D). Bristol–Myers (D) acted as MEC's (D) banker, set its employment policies and wages, approved upper management hires, and permitted MEC (D) employees to participate in Bristol–Myers' pension and savings plans. Bristol–Myers (D) also funded tests on implant safety, monitored FDA regulations, audited MEC (D), tested MEC's manufacturing process, and helped MEC (D) respond to concerns over implant safety. Package inserts displayed Bristol–Myers' (D) name and logo. Bristol–Myers (D) included MEC's (D) income on its federal tax returns, but MEC (D) prepared and filed its own Wisconsin state returns. MEC stopped manufacturing breast implants in 1991 and sold its assets with Bristol–Myers' (D) approval. At no time did Bristol–Myers (D) manufacture or distribute implants, and it claims that the plaintiffs should not be permitted to proceed against it.

■ **ISSUE**

If a parent corporation exercised almost total control over the activities of its subsidiary, should the court allow the plaintiffs to pierce the corporate veil between the parent and its subsidiary?

■ DECISION AND RATIONALE

(Pointer, C.J.) Yes. Because multiple forum states are involved, the court must consult several states' laws. If a corporation is owned by a single shareholder, the potential for abuse is great, but the court must recognize both that a parent must control its subsidiary and that the law presumes limited liability. In determining the existence of an alter ego, a court should consider whether the entities had common directors or officers, common business departments, or consolidated financial statements and tax returns. The court may also consider whether the subsidiary is adequately capitalized or relies on the parent for its business, whether the parent pays the subsidiary's expenses or uses the subsidiary's property as its own, whether the subsidiary has separate daily operations, and whether the subsidiary observes basic corporate formalities. Evidence here establishes many of these factors and supports a finding that MEC (D) was Bristol–Myers' (D) alter ego. Bristol–Myers (D) contends that the plaintiffs may not pierce the corporate veil without showing fraud, but that is not the law in Delaware, the jurisdiction Bristol–Myers (D) itself argues should control. Moreover, even in jurisdictions in which the plaintiff must prove fraud, it is necessary only in contract cases, not torts. Courts in most jurisdictions would also find that Bristol–Myers (D) is directly liable to the plaintiffs under the theory of negligent undertaking, which includes rendering services to another that are used to protect a third party. Under that theory, if a third party sustains an injury, the party indirectly involved may be liable for the harm that results from an absence of due care if the actor increases another's risk of harm, performs a duty owed to another, and causes harm to a third party who relied on the actor to perform his actions properly. Here, Bristol–Myers (D) allowed its name to be placed on the packaging in an effort to increase customer confidence and conducted investigations and issued press releases about the product's safety. It cannot now complain when customers claim they relied on Bristol–Myers' reputation. Summary judgment denied.

Analysis:

The parent-subsidiary relation alone is never sufficient to hold a parent responsible for its subsidiaries' torts. However, this case presents an extreme case in which the activities of a parent and its subsidiary were so interwoven that it was difficult to determine where one entity left off and the other began. By contrast, in *American Trading & Prod. Corp. v. Fischbach & Moore, Inc.*, 311 F. Supp. 412 (D.C. III. 1970), the court declined to impose liability on the parent, noting that the parent did not operate the subsidiary's business and did not share equipment or employees. Therefore, the court found only a relationship of supervision and guidance, and did not hold that the parent was responsible for its subsidiary's obligations.

■ CASE VOCABULARY

DUE DILIGENCE: A prospective buyer's or broker's investigation and analysis of a target company, a piece of property, or a newly issued security.

PARENT CORPORATION: A corporation that has a controlling interest in another corporation (called a subsidiary corporation), usually through ownership of more than one-half the voting stock.

SUBSIDIARY CORPORATION: A corporation in which a parent corporation has a controlling share.

Frigidaire Sales Corp. v. Union Prop., Inc.

(Creditor) v. *(Debtor)*

88 Wash.2d 400, 562 P.2d 244 (1977)

LIMITED PARTNERS ARE NOT LIABLE FOR A LIMITED PARTNERSHIP'S DEBTS

■ **INSTANT FACTS** Frigidaire Sales Corp. (P), a creditor of Commercial Investors, a limited partnership, brought an action against the corporate general partner and its limited partners individually when the partnership failed to pay installments due on contract.

■ **BLACK LETTER RULE** Limited partners are not liable for the debts of a limited partnership simply by their status as officers, directors, or stockholders of the corporate general partner as long as they conscientiously keep the corporate matters separate from their personal business and no fraud or manifest injustice results.

■ **PROCEDURAL BASIS**

On appeal from an appellate court's dismissal of the plaintiff's claim against the limited partners.

■ **FACTS**

Frigidaire Sales Corp. (Frigidaire) (P) contracted with Commercial Investors (Commercial), a limited partnership. Mannon (D) and Baxter (D) were limited partners of Commercial and served as officers and directors of Union Properties, Inc. (D). Mannon (D) and Baxter (D) also held shares in Union Properties (D) and ran Commercial's day-to-day activities. When Commercial breached its contract with Frigidaire (P), Frigidaire (P) sued Union Properties (D), Mannon (D) and Baxter (D). Frigidaire (P) contends that because the named defendants exercised day-to-day control over Commercial, they were Commercial's alter ego and should be treated as general partners. Mannon (D) and Baxter (D) argue that Commercial was controlled by Union Properties (D). The lower court entered judgment for Frigidaire (P) against Union Properties (D), the corporate general partner, but dismissed the claim against the limited partners (D), and the appellate court affirmed.

■ **ISSUE**

If a limited partnership's general partner is a corporation, whose controlling members are also the limited partners in the partnership, may a creditor treat the limited partners as additional general partners?

■ **DECISION AND RATIONALE**

(Hamilton, J.) No. Limited partnership statutes permit a corporation to be its general partner. Minimal capitalization of the general partner does not necessarily mean that the limited partners must incur general liability because they control the general partner. If the general partner has been inadequately capitalized a creditor without a remedy may pierce the corporate veil to recover its loss. Here, Frigidaire (P) was not misled into believing the defendants were acting as anything other than corporate officers. To find the individual defendants liable for this obligation would be ignore the existence of Union Properties (D). Also, Commercial signed the contract. Frigidaire (P) knew Union Properties (D) was the sole general partner of Commercial and did not ask for the personal guarantees of the individual defendants. Frigidaire (P) must look to Commercial and Union Properties (D) to recover. Affirmed.

Analysis:

Compare this case with *Delaney v. Fidelity Lease Ltd.*, 526 S.W.2d 543 (Tex. 1975), in which a court reached the opposite result. The *Delaney* plaintiffs alleged that three limited partners controlled the limited partnership, but the limited partners argued their only actions were taken through the corporation and that the corporation ran the limited partnership's business. While the individual limited partners in *Delaney* argued that they did not hold themselves out as general partners and that the plaintiffs signed their contract with the partnership, those facts were not controlling. The court found that the corporation was formed *solely* to serve as the general partner, and, as such, it must act in the limited partnership's benefit.

■ CASE VOCABULARY

GENERAL PARTNER: A partner who ordinarily takes part in the daily operations of the business, shares in the profits and losses, and is personally liable for the partnership's debts and liabilities.

GENERAL PARTNERSHIP: A partnership in which all partners participate fully in running the business and share equally in profits and losses (though the partners' monetary contributions may vary).

LIMITED PARTNER: A partner who receives profits from the business but does not take part in managing the business and is not liable for any amount greater than his or her original investment.

Cohen v. Beneficial Indus. Loan Corp.

(Shareholder) v. *(Corporation)*

337 U.S. 541, 69 S.Ct. 1221, 93 L.Ed. 1528 (1949)

A COURT MAY REQUIRE A PLAINTIFF TO POST A BOND IN A DERIVATIVE SUIT

IT'S A LOSE-LOSE SITUATION: IF I LOSE, I PAY THE CORPORATION'S LAWYER; IF I WIN, I PAY MY LAWYER

SHAREHOLDER

■ **INSTANT FACTS** David E. Cohen brought a shareholder's derivative suit against Beneficial Industrial Loan Corp. (Beneficial) (D) and others, and Beneficial brought a motion seeking to have Hannah Cohen (P), David's executrix, post security for the expenses associated with prosecuting the lawsuit.

■ **BLACK LETTER RULE** A New Jersey statute that requires a holder of less than five per cent of a corporation's outstanding shares who brings a derivative suit to pay for all expenses of defending the suit and that requires security for the payment of these expenses should be enforced in cases prosecuted under federal diversity jurisdiction.

■ PROCEDURAL BASIS

On appeal from a writ of certiorari.

■ FACTS

David E. Cohen brought suit against Beneficial Industrial Loan Corporation (Beneficial) (D) and certain of Beneficial's managers, alleging that the managers were engaged in a plan to enrich themselves at the corporation's expense. David Cohen charged that the mismanagement and fraud that extended over an eighteen-year period had cost the company over $100 million through waste and diversions. David Cohen held only 100 shares of Beneficial (D) stock, accounting for approximately 0.0125% of the company's stock. After David Cohen died, Hannah Cohen (Cohen) (P) continued the suit as the executrix of David's estate. Two years after David Cohen brought the action, New Jersey passed a statute providing that any plaintiff with a minimal ownership interest who brings a derivative action is responsible for the defense of his action if he is unsuccessful and must indemnify the corporation against those costs before proceeding. Beneficial (D) brought a motion to require Cohen (P) to post a bond of $125,000.

■ ISSUE

Must a federal court hearing a stockholder's derivative action based only on diversity jurisdiction apply the law of the forum state and require a plaintiff to provide security for the payment of costs if he or she is ultimately unsuccessful?

■ DECISION AND RATIONALE

(Jackson, J.) Yes. Stockholder's derivative actions are intended to help stockholders in large corporations hold managers and directors responsible for wrongs they committed. If a shareholder has no success in demanding the company take actions to stop wrongful conduct, the shareholder may bring an action. However, plaintiffs with small ownership interests may also abuse their rights to bring a derivative action to recover only nuisance claims. In an effort to control these abuses, the New Jersey legislature enacted remedial measures by requiring that a shareholder with minimal ownership interest who brings a derivative suit must provide security for the payment of costs if he or she is unsuccessful.

The U.S. Constitution does not require the state to open its courts to derivative suits without requiring some accountability to protect other injured stockholders, as long as the state statutes do not offend due process. The New Jersey statute places responsibility for the defendant's reasonable expenses on the losing plaintiff and allows the defendant to demand security for their payment. While the plaintiff argues that the New Jersey law denies equal protection based on a shareholder's ownership interest, that argument is without merit. The shareholder's stock ownership determines his or her stake in the outcome and the amount of injury. Therefore, it is not an unconstitutional means to limit access. A federal court may disregard state laws only if federal laws are directly on point or if the state's laws are procedural, although even then, federal courts may find the state laws relevant. This state law creates a remedy where one did not previously exist. It extends beyond what was previously recognized as costs and provides a method for ensuring that the costs are paid. Therefore, it is more than a procedural rule and should be followed in the federal courts. Affirmed.

Analysis:

Most rights and privileges come with obligations. Here, the right to proceed with a lawsuit that the real party in interest does not want to pursue comes with the obligation that if the plaintiff loses, he or she will be responsible for the costs incurred in defending the lawsuit. While the derivative action concept serves a valid purpose, the process can be long, drawn out and expensive. Statutes like the one applied here require the plaintiff to pause before bringing a suit with little potential for significant payback. Derivative lawsuits are not appropriate to prove a point or make an example of a company's business practice if the practice has little effect

■ CASE VOCABULARY

DERIVATIVE ACTION: A suit by a beneficiary of a fiduciary to enforce a right belonging to the fiduciary; especially, a suit asserted by a shareholder on the corporation's behalf against a third party (usually a corporate officer) because of the corporation's failure to take some action against the third party.

Eisenberg v. Flying Tiger Line, Inc.

(Passive Corporation's Shareholder) v. *(Operating Company)*

451 F.2d 267 (2d Cir. 1971)

AN ACTION TO REVERSE CORPORATE ACTIONS THAT DEPRIVED SHAREHOLDERS OF A VOICE IN OPERATIONS IS NOT DERIVATIVE

■ **INSTANT FACTS** A stockholder in a corporation that ceased to exist post-merger, brought an action on behalf of himself and all other stockholders of the dissolved corporation, to enjoin the plan of reorganization and merger.

■ **BLACK LETTER RULE** An action seeking to overturn a reorganization and merger that deprived an acquired corporation's shareholders from having a voice in the surviving corporation's business operations is a personal action rather than a derivative action under the New York statute requiring the posting of security for the corporation's costs.

■ **PROCEDURAL BASIS**

On appeal following the dismissal of the plaintiff's action for failure to post the required security.

■ **FACTS**

In July 1969, Flying Tiger Line, Inc. (Flying Tiger) formed Flying Tiger Corporation (FTC) under Delaware law as a subsidiary corporation. The following month, FTC organized its own subsidiary, FTL Air Freight Corporation (FTL). Under a plan to reorganize the three companies, the management merged Flying Tiger into FTL, and Flying Tiger Line ceased to exist. The shareholder vote on the matter received the two-thirds votes necessary to pass, and FTL took over the daily operations of the business. FTL then changed its name to Flying Tiger Line, Inc. (Flying Tiger Line) (D) and continued the former Flying Tiger's business. As a result, the shares traded in the business known as Flying Tiger Line were actually shares in FTC, the holding company for FTL. The holding company's stockholders were the owners of the former Flying Tiger. Eisenberg (P) brought an action against Flying Tiger Line (D) to enjoin the merger plan. Flying Tiger Line (D) removed the action to federal court and alleged several affirmative defenses. Flying Tiger Line (D) then sought an order to require Eisenberg (P) to comply with the New York law requiring a plaintiff to post a bond when bringing a derivative action. The trial judge granted the motion and gave Eisenberg (P) thirty days to post bond. When Eisenberg (P) failed to post the bond, his action was dismissed.

■ **ISSUE**

Is an action seeking to enjoin a reorganization and merger brought by the former stockholders of the corporation to be acquired, a derivative action subject to the rules requiring the plaintiff in a derivative action to post security?

■ **DECISION AND RATIONALE**

(Kaufman, J.) No. Eisenberg's (P) suit concerns Flying Tiger's reorganization plan, which included a merger. Eisenberg (P) argues that the reorganization was designed to dilute his voting rights. As a result of this plan, Eisenberg (P) argues that the minority stockholders had no voice in the new company. Instead, they now have a voice only in FTC, the holding company. Flying Tiger Line (D) insists the plan was needed to provide greater diversification without interference from the Civil Aeronautics Board. The merits of the merger are not relevant. The important issue is whether the statute requiring the plaintiff to post a bond against costs applies. Eisenberg (P) argues that Delaware law should apply, but New York law applies. Eisenberg (P) also argues that New York courts should enforce the provision requiring him to post a bond against expenses only if his action were a derivative suit and that his claim is a representative, not a derivative, suit. If the suit is based on an injury to a corporation, the suit is derivative; if it is based on an injury to an individual stockholder, the suit is a representative action. Eisenberg (P) insists that his complaint concerns his right to vote on the company's affairs, which is a shareholder's privilege. Flying Tiger Line (D) argues that if the court finds the stockholders were harmed when the target company was dissolved, the court would have to revive the former corporation to provide a remedy to the plaintiffs so the suit is derivative. The defendant's argument misstates the matter. *Gordon v. Elliman*, 306 N.Y. 456, 119 N.E.2d 331 (1954), found that an action to compel the payment of a dividend was derivative because the suit's goal was to compel the performance of an act owed to the corporation for its shareholders' benefit. Flying Tiger Line (D) argues that any duty not to merge was owed to the company, not to its stockholders. However, since *Gordon*, the legislature added the words "in its favor" to its "derivative action" definition, so that a suit is derivative only if the result is a judgment in the corporation's favor, which is not true here. *Gordon* is no longer good law. The complaint's allegations state a claim for a representative cause of action. Reversed.

Analysis:

While the distinction between derivative actions and personal actions is important in publicly-held corporations where litigation can quickly drain a corporation's resources, the same considerations are not usually a problem in smaller, closely-held corporations. In *Horizon House–Microwave, Inc. v. Bazzy*, 486 N.E.2d 70 (Mass. Ct. App. 1985), the court declined to force a minority shareholder to bring a derivative suit to dismiss. It permitted the shareholder to move directly against that corporation and majority stockholder.

■ CASE VOCABULARY

ACQUIRED CORPORATION: The corporation that no longer exists after a merger or acquisition.

DIRECT ACTION: A lawsuit to enforce a shareholder's rights against a corporation.

MERGER: The absorption of one company (especially a corporation) that ceases to exist into another that retains its own name and identity and acquires the assets and liabilities of the former.

SURVIVING CORPORATION: A corporation that acquires the assets and liabilities of another corporation by a merger or takeover.

Grimes v. Donald

(Shareholder) v. *(Well–Paid Executive)*

673 A.2d 1207 (Del. 1996)

A STOCKHOLDER GENERALLY MUST DEMAND THE BOARD BRING AN ACTION BEFORE HE OR SHE BRINGS A DERIVATIVE SUIT

OH, I DON'T CARE... DO WHATEVER YOU WANT WITH THE COMPANY...

■ **INSTANT FACTS** Grimes (P), who learned of the extremely generous compensation package DSC Communications (DSC) (D) had extended to Donald (D), demanded DSC cancel Donald's (D) contract.

■ **BLACK LETTER RULE** A shareholder need not make a demand that a company's board institute a lawsuit before bringing a derivative suit on behalf of the corporation on a showing the demand would be futile, and if a demand is made and rejected, a shareholder may still proceed by establishing that the board's refusal was wrongful.

■ PROCEDURAL BASIS

On appeal following dismissal of the plaintiff's derivative claim.

■ FACTS

In 1990, DSC Communications (DSC) (D) entered into an Employment Agreement providing that Donald (D), its CEO, would manage DSC (D). In exchange, the agreement provided Donald (D) with guaranteed employment through the age of seventy-five and provided for early termination, allowing Donald (D) to declare a "constructive termination without cause" if either the board or a major shareholder unreasonably interfered with his management of DSC. Upon termination without cause, Donald (D) would receive a generous severance package. If corporate control changed, Donald (D) would have the right to cash payments for his ownership units, valued at approximately $60 million. Grimes (P), a DSC (D) shareholder, asked the board to abrogate Donald's (D) agreement. The board refused his demand, claiming that Donald's (D) compensation is fair and that his duties, as described in his employment contract, do not constitute an impermissible delegation of the board's duties. Grimes (P) appealed the dismissal of his complaint.

■ ISSUE

Must a shareholder make a demand of the company's board before pursuing a derivative claim if he or she has no reason to believe the demand would be futile, and may the shareholder pursue his or her claim if the board's decision is not the result of considered business judgment?

■ DECISION AND RATIONALE

(Veasey, C.J.) Yes. Grimes' (P) action raises both derivative claims and a claim for abdication, which is a direct claim. Grimes' (P) abdication claim, in which he seeks a declaration that the agreement is invalid, fails as a matter of law. Grimes (P) claims that Donald's "golden parachute" terms are so expensive that the board may hesitate to interfere with Donald's (D) management and overlook DSC's long-term best interests, for fear of triggering the contract's "constructive termination without cause" clause. Directors may not delegate their duty to manage the corporation, and a court cannot enforce an agreement that permits the board to do so. However, this agreement does not preclude DSC's (D) board from performing its duties. Their delegation of responsibility to Donald (D) is protected by the business judgment rule and is not an abdication of the board's authority simply because it may limit the board's choices in the future. Similarly, if a board determines that an executive's services are sufficiently valuable to justify a sizeable salary and benefits, that determination is protected by the business judgment rule. For those portions of Grimes' (P) claims that are derivative, Grimes (P) must make a demand of the corporation before instituting his own action, and his complaint must either allege that the board denied his request or offer a reason why the demand would be futile. The demand is excused only if the shareholder has reasonable doubt that the board could exercise appropriate judgment. If the shareholder's demand is rejected, the presumption is that the board acted properly unless the shareholder can allege a basis from which reasonable doubt would be raised. If evidence suggest the board did not act properly, the shareholder may bring his claim based on wrongful refusal. The plaintiff here made a pre-suit demand and cannot later contend the demand was excused. Because DSC (D) made an effort to consider Grimes' (P) claims, its decision must be reviewed under the business judgment rule. Grimes (P) cannot succeed without providing a reason to doubt that the board reached its decision through the exercise of valid business judgment. Affirmed.

Analysis:

Proving the inability of a director to exercise independent judgment is not an easy burden for a plaintiff to carry, even though courts are required to draw all reasonable inferences in the plaintiff's favor in deciding the issue. In *Beam ex rel. Martha Stewart Living Omnimedia, Inc. v. Stewart*, 845 A.2d 1040 (Del. 2004), the court was asked to find that when it came to pursuing a claim against Martha Stewart for damage to the corporation's reputation based on the founder's unlawful securities trading, the corporate directors would fail to rule against Stewart because the directors were all Stewarts' friends. By failing to excuse the plaintiff from making demand on Omnimedia's directors to pursue the claim against Stewart, the court noted that corporate directors are entitled to a presumption that they were faithful to their fiduciary duties. Proof that this independence was compromised requires more than a showing that the directors all ran in the same social circles.

■ CASE VOCABULARY

ABDICATION: The act of renouncing or abandoning privileges or duties, especially those connected with high office.

ABROGATE: To abolish (a law or custom) by formal or authoritative action; to annul or repeal.

BUSINESS JUDGMENT RULE: The presumption that in making business decisions not involving direct self-interest or self-dealing, corporate directors act on an informed basis, in good faith, and in the honest belief that their actions are in the corporation's best interest. The rule shields directors and officers from liability for unprofitable or harmful corporate transactions if the transactions were made in good faith, with due care, and within the directors' or officers' authority.

GOLDEN PARACHUTE: An employment-contract provision that grants an upper-level executive lucrative severance benefits—including long-term salary guarantees or bonuses—if control of the company changes hands (as by a merger).

Marx v. Akers

(Shareholder) v. *(Directors)*

644 N.Y.S.2d 121, 666 N.E.2d 1034 (1996)

THE PLAINTIFF MUST PROVIDE MORE THAN CONCLUSORY STATEMENTS TO ESTABLISH THAT A DEMAND WOULD BE FUTILE

■ **INSTANT FACTS** A shareholder brought a derivative action charging breach of fiduciary duty and corporate waste by International Business Machines' (IBM) board of directors for excessive compensation of IBM's executives and outside directors.

■ **BLACK LETTER RULE** A plaintiff establishing that a demand on a company's board would have been futile must show either that the measure furthered the board's self-interest, that the directors did not fully inform themselves about the challenged transaction, or that the challenged transaction was so egregious on its face that it could not have been the product of the directors' sound business judgment.

■ PROCEDURAL BASIS

Appeal from an order dismissing a shareholder's complaint.

■ FACTS

Sylvia Marx (P) brought a shareholder derivative suit against International Business Machines (IBM) (D) and its directors without first demanding the board pursue the action. The complaint alleges the board paid excessive compensation to the company's executives and directors, wasting corporate assets. The plaintiff bases her case on the fact that while profits declined at IBM, the outside directors were paid excessive compensation and violated their fiduciary duties by voting for excessive compensation for IBM (D) executives.

■ ISSUE

Must a derivative complaint be dismissed if the plaintiff failed to make a demand of the board to pursue the action on its own?

■ DECISION AND RATIONALE

No. New York statutes require that a shareholder derivative action must either allege the efforts the plaintiff took to have the company institute the suit or the reasons the plaintiff took no actions. Because of derivative suits' impact on the director's ability to govern, courts have been reluctant to permit shareholder derivative suits. Requiring a shareholder to make a demand of the corporation before proceeding serves three purposes: courts are freed from responsibility for internal decisions; boards are protected from harassment in handling discretionary matters; and shareholders are discouraged from instituting suits for personal gain. If a stockholder successfully describes situations in which a demand of the company's board would be futile, the court will substitute its judgment for that of the board and may permit the suit to go forward. Pursuant to Delaware law, if the plaintiff establishes director interest, the business judgment rule will not shield the board and the court may excuse the demand. A court determines whether the board made its decision by validly exercising its business judgment by examining the steps the board took to evaluate the issue. In other jurisdictions, the law universally requires stockholders make a demand of the corporation. (The ABA supports this simple rule and would permit a shareholder to commence action ninety days after its demand unless it is rejected earlier or suit is necessary to prevent irreparable injury.) New York follows neither the universal demand approach nor the Delaware approach. In New York, demand is excused if it would be futile. Pursuant to *Barr v. Wackmam*, 36 N.Y.2d 371, 368 N.Y.S.2d 497, 329 N.E.2d 180 (1975), demand is futile if a majority of the directors have an interest in the transaction, the directors fail to make a reasoned inquiry about the transaction, or the transaction is approved without the exercise of reasoned business judgment. In *Barr*, the directors rejected one merger proposal in favor of another with less favorable terms because the principals associated with the second merger agreed to favorable employment contracts for the directors. *Barr* found that the board's self-dealing excused demand. However, under *Barr*, to have demand excused requires particular pleading of the reasons for excusing demand. Demand is excused as futile only if the complaint alleges the self-interest of a majority of the board members, that the board members failed to inform themselves about the transaction under the circumstances, or that the offending transaction is so patently improper that it could not be justified by any sound business judgment. Here, the plaintiff argues that the compensation paid to IBM's outside directors was excessive, but he failed to make demand that the directors pursue his claim. Only three directors purportedly received benefit from the alleged compensation scheme, and the plaintiff did not allege that a majority of the board was involved in the abuse. The plaintiff's other statements in support of his assertions are merely conclusory. He makes no allegations that the board failed to properly exercise its business judgment in setting the compensation. However, directors are deemed self-interested if their benefits from a transaction are different from the shareholder's benefits, so that directors' votes regarding director compensation are *always* interested. Therefore, demand is excused for the plaintiff's claims that the outside directors received excessive compensation, but the question remains as to whether the allegations state a cause of action. To present a valid cause of action, the alleged compensation must state facts that tend to establish that the compensation was unfair to the corporation. The plaintiff's allegations here state a conclusion but fail to provide any basis for finding them indicative of waste. Affirmed.

Analysis:

Courts presume that business decisions are made with due regard for the company's welfare. When shareholders seek to bring a derivative claim, they are fighting against that presumption. In *Grimes v. Donald*, 673 A.2d 1207 (Del. 1996), the court found that if a shareholder wanted to bring a derivative suit, he or she must first ask the corporation to bring the action unless to do so is futile. If the corporation decides against the suit, the court will presume the decision was rendered through reasoned judgment. In many cases, it may be better for a shareholder to make the effort to show the board's inability to issue an impartial decision than to later be required to prove that its decision not to go forward was a wrongful decision.

■ CASE VOCABULARY

INSIDE DIRECTOR: A director who is also an employee, officer, or major shareholder of the corporation.

OUTSIDE DIRECTOR: A nonemployee director with little or no direct interest in the corporation.

Auerbach v. Bennett

(Shareholder) v. *(Director)*

47 N.Y.2d 619, 393 N.E.2d 994, 419 N.Y.S.2d 920 (1979)

A BOARD OF DIRECTORS MAY GRANT AUTHORITY TO A SPECIAL COMMITTEE TO MAKE RECOM-
MENDATIONS ON A DERIVATIVE CLAIM

■ **INSTANT FACTS** A corporation appointed a special committee to investigate the basis of a shareholders' derivative suit charging misman-agement of corporate funds, and the committee determined the suit should be terminated.

■ **BLACK LETTER RULE** A special litigation committee's determination forecloses further in-quiry into a matter, provided the committee's investigation is bona fide.

■ **PROCEDURAL BASIS**

Appeal from trial court's ruling dismissing the plaintiff's derivative action.

■ **FACTS**

General Telephone & Electronics (GTE) performed an internal investigation to determine whether bribes had been paid to foreign public officials or political parties. Based on the report, matters were brought to the attention of GTE's board, which referred the matter to its audit committee. With the assistance of a Washington, D.C., law firm that acted as special counsel and Arthur Andersen & Co., the committee investigated whether bribes had been paid. Several months later, the audit group released and filed with the SEC a report stating that GTE and its subsidiaries had made foreign payments of more than $11 million and that some of the transactions were handled by GTE's directors. Based on the report, Auerbach (P), a GTE shareholder, filed a derivative suit seeking to have those corporate officials and members of Arthur Andersen reimburse GTE for the bribes. The board later established a special litigation committee, which was to be a liaison between the board and the general counsel addressing GTE's position on the shareholder derivative claims. The committee was comprised of three of GTE's newest directors, who were elected after the scandal. The committee reported that Arthur Anderson had performed its audit in good faith. It found that none of the individual defendants gained personally from the money paid to foreign officials, and concluded that absent any valid claims against these individuals, the derivative suits would simply pose a drain on management's time and resources. Auerbach (P), the initial plaintiff, decided against appeal, but Wallenstein (P), another shareholder, proceeded with the action.

■ **ISSUE**

May a board appoint a special committee to investigate the allegations contained in a derivative suit and to determine whether the lawsuit should be dismissed?

■ **DECISION AND RATIONALE**

(Jones, J.) Yes. The business judgment rule is grounded on the realization that a business is in a better position than a court to determine its best course. The question here is whether an assessment by a three-person subcommittee of the board is sufficient to foreclose judicial scrutiny into a shareholder's derivative action. GTE's board has 15 members and the derivative suit was brought against four of those members (D). According to the audit group's report, none of the other members of the current board were even aware of the foreign payments and only members of the board that joined GTE *after* the payments were made were allowed to serve on the litigation committee. The business judgment rule will shield the committee's decisions only if the members are found to have a disinterested independence. Examining the facts here, it is clear that the special committee members did not participate in the questionable transactions. No reasons have been given to distrust their independence. The plaintiff's argument that the authority granted to the subcommittee was an excessive delegation of power is without merit. Choosing a committee so that it excluded those members with potential personal prejudice exhibited prudent business practice. To hold, as the plaintiff suggests, that the committee contain *no* members of GTE's board of directors, would make the board powerless to make its own decision regarding derivative actions. The ultimate decision reached by the committee is protected by the business judgment rule, and the committee's decision is beyond the court's scope of review. However, the court may review the process and methods the committee used to reach its decision to ensure the committee exercised good faith in its investigation. Proof that the investigation was a sham would raise questions of good faith that would not be shielded by the business judgment rule. However, Wallenstein (P) has not offered any such proof. The defendants' evidence is sufficient to prove that their actions were guided by a desire for accuracy. Nothing establishes a lack of good faith by the committee. Affirmed, as modified.

■ DISSENT

(Cooke, C.J.) Summary judgment should not be granted if only the committee members know the special committee members' motives and actions.

Analysis:

The approach discussed here is considered the traditional approach in dealing with a company's ability to use committees. In *In re PSE & G Shareholder Litigation*, 173 N.J. 258, 285, 801 A.2d 295 (N.J. 2002), the court explained that the appeal of the traditional rule is that "it recognizes that courts are not equipped to handle sophisticated corporate decision making." However, the traditional rule has its critics. Many argue that the traditional approach provides too much deference to the board's decisions and makes the initial hurdle facing a shareholder unrealistically high. The *PSE & G* court chose instead to apply a "modified business judgment rule" that imposes an initial burden on a corporation to demonstrate that the board members were independent and disinterested, that they acted in good faith and with due care in their investigation of the shareholder's allegations, and that the board's decision was reasonable. Also, *PSE & G* provides shareholders with access to corporate documents and other discovery for the narrow issues of what steps the directors took to inform themselves of the shareholder demand and the reasonableness of their decision.

■ CASE VOCABULARY

GENERALLY ACCEPTED ACCOUNTING PRINCIPLES (GAAP): The conventions, rules, and procedures that define approved accounting practices at a particular time.

Zapata Corp. v. Maldonado

(Corporation) v. *(Shareholder)*

430 A.2d 779 (Del. 1981)

INTERESTED BOARD MEMBERS MAY APPOINT A DISINTERESTED COMMITTEE TO INVESTIGATE LITIGATION

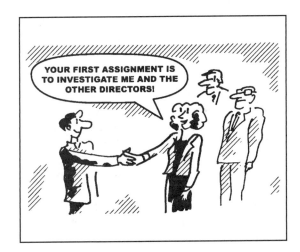

■ **INSTANT FACTS** Maldonado (P), a Zapata Corp. (D) shareholder, sued Zapata's officers and directors for breach of fiduciary duty, but Maldonado (P) did not ask Zapata's board to bring the action, considering the request to be futile.

■ **BLACK LETTER RULE** While a majority of a board may lack the independence to evaluate a derivative claim, the taint of self-interest is not necessarily sufficient to prevent the board from delegating the evaluation to an independent committee comprised of disinterested board members who may recommend dismissal of a shareholder's action.

■ PROCEDURAL BASIS

On appeal from denial of the corporation's motions to dismiss the derivative complaint.

■ FACTS

Maldonado (P), a shareholder in Zapata Corp. (D), sued ten of Zapata's officers and directors charging they had breached their fiduciary duty to the company. He did not demand that Zapata (D) bring the action first, alleging that the action would be futile because all of the directors were named as defendants and all had participated in the activities. Four years later, four of the defendant-directors were no longer on Zapata's (D) board. The remaining directors replaced those directors with two outside directors. The board then created a committee to investigate the merits of Maldonado's (P) lawsuit. The board agreed that the committee's decision would be final, binding and nonreviewable. The committee determined that Maldonado's (P) action should be dismissed, and Zapata (D) brought a motion for dismissal.

■ ISSUE

Must a trial court, when facing a motion brought by a committee appointed by a corporation's board of directors, demanding the dismissal of a shareholder suit, grant that motion notwithstanding the fact that members of the board may have had an interest in the committee's result?

■ DECISION AND RATIONALE

(Quillen, J.) Yes. In this case, when the corporation moved for summary judgment to dismiss the action, their decision was an application of the board's business judgment, as determined by the committee. Whether the corporation has the authority to demand the suit be dismissed depends on the conclusion of the trial court concerning the independence of a stockholder bringing a derivative action, the corporate power to force a dismissal of the litigation, and the court's role in resolving internal corporate controversies. Here, the trial court was incorrect in holding that once a shareholder's demand is refused, he or she obtains an independent right to pursue a derivative action. Maldonado (P) failed to make a prior demand. Consistent with the requirement for demand, a board's decision to dismiss a detrimental suit will be respected unless the decision was wrongful. Unless the board wrongfully refused or the plaintiff brought the action without board consent because of futility, a shareholder cannot override the company's decision. However, neither of those principles resolves the matter here. Simply because a shareholder can bring a suit, it does not follow that the shareholder has the right to control the litigation throughout. The appropriate issue is when may a corporate committee demand litigation initiated by one of its stockholders be terminated. A board always has the option to decline to pursue litigation it believes would be detrimental. Even if the refusal to pursue litigation is wrongful or the initial demand was excusable, litigation that may have seemed wise may become detrimental. To fail to permit a check on derivative suits would vest in a small group of stockholders the ability to tie the board's hands simply by instituting a lawsuit. Under state law, a board is permitted to delegate its powers to a committee, and, with properly delegated authority, a committee may move to dismiss a lawsuit. Similarly, a board tainted with self-interest can delegate to a disinterested committee the power to act in its place. Allowing a corporation to use litigation committees to stop well-meaning plaintiffs takes the power from a derivative suit; but forcing corporations to deal with frivolous suits is also undesirable. The court must find the balance between a valid exercise of stockholder power and the shield of corporate interests from detrimental litigation. Therefore, if an independent committee of disinterested directors determines in good faith that an action must be dismissed, the court must oblige, absent a claim of bad faith, a lack of independence or a less-than-full investigation. However, more than a business judgment must be shown to excuse the suit, especially if the plaintiff properly brought the suit. Whether to dismiss a case based on a committee's recommendation must be at the trial court's discretion. The motion to dismiss must include a summary of the investigation and its findings. The court may grant the motion if it is satisfied as to the committee's independence and good faith, but it must exercise its own independent business judgment in determining whether a motion should be granted in order to assure that a legitimate claim is not deprived of full consideration. Reversed and remanded.

Analysis:

Zapata has its critics. While the law may provide a shareholder with the opportunity to prosecute a claim against a recalcitrant board of directors, it also provides the corporation with a simple means to attempt to defeat the litigation. As the court here recognizes, regardless of how independent the committee members are, the temptation is to side with the directors. In *Houle v. Low*, 556 N.E.2d 51 (Mass. 1990), the court recognized the shortcomings of *Zapata* and concluded that when a corporation seeks to terminate litigation based on the recommendations of a special committee, the court must ensure that the committee was truly independent and unbiased and acted in good faith.

■ CASE VOCABULARY

BUSINESS JUDGMENT RULE: The presumption that in making business decisions not involving direct self-interest or self-dealing, corporate directors act on an informed basis, in good faith, and in the honest belief that their actions are in the corporation's best interest. The rule shields directors and officers from liability for unprofitable or harmful corporate transactions if the transactions were made in good faith, with due care, and within the directors' or officers' authority.

A.P. Smith Mfg. Co. v. Barlow

(*Corporation*) v. (*Shareholder*)

13 N.J. 145, 98 A.2d 581 (1953)

A CORPORATION NEED NOT HAVE SPECIFIC AUTHORITY TO MAKE VALID CHARITABLE CONTRIBUTIONS

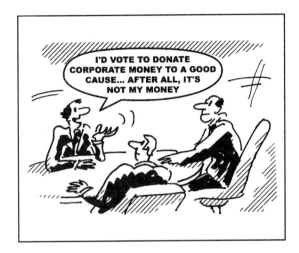

■ **INSTANT FACTS** Barlow (P), an A.P. Smith Manufacturing (D) shareholder, brought an action seeking to find that a charitable donation made by the corporation was invalid.

■ **BLACK LETTER RULE** A corporation may make reasonable charitable contributions, even in the absence of express statutory provisions.

■ **PROCEDURAL BASIS**

On appeal from a decision that the defendant's donation was intra vires.

■ **FACTS**

A.P. Smith Manufacturing Co. (A.P. Smith) (D) is a well-established company that manufactures fire hydrants and other equipment. A.P. Smith (D) contributes regularly to the local community chest, to Princeton University, and occasionally to Upsala College. On one occasion, the board resolved to donate $1500 to Princeton University, and A.P. Smith's (D) shareholders objected. A.P. Smith's (D) president considered the donation part of a sound business practice to establish good will in the community. The donation also helped ensure interest in the company by recent top graduates of the college, ultimately promoting the interests of its stockholders, employees and customers. The objecting shareholders argue that A.P. Smith's (D) certificate of incorporation does not give the company the power to make such donations and that the New Jersey statutes that A.P. Smith (D) purportedly relied on in making the donations should not apply to a corporation formed before the laws were enacted.

■ **ISSUE**

May a corporation make charitable contributions in the absence of any specific authorization in the company's charter or the state's statutes?

■ **DECISION AND RATIONALE**

(Stein, J.) Yes. In the early history of business corporations, the general belief was that a corporation should not make a charitable donation unless the company itself benefited from the gift. However, as corporate economic wealth has increased, many find public support for corporate charitable donations. In times of crisis, corporations have provided charitable donations in order to ensure the survival of society. In 1930, New Jersey passed a statute expressly authorizing corporations to help charitable concerns and requiring that donations of more than one percent of the company's capital must receive shareholder approval. The plaintiffs argue that the new statute cannot be applied to corporations that were formed without the ability to plan for the law in its corporate structure. However, the law does not demand donations and affects no contractual rights. Public policy supports these types of laws. The plaintiffs do not argue that A.P. Smith's (D) donations furthered personal, rather than corporate, interests. Therefore, the donation represents a lawful exercise of the company's authority. Affirmed.

Analysis:

While the shareholders in this case argued that the company's charter prohibited its officers from making charitable donations, the same argument has been raised to prevent a company's management from making political contributions designed to affect legislation, *see, e.g.,* Marsili v. Pacific Gas & Elec. Co., 124 Cal. Rptr. 313 (Cal. Ct. App. 1975), or from engaging in business endeavors that were not contemplated by the company when it was organized, *see, e.g., Network Affiliates, Inc. v. Robert E. Schack, P.A.*, 682 P.2d 1244 (Colo. Ct. App.1984). As a result of these types of cases, many entrepreneurs are advised by their legal counsel to provide in their corporation's charter that the company has the right to engage in any legitimate purpose for which a corporation may be organized.

■ CASE VOCABULARY

INTRA VIRES: Of or referring to an action taken within a corporation's or person's scope of authority.

Dodge v. Ford Motor Co.

(Defendant Shareholders) v. *(Corporation)*

204 Mich. 459, 170 N.W. 668 (1919)

A FOR–PROFIT CORPORATION MUST PAY DIVIDENDS ABSENT A JUSTIFIABLE BUSINESS REASON

■ **INSTANT FACTS** Ford Motor Company (D) made extraordinary profits and its founder, Henry Ford (D), intended to use those profits to lower the price of its cars and expand its factories' capabilities by adding a steel plant, but Ford Motor's shareholders (P) objected to these policies claiming that the company's first obligation was to make profits for its shareholders.

■ **BLACK LETTER RULE** Although a corporation's directors have discretion in the means they choose to make products and earn a profit, the directors may not reduce profits or withhold dividends from the corporation's shareholders in order to benefit the public.

■ **PROCEDURAL BASIS**

On appeal from trial court's ruling in favor of the plaintiffs.

■ **FACTS**

Ford Motor Co. (D) was incorporated in 1903 with $150,000. Its majority shareholder was Henry Ford (D). Horace E. Dodge (P) and John F. Dodge (P) were among the minority shareholders. The company made extraordinary profits and paid sizeable dividends to its shareholders. In 1915 alone, the Dodge brothers' (P) share of Ford Motor's (D) special dividends was $1 million. Henry Ford (D) wanted to use its profits to purchase an iron ore plant to enable the company to make its own metal parts. Despite indications that Ford Motor (D) could continue to sell more cars each year even with price increases, Henry Ford (D) also expressed a desire to lower the price of his cars. In view of his aspirations for the company, Henry Ford (D) told his fellow shareholders that their dividends would be limited to $120,000 per year for the foreseeable future, allowing him to reshape the company's focus. The Dodge brothers (P) sued to stop Ford Motor (D) from expanding and to force it to resume compensating its shareholders.

■ **ISSUE**

May courts interfere with a corporation's internal operations by reviewing a board's decision and ordering the payment of dividends to its shareholders?

■ **DECISION AND RATIONALE**

Yes. The plaintiffs must show that Henry Ford's (D) business expansion is inimical to the company's best interest and that withholding the dividends that the shareholders expect is arbitrary. At the time the Dodge brothers (P) demanded additional dividends, Ford Motor (D) had completed its most profitable year to date. Its profits were approximately $60 million, with cash assets of almost $54 million. In the company's short operating history, its practice was to declare large dividends. Reviewed in isolation, the decision to withhold dividends seems arbitrary. The company had a practice of increasing the quality of its cars annually in conjunction with lowering the cars' prices. Discussions throughout the year led to the conclusion that the company should accumulate a surplus to expand the plant so it could manufacture its own metal parts. This effort at saving, combined with a reduction in the price of Ford

---

cars, would make the company less profitable. The plaintiffs contend these policies will turn the company into a charitable concern rather than maintain its character as a business institution. Ford (D), on the other hand, believes the gains his shareholders have made to date have been generous and that they should be content to receive regular dividends and forego the special dividends for a time. Ford's proposal is not the same as donating money for charitable purposes. A corporation is organized for the benefit of its shareholders. While a corporation's directors may exercise discretion in deciding how to reach that goal, it cannot divert profits from its shareholders and devote them to other purposes. The corporation argues that as long as the directors' purposes are lawful, a court may not second-guess them, but it is not lawful for a company to direct profits from the shareholders to others. Diverting profits for future expansion is a decision that should not be overridden, because future profitability is often pursued at the cost of short-term gains. However, if the contemplated expenditures were not made immediately, significant cash would accumulate quickly, and the large sum appropriated for the smelter plant was payable over the long-term. The money should be distributed to the shareholders. Affirmed in part and reversed in part.

Analysis:

While the court in *A.P. Smith Mfg. Co. v. Barlow*, 13 N.J. 145, 98 A.2d 581 (1953) recognized the benefits that accrue to a company by its commitment to help the community, the court here seemed oblivious to the customer loyalty Ford Motor (D) was generating by lowering its prices and ensuring a steady, less expensive supply of metal parts from the new plant. Certainly, the original stockholders were seeing a return on their investments. In 1915 alone, the Dodge brothers (P) received $1.12 million in dividends on their capital, notwithstanding the fact that the brothers had already been operating a competing business with Ford Motor (D) for nearly two years. One would have to wonder whether the Dodge brothers' (P) concerns were truly motivated by a desire to maximize their dividends, or if they did not arise, at least partially, out of their concern to keep their competitor from outpacing their own company.

■ CASE VOCABULARY

DIVIDEND: A portion of a company's earnings or profits distributed pro rata to its shareholders, usually in the form of cash or additional shares.

SPECIAL DIVIDEND: A dividend paid in addition to a regular dividend, usually because of exceptional corporate profits during the dividend period.

Shlensky v. Wrigley

(Shareholder) v. *(Chicago Cubs' Director)*
95 Ill.App.2d 173, 237 N.E.2d 776 (1968)

OFFICERS' AND DIRECTORS' DECISIONS ARE PROTECTED BY THE BUSINESS JUDGMENT RULE

■ **INSTANT FACTS** Shlensky, a Chicago Cubs' shareholder, brought a derivative suit against the Chicago Cubs and its directors for negligence and mismanagement and for an order that the defendant install lights for night baseball games.

■ **BLACK LETTER RULE** A shareholder fails to state a cause of action unless it alleges that a corporation's directors' conduct was causing financial loss to the shareholder and was based upon fraud, illegality or conflict of interest.

■ PROCEDURAL BASIS

On appeal from a dismissal of the shareholder's complaint.

■ FACTS

Shlensky (P) is a minor shareholder in the Chicago National League Ball Club, Inc, (D), which manages the Chicago Cubs baseball team. The defendant corporation also manages Wrigley Field and is responsible for the concession sales, television and radio broadcasts, and revenue from other events held at Wrigley Field. Shlensky's (P) complaint alleges that more than half the scheduled baseball games throughout the league are played at night and that the Chicago Cubs are the only team that does not play night games at home. The complaint also alleges that playing night games would increase revenue. During the previous four seasons, the Cubs have experienced a loss that the plaintiffs attribute to poor home attendance. Shlensky (P) also states that financing would be readily available to install lights and that the expense associated with the upgrade would be recaptured by increased ticket sales. Philip K. Wrigley (D), president and majority stockholder of the corporation, contends that his resistance to add lights to the baseball field is due to his concern about the quality of the neighborhood surrounding the park. Wrigley (D) asserts that he would be willing to have the team play night games if the stadium were located in a different area.

■ ISSUE

Does a shareholder's action that seeks to overturn a board's decision and does not make allegations of fraud, illegality or conflict of interest state a cause of action?

■ DECISION AND RATIONALE

(Sullivan, J.) No. Based on Wrigley's (D) statements, the plaintiff argues that the board's refusal to arrange for lights is based on considerations other than the corporation's financial health. Courts have historically given broad discretion to corporate managers for making policy decisions and typically give due regard for the board's decisions unless the decisions are tainted. The plaintiff insists he has stated a valid cause of action based on *Dodge v. Ford Motor Co.*, 204 Mich. 459, 170 N.W. 668 (1919), in which the court demanded the company pay out dividends rather than retain profits in order to finance future corporate expansion. Although the *Dodge* court found that the company's goals of helping the surrounding community amounted to placing community goals ahead of the shareholders, the court refused to interfere with the company's decision to expand its business. In this case, Wrigley's (D) recognizes that lighting the field may negatively impact the neighborhood and that unhappy neighbors may not attend the Cubs' games. Without some showing that the defendant's actions are based on fraud, illegality or a conflict of interest, a court should not interfere, especially because the plaintiff did not prove that the Cubs' revenues would increase with night games. With no correlation between installing lights and an increase in the company's revenues, the plaintiff has failed to establish serious and irreparable harm to the shareholders. Directors are elected for their business judgment and courts cannot order their decisions to be disregarded simply because others may disagree. Affirmed.

Analysis:

The plaintiff here argues that *Dodge v. Ford Motor Co.*, 204 Mich. 459, 170 N.W. 668 (1919) provides support for disregarding Wrigley's (D) stated concern for the neighborhood over the interests of his shareholders. To distinguish this case from *Dodge*, the court notes that the Cubs' recognition of the need to preserve the neighborhood would likely translate into more fans from the neighborhood. Certainly, the *Dodge* court could have similarly recognized that Ford's generosity and desire to charge a fair price similarly provided benefits to Ford Motor in the form of more customers.

■ CASE VOCABULARY

CONFLICT OF INTEREST: A real or seeming incompatibility between one's private interests and one's public or fiduciary duties.

CHAPTER FOUR

The Limited Liability Company

Water, Waste & Land, Inc. d/b/a Westec v. Lanham

Instant Facts: Westec (P) negotiated with Larry Clark (D), believing Clark (D) was Lanham's (D) agent, but Lanham (D) and Clark (D) were both members of Preferred Income Investors, a limited liability company.

Black Letter Rule: If a limited liability company's agent fails to inform a third party that he is acting as the company's agent, the Limited Liability Company Act's notice provision does not relieve the agent of liability to the third party.

Elf Atochem N. Am., Inc. v. Jaffari

Instant Facts: Elf Atochem North America, Inc., (P) engaged in a joint venture with Cyrus A. Jaffari (D), the president of Malek, Inc., and the two entities formed a limited liability company, but the company did not sign its operating agreement.

Black Letter Rule: A limited liability company (LLC) is bound by the terms of an operating agreement that is signed by some of its members and that defines the LLC's governance and operation, even if the LLC did not execute the agreement.

Kaycee Land and Livestock v. Flahive

Instant Facts: Roger Flahive (D), through Flahive Oil & Gas (D), a limited liability company, leased undeveloped property from Kaycee Land and Livestock (P) and contaminated the property.

Black Letter Rule: The common law doctrine of piercing the corporate veil is not abrogated by the limited liability company act and may be used against limited liability company members in appropriate cases.

McConnell v. Hunt Sports Enter.

Instant Facts: Several individuals formed a limited liability company to try to attract an NHL team to Columbus, Ohio, but when the company's principal did not enter into the necessary agreements in time to be considered by the NHL, a subgroup of the company secured the needed facilities and was awarded the NHL franchise.

Black Letter Rule: Limited liability company members are bound by the terms of their operating agreement, and if the agreement expressly allows them to engage in "any other business venture of any nature," they are not prohibited from participating in a competing venture.

New Horizons Supply Coop. v. Haack

Instant Facts: Kickapoo Valley Freight LLC (Kickapoo) obtained a credit card for gasoline purchases from New Horizons Supply Cooperative's (New Horizons) (P) predecessor, and when Kickapoo (D) was no longer able to make payments, New Horizons (P) sought payment from Allison Haack (D).

Black Letter Rule: A limited liability company member may be responsible for the company's debts if the member fails to take the appropriate steps to dissolve the company when it winds up its operations.

Water, Waste & Land, Inc. d/b/a Westec v. Lanham

(Developer) v. (Undisclosed LLC Member)

955 P.2d 997 (Colo. 1998)

IF A THIRD PARTY IS NOT AWARE THAT AN AGENT IS ACTING FOR A PRINCIPAL, THE AGENT MAY BE LIABLE TO THE THIRD PARTY

■ **INSTANT FACTS** Westec (P) negotiated with Larry Clark (D), believing Clark (D) was Lanham's (D) agent, but Lanham (D) and Clark (D) were both members of Preferred Income Investors, a limited liability company.

■ **BLACK LETTER RULE** If a limited liability company's agent fails to inform a third party that he is acting as the company's agent, the Limited Liability Company Act's notice provision does not relieve the agent of liability to the third party.

■ **PROCEDURAL BASIS**

On appeal from a district court's ruling in favor of the defendants, reversing the trial court's decision.

■ **FACTS**

Water, Waste, & Land, Inc. (P) was a land development and engineering company, doing business as Westec. Donald Lanham (D) and Larry Clark (D) were members and managers of Preferred Income Investors, L.L.C. (Preferred Income) (D), a Colorado limited liability company (LLC). Clark (D) contacted Westec (P), hoping to hire it to perform engineering work on a development project. Clark (D) gave Westec (P) a business card that showed Lanham's (D) address as Clark's place of business. Preferred Income's (D) name was not on the business card, but the letters "P.I.I." were above the address. The card did not describe P.I.I. as an LLC, nor was the designation "LLC" located on the card. Clark (D) and Westec (P) reached an agreement for services, and Clark (D) asked Westec (P) to send the written proposal to Lanham (D). The defendants did not return the contract to Westec (P), but authorized Westec (P) to start the work. Upon completion, Westec (P) billed Lanham (D), but Lanham (D) did not pay the bill. Westec (P) filed suit against Clark (D), Lanham (D), and Preferred Income (D). The trial court found that no one told Westec (P) that Lanham's (D) company was an LLC, and that the letters "P.I.I." on the business card were not sufficient to give Westec (P) notice it was dealing with an LCC. Based on these findings, the trial court ruled that Clark (D) was the agent of both Lanham (D) and Preferred Income (D), that Westec (P) dealt with Clark (D) and Lanham (D) as individuals, and that, because Westec (P) believed Clark (D) was Lanham's (D) agent, Clark (D) was not personally liable. Therefore, the judge entered judgment in favor of Westec (P) against Lanham (D) and Preferred Income (D), and dismissed the action against Clark (D). Lanham (D) appealed. The district court reversed the trial court's decision as to the second agent based on its reading of the state Limited Liability Company Act (the Act), which provided that filing a company's articles serve as notice of its status as an LLC.

■ **ISSUE**

Is a member of an LLC personally liable under a contract if the other party to the contract was not aware that the member was negotiating on behalf of an LLC?

■ **DECISION AND RATIONALE**

(Scott, J.) Yes. The trial court concluded that the Act's notice provision effectively notified Westec (P) of Lanham's (D) agency with Preferred Income (D), but the court failed to recognize that the Act did not eliminate common law agency doctrines. The statutory notice provision applies only to parties looking to impose personal liability on the members or managers of an LLC when they *know* the individuals have formed an LLC. At common law, an agent is liable on a contract made for his principal if the agent did not disclose his or her principal's identity. Here, the trial court found Westec (P) had no knowledge that Clark (D) was an agent for Preferred Income (D) or that the letters "P.I.I." on his business card stood for "Preferred Income Investors." Westec (P) believed Clark (D) was Lanham's (D) agent. Because Clark (D) and Lanham (D) failed to disclose the LLC, they remain liable as individuals. The fact that Preferred Income (D) filed organizational papers with the Secretary of State did not put Westec (P) on notice that it was dealing with an LLC. The Act's presumption prevents a third party from pleading ignorance only once it knows the entity's name. To find otherwise would invite fraud and encourage principals to keep their LLC's name secret. Remanded to reinstate the county court's decision.

Analysis:

This case's holding is nearly universally accepted and states the position adopted by the Restatement on Agency. Unless the third party and the agent agree otherwise, an agent who makes a contract on behalf of a disclosed principal is not a party to the contract. In contrast, an agent who makes a contract for an unidentified principal becomes a party to the contract unless the third party and the agent agree otherwise. These rules recognize that a contracting party often needs to evaluate the other party's creditworthiness. As noted in the Restatement (Third) of Agency § 6.02 cmt. B (Tentative Draft No. 4, 2003), without the party's true identity, it cannot make that judgment.

■ CASE VOCABULARY

ASSUMED NAME: Alias; the name under which a business operates or by which it is commonly known.

LIMITED LIABILITY COMPANY: A company—statutorily authorized in certain states—that is characterized by limited liability, management by members or managers, and limitation on ownership transfer.

Elf Atochem N. Am., Inc. v. Jaffari

(Aerosol Scents Manufacturer) v. (Environmentally–Preferred Scent Designer)

727 A.2d 286 (Del. 1999)

A LIMITED LIABILITY COMPANY'S OPERATING AGREEMENT GOVERNS ITS MEMBER'S ACTS

■ **INSTANT FACTS** Elf Atochem North America, Inc., (P) engaged in a joint venture with Cyrus A. Jaffari (D), the president of Malek, Inc., and the two entities formed a limited liability company, but the company did not sign its operating agreement.

■ **BLACK LETTER RULE** A limited liability company (LLC) is bound by the terms of an operating agreement that is signed by some of its members and that defines the LLC's governance and operation, even if the LLC did not execute the agreement.

■ PROCEDURAL BASIS

On appeal from dismissal by Court of Chancery, holding that the matter should be arbitrated.

■ FACTS

Elf Atochem North America, Inc. (Elf) (P) manufactured chemicals to mask odors ("maskants"), which it sold to aerospace and aviation industries throughout the world. Industries have used Elf's (P) solvent-based maskants for decades, but they contain chemicals that may be hazardous. Elf (P) approached Jaffari (D), the president of Malek, Inc., to work on developing alternate maskant formulae. Elf (P) and Jaffari (D) agreed to form a joint venture using an LLC to operate their enterprise. Elf contributed $1 million in exchange for a thirty percent ownership interest in the LLC. Malek, Inc. contributed the rights to its water-based maskant in exchange for a seventy percent ownership interest. Malek, Inc., filed the LLC's Certificate of Formation with the Delaware Secretary of State, forming Malek LLC (D). Elf (P) and Malek LLC (D) signed an Exclusive Distribution Agreement allowing Elf (P) to be the exclusive, worldwide distributor for Malek LLC (D). Jaffari (D) was designated the manager of Malek LLC (D), and Malek LLC (D) and Jaffari (D) entered into a contract for Jaffari's employment. The members also signed an extensive Operating Agreement (the Agreement), but the LLC did not sign it. Under the Agreement, all company disputes were to be resolved through arbitration, and the parties could bring a court action only to compel arbitration or to enforce an award. Elf (P) sued Jaffari (D) and Malek LLC (D), individually and derivatively on behalf of Malek LLC, seeking equitable remedies based on a number of claims, many involving mismanagement and fraud. The Court of Chancery granted the defendants' motion to dismiss based on lack of subject matter jurisdiction, holding that Elf's (P) claims arose under the Agreement and were directly related to Jaffari's (D) acts as the LLC's manager. Because the Agreement provided that disagreements would be settled through arbitration in California, Delaware courts had no authority to decide the claims. Elf (P) appeals.

■ ISSUE

If an LLC fails to execute its Operating Agreement, are the provisions nevertheless binding on the LLC?

■ DECISION AND RATIONALE

(Veasey, C.J.) Yes. The Agreement requires all LLC members to consent exclusively to the jurisdiction of California's state and federal courts for any action arising out of the rights and privileges contained in the Agreement or any of the transactions contemplated by the Agreement provided the claim is "not required to be arbitrated." Delaware allows LLC members to draft an operating agreement to control their relationships. Under the LLC Act (the Act), the Court of Chancery has jurisdiction over LLC disputes, but the Act allows members to determine whether arbitration may better suit their needs in resolving internal disputes. Elf (P) contends it is bringing its claims on behalf of Malek LLC (D), and, because Malek LLC (D) is not a party to the Agreement, the Agreement's arbitration provision does not control. However, Malek LLC's members signed the Agreement, and the Act provides that an operating agreement is an agreement by LLC members regarding the company's business operations. Therefore, the LLC members are the real parties in interest in any controversy over the business operations. Malek, Inc., and Elf agreed to settle controversies through arbitration, so the claims must be submitted to arbitration based on the Agreement's terms. The parties also argued whether Elf's (P) claims are derivative. Elf (P) insists that its claims are derivative and, as such, the arbitration and forum selection clauses do not bar suit in Delaware. However, the Agreement does not provide that Delaware is the appropriate forum and provides that a party may not bring an action based on any claim arising out of or related to the Agreement, except an action to compel arbitration or to enforce an arbitration award. Furthermore, Elf (P) consented to the exclusive jurisdiction of the California courts in *any* action on a claim arising out of or in connection with the Agreement or with any transactions contemplated by the Agreement. The Agreement does not distinguish between direct and derivative actions, and the Agreement's provisions are broad enough to encompass disputes under the Distributorship Agreement, even though it has no similar provision. Therefore, the Court of Chancery's decision is correct. Because no specific statutory provision prohibits the parties from agreeing to arbitration in California, the court will not permit a party to avoid the arbitration process by characterizing its claims as derivative. Affirmed.

Analysis:

An operating agreement is a similar to an owner's manual for an LLC's operations. As the Elf court noted, an operating agreement is drafted for the member's benefit. If the LLC needs to remove a member for illegal activity or replace an officer because of illness, a properly drafted operating agreement should provide the appropriate procedure. The agreement's terms frequently mirror statutory default provisions, but if the parties want to require certain procedures, to have disputes settled in a non-traditional manner, or to require member consent for certain corporate actions, the parties should carefully consider the agreement's terms.

■ CASE VOCABULARY

JOINT VENTURE: A business undertaking by two or more persons engaged in a single defined project. The necessary elements are: (1) an express or implied agreement; (2) a common purpose that the group intends to carry out; (3) shared profits and losses; and (4) each member's equal voice in controlling the project.

Kaycee Land and Livestock v. Flahive

(*Real Estate Lessor*) v. (*Judgment–Proof Lessee*)

46 P.3d 323 (Wyo. 2002)

A COURT MAY PIERCE THE CORPORATE VEIL OF A LIMITED LIABILITY COMPANY

■ **INSTANT FACTS** Roger Flahive (D), through Flahive Oil & Gas (D), a limited liability company, leased undeveloped property from Kaycee Land and Livestock (P) and contaminated the property.

■ **BLACK LETTER RULE** The common law doctrine of piercing the corporate veil is not abrogated by the limited liability company act and may be used against limited liability company members in appropriate cases.

■ **PROCEDURAL BASIS**

On appeal from the district court's certification of a question of law to the Wyoming Supreme Court.

■ **FACTS**

Roger Flahive (D) was the managing member of Flahive Oil & Gas (Flahive Oil) (D), a limited liability company (LLC), which negotiated a lease with Kaycee Land and Livestock (Kaycee) (P) for certain real estate. Kaycee (P) contended that Flahive Oil (D) contaminated the property. Kaycee (P) did not allege that Flahive Oil (D) acted fraudulently, but wanted to pierce Flahive Oil's (D) corporate veil to reach Roger Flahive's (D) personal assets to satisfy the LLC's debt for cleaning up the property.

■ **ISSUE**

May a court pierce the corporate veil of a limited liability company to reach its members' assets?

■ **DECISION AND RATIONALE**

Yes. Courts have long recognized the common law doctrine of piercing the corporate veil as an equitable remedy. Roger Flahive (D) argues that the Wyoming Limited Liability Company Act (the Act) was designed to prevent the doctrine from being used against LLC members. He notes that unless an LLC's articles of incorporation require its members to assume personal liability for the company's debts, its members may not be personally liable unless the member's acts or conduct are fraudulent. Further, Flahive (D) contends that the Act exempts an LLC's members and managers from personal liability for the LLC's judgments or obligations. Although the Act generally prevents personal liability, nothing restricts a court from piercing the LLC veil if the LLC is used improperly. Wyoming enacted the first LLC Act, even before the IRS allowed an LLC to be taxed as a partnership. The Act has only minimal requirements, and it is unlikely the legislature even considered the common-law doctrine that governs piercing the corporate veil. Other states' statutes apply the doctrine to an LLC, but Wyoming's silence is more likely a result of its statute being the first LLC act, rather than the legislature rejecting the doctrine. In the absence of specific Wyoming legislation on the subject, the court will look to other states, where the common law principle is frequently applied. However, not every consideration that applies to piercing a corporate veil applies to an LLC, and this is not an appropriate case in which to establish LLC rules because of the limited facts provided on appeal. The district court must inquire further. Remanded.

Analysis:

Some state statutes, such as Colorado and Minnesota, specifically contain provisions that allow courts to apply the common law principles of piercing the corporate veil to an LLC. Because tax or other financial considerations drive most choice-of-entity decisions, it makes sense to treat all entities alike and, if the entity is misused, to allow creditors to make claims directly against the LLC membership for moneys owed. The Internal Revenue Service, however, is not entitled to disregard the LLC for collection purposes, even though it ignores the LLC when LLC members file their individual returns. However, as noted in I.R.S. Chief Couns. Adv. 199930013, 1999 WL 554351 (July 30, 1999), and I.R.S. Chief Couns. Adv. 199922053, 1999 WL 358245 (June 4, 1999), in the case of a single-person LLC, the IRS will pursue a claim for unpaid employment taxes against the single member.

■ **CASE VOCABULARY**

ABROGATE: To abolish (a law or custom) by formal or authoritative action; to annul or repeal.

McConnell v. Hunt Sports Enter.

(New NHL Franchisee) v. *(Losing Bidder for NHL Franchise)*

132 Ohio App.3d 657, 725 N.E.2d 1193 (1999)

IF AN OPERATING AGREEMENT PERMITS COMPETITION, LIMITED LIABILITY COMPANY MEMBERS MAY ENGAGE IN A COMPETING VENTURE

■ **INSTANT FACTS** Several individuals formed a limited liability company to try to attract an NHL team to Columbus, Ohio, but when the company's principal did not enter into the necessary agreements in time to be considered by the NHL, a subgroup of the company secured the needed facilities and was awarded the NHL franchise.

■ **BLACK LETTER RULE** Limited liability company members are bound by the terms of their operating agreement, and if the agreement expressly allows them to engage in "any other business venture of any nature," they are not prohibited from participating in a competing venture.

■ **PROCEDURAL BASIS**

On appeal from a directed verdict in favor of the defendant.

■ **FACTS**

Several wealthy individuals and their legal entities formed Columbus Hockey Limited, L.L.C. (CHL) (D) in an effort to obtain a National Hockey League (NHL) franchise for Columbus, Ohio. Two of the leading investors were John H. McConnell (P) and Lamar Hunt (D). In order to obtain the NHL franchise, the investors needed an arena and sought a sales tax surcharge to pay for its construction. The Columbus voters rejected the proposal. Nationwide Insurance Enterprise (Nationwide) expressed an interest in building the arena and leasing it to the team. Hunt (D), purporting to act for CHL (D), met with Nationwide's CEO, Dimon McPherson, to discuss Nationwide's lease proposal. Hunt (D) rejected the proposal and rebuffed Nationwide's further attempts to contact him. As the NHL deadline neared, McConnell (P) contacted McPherson and told him that he would accept Nationwide's offer. Hunt (D) told McPherson that the proposal was still unacceptable, but that he was interested in negotiating further. Based on McPherson's preliminary agreement with McConnell (P), the NHL awarded Columbus an NHL franchise. CHL's (D) members met and Hunt (D) reiterated his belief that McPherson's offer was unacceptable. McConnell's (P) group accepted Nationwide's offer, signed an agreement without using CHL's name, and then filed this suit seeking to exclude Hunt (D) and CHL (D) from the franchise under the terms of CHL's Operating Agreement (the Agreement). Hunt (D) answered the suit and filed a counterclaim. The NHL ultimately awarded the Columbus franchise to McConnell (P). The lower court granted a directed verdict in McConnell's (P) favor, and Hunt (D) appealed.

■ **ISSUE**

Should a court allow extrinsic evidence of the meaning of an operating agreement's terms that purport to do away with the fiduciary protections ordinarily afforded the members of a business organization such as a limited liability company?

■ **DECISION AND RATIONALE**

(Tyack, J.) No. Courts permit extrinsic evidence only if the language is not clear or if the agreement's circumstances suggest the contract language has special meaning. In deciding whether to give words their ordinary meaning, the court must determine whether doing so would result in an absurd meaning or whether another meaning should be gathered from the contract. Here, the Agreement states that the parties agree that its members will not be restricted from engaging in any business of any nature—even a business that may compete with the company's business. Hunt (D) argues that the words "other ventures" should be read to mean ventures that are different from the company's business. However, the contract language was drafted very broadly and cannot be read as prohibiting the company's members from creating their own organization to operate the NHL franchise. Hunt (D) also argues that the lower court erred in refusing to instruct the jury as to the impropriety of McConnell's (P) group forming a limited partnership to compete, but that instruction would not have been proper because the members had the right to compete. Generally, fiduciary obligations prohibit members of a business organization, including an LLC, from competing with one another and interfering with prospective business relationships. However, here, the Agreement's explicit terms eliminate that protection. Similarly, although tortious interference with a prospective business relationship is committed if a person, absent a privilege, encourages a third person to abandon a business relationship, the Agreement here granted the members the right to compete, so the privilege existed. Also, notwithstanding the privilege, Nationwide approached McConnell (P), and McConnell (P) dealt with Nationwide only after Hunt (D) and his group refused to come to terms. Even then, McConnell's (P) acceptance of Nationwide's offer was contingent on Hunt's (D) refusal to accept it, and Nationwide continued to negotiate with Hunt's (D) group. The trial court awarded a directed verdict in favor of McConnell (P), finding that Hunt (D) had violated the Agreement by unilaterally rejecting Nationwide's offer and allowing the NHL deadlines to pass without securing the necessary facilities. Hunt (D) had no right to respond to this suit unilaterally and to file a counterclaim; pursuant to the terms of the Agreement, Hunt (D) was required to obtain *all* CHL members' authorization before filing an answer or counterclaim. Hunt (D) argued that, absent willful misconduct, he is not liable to McConnell (P) and his group, and that as the group's "operating member," he had the discretion to act on CHL's behalf. However, the Agreement does not designate Hunt as the operating member, and because Hunt (D) lacked authority to act, his conduct does not deserve protection as an "official" duty. In light of Hunt's (D) knowledge that the Agreement required a majority vote before he acted on behalf of the company, he acted willfully when he filed his answer and counterclaim without a vote. Reversed.

Analysis:

The Agreement's provisions were broadly drafted, although such broad language is not always necessary to justify a member's competition. The primary concern when an officer, director or other fiduciary competes with its company is the existence of good faith. Courts have frequently not found bad faith when a fiduciary later secured a missed corporate opportunity. If a fiduciary misappropriated a business opportunity, the corporation may ask the court to impose a constructive trust within which it may accumulate the fiduciary's profits to be distributed to the corporation.

■ CASE VOCABULARY

FIDUCIARY: One who owes to another the duties of goof faith, trust, confidence, and candor.

TORTIOUS INTERFERENCE WITH CONTRACTUAL RELATIONS: A third party's intentional inducement of a contracting party to break a contract, causing damage to the relationship between the contracting parties.

New Horizons Supply Co-op. v. Haack

(Credit Card Company) v. *(Member of Abandoned LLC)*

224 Wis.2d 644, 590 N.W.2d 282 (App. 1999)

A LIMITED LIABILITY COMPANY MEMBER MAY BE LIABLE FOR THE COMPANY'S DEBTS

ANYBODY HERE? WE'RE YOUR CREDITORS

■ **INSTANT FACTS** Kickapoo Valley Freight LLC (Kickapoo) obtained a credit card for gasoline purchases from New Horizons Supply Cooperative's (New Horizons) (P) predecessor, and when Kickapoo (D) was no longer able to make payments, New Horizons (P) sought payment from Allison Haack (D).

■ **BLACK LETTER RULE** A limited liability company member may be responsible for the company's debts if the member fails to take the appropriate steps to dissolve the company when it winds up its operations.

■ **PROCEDURAL BASIS**

Appeal from a small claims judgment of $1009.99 plus costs.

■ **FACTS**

Allison Haack (D) signed a Cardtrol Agreement (the Agreement) pursuant to which she agreed to be responsible for all fuel purchased on the credit card. The Agreement was initially made with a predecessor to New Horizons Supply Cooperative (New Horizons) (P). Kickapoo Valley Freight LLC (Kickapoo) (D) is indicated as a patron in the Agreement, but the signature block at the end of the Agreement bears Haack's signature with no corporate designation. When the account became delinquent, New Horizons (P) contacted Kickapoo (D) and was referred to Haack (D), who handled the company's accounts payable. Haack (D) promised New Horizons (P) she would send them $100 per month on the account, but she failed to make the first payment. New Horizons (P) followed up and was told that Kickapoo (D) had dissolved, and that Haack (D), as a partner, would take responsibility for the company and start making payments the next month using proceeds from the remaining business assets. Haack (D) never made the payments, and New Horizons (P) sued Haack (D) under the designation, "dba Kickapoo Valley Freight." At trial, Haack (D) did not produce incorporation documents for Kickapoo, but she did offer documents from the Wisconsin Department of Revenue showing that the department recognized Kickapoo as a limited liability company (LLC). Haack (D) argued she was not personally liable for the LLC's debts. Haack (D) explained that her brother had suffered a breakdown over the business, and the company's assets were sold. After paying the liens against the assets, no funds remained for the unsecured creditors. Haack (D) acknowledged that she had tried to take care of the New Horizons (P) account herself. She also admitted not filing articles of dissolution or notifying creditors when the business's operations ceased. Both Haack (D) and her brother allegedly lost their entire investment in the company. At trial, the judge found for Kickapoo, concluding that in the absence of any company documents, the corporation was no more than a shell.

■ **ISSUE**

Should an LLC member who fails to take the appropriate steps to dissolve the company be permitted to defend against an action to recover against her personally by establishing that the debts in question were the LLC's obligation?

■ DECISION AND RATIONALE

(Curry, J.) No. The doctrine of piercing the corporate veil has been expressly adopted in the state's LLC law, and New Horizons (P) insists the trial judge applied it correctly here. The trial court's contention that the Revenue Department's tax treatment of Kickapoo (D) as a partnership resolved the matter was not correct. However, there is little other evidence that Kickapoo (D) was operated formally, as required by law. Haack (D) did not keep her obligations separate from the company's obligations and took no steps to insulate herself properly from liability for the company's debts, such as signing contracts as an officer, rather than as an individual. Haack (D) offered no evidence that articles of organization were ever filed with the Department of Financial Institutions. On dissolution, no formal steps were taken to dissolve the corporation. While dissolution is optional, when the action is taken, the process for distributing the company's assets is fixed and creditors are given first shot at the company's assets. When an LLC files articles of dissolution, the creditors receive written notice of the dissolution, and all known claims are resolved under those articles. If the LLC's assets are distributed in liquidation, any claim not resolved by the dissolution may be satisfied only to the extent that a member of the LLC receives assets in distribution and only in an amount that does not exceed the value of those distributed assets. In this case, Kickapoo's assets were sold and lienholders took the proceeds in satisfaction of their liens. No evidence indicated what the company did with any remaining cash. With no evidence that the company was properly wound up, Haack (D) remains liable for the obligation to New Horizons (P). Affirmed.

Analysis:

This decision represents a "last straw" result. Haack (D) did nothing right. She could not prove her organizational papers were filed with the Wisconsin state offices, she did not sign contracts so as to indicate she was obligating the LLC, and when she spoke with the LLC's creditors, she personally offered to try to make good on the debts. The court here admitted that the dissolution process was optional, yet it concluded the imposition of personal liability was correct because of Haack's (D) failure to file the dissolution documents. The problem with requiring dissolution documents be filed in order to protect a member from an LLC's creditors is that the documents frequently need to be prepared by an attorney and the dissolution fees can exceed $100. When a company is already having financial problems, scraping together the money to pay an attorney and record the documents can be difficult.

■ CASE VOCABULARY

DISSOLUTION: The termination of a corporation's legal existence by expiration of its charter, by legislative act, by bankruptcy, or by other means; the event immediately preceding the liquidation or winding-up process.

LIQUIDATION: The act or process of converting assets into cash, especially to settle debts.

CHAPTER FIVE

The Duties of Officers, Directors, and Other Insiders

Kamin v. American Express Co.

Instant Facts: Stockholders brought a derivative action, asking for a declaration that a certain dividend in kind was a waste of corporate assets.

Black Letter Rule: A complaint alleging that some course of action other than that taken by the board would have been more advantageous does not give rise to a cause of action for damages.

Smith v. Van Gorkom

Instant Facts: Trans Union's (D) stockholders brought a class action suit against the company's board of directors for negligent decision-making.

Black Letter Rule: The business judgment rule presumes that, when making business decisions, directors act on an informed basis, in good faith and in the company's best interests.

Brehm v. Eisner

Instant Facts: The shareholders sued the Walt Disney Co. directors for breach of fiduciary duty in committing waste by agreeing to an agreement's severance terms.

Black Letter Rule: In order to constitute waste, an exchange must be so one-sided that no person of a reasonable mind would have entered into it.

Francis v. United Jersey Bank

Instant Facts: The bankruptcy trustee of various creditors brought suit against Pritchard's estate to recover misappropriated funds.

Black Letter Rule: Directors have the duty to act honestly and in good faith and with the same degree of diligence, care, and skills that a reasonably prudent person would use in similar circumstances.

In re Caremark Int'l Inc. Derivative Litigation

Instant Facts: Caremark International, Inc.'s shareholders (P) brought a consolidated derivative action against Caremark's (D) board members, alleging breach of fiduciary duty related to allegations of violations of federal and state laws by Caremark's (D) employees.

Black Letter Rule: Although directors have a duty to monitor a corporation's ongoing operation, they are not liable for wrongdoings of which they had no real or constructive knowledge.

Bayer v. Beran

Instant Facts: Shareholders brought a derivative suit against the Celanese Corporation of America's directors (D) for breach of fiduciary duty for approving and extending a $1,000,000 per year radio advertising program.

Black Letter Rule: A director does not breach his or her fiduciary duty by approving a radio advertising program in which the wife of the corporate president, who was also member of board of directors, was one of the featured performers.

Lewis v. S. L. & E., Inc.

Instant Facts: Donald (P), Carol, and Margaret Lewis brought a shareholder derivative action against Richard (D), Alan (D), and Leon Lewis, Jr. (D), alleging waste.

Black Letter Rule: A transaction in which a director has an interest, other than as the corporation's director, is automatically suspect and subject to further review.

Broz v. Cellular Info. Sys., Inc.

Instant Facts: Cellular Information Systems, Inc. filed suit against Broz for breach of fiduciary duty, alleging he put his own interests before that of the corporation.

Black Letter Rule: Under the doctrine of corporate opportunity, a corporate fiduciary must place the corporation's interests before his or her own interests in appropriate circumstances, but a corporate fiduciary does not breach his or her fiduciary duty by not considering the interests of another corporation proposing to acquire the corporation in deciding to make a corporate purchase.

Sinclair Oil Corp. v. Levien

Instant Facts: Shareholders brought a derivative action against Sinclair Oil Corp. (D) to require an accounting for damages sustained by its subsidiary, Sinclair Venezuelan Oil Company.

Black Letter Rule: If, in a transaction involving a parent company and its subsidiary, the parent company controls the transaction and fixes the terms, the transaction must meet the intrinsic fairness test.

Zahn v. Transamerica Corp.

Instant Facts: Stockholders of the Axton–Fisher Tobacco Company sued Transamerica Corporation (D) claiming Transamerica (D) caused Axton–Fisher to redeem its Class A stock at $80.80 per share, instead of allowing them to participate in the liquidation of company assets, in which case they content they would have received $240 per share.

Black Letter Rule: If a stockholder who is also a director is voting as a director, he or she represents all stockholders in the capacity of a trustee and cannot use the director's position for his or her personal benefit to the stockholders' detriment.

Fliegler v. Lawrence

Instant Facts: A shareholder brought a derivative action against the officers and directors of Agau Mines, Inc. and the United States Antimony Corp. (USAC) to recover 800,000 shares of Agau stock transferred to USAC.

Black Letter Rule: A majority of disinterested shareholders must ratify corporate transactions with an interested director.

In re Wheelabrator Technologies, Inc. Shareholders Litigation

Instant Facts: The shareholders of Wheelabrator Technologies, Inc. (D) sued the company's directors for breach of fiduciary duty, alleging the proxy statement issued in connection with its merger was misleading.

Black Letter Rule: An interested transaction between a corporation and its directors is not voidable if it is approved in good faith by a majority of fully informed, disinterested stockholders.

Great Lakes Chemical Corp. v. Monsanto Co.

Instant Facts: Great Lakes Chemical Corporation (P) sued Monsanto Company (D) and its subsidiary, Sweet Technologies, Inc. (STI) (D), for failure to disclose information relating to the sale of NSC Technologies, Inc. to Great Lakes (P).

Black Letter Rule: Interests in a limited liability company are not securities if they lack the five common features of stock: (1) the right to receive dividends contingent upon an appointment of profits; (2) negotiability; (3) the ability to be pledged or hypothecated; (4) voting rights in proportion to the number of shares owned; and (5) the ability to appreciate in value.

Doran v. Petroleum Mgmt. Corp.

Instant Facts: Doran (P) sued Petroleum Management Corporation (D) for breach of contract and rescission of contract based on violations of the Securities Acts of 1933 and 1934.

Black Letter Rule: In determining whether an offer to participate in a limited partnership was a private offer, the court must consider the number of offerees and their relationship to each other and to the issuer, the number of units offered, the offering's size, and the manner of the offering.

Escott v. BarChris Construction Corp.

Instant Facts: Purchasers of convertible, subordinated debentures of BarChris Construction Corporation (D) sued BarChris (D), claiming the filed registration statement contained material false statements and omissions.

Black Letter Rule: If false statements made in a registration statement or omitted facts that should have been included are material, the registration statement is misleading.

Basic Inc. v. Levinson

Instant Facts: Former Basic Inc. shareholders brought a class action suit against Basic Inc. (D) and its directors, claiming the directors issued three false statements and forced the former shareholders to sell their shares at depressed prices based on their reliance on Basic's statements that it was not engaged in merger discussions.

Black Letter Rule: An omitted fact is material if there is a substantial likelihood that the average, reasonable shareholder would have considered it important knowledge to have before deciding how to vote.

West v. Prudential Sec., Inc.

Instant Facts: West (P) brought a class action suit against Prudential Securities, Inc. (D) for securities fraud, alleging that a stockbroker had falsely told several clients that a corporation's stock was certain to be acquired at a premium, artificially inflating its price.

Black Letter Rule: The fraud-on-the-market doctrine and its presumption of reliance on misstatements do not apply in a securities fraud class action against a securities brokerage firm alleging that a stockbroker had falsely told several clients that a particular corporation was certain to be acquired at a premium in the near future.

Pommer v. Medtest Corp.

Instant Facts: Medtest Corporation's (D) investors sued the corporation under § 10(b) of the Securities Act of 1934, claiming they were the victims of fraud.

Black Letter Rule: Statements are material if a substantial likelihood exists that the whole of the information, as considered by a reasonable investor, would have been significantly altered if the omitted fact had been disclosed.

Santa Fe Indus., Inc. v. Green

Instant Facts: Kirby Lumber Co.'s minority shareholders (P) sued Santa Fe Industries, Inc. (D), which was Kirby's majority shareholder, seeking to set aside the merger of Kirby with Santa Fe (D) and alleging that their stock was worth more than they were offered when the companies merged.

Black Letter Rule: Under the short-form merger statute, a parent company may merge itself with its subsidiary if the parent owns at least ninety percent of the subsidiary's stock and if the parent company's board of directors approves the action.

Deutschman v. Beneficial Corp.

Instant Facts: Deutschman (P) sued Beneficial Corporation (D) and two of its directors for breach of fiduciary duty, alleging a violation of the Securities Exchange Act of 1934 and claiming that he suffered losses when call options he purchased on Beneficial's (D) stock in reliance on the market price became worthless.

Black Letter Rule: An options trader purchases or sells a security and has standing to sue for damages under § 10–b and the related rules.

Goodwin v. Agassiz

Instant Facts: Goodwin (P), a shareholder in Cliff Mining Company, filed suit against Agassiz (D) for damages suffered during the sale of his stock.

Black Letter Rule: A director's knowledge of the corporation's condition requires that he engage in fair dealing when directly buying or selling the corporation's stock.

Securities and Exchange Comm'n v. Texas Gulf Sulfur Co.

Instant Facts: The Securities and Exchange Commission (P) filed suit against Texas Gulf Sulfur Co. (D) for violation of the insider-trading provisions of Rule 10b–5.

Black Letter Rule: A person who is trading a corporation's securities for his own benefit and who has access to information intended to be available for business use only, may not take advantage of the information, knowing it is not available to those with whom he is dealing.

Dirks v. Securities and Exchange Comm'n

Instant Facts: The Securities and Exchange Commission (SEC) (P) accused Dirks (D) of violating the antifraud provisions of the federal securities laws for disclosing to investors material nonpublic information he received from insiders.

Black Letter Rule: A tippee does not inherit a duty to disclose material non-public information merely because he knowingly received the information.

United States v. O'Hagan

Instant Facts: The SEC indicted O'Hagan (D), an attorney, on fifty-seven counts, including seventeen counts of securities fraud and seventeen counts of fraudulent trading in connection with a tender offer, for his trading on nonpublic information in breach of the duty of trust and confidence he owed to his law firm and its clients.

Black Letter Rule: An attorney who, based on inside information he acquired as an attorney representing an offeror, purchased stock in a target corporation before the corporation was purchased in a tender offer is guilty of securities fraud in violation of Rule 10b–5 under the misappropriation theory.

Reliance Electric Co. v. Emerson Electric Co.

Instant Facts: Emerson Electric Co. (P), which acquired 13.2 percent of the outstanding stock of Dodge Manufacturing Co. (which later merged with Reliance Electric Co. (D)) and was faced with the failure of its takeover attempt, disposed of enough shares to bring its holdings below ten percent in order to avoid liability under § 16(b).

Black Letter Rule: A corporation may recover the profits realized by an owner of more than ten percent of its outstanding shares from a purchase and sale of its stock within any six-month period, provided the owner held more than ten percent at the time of both the purchase and the sale.

Foremost–McKesson, Inc. v. Provident Sec. Co.

Instant Facts: Foremost–McKesson, Inc. (P) sued Provident Securities Co. (D) to recover profits realized on the sale of debentures to the underwriters.

Black Letter Rule: A corporation may capture for itself the profits realized on a purchase and sale of its securities within six months by a director, officer, or beneficial owner, but a beneficial owner is accountable to the issuer only if it was a beneficial owner before the purchase.

Kern County Land Co. v. Occidental Petroleum Corp.

Instant Facts: Kern County Land Co. (P) sued Occidental Petroleum Corp. (D) under § 16(b) to recover the profits Occidental (D) realized from its sale of Kern (P) stock, alleging that the execution of the Occidental–Tenneco option and the exchange of Kern (P) shares for Tenneco shares were both subject to § 16(b).

Black Letter Rule: A corporation is liable for short-swing profits only if the sale creating the profits resulted from inside information.

Waltuch v. Conticommodity Services, Inc.

Instant Facts: Waltuch (P) sued his employer for indemnification of the legal expenses he incurred in defending himself from numerous civil lawsuits and an enforcement proceeding brought by the Commodity Futures Trading Commission.

Black Letter Rule: A corporation must indemnify its officers, directors, and employees against legal expenses related to the defense of any legal action brought against them by reason of their position or capacity, provided the individual acted in good faith.

Citadel Holding Corp. v. Roven

Instant Facts: Roven (P), a former director of Citadel Holding Corp. (D), sued Citadel (D) for indemnification of sums he paid to defend a federal court action Citadel (D) brought against him.

Black Letter Rule: A corporation may advance a director the costs of defending a lawsuit.

Kamin v. American Express Co.

(Stockholder) v. *(Company)*

86 Misc.2d 809, 383 N.Y.S.2d 807 (N.Y. Sup. Ct. 1976)

A CORPORATION'S DIRECTORS ARE NOT LIABLE MERELY BECAUSE A BETTER COURSE OF ACTION EXISTED

■ **INSTANT FACTS** Stockholders brought a derivative action, asking for a declaration that a certain dividend in kind was a waste of corporate assets.

■ **BLACK LETTER RULE** A complaint alleging that some course of action other than that taken by the board would have been more advantageous does not give rise to a cause of action for damages.

■ **PROCEDURAL BASIS**

On appeal to review dismissal of action.

■ **FACTS**

American Express (D) acquired 1,954,418 shares of the common stock of Donaldson, Lufken, and Jenrette, Inc. at a cost of $29.9 million in 1972. At the time of the suit, the shares' market value was approximately $4 million. The complaint alleged that on July 28, 1975, the board of directors declared a special dividend in which those acquired shares would be distributed to the stockholders in kind. Howard (P) and Robert (P) Kamin, who were both American Express (D) shareholders, contended that if American Express (D) had sold the shares on the market, the sale would result in a loss of $25 million, which could be used to offset capital gains and result in an $8 million tax saving. On October 8 and again on October 16, the stockholders demanded the directors rescind the distribution and preserve the capital loss. The board rejected their demand and paid the dividend on October 31. The American Express (D) directors moved to dismiss the plaintiffs' action for failure to state a claim and for summary judgment.

■ **ISSUE**

Are directors liable to stockholders for losses if a different action than that taken would have been more advantageous?

■ **DECISION AND RATIONALE**

(Judge Undisclosed) No. A complaint that alleges merely that some course of action other than that taken by the board would have been more advantageous does not give rise to a cause of action for damages against those directors. Directors are liable only if their actions were illegal or unconscionable. Errors in judgment do not warrant suits in equity. In order for a director to be negligent for his decision-making process, the plaintiff must show that fraud, dishonesty, or malfeasance was present. Summary judgment granted and complaint dismissed.

Analysis:

Corporate decision making is, by nature, largely discretionary. Directors exist to make decisions for the corporation, which as an entity has no decision-making ability. If potential for liability were expanded to include situations in which other avenues later turned out to be more advantageous, the liability could encompass virtually every decision made in a corporate setting. If a director is to be open to liability for his or her uncompromised decisions, few people will seek out or accept a position on a board.

■ CASE VOCABULARY

BOARD OF DIRECTORS: The governing body of a corporation, elected by the shareholders to establish corporate policy, appoint executive officers, and make major business and financial decisions.

Smith v. Van Gorkom

(Stockholder) v. *(CEO)*

488 A.2d 858 (Del. 1985)

THE BUSINESS JUDGMENT RULE PRESUMES ALL DECISIONS MADE BY A COMPANY'S DIRECTORS ARE INFORMED

WELL, I THINK 15 MINUTES OF DISCUSSION IS PLENTY. I HAVE A TEE TIME IN TWENTY MINUTES

■ **INSTANT FACTS** Trans Union's (D) stockholders brought a class action suit against the company's board of directors for negligent decision-making.

■ **BLACK LETTER RULE** The business judgment rule presumes that, when making business decisions, directors act on an informed basis, in good faith and in the company's best interests.

■ **PROCEDURAL BASIS**

On appeal from the lower court's decision granting judgment in favor of the defendants.

■ **FACTS**

Trans Union (D) was a publicly traded, diversified holding company. The company had an annual cash flow of hundreds of millions of dollars, but it had difficulty generating sufficient taxable income to enable it to use investment tax credits. On August 27, 1980, Van Gorkam (D), Trans Union's (D) CEO, and the company's senior management met to discuss alternative courses of action, including a leveraged buyout of Trans Union (D) by a company with a large amount of taxable income. The parties met again on September 5 to discuss the plausibility of a leveraged buyout, but no price was determined. However, the parties "ran the numbers" at $50 a share and at $60 a share to determine whether a leveraged buyout was a viable option. During this meeting, Van Gorkam (D) indicated he would take $55 per share for his 75,000 shares. Van Gorkam (D), who vetoed the option of a management buyout, met with Pritzker, a corporate takeover specialist and personal acquaintance. Before the meeting, Van Gorkam (D) determined a per-share price for the sale and set up a financing structure by which to complete the sale. Van Gorkam (D), who consulted with Trans Union's (D) comptroller before setting this price but did not consult with the Board of Directors or any other members of senior management, asked the comptroller not to let anyone else on the staff know what he was doing. Van Gorkam multiplied $55 per share by the number of outstanding shares and told the comptroller to use the $690 million figure to find a buyer, assuming a $200 million equity contribution by the buyer. Pritzker offered to enter into a cash-out merger at $55 per share, and when the merger proposal came from Pritzker, the parties negotiated number of shares down to one million shares and set the price at $0.75 above the per share market price on the proposal. The board needed to accept Prizker's proposal by September 21. Van Gorkam (D) met with the company's senior members on September 20 and disclosed the offer and its terms, but he did not furnish copies of the proposed merger agreement. Senior management's reaction to the proposal was negative. Van Gorkam (D) then met with the board and provided the directors copies of the proposed merger agreement, but the directors did not have time to review the proposal. Van Gorkam (D) did not explain to the board members how he arrived at the $55 price and that he first proposed the price in his meetings with Pritzker. Van Gorkam (D) outlined the terms of the agreement as providing that Pritzker would pay $55 per share for all outstanding Trans Union (D) shares and that, upon completion of the transfer, Trans Union (D) would be merged into New T Company, Prizker's wholly owned subsidiary. For ninety days, Trans Union (D) could receive, but not actively solicit, competing offers, and it had to accept the offer by September 21. The board, relying on numerous testimonials, approved the proposed merger agreement. The corporation publicly announced the merger on September 22, upsetting senior management. Several key officers threatened to resign. Pritzker and Van Gorkam (D) met, and Pritzker agreed to modify the agreement if Van Gorkam (D) could persuade the dissidents to remain with the company for at least six months following the merger. The board approved the amendments, even though they placed serious constraints on Trans Union's (D) ability to negotiate a better deal and withdraw from the Pritzker agreement. Pritzker continued to execute amendments without conferring further with the board members. During the ninety-day open-market period in which Trans Union (D) could receive other offers, it received only one offer from General Electric Credit Corporation. However GE Credit refused to make an official offer unless Trans Union (D) rescinded its agreement with Pritzker. GE Credit terminated further discussion with Trans Union (D). Shareholders Smith (P) and Gosselin (P) brought this class action, seeking rescission of the merger or damages.

■ ISSUE

Is a board negligent in approving a proposed cash-out merger, if the merger was not the product of informed business judgment, the board acted in a grossly negligent manner in approving amendments to the proposal, and the board failed to disclose all material facts that they knew or should have known before obtaining the stockholders' approval?

■ DECISION AND RATIONALE

(Horsey, J.) Yes. The business judgment rule presumes that in making business decisions, directors act on an informed basis, in good faith and in the company's best interests. A party alleging a board's decision is not informed must rebut that presumption. In order for a decision to be considered informed, the directors must have considered all information reasonably available to them before making the decision. If the directors do not make an informed decision, they must immediately cure any defects in their decision-making process as soon as they learn of the problem. The directors here approved the merger without determining Van Gorkam's (D) role in the decision-making process, being informed as to the corporation's intrinsic value, or having prior notice of the decision. This cannot be considered an informed decision. The board also failed to cure the defects in its decision and approved amendments without waiting for them to be drafted for their review.

■ DISSENT

(McNeilly, J.) The Trans Union (D) board consisted of five inside members and five outside members. At the time of the merger, the inside directors had a combined 116 years of employment with the company and sixty-eight years of experience as directors. Four of the five outside directors were CEO's of large, Chicago-based corporations, with seventy-eight combined years of CEO experience. It is unlikely that directors with this much experience were swindled or taken in by Pritzker's fast sales pitch. These men were qualified to make on-the-spot decisions concerning Trans Union's (D) welfare.

Analysis:

This ruling emphasizes the importance of the business judgment rule. Directors often must make quick decisions with huge impacts. For that reason, directors usually have long-term ties to the company and a great deal of successful business experience. Directors must trust that if their decision looks poor in hindsight, they cannot be sued if they made their best efforts to understand the factors relating to the issue. If they are not shielded from liability in those situations, business decision-making processes will be hindered by directors worrying whether they have adequately covered their steps.

■ CASE VOCABULARY

BUSINESS JUDGMENT RULE: The presumption that in making business decisions not involving direct self-interest or self-dealing, corporate directors act on an informed basis, in good faith, and in the honest belief that their actions are in the corporation's best interest.

Brehm v. Eisner

(Shareholder) v. *(Disney CEO)*

746 A.2d 244 (Del. 2000)

THE "WASTE TEST" IS VERY STRINGENT

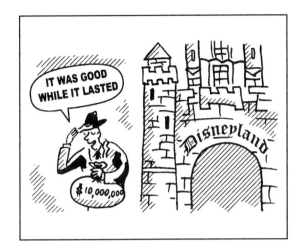

■ **INSTANT FACTS** The shareholders sued the Walt Disney Co. directors for breach of fiduciary duty in committing waste by agreeing to an agreement's severance terms.

■ **BLACK LETTER RULE** In order to constitute waste, an exchange must be so one-sided that no person of a reasonable mind would have entered into it.

■ PROCEDURAL BASIS

On appeal to review the lower court's decision to dismiss the claim.

■ FACTS

The Walt Disney Company (D) hired Ovitz (D), a longtime friend of Disney's CEO, Eisner (D), as its president. Ovitz (D) had been a talent broker in Hollywood, and although several other entertainment companies expressed an interest in hiring Ovitz (D) for high level executive positions, he did not have experience managing a diversified public company. Eisner (D) negotiated Ovitz's (D) employment agreement, which the board approved. The contract was extremely lucrative and had a five-year term. The agreement required Ovitz (D) to give his best efforts exclusively to the company in exchange for a base salary of $1 million per year, a discretionary bonus, and two sets of stock options that would enable Ovitz (D) to purchase 5 million shares of Disney (D) common stock. The "A" options vested in three annual increments of 1 million shares each, beginning on September 30, 1998. If Disney terminated Ovitz (D) employment without fault, the "A" options vested immediately. The "B" options, which were conditioned upon the extension of Ovitz's (D) employment beyond the five-year term provided in the employment agreement, consisted of 2 million shares to vest annually beginning in September 2001. The "B" options would be forfeited if the initial five-year employment term ended prematurely for any reason. Pursuant to the employment agreement Ovitz's (D) employment might terminate (a) if Disney (D) decided against offering him a new contract at the end of five years, in which case Disney (D) would pay Ovitz (D) $10 million, (b) if Disney (D) terminated Ovitz (D) before the end of his initial term for good cause, or (c) if Ovitz voluntarily resigned. If the company terminated Ovitz for good cause, Disney (D) would owe him no additional compensation, but if the company terminated him without cause, Disney (D) would pay him the present value of his remaining salary payments through September 30, 2000, a $10 million severance payment, and $7.5 million for each fiscal year remaining under the agreement, and the first 3 million stock options would immediately vest. Ovitz (D) experienced problems that continued throughout his first year of employment. He began seeking other employment and sent a letter to Eisner (D), expressing his dissatisfaction and his desire to leave the company. On December 11, 1996, Eisner (D) and Ovitz (D) agreed that Ovitz (D) would leave the company on a non-fault basis, and the board consented and formalized the terms in a letter. Ovitz (D) received the $10 million termination payment, $7.5 million for the partial year remaining under the agreement, and the immediate vesting of 3 million "A" stock options. Brehm (P) and other shareholders brought a derivative action, alleging breach of fiduciary duty and nondisclosure claims against the directors and a breach of contract claim against the president.

■ ISSUE

Are corporate directors personally liable for lack of adequate care in the decision-making process that results in a waste of corporate assets?

■ DECISION AND RATIONALE

(Judge Undisclosed) Yes. If directors fail to use adequate care in the decision-making process and waste corporate assets, they are personally liable to the corporation for their breach of fiduciary duty. The test for waste is very stringent, and courts give officers and directors the benefit of the doubt. In order to constitute waste, the exchange must be so one-sided that no person of a reasonable mind would have entered into the transaction. The size and structure of executive compensation are matters of judgment, so waste regarding executive compensation generally involves squandering money irrationally or giving away corporate assets. The board's decision to approve Ovitz's (D) employment agreement does not constitute waste. Each director has a fiduciary duty to be adequately informed of all information material to his or her decisions. The board members here relied on expert testimony in determining the financial pitfalls posed by the agreement, and reliance on expert testimony is reasonable. The board's decision to approve the employment agreement does not constitute waste. Affirmed in part, reversed in part, and remanded.

Analysis:

The plaintiffs in shareholder derivative suits originally sought to use the doctrine of waste as a way of making directors personally liable for their decisions. However, courts have always stringently tried to avoid this sort of personal liability for official business decisions. The court here acknowledges this approach for what it is and clarifies the stringent factors required to prove waste. Courts clearly will not use the doctrine of waste to punish directors simply because a decision results in economic hardship to the corporation or its stockholders.

■ CASE VOCABULARY

FIDUCIARY DUTY: One who owes to another the duties of good faith, trust, confidence, and candor.

Francis v. United Jersey Bank

(*Bankruptcy Trustee*) v. (*Estate Administrator*)
87 N.J. 15, 432 A.2d 814 (1981)

DIRECTORS MUST DILIGENTLY DISCHARGE THEIR DUTIES

■ **INSTANT FACTS** The bankruptcy trustee of various creditors brought suit against Pritchard's estate to recover misappropriated funds.

■ **BLACK LETTER RULE** Directors have the duty to act honestly and in good faith and with the same degree of diligence, care, and skills that a reasonably prudent person would use in similar circumstances.

■ PROCEDURAL BASIS

On appeal to review the appellate court's affirmance of the lower court's holding in favor of the plaintiff.

■ FACTS

Pritchard & Baird Intermediaries Corp. was a reinsurance brokerage company. Lillian Pritchard inherited a forty-eight percent interest in Pritchard & Baird from her husband, Charles Pritchard, Sr. Although Lillian was the largest single shareholder and a director, she was not active in the business and knew virtually nothing of its dealings. She paid no attention to her duties as director. Her sons, Charles, Jr. and William, owned the remaining shares and served as directors. Charles, Jr. became the corporation's manager after his father died. Charles, Jr. and William withdrew large sums of money from the corporation in the form of loans over several years. These loans totaled more than $12 million. The brothers used the funds the corporation should have held in trust for its clients to finance the loans. The company went bankrupt shortly after discovering the misappropriation of the funds, and Lillian died shortly thereafter. During her life, Lillian made no efforts to ensure that the company's policies and practices complied with industry custom or applicable laws. Before his death, Lillian's husband had warned her that Charles, Jr. would "take the shirt off" his back. The corporation's bankruptcy trustee (P) sued to recover the funds for the benefit of the bankrupt estate.

■ ISSUE

Can an inattentive and uninterested director be held personally liable for a corporation's actions?

■ DECISION AND RATIONALE

(Judge Undisclosed) Yes. Directors have the duty to act honestly and in good faith and with the same degree of diligence, care, and skills that a reasonably prudent person would use in similar circumstances. Corporate directors are generally afforded broad immunity for their decisions and actions related to corporate matters. However, the issue of director liability is difficult when a director shirks his duties and allows a third party to act on behalf of the corporation, particularly if the third party's actions are not closely monitored. Directors are under a continuing duty to keep informed about the corporation's activities. Lillian blatantly ignored her duty to the company's shareholders. Affirmed.

Analysis:

The court emphasized that a director has options if faced with a task or problem of which he or she has no working knowledge. The director may either make an inquiry to gain the necessary knowledge or refuse to act and step down. It is obvious that if the director refuses to act, someone needs to act in his or her place. However, the director must make a wise choice if delegating duties and must closely monitor persons making decisions on the corporation's behalf.

■ CASE VOCABULARY

TRUSTEE IN BANKRUPTCY: Also termed "bankruptcy trustee." A person appointed by the U.S. Trustee or elected by creditors or appointed by a judge to administer the bankruptcy estate during a bankruptcy case.

In re Caremark Int'l Inc. Derivative Litigation

(Shareholders) v. *(Corporation)*

698 A.2d 959 (Del. Ch. 1996)

DIRECTORS NEED NOT FERRET OUT WRONGDOINGS AT EVERY LEVEL OF THE BUSINESS

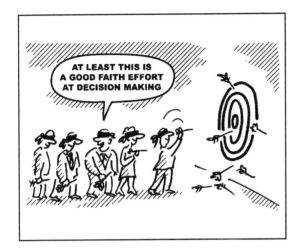

■ **INSTANT FACTS** Caremark International, Inc.'s shareholders (P) brought a consolidated derivative action against Caremark's (D) board members, alleging breach of fiduciary duty related to allegations of violations of federal and state laws by Caremark's (D) employees.

■ **BLACK LETTER RULE** Although directors have a duty to monitor a corporation's ongoing operation, they are not liable for wrongdoings of which they had no real or constructive knowledge.

■ **PROCEDURAL BASIS**

On hearing to approve a settlement offer.

■ **FACTS**

Caremark International Inc. (D), which provided patient care and managed care services, obtained a substantial part of its business revenues from third party payments, insurers, Medicare, and Medicaid. Medicare and Medicaid reimbursement payments were subject to the Anti–Referral Payments Law (ARPL), which prohibited health care providers from inducing Medicare or Medicaid referrals. Caremark (D) routinely entered into a variety of agreements with hospitals, physicians, and healthcare providers for advice and services. Occasionally, Caremark (D) entered into contracts for services with physicians who prescribed or recommended products or services that Caremark (D) provided to Medicare recipients. These contracts were not illegal under ARPL, but they brought up questions of fraud. In 1989, Caremark (D) issued an internal "Guide to Contractual Relationships" to govern contracts with physicians. Attorneys reviewed and updated the guide each year. In August 1991, the Inspector General began investigating Caremark's (D) predecessor. During the period under investigation, Caremark (D) had more than ninety offices and 7,000 employees and operated under a decentralized management system. On October 1, 1991, Caremark's (D) predecessor announced that it would no longer pay management fees to physicians for services to Medicare and Medicaid patients. The government suspected Caremark's (D) predecessor had paid physicians for monitoring patients who were receiving Medicare and Medicaid. The Department of Justice began an investigation into this matter in March 1992. On August 4, 1994, a federal grand jury in Minnesota indicted Caremark (D), Brown (a physician practicing in Minneapolis), and others for violating ARPL over a long time period. The indictment alleged that Brown had been paid more than $1.1 million to induce him to distribute Protropin, a human growth hormone drug marketed by Caremark (D). The indictment also alleged that Brown received payment for telephone answering services and fax rental expenses. Caremark's (D) shareholders brought a derivative suit, and this opinion addresses a motion to approve a settlement.

■ **ISSUE**

Are directors always liable for breach of duty for their failure to monitor the corporation's ongoing business operations?

■ DECISION AND RATIONALE

(Allen, C.) No. Although directors have a duty to monitor the ongoing operation of a corporation's affairs, they are not liable for wrongdoings of which they had no knowledge or reason to have knowledge. If directors have no grounds to suspect deception by their employees, they cannot be liable for assuming their employees are acting honestly and diligently on their behalf. Directors have no duty to question continually the integrity of each employee. The degree to which directors monitor employees at each level of the organization is a question of business judgment, best left up to individual corporations, not the courts. No evidence shows that Caremark's (D) directors knew of any wrongdoing, or that given the circumstances, they should have known of the alleged wrongdoing. Caremark's (D) managers indicate they did not believe their activities were illegal. The Caremark (D) board has a committee to oversee corporate compliance. The directors are not responsible for any illegal actions. Settlement approved.

Analysis:

This rule makes common sense. Requiring directors to manage the day-to-day activities of each employee would waste resources and is simply not feasible in large corporations. Also, constant employee monitoring would hinder workplace progress, as employees would constantly worry about their performance. However, corporations must establish practices to deal with complaints or allegations when they do arise.

■ CASE VOCABULARY

COMPLIANCE AUDIT: An audit conducted by a regulatory agency, an organization, or a third party to assess compliance with one or more sets of laws and regulations.

Bayer v. Beran

(Shareholders) v. *(Director)*

49 N.Y.S.2d 2 (N.Y. Sup. Ct. 1944)

RULE REQUIRING DIRECTORS' UNDIVIDED LOYALTY AVOIDS POSSIBILITY OF FRAUD AND THE TEMPTATION OF SELF–INTEREST

■ **INSTANT FACTS** Shareholders brought a derivative suit against the Celanese Corporation of America's directors (D) for breach of fiduciary duty for approving and extending a $1,000,000 per year radio advertising program.

■ **BLACK LETTER RULE** A director does not breach his or her fiduciary duty by approving a radio advertising program in which the wife of the corporate president, who was also member of board of directors, was one of the featured performers.

■ **PROCEDURAL BASIS**

Complaint of breach of fiduciary duty.

■ **FACTS**

In early 1942, Celanese Corporation of America (D) embarked on a radio advertising campaign at an annual cost of $1,000,000. At the time, the company had not previously engaged in radio advertising, but it had spent large sums of money on other advertising. One of the radio campaign's singers was the wife of Celanese's president, who also served as one of its directors. The Celanese (D) directors indicated that they decided to try radio advertising when the FTC announced that all celanese products had to be designated and labeled as "rayon." The company had always called its products "celanese" and contended that celanese was physically and chemically different from rayon. The company believed that celanese products had special qualities that made them superior to rayon. The company was concerned with the FTC announcement, and believed its only option was to get its message out to the public through advertising. Before making their decision to use radio, the directors reviewed reports of studies conducted by their advertising department beginning in 1939. They also employed a radio consultant to advise them on the program. The company decided to expend approximately $1,000,000 per year on the program, but the commitments were subject to cancellation every thirteen weeks. Bayer (P) and another shareholder brought a derivative suit against Beran (D) and other directors for breach of fiduciary duty for approving the radio advertising program and budget.

■ **ISSUE**

Does a director breach his or her fiduciary duty by approving a radio advertising program in which the wife of the corporate president, who was also member of board of directors, was one of the featured performers?

■ **DECISION AND RATIONALE**

(Judge Undisclosed) No. Directors have a duty not to act out of self-interest, which is known as the rule of undivided loyalty. The rule's purpose is to avoid the possibility of fraud. The court may apply the rule of undivided loyalty in situations in which the director stands to benefit personally from the transaction or works so closely with the third person that he may take advantage of that person for his or her own benefit. The directors here have not breached their fiduciary duty by authorizing the radio campaign, even though the president's wife was one of the paid performers on the campaign. The evidence does not show that the program's purpose is to enhance the president's wife's career or to give her a financial benefit. She is only one of several performers on the campaign and is a well-known singer prior to the campaign. Her wages are comparable to what similar performers are paid. Complaint dismissed.

Analysis:

During litigation, the shareholders claimed the expenditures were not valid because they were not made by resolution at a formal board meeting, and the court agreed that the initial radio campaign expenditures were made without resolution at a formal board meeting. However, the board met eighteen months later and ratified the expenditures. The court also noted that acceptance and retention of eighteen-months' worth of benefits from the radio advertising campaign were enough to serve as ratification.

■ CASE VOCABULARY

RATIFICATION: Confirmation and acceptance of a previous act, thereby making the act valid from the moment it was done.

Lewis v. S. L. & E., Inc.

(*Shareholder*) v. (*Directors*)

629 F.2d 764 (2d Cir. 1980)

DIRECTORS MAY NOT ENGAGE IN SELF–DEALING

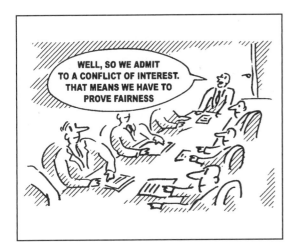

■ **INSTANT FACTS** Donald (P), Carol, and Margaret Lewis brought a shareholder derivative action against Richard (D), Alan (D), and Leon Lewis, Jr. (D), alleging waste.

■ **BLACK LETTER RULE** A transaction in which a director has an interest, other than as the corporation's director, is automatically suspect and subject to further review.

■ PROCEDURAL BASIS

On appeal to review the district court's judgment in favor of the defendants.

■ FACTS

Lewis General Tires, Inc. (LGT) operated a tire dealership and leased space from S. L. & E., Inc. (SLE) (D), which owned a building complex in Rochester, New York. Before 1956, LGT occupied SLE's (D) premises without a lease, at a rent that started at $200 per month and increased to $800 per month by 1956. The property was remodeled, and, on February 28, 1956, LGT signed a ten-year lease at the rate of $1200 per month. The lease agreement provided that SLE (D) was responsible for the real estate taxes on the property and LGT was to bear all other property expenses. Before 1962, Leon Lewis, Sr. had been the principal shareholder of both SLE (D) and LGT. In 1962, he transferred all ninety shares of his SLE (D) stock to his six children (Richard (D), Alan (D), Leon (D), Donald (P), Margaret, and Carol), giving each child fifteen shares. At the time of the transfer, Richard (D), Alan (D), and Leon, Jr. (D) were already shareholders, officers, and directors of LGT. In 1996, when the lease expired, LGT did not enter into a new lease with SLE (D), but continued to occupy the property and pay rent in the amount of $1200 per month. The SLE (D) shareholders had not met since 1962. Richard (D), Alan (D), and Leon, Jr. (D) ignored SLE's (D) separate corporate existence and did not take into account that SLE (D) had other shareholders when they made decisions on behalf of SLE (D), most of which largely benefited LGT. Donald (P), Margaret, and Carol never owned LGT stock. In June 1972, Donald (P), Carol, and Margaret were supposed to sell their SLE (D) stock to LGT. Donald (P) requested SLE (D) financial information from Richard (D) before the sale, but Richard (D) refused to provide it. Donald (P) refused to sell his SLE (D) shares. Donald (P) brought a derivative suit regarding the management of LGT and SLE (D), and the lower court entered judgment in favor of the defendants. Donald (P) appealed.

■ ISSUE

Do directors commit waste by failing to charge adequate rent for property out of self-interest?

■ DECISION AND RATIONALE

(Judge Undisclosed) Yes. A transaction in which a director has an interest, other than as director of the corporation, is automatically suspect and subject to review. Such a transaction is voidable unless the director can prove it is fair and reasonable to the corporation. From 1966 to 1972, Richard, Alan, and Leon, Jr. (D) were directors and shareholders of both SLE (D) and LGT. During that period, SLE (D) had no directors who were not also LGT directors. Therefore, the SLE (D) directors had a personal interest in the amount of rent that LGT paid, and they bear the burden of proving that the $1200 a month rent on the property from 1966 to 1972 was reasonable. No evidence indicates that the parties made any effort between 1966 and 1972 to determine the fair rental value of the property.

Analysis:

Self-dealing is particularly troublesome in closely held corporations, where mostly family members and close acquaintances hold stock and the directors are family members. These situations provide a greater possibility for abuse because the shareholders may not be keeping up with the organization's day-to-day operations if they are not also directors. Thus, if one person owns a large quantity of the stock and is also a director, there is plenty of opportunity for abuse, especially if the corporation has related entities that share directors, but do not include all family members.

■ CASE VOCABULARY

SELF–DEALING: Participation in a transaction that benefits oneself instead of another who is owed a fiduciary duty.

Broz v. Cellular Info. Sys., Inc.

(Outside Director) v. *(Corporation)*

673 A.2d 148 (Del. 1996)

DIRECTORS MUST PUT A CORPORATION'S INTERESTS BEFORE THEIR OWN

■ **INSTANT FACTS** Cellular Information Systems, Inc. filed suit against Broz for breach of fiduciary duty, alleging he put his own interests before that of the corporation.

■ **BLACK LETTER RULE** Under the doctrine of corporate opportunity, a corporate fiduciary must place the corporation's interests before his or her own interests in appropriate circumstances, but a corporate fiduciary does not breach his or her fiduciary duty by not considering the interests of another corporation proposing to acquire the corporation in deciding to make a corporate purchase.

■ **PROCEDURAL BASIS**

On appeal to review the lower court's decision in favor of the plaintiff.

■ **FACTS**

Broz (D) was the president and sole stockholder of RFB Cellular, Inc. (RFBC) (D), a cellular telephone service provider. Broz (D) was also an outside director on the board of Cellular Information Systems (CIS) (P). RFBC (D) owned and operated an FCC license area, the Michigan–4 Rural Service Area Cellular License (Michigan–4). The license gave RFBC (D) permission to provide cellular phone service to a rural portion of Michigan. In April 1994, Mackinac Cellular Corp. put its Michigan–2 license on the market. Michigan–2 was the license area adjacent to Michigan–4. Mackinac had a brokerage firm, Daniels & Assoc., compile a list of potential purchasers, which included RFBC (D). Rhodes, a Daniels representative, contacted Broz (D) to discuss the potential sale of Michigan–2. CIS (P) was not offered an opportunity to purchase Michigan–2. CIS (P) had experienced financial difficulties and was not considered a viable buyer. On June 14, 1994, Broz (D) spoke with Treibick, CIS's (P) CEO, concerning his desire to acquire the Michigan–2 license, but he told Broz (D) that CIS (P) was not interested in purchasing Michigan–2. On June 28, 1994, six CIS (P) directors entered into agreements to sell their CIS (P) shares to PriCellular for $2 per share. PriCellular delayed the closing because of financial difficulties from September 16 to November 9. Broz (D) submitted offers for the purchase of Michigan–2 to Mackinac on August 6, September 6, and September 21, 1994. During this period, PriCellular also made offers to Mackinac to purchase Michigan–2. Treibick was aware of PriCellular's desire to purchase Michigan–2. PriCellular reached an agreement with Mackinac in September 1994 on an option to purchase Michigan–2. The option price was set at $6.7 million, and the option was to remain open until December 15, 1994. The option agreement also provided that Mackinac could sell Michigan–2 to any party who was willing to exceed the option price by $500,000. On November 14, 1994, Broz (D) agreed to pay Mackinac $7.2 million for the Michigan–2 license, and the parties executed a purchase agreement. On November 23, 1994, PriCellular closed on its purchase of CIS (P) stock. CIS (P) sued to prevent Broz (D) and RFBC (D) from acquiring the license, and the lower court entered judgment for CIS (P). The defendants appealed.

■ ISSUE

Does a corporate fiduciary breach his or her fiduciary duty by not considering the interests of a corporation proposing to acquire the corporation in reaching a decision to make a corporate purchase?

■ DECISION AND RATIONALE

(Judge Undisclosed) No. Under the doctrine of corporate opportunity, a corporate fiduciary agrees to place the interests of his or her corporation before his or her personal interests in appropriate circumstances. As an outside director of CIS (P), Broz (D) owed CIS (P) a fiduciary duty to put its interests before his own. However, CIS (P) did not have a valid expectancy interest in the license. CIS (P) was not offered an option to purchase Michigan–2, and Broz's (D) interest in acquiring Michigan–2 did not create any duties that conflicted with his obligations to CIS (P). Broz (D) did not usurp any opportunity that CIS (P) was willing and able to pursue. During the competition for the option to purchase Michigan–2, PriCellular did not have an equity interest in CIS (P). Reversed.

Analysis:

The lower court held that CIS's (P) interests in the Mackinac opportunity merged with those of PriCellular before the closing on its offer to purchase stock. The higher court ruled that that finding was incorrect. At the time of purchase, PriCellular had not yet closed on the CIS (P) stock. In fact, it had voluntarily pushed back its closing date by three months. The court believed that extending the corporate opportunity doctrine to entities with an option to purchase a portion of the organization would be too complicated and would extend the doctrine too far.

■ CASE VOCABULARY

CORPORATE OPPORTUNITY DOCTRINE: The rule that a corporation's directors, officers, and employees are precluded from using information gained in corporate capacity to take personal advantage of any business opportunity that the corporation has an expectancy right or property interest in, or that in fairness should otherwise belong to the corporation.

Sinclair Oil Corp. v. Levien

(*Parent Company*) v. (*Subsidiary's Minority Shareholder*)

280 A.2d 717 (Del. 1971)

A TRANSACTION BETWEEN A PARENT AND ITS SUBSIDSIARY MUST BE INTRINSICALLY FAIR

BUT, EQUAL DIVIDEND PAYMENTS TO ALL SHAREHOLDERS MEANS NO SELF-DEALING, AND SO NO INTRINSIC FAIRNESS TEST

■ **INSTANT FACTS** Shareholders brought a derivative action against Sinclair Oil Corp. (D) to require an accounting for damages sustained by its subsidiary, Sinclair Venezuelan Oil Company.

■ **BLACK LETTER RULE** If, in a transaction involving a parent company and its subsidiary, the parent company controls the transaction and fixes the terms, the transaction must meet the intrinsic fairness test.

■ **PROCEDURAL BASIS**

On appeal to review the lower court's judgment in favor of the plaintiff.

■ **FACTS**

Sinclair Oil Corp. (Sinclair) (D), which was in the business of exploring for oil and producing and marketing crude oil and oil products, was primarily a holding company. Sinclair's (D) subsidiary, Sinclair Venezuelan Oil Company (Sinclair Venezuelan), was organized for the sole purpose of performing Sinclair's (D) operations in Venezuela. Sinclair (D) owned approximately ninety-seven percent of Sinclair Venezuelan's stock, and Sinclair (D) nominates all of Sinclair Venezuelan's directors. Almost all of Sinclair Venezuelan's directors were officers, directors, or employees of corporations Sinclair Venezuelan owned. Levien (P) owned about 3,000 of the 120,000 publicly traded shares of Sinclair Venezuelan. In the period from 1960 through 1966, Sinclair (D) caused Sinclair Venezuelan to pay out $108 million in dividends, $38 million greater than Sinclair Venezuelan's earnings during that same period. As a result, Sinclair Venezuelan paid much money to Sinclair (D). In 1961, Sinclair (D) created Sinclair International Oil Company (International), for the purpose of coordinating all of Sinclair's (D) foreign operations. Sinclair (D) then caused Sinclair Venezuelan to enter into a contract to sell all of its crude oil and refined products to International at specified prices. The contract required International to pay for the oil upon receipt and to purchase at least a minimum amount of crude and refined products. Sinclair Venezuelan contended that International was more than thirty days' late with its payments and that it did not purchase the fixed minimum amount of goods required by the contract. Pursuant to this contract, Sinclair (D) received Sinclair Venezuelan products, but Levien (P) and Sinclair Venezuelan's other minority shareholders did not share in the profits generated by the sales. Levien (P) sued Sinclair (D) for breach of contract and for damages Sinclair Venezuelan sustained because Sinclair (D) denied industrial development to Sinclair Venezuelan. The lower court entered judgment against Sinclair (D), and the defendant appealed.

■ **ISSUE**

If, in a transaction involving a parent company and its subsidiary, the parent company controls the transaction and fixes the terms, must the transaction be intrinsically fair?

■ **DECISION AND RATIONALE**

(Judge Undisclosed) Yes. If a transaction involves a parent company and a subsidiary, with the parent company controlling the transaction and fixing the terms, the transaction must meet the intrinsic fairness test. Under the intrinsic fairness standard, the dominant company must prove that its transaction with the subsidiary was objectively fair. The intrinsic fairness standard is invoked only if the parent company is on both sides of a transaction with its subsidiary, and self-dealing is suspected. Self-dealing will be deemed to be present if the parent company uses its power to enter into a transaction with the subsidiary and the parent company receives a benefit from the subsidiary to the subsidiary's detriment. Although the dividends paid out here may have been excessive, they violate no law because Delaware law allows payments of dividends out of surplus or net profits. Also, Sinclair (D) did not receive anything from Sinclair Venezuelan to the exclusion of Sinclair Venezuelan's minority shareholders. The minority shareholders were paid the same dividend percentage per share that Sinclair (D) received. Thus, the dividend payments were not self-dealing. However, Sinclair's (D) forcing Sinclair Venezuelan's sale to International was self-dealing. Sinclair (D) caused the sale to happen, and Sinclair (D) received the products from the sale. Sinclair Venezuelan's minority shareholders received little from this transaction. Therefore Sinclair failed to prove that transaction was intrinsically fair to Sinclair Venezuelan's minority shareholders. Reversed in part and affirmed in part.

Analysis:

The court emphasizes that the proper standard to apply in this case should have been the business judgment rule, but that even under the business judgment rule, the dividends would not have been considered self-dealing. The court further notes that the motives for issuing dividends are immaterial unless the dividends amount to waste and arise out of improper motives. The plaintiff did not contend waste, but rather contended that the dividends drained Sinclair Venezuelan of money for expansion.

■ CASE VOCABULARY

INTRINSIC: Belonging to a thing by its very nature; not dependent on external circumstances; inherent; essential.

SUBSIDIARY: A corporation in which a parent corporation has a controlling share.

Zahn v. Transamerica Corp.

(*Stockholder*) v. (*Acquiring Corporation*)

162 F.2d 36 (3d Cir. 1947)

A STOCKHOLDER VOTING AS A DIRECTOR MUST VOTE IN ALL SHAREHOLDERS' BEST INTERESTS

■ **INSTANT FACTS** Stockholders of the Axton–Fisher Tobacco Company sued Transamerica Corporation (D) claiming Transamerica (D) caused Axton–Fisher to redeem its Class A stock at $80.80 per share, instead of allowing them to participate in the liquidation of company assets, in which case they content they would have received $240 per share.

■ **BLACK LETTER RULE** If a stockholder who is also a director is voting as a director, he or she represents all stockholders in the capacity of a trustee and cannot use the director's position for his or her personal benefit to the stockholders' detriment.

■ **PROCEDURAL BASIS**

On appeal to review the lower court's decision granting the defendant's motion to dismiss.

■ **FACTS**

Zahn (P) holds shares of Class A common stock of Axton–Fisher Tobacco Company. Before April 30, 1943, Axton–Fisher had three classes of outstanding stock—preferred stock, Class A stock, and Class B Stock. The preferred stock shares were valued at $100 and were entitled to cumulative dividends at the rate of $6 per annum. The preferred stock had a liquidation value of $105 per share plus accrued dividends. Class A shares were entitled to an annual cumulative dividend of $3.20 per share, and Class B shares were entitled to an annual dividend of $1.60 per share. Class A and Class B shares were equally entitled to any additional declared dividends. In the event of liquidation, both Class A and Class B would receive distribution of the remaining assets after the preferred stock received payment, with Class A receiving twice as much per share as Class B. Shareholders could convert shares of Class A stock into Class B stock, and the corporation could call Class A stock at the rate of $60 per share plus accrued dividends upon sixty days' notice. Class A and Class B shares possessed equal voting rights. On May 16, 1941, Transamerica (D) purchased approximately 71.5 percent of Axton–Fisher's outstanding shares of Class B stock, which constituted approximately 46.7 percent of Axton–Fisher's total voting stock. By 1943, Transamerica (D) owned approximately 66 percent of the total Class A stock outstanding. Transamerica (D) dominated Axton–Fisher's management, directorate, and business affairs, and elected the majority of its directors, most of whom were also Transamerica (D) officers. At that time, Axton–Fisher's principal asset was leaf tobacco, which it had purchased for $6,361,981. By April 1943, unbeknownst to the public holders of Transamerica (D) Class A stock, the tobacco's value had soared to $20 million. Upon learning this, Transamerica (D) called Axton–Fisher's Class A stock at $60 per share and sold a large portion of the tobacco to Phillip Morris, Co., Ltd., along with almost all of Axton–Fisher's assets. Shortly thereafter, Axton–Fisher was liquidated, the preferred stock was paid off, and Transamerica (D) pocketed the rest of the profits from the sale. Class B stockholders received warehouse receipts for the remainder of the tobacco. Zahn (P), a holder of Axton–Fisher Class A common stock, sued Transamerica (D), asserting that Transamerica (D) caused Axton–Fisher to redeem its stock at $80.80 per share instead of permitting the Class A shareholder to participate in the assets upon liquidation of the company. The lower court granted Transamerica's (D) motion to dismiss, and Zahn (P) appealed.

■ ISSUE

May a stockholder, who is also a director and is voting as a director, use the director's position for his or her personal benefit to the stockholders' detriment?

■ DECISION AND RATIONALE

(Judge Undisclosed) No. If a stockholder, who is also a director, is voting as a director, he represents all stockholders as their trustee, and he cannot use his position as director for his own personal benefit to the stockholders' detriment. The directors knew of Axton–Fisher's right to call shares of Class A stock for redemption because it was in the corporate charter, but the right was not expressly disclosed to the stockholders. The Axton–Fisher directors were instruments of Transamerica (D) and were voting in favor of Transamerica's (D) interests, not the corporation's and its shareholders' interests. There was no reason for Axton–Fisher to liquidate after the redemption of Class A stock, other than to ensure only Class B stockholders would benefit from the liquidation. The redemption of Class A stock was not necessary for the financial welfare of the company. The decision to call Class A stock was made by Class B shareholders, right before a liquidation sale, so that as a result of the call, only Class B shareholders profited. Reversed.

Analysis:

The events that transpired here constituted a hostile takeover. In a hostile takeover, another company or entity, usually a larger one, slowly acquires a majority share of the another company's stock and then appoints its own employees and directors as directors of the other company. The acquired company's shareholders lose power and are usually forced to sell their shares at a substantially reduced price from what they may have received if the takeover had not occurred.

■ CASE VOCABULARY

CONVERTIBLE STOCK: A security (usually a bond or preferred stock) that may be exchanged by the owner for another security, especially common stock from the same company, and usually at a fixed price on a specified date.

Fliegler v. Lawrence

(Shareholder) v. *(Corporate President)*

361 A.2d 218 (Del. 1976)

INTERESTED SHAREHOLDERS CANNOT RATIFY THEIR OWN TRANSACTIONS WITH THEIR CORPO-
RATION

■ **INSTANT FACTS** A shareholder brought a derivative action against the officers and directors of Agau Mines, Inc. and the United States Antimony Corp. (USAC) to recover 800,000 shares of Agau stock transferred to USAC.

■ **BLACK LETTER RULE** A majority of disinterested shareholders must ratify corporate transactions with an interested director.

■ **PROCEDURAL BASIS**

On appeal of the lower court's judgment in favor of the defendants.

■ **FACTS**

Agau Mines, Inc. (D) was engaged in exploratory mining for gold and silver. In 1969, Lawrence (D), Agau's (D) president, acquired antimony properties under a lease option for $60,000. The properties were a "raw prospect" that Lawrence (D) initially acquired in his individual capacity. Lawrence (D) offered to transfer the properties to Agau (D), but Agau (D) was not in a financial position to acquire and develop the properties. Agau's board decided to transfer the properties to USAC, which was a closely held corporation they formed for the specific purpose of holding the properties. Agau's (D) board owned the majority of USAC's stock. The members formed USAC to hold the property so they could raise the capital necessary to develop the properties without risk to Agau (D). Agau (D) was granted a long-term option to purchase USAC, which it exercised in January 1970. Pursuant to the option, Agau (D) was to deliver 800,000 shares of its restricted investment stock for all authorized and issued shares of USAC. The basis for this exchange was to reimburse the USAC shareholders for their costs in developing the properties so they could become profitable. A majority of the Agau (D) shareholders approved its exercise of the option in October 1970. Fliegler (P) brought a derivative action on behalf of the corporation against its officers and directors, and the lower court entered judgment in favor of the defendants. The plaintiff appealed.

■ **ISSUE**

If officers, directors, and shareholders of a corporation hold a significant interest in a second corporation that the first corporation acquired, must the defendants show the intrinsic fairness of the transaction?

■ **DECISION AND RATIONALE**

(Judge Undisclosed) Yes. A majority of disinterested shareholders must ratify corporate transactions with an interested director in order for the transaction to be valid. It is not sufficient for the majority of all shareholders to ratify the action if the majority of shareholders are interested in the transaction. This rule is meant to protect against invalidation of an action solely because a director is involved, not to provide a means for interested shareholders to approve actions in their own personal interests. However, Agau's (D) directors did nothing in their personal interests here. Agau (D) received valuable properties and an enterprise that will likely generate large profits. Given the substantial value received by Agau (D), 800,000 shares of stock was a fair price to pay to USAC. Affirmed.

Analysis:

The court here interprets the law to read that the provision permitting immunity from judicial review if an action is ratified by the majority of shareholders does not apply if the majority of the shareholders are interested. To allow such a provision to apply in such situations would be a mockery of the law. The judicial review of interested transactions is meant to protect minority shareholders from being trampled by the majority shareholders. If a majority of interested shareholders can approve an interested transaction, especially if only one or a few entities hold the majority of the shares, minority shareholders would not be adequately protected.

■ CASE VOCABULARY

DISINTERESTED: Free from bias, prejudice, or partiality; not having a pecuniary interest.

In re Wheelabrator Technologies, Inc. Shareholders Litigation

(Target Corporation's Shareholders) v. *(Target Corporation)*

663 A.2d 1194 (Del. Ch. 1995)

STOCKHOLDERS MUST BE FULLY INFORMED WHEN THEY RATIFY AN INTERESTED TRANSACTION

FROM WHAT I'VE PICKED UP, RATIFICATION OF A DUTY OF CARE PROBLEM KILLS THE CLAIM, BUT RATIFICATION OF A SHAREHOLDER CONFLICT LOWERS THE STANDARD --NO, SHIFTS THE BURDEN--OH, I DON'T KNOW...

■ **INSTANT FACTS** The shareholders of Wheelabrator Technologies, Inc. (D) sued the company's directors for breach of fiduciary duty, alleging the proxy statement issued in connection with its merger was misleading.

■ **BLACK LETTER RULE** An interested transaction between a corporation and its directors is not voidable if it is approved in good faith by a majority of fully informed, disinterested stockholders.

■ **PROCEDURAL BASIS**

Hearing on motion for summary judgment.

■ **FACTS**

Waste Management, Inc. bought twenty-two percent of Wheelabrator Technologies, Inc. (D) (WTI) and elected four of its own directors to serve on WTI's (D) board, which consisted of eleven directors. In 1990, WTI (D) and Waste Management negotiated a merger agreement pursuant to which Waste Management would acquire another thirty-three percent of WTI's (D) stock, and WTI (D) shareholders would receive .574 WTI (D) shares and .469 Waste Management shares for each WTI (D) share they held. WTI's (D) board held a special meeting to consider the agreement. The Waste Management designees did not attend the meeting. The directors reviewed copies of the agreement and heard from WTI's (D) investment bankers and attorneys, who indicated the transaction was fair. The seven directors present unanimously approved the merger agreement. The Waste Management directors then joined the meeting, and the full board unanimously approved the agreement. At a special shareholder meeting, the majority of WTI (D) shareholders also approved the agreement. The shareholders brought an action against WTI (D), alleging breach of fiduciary obligations to disclose material information concerning the merger and breach of duties of loyalty and due care. The defendants moved for summary judgment.

■ **ISSUE**

Do directors breach their duty of loyalty to shareholders if a majority of the fully informed and disinterested stockholders approve an interested transaction between a corporation and its directors?

■ **DECISION AND RATIONALE**

(Jacobs, V.C.) No. An interested transaction between a corporation and its directors is not voidable if a majority of the fully informed, disinterested stockholders approved it in good faith. However, if material information was withheld from the stockholders before their ratification of the action and the withheld information may have had an effect on the stockholder's decision, then the decision was not informed and will not validate the interested action. The plaintiff's sole basis for believing the proxy statement is misleading is the fact that the WTI (D) board deliberated for only three hours before approving the merger agreement and recommending it to its shareholders. However, a speedy decision is not sufficient evidence to support a contention that the board's decision was not informed. The directors

---

heard from WTI's (D) investment bankers and attorneys before making its decision, and the proxy statement described in detail everything the board considered before making a decision.

Analysis:

The standard for proving a decision was not informed is fairly high. There must be direct evidence of information intentionally being withheld from stockholders or being so grossly distorted that no reasonable person could determine it was not the truth. Allegations of not taking sufficient time are not enough to deem the decision uninformed. A court must determine whether a decision was informed on a case-to-case basis. It is impossible to set out a bright-line rule that encompasses all possible scenarios and all levels of the recipient's intelligence and understanding.

■ CASE VOCABULARY

DUTY OF LOYALTY: A person's duty not to engage in self-dealing or otherwise use his or her position to further personal interests rather than those of the beneficiary. For example, directors have a duty not to engage in self-dealing to further their own personal interests rather than the interests of the corporation.

Great Lakes Chemical Corp. v. Monsanto Co.

(Purchaser) v. *(Seller)*

96 F.Supp.2d 376 (D. Del. 2000)

AN INTEREST IN A LIMITED LIABILITY COMPANY IS NOT A SECURITY

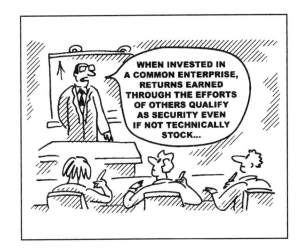

WHEN INVESTED IN A COMMON ENTERPRISE, RETURNS EARNED THROUGH THE EFFORTS OF OTHERS QUALIFY AS SECURITY EVEN IF NOT TECHNICALLY STOCK...

■ **INSTANT FACTS** Great Lakes Chemical Corporation (P) sued Monsanto Company (D) and its subsidiary, Sweet Technologies, Inc. (STI) (D), for failure to disclose information relating to the sale of NSC Technologies, Inc. to Great Lakes (P).

■ **BLACK LETTER RULE** Interests in a limited liability company are not securities if they lack the five common features of stock: (1) the right to receive dividends contingent upon an appointment of profits; (2) negotiability; (3) the ability to be pledged or hypothecated; (4) voting rights in proportion to the number of shares owned; and (5) the ability to appreciate in value.

■ PROCEDURAL BASIS

Hearing on the defendant's motion to dismiss.

■ FACTS

Monsanto (D) was the world's largest manufacturer of L-phenylalanine (L-phe), an amino acid that is the main ingredient in aspartame, an artificial sweetener, which can also be used in many other pharmaceutical products. Monsanto (D) manufactured the aspartame and marketed it as NutraSweet. In 1985, Monsanto (D) created NSC to develop specialized pharmaceutical intermediates and pharmaceutical active compounds derived from L-phe. L-phe and Tic–D, a pharmaceutical intermediate derived from L-phe, became NSC's core business. In 1998, Monsanto (D) and STI (D) agreed to establish NSC as a limited liability company and each contributed assets to NSC. In exchange for their contributions, Monsanto (D) obtained an 81.5 percent interest in NSC, while STI (D) received an 18.5 percent interest. Income, profits, gains, losses, deductions, and credits were to be allocated pro rata to the members in accordance with their membership interests. In October 1998, Monsanto (D) and STI (D) presented an offer for the sale of NSC to Great Lakes. Great Lakes sent a letter indicating its interest in NSC on November 12, 1998. While the parties were still negotiating the sale of NSC, the market price of L-phe began decreasing. On January 15, 1999, Monsanto (D) provided Great Lakes with revised sales projections, reducing the original forecast of $93.2 million to $78 million. On April 8, 1999, the parties entered into a purchase agreement, and Great Lakes closed the NSC sale on May 3, 1999. Great Lakes (P) sued, alleging that the defendants violated the Securities Exchange Act by failing to disclose material information, among other claims, and Monsanto (D) and STI (D) moved to dismiss the complaint for failure to state a claim.

■ ISSUE

Are interests in a limited liability company securities even if they lack the five common features of stock?

■ DECISION AND RATIONALE

(Judge Undisclosed) No. "Stock" has five common features: (1) the right to receive dividends contingent upon an appointment of profits; (2) negotiability; (3) the ability to be pledged or hypothecated; (4) voting rights in proportion to the number of shares owned; and (5) the ability to appreciate in

---

value. Although the interests in NSC may look like stock, they are not. The primary goal of securities laws is to regulate investments, not commercial ventures. Although some of the characteristics of the NSC interest are similar to stock, such as the members' entitlement to share equally in the distributions of profits and earnings and the fact that interests may be pleaded or hypothecated, those factors are not sufficient. They do not outweigh the purpose behind the transaction, which was a commercial transaction to acquire ownership of an entity, not to use it merely for an investment purpose. Motion granted.

Analysis:

There can be a fine line between stock, which is generally purchased for investment purposes, and buying stock in a company for the commercial purpose of acquiring control and ownership of the entity. Most people purchasing stock in a company are not motivated by obtaining control of the entity's affairs beyond ensuring that the company's revenues increase so their stock value increases. However, if one desires to purchase a company or obtain significant control over it, the purchase of a majority of the stock in the company can achieve that purpose if an outright purchase of the entity is not an option.

■ CASE VOCABULARY

STOCK: The capital or principal fund raised by a corporation through subscriber's contributions of the sale of shares.

SECURITY: An instruments that evidences the holder's ownership rights in a firm (e.g., a stock), the holder's creditor relationship with a firm or government (e.g., a bond), or the holder's other rights (e.g., an option).

Doran v. Petroleum Mgmt. Corp.

(Special Partner) v. *(Oil Drilling Company)*

545 F.2d 893 (5th Cir. 1977)

THE STATUS OF PRIVATE OFFERINGS RESTS ON THE OFFEREE'S KNOWLEDGE

■ **INSTANT FACTS** Doran (P) sued Petroleum Management Corporation (D) for breach of contract and rescission of contract based on violations of the Securities Acts of 1933 and 1934.

■ **BLACK LETTER RULE** In determining whether an offer to participate in a limited partnership was a private offer, the court must consider the number of offerees and their relationship to each other and to the issuer, the number of units offered, the offering's size, and the manner of the offering.

■ PROCEDURAL BASIS

On appeal to review the district court's judgment in favor of the defendant.

■ FACTS

Petroleum Management Corporation (PMC) (D) organized a limited partnership in California for the purpose of drilling and operating four oil wells in Wyoming. PMC (D) contacted five individuals with an offer to participate in the venture. Only one of those individuals accepted. Doran (P) received a call from Kendrick, a California securities banker. Kendrick informed Doran (P) of the opportunity to become a "special participant" in the partnership. PMC (D) sent Doran (P) drilling logs and technical maps of the proposed drilling area and told him two of the four wells had already been completed. Doran (P) agreed to become a "special partner" and to pay PMC (D) $125,000 in consideration for his partnership interest, paying $25,000 as a down payment and assuming responsibility for the payment of a $113,643 note owed by PMC (D) to Mid–Continent Supply Company. Over the next two years, PMC (D) periodically sent Doran (P) information on the completed wells. However, during that time, the wells were continuously overproduced in violation of production allowances established by the Wyoming Oil and Gas Conservation Commission. On November 16, 1971, the Commission sealed the partnership's wells. The Commission permitted the wells to resume production on August 9, 1972, but they were not as productive as they had been prior to being sealed. Because of the wells being sealed and the decreased production thereafter, the note for which Doran (P) was responsible went into default. Mid–Continent received a judgment against Doran (P) and PMC (D), and Doran (P) sued PMC (D) for rescission and damages. The lower court found in favor of the defendant, and the plaintiff appealed.

■ ISSUE

In determining whether an offer to participate in a limited partnership was a private offer exempt from registration, must the court consider the number of offerees and their relationship to each other and to the issuer, the number of units offered, the offering's size, and the manner of the offering?

■ DECISION AND RATIONALE

Yes. A court determining whether an offer to participate in a limited partnership is a private offer must consider four factors: the number of offerees and their relationship to each other and to the issuer, the number of units offered, the offering's size, and the manner of the offering. Private offerings have traditionally been considered to be those offered to persons who have knowledge or expertise in the area and are thus able to fend for themselves. The purpose behind the Securities Act of 1933 was to promote full disclosure of information necessary to make informed investment decisions. Thus, the question of whether an offering is private turns on the offeree's knowledge. Remanded to determine whether the plaintiff had knowledge of or access to all information so as to make registration unnecessary.

Analysis:

The rule that public offerings must be registered evolved to protect the common investor. Legislatures are willing to let companies make private offerings to a limited number of people without registration, because the private offerings are often made to experienced investors who may already be familiar with the company. The legislatures and courts have believed these investors do not need the protections of a registration requirement, because they will likely obtain the information on their own before investing.

■ CASE VOCABULARY

PRIVATE OFFERING: An offering made only to a small group of interested buyers. Also termed "private placement."

REGISTRATION: The complete process of preparing to sell a newly issued security to the public.

REGISTRATION STATEMENT: A document containing detailed information required by the SEC for the public sale of corporate securities. The statement includes the prospectus to be supplied to prospective buyers.

Escott v. BarChris Construction Corp.

(Stockholder) v. *(Construction Company)*

283 F.Supp. 643 (S.D.N.Y. 1968)

FALSE STATEMENTS MUST BE MATERIAL FOR A REGISTRATION STATEMENT TO BE MISLEADING

■ **INSTANT FACTS** Purchasers of convertible, subordinated debentures of BarChris Construction Corporation (D) sued BarChris (D), claiming the filed registration statement contained material false statements and omissions.

■ **BLACK LETTER RULE** If false statements made in a registration statement or omitted facts that should have been included are material, the registration statement is misleading.

■ **PROCEDURAL BASIS**

Hearing on the defendant's motion to dismiss.

■ **FACTS**

BarChris Construction Corporation (D) built large bowling centers that contained bars and restaurant facilities. The advent of the automatic pin-setting machine, caused BarChris's (D) sales to increase dramatically because of the increased interest in bowling. In 1956, BarChris's (D) sales were approximately $800,000, but by 1960, they had jumped to more than $9,165,000. BarChris (D) had to expend large sums of money to finance construction projects before it received reimbursement. As a result, BarChris (D) was in need of an ever-increasing amount of money to finance its operations. In 1959, BarChris (D) offered stock for sale to the public at $3 per share. Peter Morgan & Company underwrote the stock issue. In early 1961, BarChris (D) needed additional working capital and decided to sell 5.5 percent convertible subordinated fifteen-year debentures. The company filed the required registration statement with the SEC on March 30, 1961, and filed amendments to the statement on May 11 and May 16. The closing occurred on May 24. By this time, BarChris (D) was having difficulty collecting payment from its customers. By 1962, the company was in serious trouble. The bowling industry was overbuilt, and many alleys were closing. In May 1962, BarChris (D) made a last attempt to raise money by selling common stock. It filed a registration statement for the stock sale with the SEC and then later withdrew it. On October 29, 1962, BarChris (D) filed for Chapter 11 Bankruptcy. The debenture buyers sued for damages.

■ **ISSUE**

Is a registration statement that contains material false statements or omitted facts misleading?

■ **DECISION AND RATIONALE**

(Judge Undisclosed) Yes. False statements made in a registration statement or omitted facts that should have been included in the statement must be material in order for a registration statement to be deemed misleading. All matters of which an average prudent investor ought reasonably to be informed before purchasing the registered security are material, including any information an investor needs to know before he can make an intelligent, informed decision as to whether to purchase the securities. The registration materials BarChris (D) filed with the SEC in 1961 contained material misstatements and omissions. The registration statement included overstated sales figures and gross profits for the first quarter, overstated orders on hand, and understated contingent liabilities, and failed to disclose the true facts related to the officers' loans, customer's delinquencies, the application of the stock-sale proceeds, and the prospective operation of some alleys. On the balance sheet, the company listed its current assets as $4,524,021 and total current liabilities as $2,413,867, a ratio of approximately 1.9 to 1. However, if correctly reported, the company's assets should have been listed as $3,924,000 and the liabilities as $2,478,000, a ration of 1.6 to 1. This is a significant difference to most investors. Motion to dismiss denied.

Analysis:

The court noted that the question of whether something is material is entirely a matter of judgment. There is no way to know what the so-called "average prudent investor" considers to be important knowledge. Therefore, the standard must be applied to the individual facts and circumstances of each case, and the trier of fact must determine the materiality of any misstatements or omissions. Since potential investors consider hundreds of facts before deciding whether or not to invest in a particular security, the court cannot set out a bright-line rule on materiality.

■ CASE VOCABULARY

MATERIAL: Of such a nature that knowledge of the item would affect a person's decision-making process; significant; essential.

REGISTER: To file a new security issue with the Securities and Exchange Commission or similar state agency.

Basic Inc. v. Levinson

(Corporation) v. *(Shareholder)*

485 U.S. 224, 108 S.Ct. 978, 99 L.Ed.2d 194 (1988)

SHAREHOLDERS DETERMINE WHICH OMITTED FACTS ARE MATERIAL

■ **INSTANT FACTS** Former Basic Inc. shareholders brought a class action suit against Basic Inc. (D) and its directors, claiming the directors issued three false statements and forced the former shareholders to sell their shares at depressed prices based on their reliance on Basic's statements that it was not engaged in merger discussions.

■ **BLACK LETTER RULE** An omitted fact is material if there is a substantial likelihood that the average, reasonable shareholder would have considered it important knowledge to have before deciding how to vote.

■ **PROCEDURAL BASIS**

On certiorari to review the Court of Appeals' decision reversing the District Court's grant of summary judgment in favor of the defendants.

■ **FACTS**

Basic Inc. (D) was a publicly traded company that manufactured chemical refractories for the steel industry. In 1976, Combustion Engineering, Inc., a company that made alumina-based refractories, initiated a strategic plan to acquire Basic (D). Combustion representatives began meeting with Basic's (D) officers and directors concerning a possible merger. In 1978, Basic (D) made three public statements denying it was engaged in merger negotiations. On December 18, 1978, Basic (D) told the New York Stock Exchange to stop trading its shares and issued a statement that it had been asked to consider a merger with another company. On December 19, Basic (D) accepted Combustion's offer of $46 per share. On December 20, it publicly announced its acceptance of Combustion's offer. Basic's (D) former shareholders, who sold their stock before Basic (D) formally announced the merger, sued alleging material misrepresentations.

■ **ISSUE**

Were the Basic (D) directors liable for making a material misstatement when they made a public statement indicating Basic (D) was not involved in merger discussions?

■ **DECISION AND RATIONALE**

(Judge Undisclosed) Yes. An omitted fact is material if there is a substantial likelihood that the average, reasonable shareholder would have considered it important knowledge to have. This materiality standard also applies to preliminary merger discussions. Preliminary merger discussions are contingent or speculative in nature, so it is difficult to determine what type of omitted information the average investor would have considered significant. However, Congress has decided that preliminary merger discussions are material and should be disclosed to investors. Investors generally are prudent people who do not need to be protected from the disclosure of preliminary merger information, because they understand that preliminary merger discussions do not always lead to mergers. Therefore, the preliminary merger should have been disclosed to the shareholders. However, under Rule 10b–5, a

---

HIGH COURT CASE SUMMARIES

plaintiff must prove reliance on a misleading statement in order for the statement to be deemed material. The shareholders claim they were injured by this omission because their stock would have been more valuable if the merger talks had been reported. Under the "fraud on the market theory," the price of a company's stock is determined by the available material information regarding the company and its business. The theory assumes that misleading information or statements will defraud stock purchasers even if they do not rely on the misstatements. A corporation can rebut this assumption by showing that the plaintiff did not rely on the market price. Vacated and remanded.

CONCURRENCE IN PART AND DISSENT IN PART

The fraud-on-the-market theory should not have been applied in this case, and the fraud-on-the-market assumption must be refutable by evidence to the contrary. The Court assumed that under the fraud-in-the-market theory, buyers rely on the integrity of the market price. This seems to mean investors should be able to rely on the stock's price as a reflection of its value, which is absurd because stock values are constantly changing and stock shares have no true value.

Analysis:

The basic rule provides that an omitted fact is material if there is a substantial likelihood that the average, reasonable shareholdor would have considered it important knowledge to have. A bright-line rule regarding preliminary merger discussions would make it much easier for corporate managers to determine what information they can keep confidential until a merger is finalized. However, the Court noted that the purposes behind the Securities Acts should not be ignored merely for the sake of convenience and ease of application.

■ CASE VOCABULARY

BRIGHT–LINE RULE: A legal rule of decision that tends to resolve issues, especially ambiguities, simply and straightforwardly, sometimes sacrificing equity for certainty.

West v. Prudential Sec., Inc.

(Client) v. *(Stock Broker)*

282 F.3d 935 (7th Cir. 2002)

FRAUD–ON–THE–MARKET DOES NOT APPLY TO NON–PUBLIC STATEMENTS

■ **INSTANT FACTS** West (P) brought a class action suit against Prudential Securities, Inc. (D) for securities fraud, alleging that a stockbroker had falsely told several clients that a corporation's stock was certain to be acquired at a premium, artificially inflating its price.

■ **BLACK LETTER RULE** The fraud-on-the-market doctrine and its presumption of reliance on misstatements do not apply in a securities fraud class action against a securities brokerage firm alleging that a stockbroker had falsely told several clients that a particular corporation was certain to be acquired at a premium in the near future.

■ **PROCEDURAL BASIS**

On appeal to review the district court's decision certifying the class.

■ **FACTS**

Hofman, a stockbroker working for Prudential Securities (D), told eleven of his customers that it was certain Jefferson Savings Bancorp would be acquired. Hofman continued to so inform his clients for seven months. No acquisition of Jefferson was ever pending. West (P) brought a class action suit against Prudential Securities, Inc. (D) for securities fraud, alleging that Hofman had falsely told several clients that Jefferson's stock was certain to be acquired at a premium, artificially inflating its price.

■ **ISSUE**

Do the fraud-on-the-market doctrine and its presumption of reliance on misstatements apply in a securities fraud class action against a securities brokerage firm alleging that a stockbroker had falsely told several clients that a particular corporation was certain to be acquired at a premium in the near future?

■ **DECISION AND RATIONALE**

(Easterbrook, C.J.) No. Under the fraud-on-the-market theory, an investor's reliance on public material misrepresentations may be presumed for purposes of Rule 10b–5 actions because most publicly available information is reflected in market price. The basic theory behind the fraud-on-the-market theory is that public information reaches professional investors and that their trades based on that information quickly influence securities' prices. Public announcements can greatly affect stock prices. If prices already incorporated effects brought about by non-public information, public announcements of the same factors would have no additional effects. Hofman announced to a handful of his own customers that Prudential (D) was going to acquire Jefferson Savings Bancorp. It is difficult to see how these private statements could have had a widespread effect on the price of Jefferson's stock. Reversed.

Analysis:

The opinion discusses the belief that Jefferson's market was inefficient. An efficient market is the foundation of the fraud-on-the-market doctrine. The court asks how one outsider's unsubstantiated lie could cause a long-term increase in the stock's price. It also theorizes that professional investigators would notice the rise and would investigate its basis, or quickly sell their stock at a decreased price to bring the market back down. In the court's opinion, one unsubstantiated lie might fool investors for a brief period, but over a period of several months the lie would be discovered.

■ CASE VOCABULARY

CAUSATION: The causing or producing of an effect.

FRAUD–ON–THE–MARKET THEORY: Fraud occurring when an issuer of securities gives out misinformation that affects the market price of stock, the result being that people who buy or sell are effectively misled even though they did not rely on the statement itself or anything derived from it other than the market price.

RELIANCE: Dependence or trust by a person, especially when combined with action based on that dependence or trust.

Pommer v. Medtest Corp.

(Minority Shareholder) v. *(Corporation)*

961 F.2d 620 (7th Cir. 1992)

STATEMENTS ARE MATERIAL IF THEY ALTER ALL OTHER INFORMATION CONSIDERED AS A WHOLE

■ **INSTANT FACTS** Medtest Corporation's (D) investors sued the corporation under § 10(b) of the Securities Act of 1934, claiming they were the victims of fraud.

■ **BLACK LETTER RULE** Statements are material if a substantial likelihood exists that the whole of the information, as considered by a reasonable investor, would have been significantly altered if the omitted fact had been disclosed.

■ **PROCEDURAL BASIS**

On appeal to review the federal magistrate's decision setting aside a lower court's verdict for the plaintiffs and entering a judgment for the defendant.

■ **FACTS**

Medtest Corp. (D) owns the intellectual property rights to a self-administered cervico-vaginal testing process. Manning, who designed the process, partnered with West (D), an attorney, to form Medtest (D) for the purpose of obtaining a patent and marketing the process. Manning owned thirty-one percent of Medtest's stock, West (D) owned twenty-six percent of the stock, and friends and relatives of the two owned the rest. In September 1982, Manning sold 250 of his Medtest shares to the Pommers (P) for $25,000. He later sold them an additional 2750 shares for $175,000, giving the Pommers (P) three percent of Medtest's (D) outstanding stock. This stock was valuable only if the firm paid dividends, went public, or was purchased by a third party. Before the Pommers' stock purchase, Manning told them Medtest (D) held a federal patent on the process and that Medtest (D) was going to be sold to Abbott Laboratories for $50 million to $100 million. Manning also told the Pommers (P) that the deal was almost complete. Had the deal actually occurred, the Pommers' (P) three-percent interest would have been worth between $1.5 million and $3 million. In reality, at the time of the sale to the Pommers (P), Medtest (D) had only applied for a patent, which was not awarded to it until August 14, 1984. Nor was Medtest (D) in the final stages of negotiation of a sale to Abbott Laboratories; it had merely discussed a potential sale with Abbott. On October 28, 1982, Abbott sent Medtest (D) a letter informing it Abbott was not interested in purchasing Medtest (D). The Pommers (P) brought a securities fraud action.

■ **ISSUE**

Are statements concerning the existence of a patent and an impending sale of the company material?

■ **DECISION AND RATIONALE**

(Easterbrook, J.) Yes. Statements are material if a substantial likelihood exists that the "total mix" of the information considered by the reasonable investor would have been significantly altered if the omitted fact had been disclosed. Pommer (P) testified that he would not have purchased his shares if he had known that Medtest (D) did not have the patent. This misstatement is not cured by the fact that Medtest (D) obtained a patent two years later. A statement that is false when made does not become legally valid simply because it later becomes true. The Pommers (P) likely also would have considered the truth about the negotiations with Abbott to have substantially altered the "total mix" of information. Medtest (D) knew the sale with Abbott was not approved; the gap between a $50 million price and a $100 million price is large. Also, if Medtest (D) really believed the sale to Abbott was nearly finalized, it would not have been willing to sell three percent of its stock for $200,000, if that stock would be worth at least $1.5 million after the sale. Reversed and remanded.

Analysis:

Requiring that an omitted piece of information must substantially alter the "total mix" of information is another way of saying that the omitted information cannot be trivial. The information must be of some consequence to the potential investor or the court will not waste its time arguing whether its omission made the transaction fraudulent. This rule is useful in preventing investors from trying to retract sales when events do not turn out as they expected. Investors cannot be allowed to purchase securities and then rescind their purchase based on a triviality or a technicality, simply because they do not earn as much profit as they would like.

■ CASE VOCABULARY

AFTERMARKET: Also "secondary market." The market for goods or services that have previously been available for buying and selling; especially the securities market in which previously issued securities are traded among investors.

Santa Fe Indus., Inc. v. Green

(*Majority Shareholder*) v. (*Minority Shareholder*)

430 U.S. 462, 97 S.Ct. 1292, 51 L.Ed.2d 480 (1977)

A PARENT MAY MERGE ITSELF WITH ITS SUBSIDIARY IN SOME CASES

TAKE IT OR LEAVE IT. IF YOU DON'T THINK THIS IS ENOUGH, YOU CAN SEEK APPRAISAL

■ **INSTANT FACTS** Kirby Lumber Co.'s minority shareholders (P) sued Santa Fe Industries, Inc. (D), which was Kirby's majority shareholder, seeking to set aside the merger of Kirby with Santa Fe (D) and alleging that their stock was worth more than they were offered when the companies merged.

■ **BLACK LETTER RULE** Under the short-form merger statute, a parent company may merge itself with its subsidiary if the parent owns at least ninety percent of the subsidiary's stock and if the parent company's board of directors approves the action.

■ PROCEDURAL BASIS

On certiorari to review the Court of Appeals' decision reversing the District Court's dismissal for failure to state a claim.

■ FACTS

Santa Fe Industries, Inc. (D) acquired sixty percent of Kirby Lumber Co.'s stock. Over the years, Santa Fe (D) acquired additional stock, and eventually owned ninety-five percent of Kirby's outstanding stock. Santa Fe (D) paid between $65 and $92.50 per share for the stock. In 1974, Santa Fe (D) used the short-form merger statute to merge itself with Kirby Lumber Co. and hired Morgan & Stanley Co. to determine the fair market value of Kirby's stock. It also obtained independent appraisals of Kirby's physical assets, which were appraised at $320 million dollars ($640 per share). Morgan Stanley valued Kirby's stock at $125 per share. Kirby's minority stockholders (P) were informed of the merger one day after it became effective and were told they could obtain an independent appraisal if they were unhappy with the $150–per–share price for their stock. The minority shareholders (P) sued the majority shareholders and the appraisal firm.

■ ISSUE

Is a short-form merger valid under SEC Rule 10b–5?

■ DECISION AND RATIONALE

(Judge Undisclosed) Yes. Pursuant to the short-form merger statute, a parent company may merge itself with its subsidiary if it owns at least ninety percent of the subsidiary's stock and the parent company's board approves the action. As a condition of the merger, the parent company must pay the minority shareholders cash for their shares and must give notice of the merger within ten days after it becomes effective. However, Rule 10b–5 prohibits any act that defrauds or deceives, but conduct is not prohibited under § 10b–5 unless it can be fairly viewed as "manipulative or deceptive." The minority shareholders here had an option under the short-form merger statute either to accept the offered price or to seek an appraisal by the Court of Chancery. The minority shareholders were provided with all the information needed to determine if the offered price was fair. The plaintiffs presented no evidence of manipulative conduct by Santa Fe. Reversed and remanded.

Analysis:

The court indicated that Congress did not provide for private actions for a violation of § 10b–5. That was not the purpose behind enacting the statute. The Securities Exchange Act promotes full disclosure in public offerings of securities, but better methods exist for bringing a claim of breach of fiduciary duty for fraud. Congress indicated that anti-fraud actions should be allowed under this statute only if they are necessary to uphold the purpose behind enacting the Securities Exchange Act.

■ CASE VOCABULARY

MERGER: The absorption of one company that ceases to exist into another that retains its own name and identity and acquires the assets and liabilities of the former.

Deutschman v. Beneficial Corp.

(Option Purchaser) v. *(Corporation)*

841 F.2d 502 (3d Cir. 1988)

A PLAINTIFF MUST DEAL IN A SECURITY TO HAVE STANDING

■ **INSTANT FACTS** Deutschman (P) sued Beneficial Corporation (D) and two of its directors for breach of fiduciary duty, alleging a violation of the Securities Exchange Act of 1934 and claiming that he suffered losses when call options he purchased on Beneficial's (D) stock in reliance on the market price became worthless.

■ **BLACK LETTER RULE** An options trader purchases or sells a security and has standing to sue for damages under § 10–b and the related rules.

■ **PROCEDURAL BASIS**

On appeal of the district court's dismissal of the plaintiff's complaint.

■ **FACTS**

Deutschman (P) was a shareholder of Beneficial Corp. (D). In 1986 and 1987, Beneficial's (D) insurance division suffered severe losses, which had a negative impact on Beneficial's (D) financial welfare. Casperson (D), Beneficial's chairman and CEO, and Halvorsen (D), its CFO, issued statements on behalf of the company in an attempt to stop the decline in its stock price. The statements indicated that the financial problems were over and covered by the company's financial reserves. Casperson (D) and Halvorsen (D) held stock and stock options in Beneficial (D). Beneficial's shares were traded on the New York Stock Exchange and on other national stock exchanges. Deutschman (P), who had purchased call options on the stock, brought a class action alleging claims under the Securities Exchange Act.

■ **ISSUE**

Do option traders have standing to sue for damages under § 10–b of the Securities Exchange Act and Rule 10b–5?

■ **DECISION AND RATIONALE**

(Judge Undisclosed) Yes. A plaintiff must purchase or sell a security in order to have standing to sue for damages under § 10–b. The purpose underlying the Securities Exchange Act is to protect participants in the securities market. Previous cases determined that anyone who had dealt in the security to which the misrepresentation related was protected. Under that standard, option traders have standing to file suit under § 10–b of the Securities Act of 1934. An option contract gives the owner a right to buy or sell a fixed number of shares of a specified underlying stock at a given price on or before the contract's expiration date. The trader pays a premium for the option, and the contract's value changes depending on the stock's market price relative to the striking price. Option contracts permit traders to engage in hedging transactions, which can reduce exposure to market fluctuations. Reversed.

Analysis:

The defendants here attempted to assert a policy argument that option traders should be entitled to less protection under the Securities Exchange Act because option trading is essentially gambling. The court declined to accept this theory, noting that the price of option contracts depends closely on the price of the underlying stock, so that the risk in trading in option contracts is not much greater than the risk in trading stock. In practice, investing in the stock market is always a gamble, and it seems unfair to treat certain investment practices as entitled to less protection than others when all investments carry a risk of loss.

■ CASE VOCABULARY

OPTION: The right (but not the obligation) to buy or sell a given quantity of securities, commodities, or other assets at a fixed price within a specified time.

Goodwin v. Agassiz

(Shareholder) v. *(Director)*

283 Mass. 358, 186 N.E. 659 (1933)

DIRECTORS' DIRECT STOCK SALES OR PURCHASES MUST BE FAIR

■ **INSTANT FACTS** Goodwin (P), a shareholder in Cliff Mining Company, filed suit against Agassiz (D) for damages suffered during the sale of his stock.

■ **BLACK LETTER RULE** A director's knowledge of the corporation's condition requires that he engage in fair dealing when directly buying or selling the corporation's stock.

■ **PROCEDURAL BASIS**

On appeal of a decree dismissing the plaintiff's bill.

■ **FACTS**

In May 1926, Agassiz (D) and the other defendants purchased seven hundred shares of stock in Cliff Mining Co. on the Boston stock exchange. Before that purchase, Goodwin (P) had owned the stock. Agassiz (D), the president and a director of Cliff, and MacNaughten (D), the general manager and a director of Cliff, knew that an experienced geologist had written up a theory regarding the possible existence of copper deposits in the vicinity of Cliff's property. The region, known as the Mineral Belt of Northern Michigan, contained several copper-mining companies. Another company of which Agassiz (D) and MacNaughten (D) are officers made extensive geological surveys of the company's lands. Upon recommendations from that survey, exploration began on Cliff's property in 1925. The exploration was unsuccessful and ceased in May 1926. Before Agassiz (D) and MacNaughten (D) further explored the geologist's theory, they decided to acquire an option in another copper company of which they were officers. Agassiz (D) and MacNaughten (D) agreed not to inform anyone of the geologist's theory that copper existed below Cliff's land because the information could reduce the number of options available to them. Agassiz (D) and MacNaughten (D) believed that if there was any truth to the geologist's beliefs, the price of Cliff stock would increase. Goodwin (P) learned of the end of explorations on Cliff's property on May 15, 1962, from an article in the newspaper and immediately sold his shares through brokers. Goodwin (P) did not know the defendants were purchasing the stock or that his stock was being bought for the defendants. Goodwin (P) would not have sold his stock if he had known of the geologist's theory.

■ **ISSUE**

Do directors' actions keeping secret knowledge regarding the corporation's condition constitute an actionable wrong when the director is dealing in the stock?

■ **DECISION AND RATIONALE**

(Judge Undisclosed) No. A director's knowledge regarding the condition of a corporation requires that he engage in fair dealing when directly buying or selling the corporation's stock. Stock sales and purchases are generally very impersonal transactions, and it would place a great burden on the stock market and stock brokers if any officer or director had to contact the party seeking to buy the shares and inform them of anything that could later affect the stock's value. However, if an officer of a corporation directly approaches a shareholder and offers to purchase his stock, the courts will closely scrutinize the interested transaction for evidence of abuse of power. No evidence here proves the defendants were guilty of fraud. The only knowledge the defendants possessed that the plaintiff did not know was the geologist's theory that the region containing the defendant's land might contain copper deposits. The theory did not state that copper would be found in any one particular location. The defendants did not tell anyone of the theory, but no duty required them to inform anyone about it. Affirmed.

Analysis:

The court noted that the law need not put all parties to a contract on equal footing when it comes to knowledge, experience, skills, and cunningness. The law does not necessarily equate with morality. While it may seem "right" to place every person to a contract in equal positions, the law simply cannot undertake the task. The parties themselves must bear some responsibility for educating themselves or seeking assistance in protecting their interests.

■ CASE VOCABULARY

BILL: A formal written complaint, such as a court paper requesting some specific action for reasons alleged.

Securities and Exchange Comm'n v. Texas Gulf Sulfur Co.

(Government Agency) v. *(Mining Company)*

401 F.2d 833 (2d Cir. 1968)

INSIDERS MAY NOT USE BUSINESS INFORMATION FOR THEIR PERSONAL TRADING

WELL, THAT'S OIL ALL RIGHT. MAYBE WE SHOULD BUY THE LAND AFTER ALL

■ **INSTANT FACTS** The Securities and Exchange Commission (P) filed suit against Texas Gulf Sulfur Co. (D) for violation of the insider-trading provisions of Rule 10b–5.

■ **BLACK LETTER RULE** A person who is trading a corporation's securities for his own benefit and who has access to information intended to be available for business use only, may not take advantage of the information, knowing it is not available to those with whom he is dealing.

■ **PROCEDURAL BASIS**

On appeal to review the trial court's judgment in favor of the defendants.

■ **FACTS**

Texas Gulf Sulfur (TGS) (D) began exploratory drilling in eastern Canada in the late 1950's. Mollison (D), who was TGS's (D) Vice President and a mining engineer, supervised the project. Clayton (D), an electrical engineer, also worked on the site. In November 1963, TGS (D) had done exploratory drilling on an area that appeared to be strong in mineral content. TGS (D) decided to buy the land, and its president, Stephens (D), ordered all employees to keep the drilling results a secret so TGS (D) would not have competition driving up the land's price. The company resumed drilling on March 27, 1964, once it had purchased enough land to protect its interests. In the period between November 1963 and March 1964, several TGS (D) employees and others they had tipped off purchased TGS (D) stock and calls on the stock. By the end of March 1964, they owned 8,235 shares and 12,300 calls. Rumors began circulating that TGS (D) was nearing a major ore strike, and on April 11, articles in the New York Herald Tribune and the New York Times indicated that TGS (D) was about to score a major strike. Stephens (D) immediately contacted others and obtained a current report on the drilling's progress. The following afternoon, TGS (D) issued a press release indicating that as of April 12, the reports of a substantial copper discovery at the Canadian job site exaggerated the scale of the operations and that most of the drilled areas revealed only barren pyrite or graphite without value, although a few had resulted in the discovery of small or marginal sulphide ore bodies. However, the insiders knew as of the evening of April 10 that TGS (D) had discovered 6.2 to 8.3 million tons of proven ore worth approximately $26 to $29 per ton. On April 13, the New York Herald ran a story titled "Copper Rumor Deflated," correcting its previous report of a major strike but indicating that recent mineral activity near the drilling site had provided favorable results. On April 13, a Canadian journalist interviewed several insiders in preparation of an article confirming a 10 million-ton ore strike. The article was published on April 16, and TGS (D) gave the Ontario Minister of Mines a statement regarding the discovery's extent for release to the media. Mollison (D) and Holyk (D), another insider, thought the statement would be released over the airways at 11p.m. on April 15, but it was not released until the next morning. An official statement announcing the discovery of at least 25 million tons of ore was released over the American airwaves, appeared on Merrill Lynch's private wire, and was announced over the Dow Jones ticker tape that morning. On April 15, Clayton (D) ordered 200 shares of TGS (D) stock through his Canadian broker. Crawford (D) ordered 300 shares at midnight on April 15 and an additional 300 shares early the next morning. Other

---

insiders similarly purchased stock before the discovery's announcement became common knowledge. The SEC sued, alleging violations of the insider trading laws.

■ ISSUE

Do insiders violate Rule 10b–5 when they purchase shares before disclosure of information intended to be available only for corporate purposes is announced to the public?

■ DECISION AND RATIONALE

(Judge Undisclosed) Yes. Anyone trading for his own benefit in a corporation's securities who has access to information intended to be available for business use only, may not take advantage of such information, knowing it is not available to those with whom he is dealing. If anyone possesses such information, they must either disclose it to the investing public, or if disclosure is not possible, they must refrain from trading in or recommending for trade the securities involved until the secret information is disclosed. The existence of a vast amount of viable ore on TGS (D) land is material information that a reasonable investor would like to know before deciding whether or not to purchase TGS (D) stock. Discovering that large a quantity of valuable ore would most certainly have an effect on a mining company's stock's value. All of the stock purchases and calls made by individuals who knew of the ore discovery before the public announcement violated Rule 10b–5.

Analysis:

The basic rule of this case is that anyone trading for his own benefit in a corporation's securities who has access to information intended to be available for business use only, may not take advantage of the information if he or she knows it is not available to the public. However, the court noted that an insider is not always foreclosed from investing in his or her own company simply because he or she is more familiar with the company's operations. Also, the rule applies only in situations where private knowledge exists and releasing the knowledge may have a substantial effect on the security's price.

■ CASE VOCABULARY

INSIDER: A person who has knowledge of facts not available to the general public.

INSIDER TRADING: The use of material, nonpublic information in trading the shares of a company by a corporate insider or other person who owes a fiduciary duty to the company.

Dirks v. Securities and Exchange Comm'n

(Tippee) v. *(Regulatory Authority)*

463 U.S. 646, 103 S.Ct. 3255, 77 L.Ed.2d 911 (1983)

TIPPEES DO NOT AUTOMATICALLY HAVE A DUTY TO DISCLOSE

■ **INSTANT FACTS** The Securities and Exchange Commission (SEC) (P) accused Dirks (D) of violating the antifraud provisions of the federal securities laws for disclosing to investors material nonpublic information he received from insiders.

■ **BLACK LETTER RULE** A tippee does not inherit a duty to disclose material non-public information merely because he knowingly received the information.

■ **PROCEDURAL BASIS**

On appeal to review the SEC's determination that the petitioner was guilty of 10b–5 violations.

■ **FACTS**

Dirks (D), an officer of a New York brokerage firm that specialized in providing investment analysis of insurance company securities to institutional investors, received information from Secrist, a former officer of Equity Funding of America, that Equity Funding's assets were vastly overstated through the corporation's fraudulent practices. Secrist told Dirks (D) that other regulatory agencies failed to act on similar claims brought by other Equity Funding employees. Dirks (D) decided to investigate Secrist's story and interviewed several Equity Funding officers and employees. Equity Funding's senior managers denied any wrongdoing, but some other Equity Funding employees verified Secrist's claims. Although Dirks (D) did not own Equity Funding stock, he informed some of his clients of the claims. As a result, some of the shareholders sold their Equity Funding shares, including five investors whose combined liquidated holdings exceeded more than $16 million. Dirks (D) investigated Equity Funding for two weeks. During that time, the price of Equity Funding's stock fell from $26 to $15 per share. This dramatic drop led the New York Stock Exchange to cease trading of Equity Funding's stock. California insurance authorities reviewed Equity Funding's financial records and uncovered evidence of fraud. After this discovery, the SEC filed a complaint against Equity Funding, and the Wall Street Journal published a front-page story on the fraudulent activity. After a hearing concerning Dirks' (D) role in exposing the fraud, the SEC (P) found that Dirks (D) had aided and abetted violations of antifraud provisions of the Securities Exchange Act by repeating the fraud allegations to members of the investment community who later sold their stock. However, because Dirks also brought the fraud to light, the SEC only censured him. On review, the Court of Appeals entered judgment against Dirks, and Dirks appealed.

■ **ISSUE**

Does an individual, who is not a fiduciary and was not in confidence with a securities' seller, always have a duty to disclose material nonpublic information of which he has knowledge?

■ **DECISION AND RATIONALE**

(Powell, J.) No. A tippee does not inherit a duty to disclose material non-public information of which he has knowledge merely because he knowingly received such information. Such an imposition could adversely impact the continued existence of market analysts. An analyst must seek out information about publicly traded corporations' practices and financial status and analyze the information. The analyst usually obtains his information by interviewing corporate officers and insiders. Analysts cannot help but obtain material, non-public information. This does not necessarily mean they should be prevented from trading on the information or passing it on to investors. Market analysts are an important part of the stock market because they promote efficiency in pricing. However, a tippee who improperly receives insider information may assume an insider's duty to disclose if the insider breached his fiduciary duty to the shareholders by disclosing the information to the tippee, and the tippee knew or should have known of the breach. Whether a disclosure is a breach of duty depends on the disclosure's purpose. The test is whether the insider will personally benefit, directly or indirectly, from the disclosure. If there is no personal benefit or gain, there is no breach of duty. Reversed.

■ DISSENT

(Blackmun, J.) The majority creates a special motivational requirement on the fiduciary duty doctrine. This new requirement excuses a knowing and intentional violation of an insider's duty to shareholders if the insider does not personally benefit. Such a requirement is not justified.

Analysis:

The decision emphasizes that this exception for tippees does not mean they are always free to trade on the information. Such a bright-line exception would leave the door wide open for abuse. Tippees may not use the information they receive for their own benefit. If they do, their exception from the duty to disclose disappears, and they will be deemed to be in violation of Rule 10b–5.

■ CASE VOCABULARY

TIP: A piece of special information; especially, in securities law, advance or inside information passed from one person to another.

TIPPEE: A person who acquires material nonpublic information from someone in a fiduciary relationship with the company to which that information pertains.

TIPPER: A person who possesses material inside information and who selectively discloses that information for trading or other personal purposes.

United States v. O'Hagan

(Federal Government) v. *(Attorney)*

521 U.S. 642, 117 S.Ct. 2199, 138 L.Ed.2d 724 (1997)

ATTORNEY BREACHES HIS DUTY OF LOYALTY IF HE USES NONPUBLIC INFORMATION TO TRADE SECURITIES

■ **INSTANT FACTS** The SEC indicted O'Hagan (D), an attorney, on fifty-seven counts, including seventeen counts of securities fraud and seventeen counts of fraudulent trading in connection with a tender offer, for his trading on nonpublic information in breach of the duty of trust and confidence he owed to his law firm and its clients.

■ **BLACK LETTER RULE** An attorney who, based on inside information he acquired as an attorney representing an offeror, purchased stock in a target corporation before the corporation was purchased in a tender offer is guilty of securities fraud in violation of Rule 10b–5 under the misappropriation theory.

■ **PROCEDURAL BASIS**

On certiorari to review the Eighth Circuit's decision, reversing all of the defendant's convictions.

■ **FACTS**

O'Hagan (D) was a partner in the Dorsey & Whitney law firm in Minneapolis, Minnesota. In July 1988, Grand Metropolitan PLC, a London company, retained Dorsey & Whitney to represent them in a potential tender offer for the common stock of the Pillsbury Company. Grand Metropolitan made a public announcement of its tender offer on October 4, 1988. On August 18, 1988, O'Hagan (D) purchased call options for Pillsbury stock, each of which gave O'Hagan (D) the right to purchase 100 shares of Pillsbury stock before a specified date in September 1988. O'Hagan (D) owned 2500 unexpired Pillsbury options by the end of September 1988, more than any other individual investor. He also purchased 5000 shares of Pillsbury common stock that September at a price of just less than $39 per share. Pillsbury stock rose to nearly $60 per share when Grand Metropolitan announced its tender offer in October. O'Hagan (D) sold his call options and common stock at a profit of more than $4.3 million.

■ **ISSUE**

Does an attorney breach his duty of loyalty to his law firm and its client in violation of Rule 10b–5 if he uses nonpublic information to trade securities?

■ **DECISION AND RATIONALE**

(Judge Undisclosed) Yes. The misappropriation theory provides that a person is guilty of fraud if he misappropriates confidential information for security trading purposes, in breach of a duty owed to the information's source. The theory behind the misappropriation doctrine is that a fiduciary's self-serving use of a principal's information to trade securities deprives the principal of its right to exclusive use of its private information. Misappropriation satisfies § 10(b)'s requirement that chargeable conduct must involve a "deceptive device or contrivance" in the purchase or sale of securities. A fiduciary who is

---

feigning loyalty to a principal while secretly using the principal's private information for his own gain defrauds the principal. Reversed and remanded.

Analysis:

The misappropriation doctrine supplements the protective sweep of the insider trading protections for securities. It was designed to protect the securities market from abuse by outsiders who have access to confidential information, but who owe no obligation or fiduciary duty to the corporation's shareholders. A defendant can overcome allegations of misappropriation by evidence of full disclosure of the use of nonpublic information for trading.

■ CASE VOCABULARY

MISAPPROPRIATION: The application of another's property or money dishonestly to one's own use.

Reliance Electric Co. v. Emerson Electric Co.

(Principal Corporation) v. *(Shareholder)*

404 U.S. 418, 92 S.Ct. 596, 30 L.Ed.2d 575 (1972)

PROFITS ARE NOT RECOVERABLE BY A SUCCESSOR UNDER INSIDER TRADING PROVISIONS

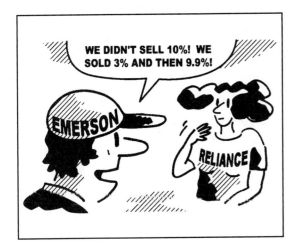

WE DIDN'T SELL 10%! WE SOLD 3% AND THEN 9.9%!

EMERSON

RELIANCE

■ **INSTANT FACTS** Emerson Electric Co. (P), which acquired 13.2 percent of the outstanding stock of Dodge Manufacturing Co. (which later merged with Reliance Electric Co. (D)) and was faced with the failure of its takeover attempt, disposed of enough shares to bring its holdings below ten percent in order to avoid liability under § 16(b).

■ **BLACK LETTER RULE** A corporation may recover the profits realized by an owner of more than ten percent of its outstanding shares from a purchase and sale of its stock within any six-month period, provided the owner held more than ten percent at the time of both the purchase and the sale.

■ PROCEDURAL BASIS

On certiorari to review the Court of Appeal's decision reversing the District Court's determination that Emerson (P) was liable.

■ FACTS

Emerson Electric Co. (P), in an unsuccessful attempt to take over Dodge Manufacturing Co., acquired 13.2 percent of the Dodge's outstanding stock on June 16, 1967, at the price of $63 per share. Dodge later approved a merger with Reliance Electric Co. (D). In an attempt to immunize its shares from liability under § 16(b), Emerson (P) planned to reduce its Dodge holdings to less than ten percent of Dodge's outstanding shares. Accordingly, on August 28, 1967, Emerson (P) sold 37,000 Dodge shares to a brokerage house for $68 per share, reducing Emerson's (P) holdings to 9.96 percent. Emerson (P) then sold the remaining shares to Dodge for $69 per share on September 11, 1967. Reliance (D) demanded the profits realized on both sales, and Emerson brought suit seeking a declaratory judgment as to its liability under § 16(b).

■ ISSUE

Are the profits from two sales, each of which constitute less than ten percent of a corporation's outstanding shares, recoverable by the corporation under § 16(b)?

■ DECISION AND RATIONALE

(Judge Undisclosed) No. Pursuant to § 16(b) of the Securities Exchange Act, a corporation may recover the profits realized by an owner of more than ten percent of its shares from a purchase and sale of its stock within any six-month period, provided the owner held more than ten percent of the shares at the time of both the purchase and the sale. The rule, which imposes strict liability on any transactions occurring within the six-month statutory time frame, prevents insiders from purchasing large quantities of stock in their company based on private information and then quickly dumping the stock when the information goes public and the stock price increases. Even if two sales are part of an interrelated plan to reduce ownership to less than ten percent, once the shareholder owns less than ten percent, any additional sales are not governed by § 16(b). Thus, Emerson is not liable for profits arising from the second sale. Affirmed.

Analysis:

Section 16(b) prevents the damages wrought by insider trading. It removes the profits from transactions where the potential for abuse is the greatest. The rule does not apply in every situation in which an investor relies on inside information in making its decision to purchase stock. For example, the rule does not apply if the investor does not qualify as an insider. Similarly, it does not apply to a plan to sell within six months of purchase if the actual sale occurred after the statutory six-month period.

■ CASE VOCABULARY

STRICT LIABILITY: Liability that does not depend on actual negligence or intent to harm, but that is based on the breach of an absolute duty to make something safe.

Foremost-McKesson, Inc. v. Provident Sec. Co.

(Purchaser) v. *(Seller)*

423 U.S. 232, 96 S.Ct. 508, 46 L.Ed.2d 464 (1976)

BENEFICIAL OWNERS HAVE NO LIABILITY FOR SHORT-TERM PROFITS IF THEIR STATUS EXISTED BOTH BEFORE AND AFTER THE SALE

- **INSTANT FACTS** Foremost-McKesson, Inc. (P) sued Provident Securities Co. (D) to recover profits realized on the sale of debentures to the underwriters.

- **BLACK LETTER RULE** A corporation may capture for itself the profits realized on a purchase and sale of its securities within six months by a director, officer, or beneficial owner, but a beneficial owner is accountable to the issuer only if it was a beneficial owner before the purchase.

■ PROCEDURAL BASIS

On certiorari to review the Court of Appeals' decision affirming the lower court's grant of summary judgment for the defendant.

■ FACTS

Provident Securities Co. (D), a personal holding company, decided to dissolve and liquidate its assets. Foremost-McKesson, Inc. (P) expressed interest in purchasing the company. The companies engaged in lengthy negotiations over the consideration. Provident (D) wanted to be paid in cash because of its imminent dissolution, but Foremost-McKesson (P) wanted to pay with its own securities. The parties executed a purchase agreement on September 25, 1969, which provided that Foremost-McKesson (P) would purchase two-thirds of Provident's (D) assets in exchange for $4.25 million in cash and $49.75 million of Foremost-McKesson's (P) convertible subordinated debentures. Foremost-McKesson (P) also agreed to register $25 million in principal amount of the debentures and to participate in an underwriting agreement pursuant to which the debentures would be sold to the public. At closing Foremost-McKesson (P) delivered the cash and a $40 million debenture, which was later exchanged for a $25 million debenture and a $15 million debenture. Foremost-McKesson (P) delivered a $2.5 million debenture to the escrow agent on the closing date and a $7.25 million debenture, representing the balance of the purchase price, to Provident (D) on October 20. The debentures were immediately convertible into more than ten percent of Foremost-McKesson's (P) common stock. On October 21, Provident (D), Foremost-McKesson (P), and a group of underwriters executed an underwriting agreement that provided for the sale to the underwriters of the $25 million debenture, to be closed on October 28. Provident (D) distributed the $15 million and $7.25 million debentures to its stockholders on October 24. The parties completed the closing on the underwriting agreement on October 28, and Provident (D) then distributed the proceeds from the debenture sale to its stockholders and dissolved. Foremost-McKesson (P) brought this action seeking a declaratory judgment of its nonliability under the "short-swing" profit provisions of the Securities Exchange Act.

■ ISSUE

Is a beneficial owner accountable to the issuer for profits if it was not a beneficial owner before the purchase?

■ DECISION AND RATIONALE

(Judge Undisclosed) No. In a purchase-sale sequence, a beneficial owner must account for profits only if it was a beneficial owner before the purchase. Historically, § 16(b) applied to short-term purchase and sale sequences by a beneficial owner only if it had beneficial owner status before the purchase. No reason is presented why this trend should change. Congress had its reasons for setting ten percent as the threshold ownership level at which the potential for insider abuse became a concern. The Court may not impose liability on the basis of a purchase made when the percentage of ownership required for beneficial ownership had not been reached before the sale.

Analysis:

The Court cited Congress's distinction between short-term trading by "mere" stockholders and similar trading by directors and officers to support its determination that beneficial owners need only account for profits if their holdings are large enough to allow them access to corporate information. Congress noted that short-swing trading by an officer or a director is always suspect, whereas such activity by other stockholders becomes suspicious only when they own large quantities of the stock.

■ CASE VOCABULARY

BENEFICIAL OWNER: A corporate shareholder who has the power to buy or sell the shares, but who is not registered on the corporation's books as the owner.

DECLARATORY JUDGMENT: A binding adjudication that establishes the rights and other legal relations of the parties without providing for or ordering enforcement.

Kern County Land Co. v. Occidental Petroleum Corp.

(Newly Formed Company) v. *(Shareholder)*

411 U.S. 582, 93 S.Ct. 1736, 36 L.Ed.2d 503 (1973)

NO LIABILITY FOR SHORT–SWING PROFITS WITHOUT ACCESS TO INSIDE INFORMATION

■ **INSTANT FACTS** Kern County Land Co. (P) sued Occidental Petroleum Corp. (D) under § 16(b) to recover the profits Occidental (D) realized from its sale of Kern (P) stock, alleging that the execution of the Occidental–Tenneco option and the exchange of Kern (P) shares for Tenneco shares were both subject to § 16(b).

■ **BLACK LETTER RULE** A corporation is liable for short-swing profits only if the sale creating the profits resulted from inside information.

■ **PROCEDURAL BASIS**

On certiorari to review the Court of Appeals' judgment, reversing the trial court's judgment and granting summary judgment for the defendant.

■ **FACTS**

Kern County Land Corp. (Old Kern) attempted to merge with Occidental Petroleum Corp. (D). When the merger attempt was unsuccessful, Occidental (D) announced an offer to buy 500,000 shares of Old Kern common stock at the price of $83.50 per share, plus a brokerage fee of $1.50 per share. The offer was on a first-come, first-serve basis and expired on June 8, 1967. By May 10, 1967, 500,000 shares had been tendered, which exceeded ten percent of Old Kern's outstanding shares. On May 11, Old Kern offered another 500,000 shares. By the close of the offer on June 8, 1967, Occidental (D) owned 887,549 shares of Old Kern common stock. Old Kern's management attempted to frustrate Occidental's (D) takeover attempt by sending a letter to its stockholders cautioning them against tender offers from Occidental (D), indicating that those offers may not be the best available. The letters also indicated that the managers were engaged in merger discussions with several companies. Also, Old Kern's president sent a telegram to all stockholders advising them against tender. On May 19, 1967, Old Kern announced it had approved a merger with Tenneco, and that Tenneco would acquire the assets, property and goodwill of Old Kern through Kern County Land Company (New Kern) (P), a company Tenneco formed to receive Old Kern's assets and carry on its business. Old Kern's shareholders were to receive a share of Tenneco cumulative convertible stock in exchange for each share of Old Kern stock. Occidental (D) negotiated an agreement with Tenneco Corp., a subsidiary of Tenneco, whereby Occidental (D) granted the subsidiary the option to purchase all of Tenneco's preference stock to which Occidental was entitled in exchange for its Old Kern stock when the merger closed at the price of $105 per share. The premium to secure the option was $10 per share, totaling $8,866,230, and was due at the time the parties signed the agreement. If the option was exercised, the premium was to be applied to the purchase price. The option could not be exercised before December 9, 1967, which was six months and one day after Occidental's (D) tender offer expired. The parties executed the option on June 2, 1967, and the Old Kern–Tenneco merger closed on August 30, 1967. The subsidiary exercised its option on December 11, 1967, and Occidental's (D) profits on the transaction were $19,506,419.22. New Kern (P) sued, seeking to recover under § 16(b), which prohibits short-swing speculation by insiders.

■ ISSUE

Is exercising an option agreement given to a corporation for stock in a target corporation subject to § 16(b) if the corporation had no inside information?

■ DECISION AND RATIONALE

(Judge Undisclosed) No. A corporation is liable for short-swing profits only if the sale resulting in those profits resulted from access to inside information. Determining whether certain types of sales are subject to § 16(b), hinges upon whether the transaction serves as a vehicle for the types of evils Congress sought to prevent by enacting the statute, which are realizing short-swing profits based on access to inside information. It is unrealistic to assume that Occidental (D) had any access to inside information. Occidental (D) was engaged in a takeover attempt of Old Kern, which Old Kern was resisting. Old Kern communicated twice with its shareholders, advising them against tender offers from Occidental (D). The merger required the share exchange, and no money changed hands. This is not a "sale" by Occidental (D). Nor is the option granted to Tenneco a "sale." The option contains no potential for Occidental (D) to abuse inside information related to this transaction because it is highly unlikely Occidental (D) had access to inside information. Affirmed.

Analysis:

The court affirmed that a corporation might be liable under § 16(b) for short-swing profits if the profits resulted from access to inside information. The court focused on the purpose behind enacting § 16(b). After analyzing the Congressional intent, the court determined it would be unjust to apply the section's restrictions to situations that were not contemplated by the drafters. Although a transaction may fit the time frame set out by the statute, it did not involve the abuse of power the doctrine was designed to prevent.

■ CASE VOCABULARY

SHORT–SWING PROFITS: Profits made by a corporate insider on the purchase and sale (or sale and purchase) of company stock within a six-month period. These profits are subject to being returned to the company.

Kern County Land Co. v. Occidental Petroleum Corp. (Continued)

208   H I G H   C O U R T   C A S E   S U M M A R I E S

Waltuch v. Conticommodity Services, Inc.

(Employee) v. *(Employer)*

88 F.3d 87 (2d Cir. 1996)

A CORPORATION MUST INDEMNIFY CERTAIN INDIVIDUALS FOR LEGAL EXPENSES IF THEY ACTED IN GOOD FAITH

■ **INSTANT FACTS** Waltuch (P) sued his employer for indemnification of the legal expenses he incurred in defending himself from numerous civil lawsuits and an enforcement proceeding brought by the Commodity Futures Trading Commission.

■ **BLACK LETTER RULE** A corporation must indemnify its officers, directors, and employees against legal expenses related to the defense of any legal action brought against them by reason of their position or capacity, provided the individual acted in good faith.

■ **PROCEDURAL BASIS**

On appeal from the district court's judgment in favor of the defendant.

■ **FACTS**

Waltuch (P), the vice president and chief metals trader for Conticommodity Services, Inc. (D), traded silver for the firm's clients, as well as for himself. Silver prices climbed rapidly in late 1979 and early 1980, and several of Waltuch's (P) clients bought silver futures contracts. The silver price then dropped rapidly, causing the silver market to crash. Numerous lawsuits were filed against Waltuch (P) and Conticommodity (D) between 1981 and 1985, alleging fraud, market manipulation, and antitrust violations. All suits were eventually settled pursuant to a settlement agreement that provided that Conticommodity (D) would pay more than $35 million to the various plaintiffs. Although Waltuch (P) was dismissed from the suits and not required to contribute, he incurred $1.2 million in legal fees defending himself. Waltuch (P) was also the subject of an enforcement proceeding by Commodity Futures Trading Commission (CFTC), which settled when Waltuch (P) agreed to pay a $100,000 fine and accept a six-month ban on buying or selling futures contracts. Waltuch's (P) legal fees in defending against this action totaled $1 million. Waltuch (P) sued Conticommodity (D) for indemification for his legal fees.

■ **ISSUE**

Must a corporation indemnify its employees against legal expenses related to the defense of any action brought against them by reason of their position or capacity, even if they did not act completely in good faith?

■ **DECISION AND RATIONALE**

(Judge Undisclosed) No. Corporations are required to indemnify its officers, directors, and employees against legal expenses related to the defense of any legal action brought against them by reason of their position or capacity, only if the individual seeking indemnification acted in good faith. A corporation may choose to provide its employees with additional indemnification rights and other forms of indemnification, but it is not required to do so.

Analysis:

The purpose behind the good-faith requirement for indemnification is that a blanket requirement of indemnification for all employees against lawsuits related their performance of their job duties would encourage large-scale abuse by employees, who would know that their only penance might be termination. On the other hand, the legislature determined that it was important to require employers to provide indemnification of some kind for their employees, especially their directors, for lawsuits brought against them for acts related to the performance of their job duties. The court recognized that some positions, by virtue of their high-profile status and high impact-level leave the individual open to lawsuits anytime a client becomes unhappy. If corporations did not indemnify its employees, directors or officers in these types of actions, no one would be willing to accept positions with great responsibility, knowing it may leave them wide open to expensive lawsuits.

■ CASE VOCABULARY

INDEMNITY: A duty to make good any loss, damage, or liability incurred by another.

Citadel Holding Corp. v. Roven

(*Employer*) v. (*Director*)
603 A.2d 818 (Del. 1992)

DIRECTORS MAY RECEIVE AN ADVANCE ON INDEMNIFICATION

■ **INSTANT FACTS** Roven (P), a former director of Citadel Holding Corp. (D), sued Citadel (D) for indemnification of sums he paid to defend a federal court action Citadel (D) brought against him.

■ **BLACK LETTER RULE** A corporation may advance a director the costs of defending a lawsuit.

■ **PROCEDURAL BASIS**

On appeal from the lower court's decision awarding damages to the plaintiff.

■ **FACTS**

Citadel Holding Corp. (D) was a savings and loan company. Roven (P), a director of the company from July 1985 to July 1988, owned approximately 9.8 percent of Citadel's (D) common stock. Citadel (D) and Roven (P) entered into an indemnity agreement in May 1987, which included Citadel's (D) general obligation to indemnify Roven (P) against any threatened or actual suit or proceeding, whether civil, criminal, administrative, or investigative, to which he is a party. The agreement placed several limitations on the general indemnity clause, including actions brought pursuant to § 16(b) of the Securities Exchange Act. The agreement also provides that Roven (P) may require Citadel (D) to advance the costs of defending certain lawsuits, but the director must repay advances if he was not entitled to indemnification. Citadel (D) sued Roven (P), alleging he violated § 16(b) by purchasing options to buy Citadel (D) stock while he was a director. Roven (P) contested the claim that his option purchases violated § 16(b) and sued to obtain advances under the indemnification agreement for his legal fees.

■ **ISSUE**

Is an employee party to an indemnity agreement with his or her employer entitled to an advance for costs related to a federal action the employer brought against him?

■ **DECISION AND RATIONALE**

(Judge Undisclosed) Yes. A corporation may advance to a director the costs of defending a lawsuit. Although the law makes this authority permissive, the parties' agreement makes it mandatory. The language clearly states that Citadel (D) *shall* pay costs and expenses incurred in defending "any action, suit, proceeding or investigation."

Analysis:

The court noted that indemnity is usually subject to a reasonableness requirement. A court will not expect an employer to pay frivolous legal expenses or legal expenses not related to the agent's role with the company. In any event, a corporation is unlikely to volunteer to pay unreasonable legal fees.

■ CASE VOCABULARY

INDEMNIFICATION: The action of compensating for loss or damage sustained.

INDEMNITY CONTRACT: A contract by which the promisor agrees to reimburse a promisee for some loss irrespective of a third person's liability.

CHAPTER SIX

Problems of Control

Levin v. Metro–Goldwyn–Mayer, Inc.

Instant Facts: Levin and five other shareholders (P) of Metro–Goldwyn–Mayer, Inc. (D) brought an action against its directors, arguing the management was using illegal and unfair methods of communicating with stockholders and had forced the corporation to bear the expenses of a proxy solicitation.

Black Letter Rule: Incumbent management may make reasonable use of corporate assets to inform shareholders of its position in a proxy contest involving corporate policy issues.

Rosenfeld v. Fairchild Engine & Airplane Corp.

Instant Facts: Stockholders brought a derivative action arising out of money paid by the corporation to defray rival factions' expenses in a proxy fight.

Black Letter Rule: Absent a claim that the expenses were unwarranted, excessive, or otherwise improper, a corporation may reimburse factions for costs associated with a proxy fight involving a policy contest, but not one involving a personal power contest.

J.I. Case Co. v. Borak

Instant Facts: Borak (P) and other shareholders found that the proxy materials used by J. I. Case Co. (D) used their names as part of the company's efforts to obtain approval of a merger with American Tractor Corporation, and Borak (P) sued to have the merger declared void.

Black Letter Rule: It is unlawful to solicit a proxy or consent authorization using false and misleading statements, and, in such event, a court may enforce a private right of action for rescission or damages.

Mills v. Electric Auto–Lite Co.

Instant Facts: The plaintiffs brought suit to undo a merger because the proxy materials submitted to the shareholders before the merger's vote failed to disclose that the board members endorsing the merger were nominees of the targeting company who had held a majority interest in the targeted company years before the merger was proposed.

Black Letter Rule: To establish a cause of action under § 14 of the Securities Exchange Act, a plaintiff need show only the misstatement's or omission's materiality and its ability to influence a shareholder's vote.

Seinfeld v. Bartz

Instant Facts: Cisco Systems, Inc. (D) issued proxy statements that failed to value the stock options granted its directors as part of their compensation.

Black Letter Rule: A company's failure to disclose in its proxy statements the value of the stock options granted to its directors does not constitute a materially false and misleading statement under Rule 14a–9 of the SEC.

Lovenheim v. Iroquois Brands, Ltd.

Instant Facts: Lovenheim (P) asked to have information about a resolution he proposed to make at an upcoming shareholders' meeting included in the company's proxy materials, but the company refused.

Black Letter Rule: Under § 14(a) of the Securities Exchange Act, shareholders may include in the company's proxy statements certain materials that have limited, if any, economic impact on the company as long as they are "otherwise significantly related" to the issuer's business.

The New York City Employees' Retirement Sys. v. Dole Food Co., Inc.

Instant Facts: A public pension fund sought permission from Dole Food Co., Inc. (D) to include information on a proposal to establish a committee to investigate current federal health insurance proposals, but Dole (D) refused the request.

Black Letter Rule: A shareholder's proposal to form a committee to evaluate health insurance proposals before Congress does not relate to the company's ordinary business operations, but the corporation must include the proposal's information in its proxy statements.

Austin v. Consolidated Edison Co. of N.Y., Inc.

Instant Facts: The issuing company's shareholders sought to force Consolidated Edison Co. of N.Y., Inc. (D) to include information in its annual meeting proxy materials about a proposal that would allow employees to retire after thirty years' service regardless of their age.

Black Letter Rule: Shareholders may not require a corporation to include materials concerning a stockholder proposal supporting an employee's right to retire with full pension benefits with thirty years' service regardless of their age, because the proposal concerns "ordinary business operations."

Crane Co. v. Anaconda Co.

Instant Facts: Crane Company (P) sought to acquire twenty percent of Anaconda Company's (D) shares and asked to have access to Anaconda's (D) shareholder list to distribute information on the tender offer directly to Anaconda's (D) shareholders.

Black Letter Rule: A corporation must grant a shareholder who wants to discuss a tender offer's terms directly with the corporation's shareholders access to the shareholder list, unless the corporation can establish a wrongful purpose.

State ex rel. Pillsbury v. Honeywell, Inc.

Instant Facts: Pillsbury (P) purchased Honeywell, Inc. (D) stock in order to bring suit to compel production of the defendant's corporate books and records.

Black Letter Rule: A stockholder who purchased stock for the sole purpose of bringing suit to compel production of corporate books and records, who was motivated by his belief that the corporation should not be manufacturing ammunition to be used in the Vietnam War, and who had no concern for the corporation's economic well being, cannot compel production of the corporation's shareholder lists or business records.

Sadler v. NCR Corp.

Instant Facts: Shareholders brought an action against a corporation to obtain its shareholder list and to demand the corporation create a list of nonobjecting beneficial owners.

Black Letter Rule: A New York law entitling resident shareholders to shareholder lists and lists of nonobjecting beneficial owners does not subject the corporation to inconsistent regulation prohibited by the commerce clause nor discriminate against or burden interstate commerce.

Stroh v. Blackhawk Holding Corp.

Instant Facts: Stroh (P) purchased shares of Blackhawk Holding Corp.'s Class B stock, which permitted voting rights in corporate matters, but did not receive dividends or other corporate assets.

Black Letter Rule: A corporation's shares of class B stock, which permit voting rights, are valid shares of stock, notwithstanding the fact that the stock is not entitled to dividends.

Wisconsin Inv. Bd. v. Peerless Sys. Corp.

Instant Facts: Peerless Systems Corp. (D) sought shareholder approval of three measures at its annual meeting, and the board had hoped all resolutions would pass, but when the votes cast would have defeated the measure addressing stock options, the board adjourned the meeting and continued the proposal's vote to another day.

Black Letter Rule: If a board takes an action designed to "interfere with or impede exercise of the shareholder franchise," the action is not protected under the business judgment rule without a compelling justification for the board's actions.

Ringling Bros.–Barnum & Bailey Combined Shows v. Ringling

Instant Facts: Edith Ringling (P) agreed to vote her stock in agreement with Haley (D), but then refused to do so.

Black Letter Rule: A shareholder may agree with another shareholder to vote his or her stock in a particular way.

McQuade v. Stoneham

Instant Facts: McQuade (P), who was employed as corporate treasurer pursuant to a shareholder's agreement, was discharged.

Black Letter Rule: A shareholder agreement may not control a board of directors' exercise of judgment.

Clark v. Dodge

Instant Facts: Clark (P), who was employed as treasurer and general manager of a corporation pursuant to a shareholder's agreement, was discharged.

Black Letter Rule: A shareholder agreement regarding employment of certain individuals as officers is enforceable if the directors are the sole shareholders.

Galler v. Galler

Instant Facts: Isadore Galler (D) entered into a shareholders' agreement with his brother, Benjamin, and later refused to abide by the agreement.

Black Letter Rule: Shareholder agreements that relate to the management of a close corporation will be upheld, even if the agreements violate corporate norms.

Ramos v. Estrada

Instant Facts: Estrada (D) did not vote her stock in accordance with a shareholders' agreement, and Ramos (P) brought suit for breach of contract.

Black Letter Rule: Voting agreements between two or more shareholders of a corporation are enforceable, even if the corporation does not qualify as a close corporation.

Wilkes v. Springside Nursing Home, Inc.

Instant Facts: Wilkes (P), who formed a real estate investment business with three other men who shared equally in the business, created disharmony and was fired when he struck a particularly hard bargain with one of the other shareholders in the sale of some corporate property.

Black Letter Rule: Majority shareholders acting to "freeze out" a minority shareholder by terminating his employment without a valid business purpose have breached their duty to act as fiduciaries.

Ingle v. Glamore Motor Sales, Inc.

Instant Facts: Ingle (P) was a sales manager at and a shareholder of Glamore Motor Sales, Inc., (D), and when the company terminated his employment, his shares were bought back under a shareholders' agreement.

Black Letter Rule: If a shareholders' agreement provides for the right to repurchase shares upon the termination of a shareholder's employment with the issuing company, the employment is treated as employment at will and the shareholder has no claim for damages upon termination.

Sugarman v. Sugarman

Instant Facts: Descendants of a corporation's original founders filed a claim for breach of fiduciary duty after the majority shareholder exercised his position to direct profits to himself and his father rather than pay dividends or employ other family members, resulting in a freeze-out.

Black Letter Rule: If a controlling shareholder uses corporate assets for his own personal benefit, an offer to purchase minority shareholders' stock at an inadequate price will be viewed as part of a plan to freeze-out the minority shareholders.

Smith v. Atlantic Props., Inc.

Instant Facts: Wolfson (D), who owned part of a corporation that purchased property for investment, blocked dividend payments to other shareholders, leading to substantial IRS penalties and limiting the others' returns from their investments.

Black Letter Rule: A minority shareholder may abuse his position by using measures designed to safeguard his position in a manner that fails to take into consideration his duty to act in the "utmost good faith and loyalty" toward the company and his fellow shareholders.

Jordan v. Duff & Phelps, Inc.

Instant Facts: Jordan (P), an employee of and stockholder in Duff & Phelps, Inc. (D), left the closely-held company and cashed in his stock according to his stockholder agreement; a pending sale of the defendant firm would have made his stock far more valuable.

Black Letter Rule: If a closely-held company withholds from an employee-stockholder material information about possible increases in stock value in breach of its fiduciary duty, the employee-stockholder may be entitled to damages if he or she can show that the nondisclosure caused the employee-stockholder to act to his or her financial detriment.

Alaska Plastics, Inc. v. Coppock

Instant Facts: Muir (P) received half of her husband's shares in Alaska Plastics, Inc. (D) in a divorce; the company offered to buy her shares at a price Muir (P) believed to be too low.

Black Letter Rule: A shareholder may require a corporation to repurchase its own shares upon the company's breach of fiduciary duty, but the remedy should be less than liquidation, if possible, and a fair price may be less than the appraised value.

Pedro v. Pedro

Instant Facts: Members of a family-run business terminated one of the shareholder's employment when he refused to ignore a substantial accounting discrepancy.

Black Letter Rule: A shareholder-employee of a closely held corporation, who was fired by other shareholders in a breach of fiduciary duty, is entitled to damages equal to the total of the difference between his stock's fair value and any lesser amount required by a stock retirement agreement, in addition to the damages arising from his loss of life-time employment.

Stuparich v. Harbor Furniture Mfg., Inc.

Instant Facts: Stuparich (P) and Tuttleton (P), minority shareholders in Harbor Furniture Mfg., Inc. (D), received regular dividends, but wanted to be bought out because they were not on good terms with the other shareholders and their family members.

Black Letter Rule: A court will not order dissolution of a close corporation if the plaintiffs fail to show the dissolution was reasonably necessary to protect their rights.

Frandsen v. Jensen–Sundquist Agency, Inc.

Instant Facts: The majority block of shares in Jensen–Sundquist Agency, Inc. (D) was owned by a group of individuals that entered into a shareholders' agreement providing them with protection in the event of a sale of the corporation's stock, and when the company attempted to transfer its primary asset, one of the shareholders demanded to exercise his right of first refusal.

Black Letter Rule: A minority shareholder's right of first refusal that is triggered by the majority shareholders' sale of their stock does not apply to a transaction in which an acquiring entity purchases the corporation's principal asset, after which the corporation is liquidated.

Zetlin v. Hanson Holdings, Inc.

Instant Facts: Zetlin (P) owned two percent of Gable Industries when Hanson Holdings, Inc. (D) and Sylvestri (D), which owned a controlling interest in Gable Industries, sold their shares to Flintkote Co. for $15 per share at a time the common stock was trading at $7.38 per share.

Black Letter Rule: In the absence of an allegation that a shareholder is looting corporate assets or has committed fraud or other acts of bad faith, a shareholder may obtain a premium price for the sale of a controlling block of shares.

Perlman v. Feldmann

Instant Facts: Feldmann (D), a majority shareholder in a steel mill business, sold a controlling interest in the mill to a company that required steel in the fabrication of its products, and the minority shareholders brought a derivative action against Feldmann (D) to recover the amounts he received in excess of the shares' market price.

Black Letter Rule: A shareholder with a controlling interest who transfers his or her shares is accountable to the minority shareholders for the amount in excess of the market price if the premium is attributable to the sale of a corporate asset.

Essex Universal Corp. v. Yates

Instant Facts: Yates (D) agreed to sell a controlling block of shares in Republic Pictures to Essex Universal Corp. (P), and the sale agreement required Yates (D) to deliver a board of directors filled with members nominated by Essex Universal (P).

Black Letter Rule: If the transfer of shares is sufficient to constitute the transfer of a controlling interest, a seller may lawfully agree to assist the buyer in installing a favorable board of directors.

Levin v. Metro–Goldwyn–Mayer, Inc.

(MGM Shareholder) v. *(Movie Studio)*

264 F.Supp. 797 (S.D.N.Y. 1967)

CORPORATE MANAGEMENT MAY USE CORPORATE ASSETS TO PROVIDE SHAREHOLDERS WITH INFORMATION THAT IS RELEVANT TO A VOTE

WE'LL SHOW THEM WHO GETS TO SPEND MONEY AROUND HERE! WE'RE SPONSORING THIS CAMPAIGN AGAINST THEIR PROXY FIGHT

■ **INSTANT FACTS** Levin and five other shareholders (P) of Metro–Goldwyn–Mayer, Inc. (D) brought an action against its directors, arguing the management was using illegal and unfair methods of communicating with stockholders and had forced the corporation to bear the expenses of a proxy solicitation.

■ **BLACK LETTER RULE** Incumbent management may make reasonable use of corporate assets to inform shareholders of its position in a proxy contest involving corporate policy issues.

■ **PROCEDURAL BASIS**

On hearing of a motion for a preliminary injunction.

■ **FACTS**

Six stockholders (P) filed suit against Metro–Goldwyn–Mayer, Inc. (MGM) and five of its board members (the O'Brien Group) (D) who are part of the company's management and are officers or members of its executive committee. Levin (P) was a director who owned large blocks of MGM's (D) common stock. Levin (P) and other shareholders (P) (the Levin Group) were battling for control of MGM (D) against the O'Brien Group (D). Each group intended to nominate its slate of candidates for directors at the MGM (D) annual stockholders' meeting. Each group had been soliciting proxies. The plaintiffs argued that the defendants used MGM (D) assets to pay for their proxy solicitation and were relying on MGM's (D) good will and business contacts to secure support for their candidates. The plaintiffs sought an injunction against the defendants, requiring them to assume financial responsibility for their campaign and to compensate MGM (D) for expenses in the amount of $2,500,000. The plaintiffs argued that the injunction was necessary to prevent the unlawful use of MGM's (D) resources, to prevent the O'Brien Group's (D) outside consultants from billing MGM (D) for their services, and to prevent special counsel from being compensated by MGM (D) instead of the O'Brien Group (D).

■ **ISSUE**

May an incumbent board and management use corporate funds to finance the expenses associated with providing shareholders with information about their position?

■ **DECISION AND RATIONALE**

(Ryan, J.) Yes. The court must weigh the merits of the plaintiff's motion against MGM's (D) history. The studio is a financial giant, and the defendants note their success directing the studio's business activities. However, whether the current management should continue to lead the company is a decision that only the stockholders can make. In order to make an informed judgment, the stockholders need information from those soliciting their proxies. A court's injunction should not influence a stockholder's decision as to which faction should receive its proxy by limiting which factions can solicit the proxy. The court must determine whether the parties have used illegal or unfair advantage to communicate with shareholders. The proxy statement states that MGM (D) is bearing all costs associated with management's solicitation and discloses the costs paid to outside consultants. The management's costs do not appear excessive, unfair or illegal. Motion denied.

Analysis:

A corporation depends on its officers' and managers' business sense to run the day-to-day business, but the corporation calls on its shareholders to cast votes that have long-range effects on the company's operations. In this case, the proxy contest centered on control issues, and the court found that the expenses associated with ensuring that the shareholders were informed were reasonable corporate expenses. In *Palumbo v. Deposit Bank*, 758 F.2d 113 (3d Cir. 1985), the matter involved a proxy contest concerning a merger, another corporate policy matter. *Palumbo* found that the corporation should reimburse the expenses in the absence of any arguments that the amounts spent were unreasonable.

■ CASE VOCABULARY

PROXY: One who is authorized to act as a substitute for another; especially, in corporate law, a person who is authorized to vote another's stock shares.

PROXY CONTEST: A struggle between two corporate factions to obtain the votes of uncommitted shareholders. A proxy contest usually occurs when a group of dissident shareholders mounts a battle against the corporation's managers.

Rosenfeld v. Fairchild Engine & Airplane Corp.

(Shareholder) v. *(Corporation)*

309 N.Y. 168, 128 N.E.2d 291 (1955)

ABSENT A CLAIM THAT PROXY FIGHT EXPENSES WERE EXCESSIVE, A COMPANY MAY REIMBURSE THE PARTIES FOR THEIR COSTS

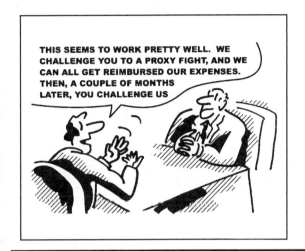

■ **INSTANT FACTS** Stockholders brought a derivative action arising out of money paid by the corporation to defray rival factions' expenses in a proxy fight.

■ **BLACK LETTER RULE** Absent a claim that the expenses were unwarranted, excessive, or otherwise improper, a corporation may reimburse factions for costs associated with a proxy fight involving a policy contest, but not one involving a personal power contest.

■ **PROCEDURAL BASIS**

On appeal from a judgment affirming a dismissal of the plaintiffs' complaint.

■ **FACTS**

Rosenfeld (P), an attorney who owned twenty-five percent of Fairchild Engine & Airplane Corp.'s (D) shares, sued to have $261,522 returned to the corporation. The corporation had paid the funds to reimburse both sides' expenses in a proxy contest. During the proxy fight, the previous board had spent $106,000 in an effort to retain their power. When the new board took over, they paid an additional $28,000 to the former board for their remaining expenses. The corporation also paid the prevailing group $127,000 for their expenses. The company's stockholders ratified the payments.

■ **ISSUE**

Following a proxy fight for control of a company, may a board authorize the reimbursement of fair and reasonable expenses incurred by both the winner and loser?

■ **DECISION AND RATIONALE**

(Froessel, J.) Yes. In order to assure that shareholders have access to the information needed to make an informed decision, proponents of both sides need to know that the company will reimburse them for their expenses. Without this knowledge, the directors may be unable to fight off challenges from anyone with sufficient funds to wage a proxy fight, which may damage the corporation. As long as the factions incurred the expenses in good faith in a contest over policy, the company may reimburse the parties for reasonable and proper expenses to solicit proxies and to defend their corporate policies. However, directors may not use unlimited corporate assets. Also, a court may disallow any expenditure that advances personal power, is against the stockholders' or the corporation's interests, or is excessive. Affirmed.

■ **DISSENT**

(Van Voorhis, J.) The stockholders did not pass any resolutions concerning paying fees to the management group that had been retained for more than the shareholders' education. Portions of the funds were spent on unnecessary entertainment, public relations and travel expenses. The court did not require the directors to justify these expenses. The majority argues that the corporation should reimburse the incumbent directors because the shareholders voted to reimburse the challenging group, but such reimbursement is not required. The shareholders did not consider reimbursing the incumbents, because they wanted to remove them because of their history of financial abuse. The management had a duty to acquaint stockholders with facts about the corporation's management, but there is a distinction between reimbursing factions for the cost of maintaining control and reimbursing them for the costs of educating the shareholders in policy matters. It can be difficult to determine the true motive for spending. Here, the proxy fight centered on pension benefits paid to a former officer and director. The challenging group argues that by reimbursing the former directors, the directors continue to reap a benefit from their misdeeds.

Analysis:

By contrast, the plaintiff in *Grodetsky v. McCrory Corp.*, 267 N.Y.S.2d 356 (1966), brought an action for reimbursement of $1,750,000 for expenses claimed to have been incurred in defeating a proposed business transaction that was alleged to pose a loss of $35 million to the corporation. McCrory Corp. had agreed to sell some of its stock. One of McCrory's large lessors heard of the proposed transaction and tried to block it, fearing it would affect McCrory's ability to fulfill its obligations under its leases. When the measure was defeated, the lessor submitted a bill to McCrory for his work in defeating the measure. The court refused to find any legitimacy in the bill, holding that the charges were incurred for the lessor's benefit.

■ CASE VOCABULARY

SOLICITATION: A request for a proxy; a request to execute, not execute, or revoke a proxy; the furnishing of a form of proxy; or any other communication to security holders under circumstances reasonably calculated to result in the procurement, withholding, or revocation of a proxy.

J.I. Case Co. v. Borak

(Corporation) v. *(Shareholder)*

377 U.S. 426, 84 S.Ct. 1555, 12 L.Ed.2d 423 (1964)

PROXY MATERIALS CONTAINING FALSE AND MISLEADING STATEMENTS GIVES RISE TO A PRIVATE RIGHT OF ACTION

■ **INSTANT FACTS** Borak (P) and other shareholders found that the proxy materials used by J. I. Case Co. (D) used their names as part of the company's efforts to obtain approval of a merger with American Tractor Corporation, and Borak (P) sued to have the merger declared void.

■ **BLACK LETTER RULE** It is unlawful to solicit a proxy or consent authorization using false and misleading statements, and, in such event, a court may enforce a private right of action for rescission or damages.

■ **PROCEDURAL BASIS**

On appeal to the U.S. Supreme Court following a decision by the Court of Appeals reversing the trial court's judgment in favor of the defendant.

■ **FACTS**

Borak (P) and other shareholders (P) brought this action alleging that the merger between Case (D) and American Tractor Corporation (ATC) was approved through false proxy statements that violated § 14(a) of the Securities Exchange Act. Borak (P) argued that the proposed merger breached the directors' fiduciary duties to its shareholders and constituted self-dealing. Borak (P) and the other plaintiffs insisted that Case (D) used their names in violation of SEC procedures and alleged that the merger would not have been approved without the false statements. Borak (P) seeks to have the merger declared void.

■ **ISSUE**

Does § 27 of the Securities Exchange Act provide a federal cause of action for rescission or damages to a corporate stockholder if approval of a corporate merger was obtained through the use of a proxy statement containing false and misleading statements?

■ **DECISION AND RATIONALE**

Yes. The defendants argue that the Securities Exchange Act (the Act) does not reference a "private right of action" and does not provide a right to seek injunctive relief. The defendants, claiming that a merger can be reversed only on proof of fraud or a showing that the merger was not beneficial, also maintain that the proxy materials resolve neither issue. However, the proxy materials' relevance is a question for the trial judge. The Act makes it unlawful for any person to solicit proxies in violation of the rules governing proxies. While the Act does not mention the phrase "private right of action," the Act's protections flow to stockholders, and it would follow that the Act would allow judicial relief to enforce the protection. Injury to a stockholder is caused by injury to the corporation, and the damage results from deceit against shareholders. Finding that derivative claims are not within the actions pondered by § 14 would foreclose private relief. The SEC has neither time nor resources to ensure every proxy statement is accurate. Many misstatements are not apparent until stockholders approve the matter. Therefore, courts must provide remedies as needed to fulfill the Act's purpose, and the remedies need not be restricted to prospective relief. Affirmed.

Analysis:

Whether a statute provides a private remedy is frequently at issue because, although some statutes may contain language discussing a private cause of action, the law is often silent. In *Cort v. Ash,* 422 U.S. 66, 95 S. Ct. 2080, 45 L.Ed.2d 26 (1975), the Supreme Court provided that a court should consider the following four factors in determining whether or not a statute should be read as containing a private right of action: "First, is the plaintiff one of the class for whose especial benefit the statute was enacted ...? Second, is there any indication of legislative intent, explicit or implicit, either to create such a remedy or to deny one? Third, is it consistent with the underlying purposes of the legislative scheme to imply such a remedy for the plaintiff? And finally, is the cause of action one traditionally relegated to state law, in an area basically the concern of the States, so that it would be inappropriate to infer a cause of action based solely on federal law?" *Id.,* 422 U.S. at 77 (citations omitted). The application of the *Cort* factors to this case would probably reach the same result.

Mills v. Electric Auto–Lite Co.

(Shareholders) v. *(Corporation)*

396 U.S. 375, 90 S.Ct. 616, 24 L.Ed.2d 593 (1970)

A PLAINTIFF MUST SHOW MATERIALITY AND RELATIONSHIP TO ESTABLISH A CLAIM FOR A MISSTATEMENT OR OMISSION UNDER § 14

■ **INSTANT FACTS** The plaintiffs brought suit to undo a merger because the proxy materials submitted to the shareholders before the merger's vote failed to disclose that the board members endorsing the merger were nominees of the targeting company who had held a majority interest in the targeted company years before the merger was proposed.

■ **BLACK LETTER RULE** To establish a cause of action under § 14 of the Securities Exchange Act, a plaintiff need show only the misstatement's or omission's materiality and its ability to influence a shareholder's vote.

■ PROCEDURAL BASIS

On appeal from a motion for summary judgment finding the omission constituted a violation of § 14 of the Securities Exchange Act.

■ FACTS

The plaintiffs held shares in Electric Auto–Lite Company (D) before its merger with Mergenthaler Linotype Co. The day before the shareholders' meeting, at which the merger vote was to occur, the plaintiffs filed suit seeking an injunction prohibiting Electric Auto–Lite (D) from casting any votes it obtained through misleading proxy statements. The plaintiffs failed to ask for a temporary restraining order, so the vote proceeded and the shareholders approved the merger. The plaintiffs brought this action to have the merger set aside, alleging that the proxy statement was misleading and in violation of § 14 of the Securities Exchange Act (the Act). The plaintiffs argued that Mergenthaler owned enough Electric Auto–Lite (D) shares that it had control of the company two years before the merger. The board's merger recommendation failed to inform the shareholders that Mergenthaler had nominated all eleven directors. The plaintiffs argued that this omission gave rise to a derivative cause of action and a breach of fiduciary duty claim. Although the trial court held that the proxy statement's defect was material, the court found it needed a hearing to determine whether there was a causal connection between the misstatement and the merger. For the merger to pass, Mergenthaler, which owned fifty-four percent of the shares, still needed enough shares to obtain two-third of the votes. In the end, more than eighty percent of the shares voted for the merger, with 317,000 votes in favor of the merger coming from minority shareholders. The trial court concluded that those numbers were sufficient to find a causal relationship between the omission and the result. The appellate court, disagreeing with the trial court's conclusion that the plaintiff had established a relationship between the omission and the merger's approval, held that as long as minority shareholders had been treated fairly, the court must conclude that the merger would have been approved, even with the omitted disclosure. The plaintiffs appealed.

■ ISSUE

If a proxy fails to disclose a relationship between the target company and the surviving company, must the plaintiff also show that the omitted facts changed the vote's outcome in order to state a cause of action for a violation of the Securities Exchange Act?

■ DECISION AND RATIONALE

No. On appeal, the plaintiff argues that the appellate court's decision frustrates the Act's policy. In *J. I. Case Co. v. Borak*, 377 U.S. 426 (1964), the court stressed the congressional belief that a shareholder's right to vote is an important right that could be exercised only when the shareholder is provided with accurate information. In *Borak*, the court declined to discuss the relationship between the proxy materials and the merger's approval; but here, that is the focus. If a misstatement or omission is deemed material, it follows that the omission would have had an impact on the ultimate vote. A shareholder cannot seek redress for every trivial defect, but impact on the ultimate vote is not needed; it is sufficient that the misstatement or omission is material. However, the Act does not require a court to unscramble a merger, and damages should be awarded only if proven. Court of Appeals' judgment vacated; case remanded.

Analysis:

Mills provides that any material misstatement or omission in a company's proxy materials is presumed to have had an effect on the shareholders' voting. However, the case still requires that the parties seeking relief must prove the extent to which they were damaged by the misstatement or omission. In *ONBANCorp, Inc. v. Holtzman*, 956 F. Supp. 250 (N.D.N.Y. 1997), the court declined to extend *Mills* to support the conclusion that shareholder damage naturally follows from any material misstatement or omission.

■ CASE VOCABULARY

INTERLOCUTORY JUDGMENT: An intermediate judgment that determines a preliminary or subordinate point or plea but does not finally decide the case.

MATERIAL: Of such a nature that knowledge of the item would affect a person's decision-making; significant; essential.

Seinfeld v. Bartz

(Parties not identified)

2002 WL 243597 (N.D. Cal. 2002)

A PROXY STATEMENT'S OMISSION OR MISSTATEMENT OF THE VALUE OF A DIRECTOR'S STOCK OPTIONS IS NOT MATERIAL

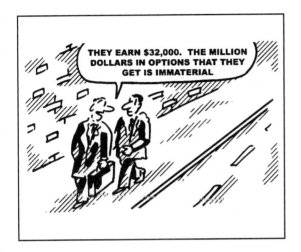

■ **INSTANT FACTS** Cisco Systems, Inc. (D) issued proxy statements that failed to value the stock options granted its directors as part of their compensation.

■ **BLACK LETTER RULE** A company's failure to disclose in its proxy statements the value of the stock options granted to its directors does not constitute a materially false and misleading statement under Rule 14a–9 of the SEC.

■ **PROCEDURAL BASIS**

Not stated.

■ **FACTS**

The plaintiff, a shareholder in Cisco Systems, Inc. (D), sued Cisco and its ten directors in a derivative action. An amendment to Cisco's (D) Automatic Option Grant Program increased stock options to new outside directors from 20,000 to 30,000 and increased annual options granted for each returning outside director from 10,000 to 15,000. The plaintiff contended that the proxy soliciting approval of the amendment was negligently prepared. The disputed statement mentioned the salary for each outside director, stated that the directors would receive periodic option grants under the company's Automatic Option Grant Program and Discretionary Option Grant Program, and gave further information on both programs. However, Cisco (D) did not value the options under the Black–Scholes option-pricing model, which would have calculated the option values at $369,500 for 1998 and $1,020,600 for 1999. Furthermore, Cisco (D) noted that it expected no value to be realized from the options.

■ **ISSUE**

Does a company's failure to attribute in its proxy statements the value of stock options granted to its directors constitute a materially false and misleading statement under Rule 14a–9 of the SEC?

■ **DECISION AND RATIONALE**

(Henderson, J.) No. The plaintiff here contends that the failure to place a value on the stock options granted to Cisco's (D) directors renders the company's proxy statements materially false and misleading. Under Rule 14a–9 of the SEC, a proxy solicitation cannot include a statement that is a false or misleading statement of material fact or that omits a fact that results in some portion of the statement being false or misleading. A fact is deemed material if a "reasonable shareholder would consider it important in deciding how to vote." It is not important whether the fact would have caused a shareholder to change or question his vote. A reasonable investor need only have viewed the fact as significantly altering the "total mix" of information at his disposal. While the plaintiff contends that the Black–Scholes values for the options are material, four other courts have rejected similar contentions under state law, using a standard similar to the federal standard. *Custom Chrome, Inc. v. Comm'r of*

Internal Revenue accepted Black–Scholes as a reliable method of valuing options, but those options were part of a loan transaction, not a compensation package. Complaint dismissed.

Analysis:

Depending on the margin between an option's buy-in price and the shares' market price, stock options can provide substantial additional income for the recipient. In this case, the directors' cost to exercise their options must have been minimal in relationship to the share's market price in order for the plaintiff to be upset that a value would not be placed on the options. In a volatile market, the shares' costs can fluctuate drastically and a price that started as a bargain may change so that exercising the option would be expensive rather than profitable. Therefore, although a company may place a value on an option today, by the time the information is delivered to the shareholders, the information may be incorrect.

■ CASE VOCABULARY

STOCK OPTION: An option that allows a corporate employee to buy shares of corporate stock at a fixed price or within a fixed period. Such an option is usually granted as a form of compensation and can qualify for special tax treatment under the Internal Revenue Code.

Lovenheim v. Iroquois Brands, Ltd.

(*Shareholder*) v. (*Corporation*)

618 F.Supp. 554 (D.D.C. 1985)

SHAREHOLDERS MAY INCLUDE SIGNIFICANTLY RELATED MATERIALS WITH A COMPANY'S PROXY STATEMENTS

AND I'M SAYING IT **IS** A POLICY DECISION WHETHER OR NOT YOU USE BALLPOINT OR FOUNTAIN PENS!

■ **INSTANT FACTS** Lovenheim (P) asked to have information about a resolution he proposed to make at an upcoming shareholders' meeting included in the company's proxy materials, but the company refused.

■ **BLACK LETTER RULE** Under § 14(a) of the Securities Exchange Act, shareholders may include in the company's proxy statements certain materials that have limited, if any, economic impact on the company as long as they are "otherwise significantly related" to the issuer's business.

■ **PROCEDURAL BASIS**

On motion for injunctive relief.

■ **FACTS**

Lovenheim (P), who owned 200 shares of common stock in Iroquois Brands, Ltd. (D), sought to have a statement concerning the force-feeding of geese as part of pâté de fois gras production included in Iroquois' (D) proxy materials. Lovenheim (P) considered the practice offensive, and Iroquois (D) imported pâté de fois gras in its business. Lovenheim (P) wanted to propose a resolution studying the French production of pâté de fois gras and whether it constituted animal cruelty. He claimed he had a right under § 14(a) of the Securities Exchange Act (the Act) to demand that information about his proposal be included in Iroquois' (D) proxy materials. (Pursuant to § 14(a), a stockholder may notify an issuer of his intention to present a proposal for action at a future meeting and allow the shareholder to include a statement of not more than 500 words in support of the proposal.) Iroquois (D) refused Lovenheim's (P) request under the Act's exception that permits a company to disallow shareholder's information if it relates to operations that constitute less than five percent of the issuer's net earnings or gross sales and is not otherwise significant.

■ **ISSUE**

May an issuer refuse to include in its proxy materials a shareholder's information on a proposed resolution if the issuer decides the materials relate to a subject that is not economically significant to the company?

■ **DECISION AND RATIONALE**

(Judge Undisclosed) No. Whether Lovenheim (P) prevails depends on the whether the proposed information falls within the exceptions to Rule 14a–8. Iroquois (D) argues that because its annual revenues are $141 million and its sales from pâté de fois gras account for only $79,000 and resulted in a loss to the company of $3,121, the item is not a significant part of its sales. Although Lovenheim (P) does not argue the pâté sales' economic significance, he contends that the treatment of the geese is still "otherwise significantly related to the issuer's business." By using the word "otherwise," the rule's drafters indicated a willingness to require distribution of information of a non-economic nature. In the past, the exception has been used to support including information on proposals related to less than one percent of a company's business and other non-economic issues. The plaintiff argues that without injunctive relief, he will suffer irreparable harm when the company mails the proxies without including his statement. While the plaintiff acknowledges his resolution is not likely to pass, the loss of an arena to voice his concerns is real and the harm is irreparable. Iroquois (D) is not likely to be injured by including the information. Lovenheim (P) argues that communicating his proposal in the proxy statement furthers the public interest, and he is correct. Motion for preliminary injunction granted.

Analysis:

In earlier cases, such as *A.P. Smith Mfg. Co. v. Barlow*, 13 N.J. 145, 98 A.2d 581 (1953) and *Dodge v. Ford Motor Co.*, 204 Mich. 459, 170 N.W. 668 (1919), companies were at odds with their shareholders over the ability to make charitable donations or price their products in a way that was both beneficial to the companies and the shareholders and helped their communities. Here, a shareholder is seeking to use the company's annual shareholder meeting as a forum for his belief that the company is fostering animal cruelty by its pâté de fois gras sales. Although Iroquois (D) argues that its revenue from the delicacy's sale is insignificant, the court finds that the issue is still sufficiently related to Iroquois' (D) business so as to give the shareholder the right to voice his concerns. Depending on the company's size, a shareholder meeting can provide a large forum for discussing social issues.

■ CASE VOCABULARY

AMBIGUITY: An uncertainty of meaning or intention, as in a contractual term or statutory provision.

SHAREHOLDER PROPOSAL: A proposal by one or more corporate stockholders to change company policy or procedure. Ordinarily, the corporation informs all stockholders about the proposal before the next shareholder meeting.

The New York City Employees' Retirement Sys. v. Dole Food Co., Inc.

(Shareholder) v. *(Issuing Company)*

795 F.Supp. 95 (S.D.N.Y. 1992)

SHAREHOLDER'S PROPOSAL TO INVESTIGATE FEDERAL EMPLOYEE HEALTH CARE PLANS SHOULD BE INCLUDED IN PROXY STATEMENT

HI, YES, WE'D LIKE YOU TO STUDY HEALTH CARE REFORM. I UNDERSTAND YOU'RE A FOOD COMPANY, BUT WE STILL THINK YOU SHOULD PAY FOR A STUDY FOR US

■ **INSTANT FACTS** A public pension fund sought permission from Dole Food Co., Inc. (D) to include information on a proposal to establish a committee to investigate current federal health insurance proposals, but Dole (D) refused the request.

■ **BLACK LETTER RULE** A shareholder's proposal to form a committee to evaluate health insurance proposals before Congress does not relate to the company's ordinary business operations, but the corporation must include the proposal's information in its proxy statements.

■ **PROCEDURAL BASIS**

On motion for injunctive relief.

■ **FACTS**

New York City Employees' Retirement System (NYCERS) (P) is a public pension fund holding 164,841 common shares in Dole Food Co., Inc. (D). The New York City Comptroller, as custodian of NYCERS's (P) assets, requested that Dole (D) include a statement concerning the impact of health care costs on employees' ability to retire. NYCERS (P) proposed a shareholder resolution on the matter and prepared a draft of the resolution and a supporting statement to include with Dole's (D) proxy statements. Dole (D) sought input from the SEC on its right to exclude the proposal based on its relationship to an "ordinary business operation." The SEC agreed with Dole (D) and issued a no-action letter on the matter. Based on the SEC's response, Dole (D) denied NYCERS's request.

■ **ISSUE**

Must a company include a shareholder proposal seeking to have the issuer create a committee to investigate federal proposals affecting employee health care and insurance with its proxy materials?

■ **DECISION AND RATIONALE**

(Conboy, J.) Yes. Under Rule 14a–8, a security holder may ask the issuer to present a proposal at a forthcoming meeting and to include information on the proposal in the company's proxy statement. The company must include the information unless it can show an exception applies. The SEC has stated that if proposals affect a business's mundane operations, the company may reject the materials, provided they do not touch on a significant strategic decision or significantly affect the manner in which the company does business. NYCERS (P) shows that the matter is not related to Dole's (D) "ordinary business operations," but Dole (D) argues that health care benefits are generally within the "ordinary business" exception. Health care is an issue of great social significance, and although NYCERS' (P) proposal does not relate specifically to health care at Dole (D), it does represent the type of issue that

Dole (D) has previously addressed. Therefore, it does not fall within the "ordinary business" exception. Dole (D) also argues that the proposal does not relate to any of its business lines, but it certainly affects more than five percent of the company's outlays. Finally, Dole (D) argues that it may reject the proposal because it concerns issues that are beyond Dole's (D) control. Injunction issued.

Analysis:

Using a shareholders' meeting as a forum for social issues has become more common over the years. Subsequent cases have broadly construed this case to give shareholders a right to use the meeting to advance their agendas. If, as here, the management wrongfully refuses to disclose a shareholder's proposal, the shareholders may seek to have a court enjoin the meeting.

■ **CASE VOCABULARY**

NO ACTION LETTER: A letter from the staff of a governmental agency stating that if the facts are as represented in a person's request for an agency ruling, the staff will advise the agency not to take action against the person. Typically, a no-action letter is requested from the SEC on such matters as shareholder proposals, resales of stock, and marketing techniques.

Austin v. Consolidated Edison Co. of N.Y., Inc.

(Shareholders) v. *(Issuing Company)*

788 F.Supp. 192 (S.D.N.Y. 1992)

SHAREHOLDER'S PROPOSAL CONCERNING EMPLOYEES' RETIREMENT BENEFITS MAY BE OMITTED FROM PROXY MATERIALS

■ **INSTANT FACTS** The issuing company's shareholders sought to force Consolidated Edison Co. of N.Y., Inc. (D) to include information in its annual meeting proxy materials about a proposal that would allow employees to retire after thirty years' service regardless of their age.

■ **BLACK LETTER RULE** Shareholders may not require a corporation to include materials concerning a stockholder proposal supporting an employee's right to retire with full pension benefits with thirty years' service regardless of their age, because the proposal concerns "ordinary business operations."

■ **PROCEDURAL BASIS**

On motion by the defendant seeking summary judgment to have the plaintiffs' motion for a preliminary injunction denied.

■ **FACTS**

Austin (P) and two other shareholders (P) were employed by Consolidated Edison Company of New York, Inc. (Con–Ed) (D). The plaintiffs wanted Con–Ed (D) to include information in its proxy materials in support of a resolution allowing an employee to retire after thirty years' service. This represented a departure from the company's policy of permitting retirement after age sixty provided the sum of an employee's age and years of service total at least seventy-five. The measure was to be part of Con–Ed's (D) upcoming labor negotiations with its employees. In support of its refusal to include information on the plaintiff's proposal, Con–Ed (D) obtained a no-action letter from the SEC.

■ **ISSUE**

May an issuer exclude from its annual proxy statement information on a proposal by the issuer's employees concerning retirement qualifications and benefits?

■ **DECISION AND RATIONALE**

(Mukasey, J.) Yes. The SEC has a long record of allowing companies to exclude pension proposal information from their proxy statements. The plaintiffs may use collective bargaining to press their issue. While the availability of collective bargaining to address an issue is not determinative, it is a more effective forum to resolve issues such as this.

Analysis:

While typical employee compensation and retirement issues are frequently found to be mundane and not fit for shareholder proposals, officer and director compensation is another matter. Nevertheless, in *Morgan Stanley Dean Witter & Co.*, SEC No–Action Letter, 1998 WL 886894 (Dec. 18, 1998), the SEC supported excluding information on shareholder proposals in favor of the board adopting a policy of tying at least half of executive management's compensation to the dividends paid out each year. In *Lucent Technologies Inc.*, SEC No–Action Letter, 1998 WL 761842 (Nov. 2, 1998), the SEC supported excluding information regarding a dividend reinvestment plan, because it relates to the company's ordinary business operations.

Crane Co. v. Anaconda Co.

(Offered to Swap Stock) v. *(Issuing Company)*

39 N.Y.2d 14, 382 N.Y.S.2d 707, 346 N.E.2d 507 (1976)

A CORPORATION MUST GRANT A REQUEST FOR ACCESS TO A SHAREHOLDER LIST TO ENABLE TENDER–OFFER DISCUSSIONS

HI, WE'D LIKE TO TAKE OVER YOUR COMPANY. BUT FIRST, CAN YOU GIVE US THE NAMES AND ADDRESSES OF ALL YOUR SHAREHOLDERS?

■ **INSTANT FACTS** Crane Company (P) sought to acquire twenty percent of Anaconda Company's (D) shares and asked to have access to Anaconda's (D) shareholder list to distribute information on the tender offer directly to Anaconda's (D) shareholders.

■ **BLACK LETTER RULE** A corporation must grant a shareholder who wants to discuss a tender offer's terms directly with the corporation's shareholders access to the shareholder list, unless the corporation can establish a wrongful purpose.

■ **PROCEDURAL BASIS**

On appeal from a decision reversing the Special Term's decision that the request was improper.

■ **FACTS**

Crane (P) announced a proposal to exchange $100 million in subordinated debentures for 5 million common shares of Anaconda (D) stock, and Anaconda's (D) management opposed the proposal. Anaconda (D) sent four letters to its shareholders, asking them to resist Crane's (P) proposal. Anaconda (D) sued Crane (P) in an action that limited Crane (P) to acquiring no more than 5 million shares, prohibited it from pursuing representation on Anaconda's board, and reminded Crane (P) of its obligations under the antitrust laws. Crane (P) began distributing its prospectus to help it obtain the Anaconda (D) stock, and it asked Anaconda (D) for a list of its shareholders. Crane (P) claimed Anaconda (D) had a fiduciary duty to inform its shareholders of Crane's (P) offer. Crane (P) owned no Anaconda (D) stock at the time, although more than two million shares had been tendered. Crane (P) renewed its demand for the shareholder list, and provided Anaconda (D) with an affidavit supporting its statement that it was not seeking the list for a purpose unrelated to Anaconda's (D) business. Anaconda (D) again refused, and Crane (P) filed this action, emphasizing its desire to communicate with Anaconda (D) shareholders to explain the tender offer and to respond to Anaconda's (D) shareholders' misconceptions. The Special Term found that Crane's (P) request was not proper, and it dismissed Crane's (P) petition. The appellate court reversed the Special Term's decision, and Anaconda (D) appealed.

■ **ISSUE**

May a qualified shareholders ask to inspect the corporation's stock register to obtain the identity of other shareholders to inform them directly of its exchange offer and to solicit stock tenders?

■ **DECISION AND RATIONALE**

(Wachtler, J.) Yes. "A shareholder desiring to discuss relevant aspects of a tender offer should be granted access to the shareholder list unless it is sought for a purpose inimical to the corporation or its stockholders—and the manner of communication selected should be within the judgment of the shareholder." Stockholders frequently litigate to obtain the company's stockholder list and the right to do so is recognized at common law and under statute as a way for shareholders to protect their investment. At common law, the shareholder had to prove the request was made in good faith for a proper purpose. As long as the shareholder properly pleaded good faith and proper purpose, the court granted the request. Early legislation in the area eliminated the "proper purpose" requirement, creating an absolute right to the list, but that right has been abandoned in favor of requiring the list to be released only to advance one of the corporation's business purposes. The current statute requires access to the list if the demand is accompanied by an affidavit stating that the only purpose for which the shareholder is seeking the list is the "business of the corporation" and that "the petitioner has not been involved in the sale of stock lists within the last five years." Anaconda (D) argues that if the plaintiff seeks to use the list in conjunction with an attempt to buy the corporation's stock, the "business of the corporation" is not involved. However, if a corporation faces a take-over attempt, the shareholders' welfare is involved. The defendant may not sustain its argument that an attempt to acquire more than twenty percent of a company's shares does not involve the company's business. Inspection of list compelled.

Analysis:

Long before the FCC's creation of a "Do Not Call" list for consumers, the SEC protected shareholders from unwarranted use of their names and addresses. Some corporate statutes have made access to the lists easier. However, as noted in *Shabshelowitz v. Fall River Gas Co.*, 412 Mass. 259, 588 N.E.2d 630 (1992), a corporation is justified in refusing to grant access if it believes the list will be sold.

■ CASE VOCABULARY

FOREIGN CORPORATION: A corporation that was organized and chartered under the laws of another state, government, or country.

State ex rel. Pillsbury v. Honeywell, Inc.

(*Shareholder*) v. (*Issuing Corporation*)

291 Minn. 322, 191 N.W.2d 406 (1971)

COMPANY MAY DENY ACCESS TO A STOCKHOLDER WHO PURCHASED STOCK SOLELY TO ACCESS CORPORATE BOOKS AND RECORDS

■ **INSTANT FACTS** Pillsbury (P) purchased Honeywell, Inc. (D) stock in order to bring suit to compel production of the defendant's corporate books and records.

■ **BLACK LETTER RULE** A stockholder who purchased stock for the sole purpose of bringing suit to compel production of corporate books and records, who was motivated by his belief that the corporation should not be manufacturing ammunition to be used in the Vietnam War, and who had no concern for the corporation's economic well being, cannot compel production of the corporation's shareholder lists or business records.

■ PROCEDURAL BASIS

On appeal from the district court's order denying the plaintiff's demand that Honeywell produce its shareholder list.

■ FACTS

Pillsbury (P) believed Honeywell, Inc. (D) should stop production of ammunition to be used in the Vietnam War. Pillsbury (P) purchased 100 shares of Honeywell (D) stock to gain a voice in the company's affairs and sent two written demands to Honeywell (D) asking for its shareholder ledger. Honeywell (D) refused. Pillsbury (P) filed this action seeking production of the list. The trial court dismissed Pillsbury's (P) petition, finding he sought the list for an improper purpose.

■ ISSUE

Does a shareholder who purchases shares in a corporation for the purpose of changing its manufacturing policies have a proper purpose for accessing shareholder lists and business records?

■ DECISION AND RATIONALE

(Kelly, J.) No. Under Delaware law, a shareholder must prove a proper purpose in order to obtain corporate records and shareholder lists. The trial court found that Pillsbury (P) showed only that he disagrees with the company's management and that he has a right to obtain the list to solicit proxies. Pillsbury (P) insists that any solicitation of proxies is a proper purpose, but Honeywell (D) argues that a proper purpose must relate to concerns over the investment represented by the shares. Possession of a shareholder list is a powerful tool. Without some method for restricting access to the list, a company would be unable to carry on its business and maintain its records. Pillsbury (P) had no interest in Honeywell's (D) affairs until he learned of their ammunition production, and he purchased stock solely to assert ownership and apply pressure to force Honeywell (D) to stop production. This contrived scenario does not constitute proper use. Shareholders with bona fide investments may have a legitimate concern over the ammunition production, and the court may support their actions if the bomb production has a negative impact on Honeywell's (D) returns. However, Pillsbury (P) has no interest in Honeywell's (D) long-term profitability. Affirmed.

Analysis:

Courts do not always view political questions in the manner that the court here viewed Pillsbury's (P) motives. For example, in *Conservative Caucus Research, Analysis & Educ. Found., Inc. v. Chevron Corp.*, 525 A.2d 569 (Del. Ch. 1987), a shareholder wanted access to the company's stockholder list in order to seek out other shareholders and discourage the management from doing business in Angola. Although there were many political ramifications associated with doing business in Angola, the court found that the shareholder's concern was reasonably related to registered stockholders' interests because the effect of war would negatively impact the company's profitability.

■ CASE VOCABULARY

MANDAMUS: A writ issued by a superior court to compel a lower court or a government officer to perform mandatory or purely ministerial duties correctly.

Sadler v. NCR Corp.

(Shareholder) v. *(Corporation)*

928 F.2d 48 (2d Cir. 1991)

NEW YORK LAW ENTITLES SHAREHOLDERS TO SHAREHOLDER AND NONOBJECTING BENEFICIAL OWNERS LISTS

■ **INSTANT FACTS** Shareholders brought an action against a corporation to obtain its shareholder list and to demand the corporation create a list of nonobjecting beneficial owners.

■ **BLACK LETTER RULE** A New York law entitling resident shareholders to shareholder lists and lists of nonobjecting beneficial owners does not subject the corporation to inconsistent regulation prohibited by the commerce clause nor discriminate against or burden interstate commerce.

■ **PROCEDURAL BASIS**

On appeal from the district court's decision in favor of the shareholders.

■ **FACTS**

AT&T (P) acquired 100 shares of stock in NCR (D), a large computer company with at least eight offices in New York. The Sadlers (P), New York residents, owned more than 6,000 NCR shares. In December 1990, AT&T (P) began a tender offer to acquire all NCR (D) shares and mailed an offer to buy shares to all NCR (D) shareholders. NCR (D) rejected the bid and declined to redeem a poison-pill plan that posed an obstacle to AT & T's (P) plans. AT&T (P) tried to solicit shareholders to install a new board of directors at NCR (D) so it could proceed with its plans. Under Maryland law, shareholders may convene a special meeting to replace directors. AT&T (P) successfully called the special meeting, but it was scheduled for the date on which NCR (D) usually holds its annual meeting. In early January 1991, the Sadlers (P) tried to obtain NCR's shareholder list so that AT&T (P) could communicate with the shareholders. AT&T (P) also sought a "CEDE list," which would include the brokerage firms and other record owners who held shares in trust, and a list of nonobjecting beneficial owners (a NOBO list), which would identify those owning beneficial interests in shares that had consented to having their identities disclosed. The SEC requires brokers and other record holders to compile NOBO lists when requested. The Sadlers (P) and AT&T (P) filed suit seeking the stockholder list.

■ **ISSUE**

Does requiring an out-of-state corporation to produce a shareholder list and a list of nonobjecting beneficial owners violate the commerce clause?

■ **DECISION AND RATIONALE**

(Newman, J.) Yes. New York law permits any resident who has held shares in a company for at least six months to require the corporation to produce a list of its shareholders and the dates they acquired ownership. The plaintiffs qualify because they are New York residents and have held NCR (D) stock for at least six months. NCR (D) argues that the plaintiffs' request is not valid, because the plaintiffs will share the information with AT&T (P), which has not held shares for the requisite time. The Sadlers'

---

agreement to share the information with AT&T (P) does not prevent them from obtaining the lists. Although a corporation may refuse to produce the information on a showing of an improper purpose, the Sadlers' use is not improper. The more difficult question is whether New York law requires NCR (D) to compile a NOBO list. If NCR (D) already had the list, producing it would be no problem, but creating the list involves a sufficient amount of work. Although the law does not mandate a company to produce a NOBO list, it does not excuse production because one has not been created.

Analysis:

Corporations are creatures of the state. Therefore, state statutes govern nearly every facet of a corporation's existence, including how a company can be formed and the manner in which it can accomplish changes in its structure, such as adding shareholders, terminating directors for cause and expanding and contracting the number of directors on its board. Concern over subjecting a company to countless rules and regulations in numerous jurisdictions where it may do business has lead to the "internal affairs doctrine." As explained by the court in *Resolution Trust Corp. v. Camhi*, 861 F. Supp. 1121, 1126 (D. Conn. 1994), there is a difference between the protection given to companies under the "internal affairs doctrine," where state law rules over issues on a corporation's internal affairs, and the laws that apply to the relationship between a company and third parties. Although this distinction may seem easy to apply, if the outcome could cost the company millions of dollars, the company will frequently argue that an unwelcome state law is attempting to interfere in the corporation's internal affairs.

■ **CASE VOCABULARY**

BENEFICIAL INTEREST: A right or expectancy in something (such as a trust or an estate), as opposed to legal title to that thing.

Stroh v. Blackhawk Holding Corp.

(Class B Stock Shareholder) v. *(Issuing Company)*

48 Ill.2d 471, 272 N.E.2d 1 (1971)

SHARES MAY REPRESENT A PROPRIETARY INTEREST EVEN IF THEY DO NOT ENTITLE THE HOLDER TO DIVIDENDS OR OTHER PROPERTY

■ **INSTANT FACTS** Stroh (P) purchased shares of Blackhawk Holding Corp.'s Class B stock, which permitted voting rights in corporate matters, but did not receive dividends or other corporate assets.

■ **BLACK LETTER RULE** A corporation's shares of class B stock, which permit voting rights, are valid shares of stock, notwithstanding the fact that the stock is not entitled to dividends.

■ **PROCEDURAL BASIS**

On appeal from an order finding for the corporation.

■ **FACTS**

Blackhawk Holding Corp. (D) was organized as an Illinois corporation authorized to issue 3,000,000 shares of Class A common stock and 500,000 shares of Class B common stock. Twenty-one promoters bought the Class A shares. The Class B shares were sold at a substantially lower price because they were not entitled to dividends under any circumstances, including voluntary or involuntary liquidation. The following year, the company sold an additional 500,000 shares of Class A stock and subsequently offered a two-for-one split for the Class A shares, bring the total number of issued Class A shares to 1,237,681.

■ **ISSUE**

May a company issue shares that do not have any economic benefits to their owners?

■ **DECISION AND RATIONALE**

(Davis, J.) Yes. The Illinois constitution provides that a shareholder in an Illinois corporation must be guaranteed the right to vote. An Illinois corporation may issue varying classes of stock with different rights, but it may not deny a shareholder the right to vote his or her shares. Pursuant to the Business Corporation Act, shares are defined as units of proprietary interest in a company. The term "proprietary" implies ownership of a property right. A proprietary right may give the shareholder the right to participate in controlling the company, to share in its profits or to obtain value upon liquidation. Under the statute, these rights are presented as alternatives. The Act allows a corporation to limit or restrict any benefits to a class of stock, subject to the state constitution's requirement that all shares must be permitted to vote. Nothing in the Act or the constitution requires shares to entitle the holder to a financial benefit. In this case, the Class B shares that gave the holder the right to vote but not provide dividends or other corporate assets were sold cheaply. The law does not forbid this. Affirmed.

DISSENT

(Schaefer, J.) Illinois law provides for a company to issue shares that provide the holder with only a voice in the company, but no monetary benefit. What the shareholder receives in that case is not a share of corporate stock.

Analysis:

The shareholder likely did not consider what he was buying when he made the decision to acquire the Class B shares. The fact that the Class B shares were acquired for a fraction of the cost of Class A shares should have tipped off the investor to investigate what he was getting. Even so, it is unlikely that Stroh (P) believed he would get only the right to vote. While it may seem unusual for an investor to purchase shares with no financial payback, an investor may still have an incentive to purchase them. For example, the shares may provide the holder with enough power to influence a vote on wages or benefits that he may be entitled to receive in the future, or the board may vote to grant Class A rights to Class B shares at a discount in the future.

■ CASE VOCABULARY

PROPRIETARY INTEREST: A legal share in something; all or part of a legal or equitable claim to or right in property. Collectively, the word includes any aggregation of rights, privileges, powers, and immunities; distributively, it refers to any one right, privilege, power, or immunity.

Wisconsin Inv. Bd. v. Peerless Sys. Corp.

(Shareholder–Investor) v. (Issuing Corporation)

2000 WL 1805376 (Del. Ch. 2000)

A COURT WILL NOT UPHOLD A BOARD'S ACTION THAT INTERFERES WITH A SHAREHOLDERS' VOTE, ABSENT A COMPELLING JUSTIFICATION

■ **INSTANT FACTS** Peerless Systems Corp. (D) sought shareholder approval of three measures at its annual meeting, and the board had hoped all resolutions would pass, but when the votes cast would have defeated the measure addressing stock options, the board adjourned the meeting and continued the proposal's vote to another day.

■ **BLACK LETTER RULE** If a board takes an action designed to "interfere with or impede exercise of the shareholder franchise," the action is not protected under the business judgment rule without a compelling justification for the board's actions.

■ **PROCEDURAL BASIS**

On cross motions for summary judgment.

■ **FACTS**

The State of Wisconsin Investment Board (SWIB) (P) invests the State Investment Fund's assets for Wisconsin's state retirement program. SWIB (P) held shares in Peerless Systems Corporation (D), representing seven to nine percent of Peerless's (D) outstanding stock. Peerless (D) is a Delaware corporation engaged in software-related businesses. In 1999, Peerless (D) had four members on its board of directors, three of whom were outside directors who received stock options. The fourth director, a Peerless (D) employee, received both a salary and stock options. Peerless (D) issued a proxy statement for three shareholder proposals, each of which the board recommended the shareholders approve. Proposal 2, the proposal at issue, would authorize a 1–million share increase in stock available for the Peerless (D) stock option plan. SWIB (P) was adamantly opposed to Proposal 2, believing it would dilute its voice in Peerless (D). Therefore, SWIB (P) wrote each Peerless (D) shareholder, recommending that they should reject the proposal. Immediately before the regular shareholders' meeting, Peerless (D) held a Special Shareholders Meeting to consider a merger, which was overwhelmingly approved with slightly over half of the eligible shares voting. The regular meeting took place as scheduled, but SWIB (P) did not attend. A vote was taken on the other two proposals and both measures passed, but the meeting was adjourned without voting on Proposal 2. If the shareholders had voted on Proposal 2 at the meeting, the measure would have been defeated by over half a million votes. Peerless's (D) bylaws permit it to reconvene a meeting and conduct any business that could have been conducted at the original meeting. Peerless (D) contends it adjourned the meeting without a vote on Proposal 2 in order to allow more votes to be cast. Voting on Proposal 2 was light because, under NYSE rules, brokers and agents holding shares for beneficial owners could not vote on non-routine matters, and Proposal 2 was deemed to be non-routine. Peerless (D) made no public statement on Proposal 2's status following the meeting, but Peerless (D) continued to solicit votes from shareholders it presumed would favor the proposal. When SWIB (P) was informed about the continued vote on Proposal 2, it sent a second solicitation letter to Peerless (D) shareholders urging the proposal's rejection. The reconvened meeting occurred thirty days later, and Proposal 2 narrowly passed with just

---

over thirty percent of the eligible shares casting a vote. SWIB (P) filed a complaint against Peerless (D), seeking to have the vote set aside.

■ ISSUE

May a corporation continue the voting on a proposal in an effort to ensure its passage when to do so breaches a duty of loyalty to its other shareholders?

■ DECISION AND RATIONALE

(Chandler, J.) No. Peerless (D) contends that SWIB (P) has no standing to bring this action because it did not attend either meeting or object to the first meeting's continuance. No case law supports this contention, and it cannot be permitted in light of the strong public policy considerations related to proxy solicitation. The proxy system ensures shareholders a voice in the business conducted and works to both large and small investors' benefit. The court must first determine what standard of review to apply to the board of director's conduct in adjourning the meeting without taking the vote on Proposal 2. The defendants argue that their decision should be protected under the business judgment rule. The plaintiffs argue that the directors' conduct should be judged under the *Blasius* rule, which provides that a court must find a "compelling justification" for the board's actions. *Blasius* presents an onerous burden and should be used only if there is a finding that the primary purpose of the board's action was to "interfere with or impede exercise of the shareholder franchise." Under *Blasius*, unless the plaintiff can establish that the board's purpose was to "interfere with or impede exercise of the shareholder franchise," the action will be subject to review under the business judgment rule. Peerless (D) argues that its reason for delaying the Proposal 2 vote was to obtain input from more shareholders. However, if the Proposal 2 vote had gone forward at the first meeting, the votes already cast exceeded the number of votes cast at the Special Shareholders Meeting on the merger. Also, Peerless's (D) failure to notify the shareholders of the meeting's adjournment did nothing to further its goal of obtaining more votes. By its own admissions, Peerless (D) focused its efforts at contacting only those shareholders it believed would vote in favor of Proposal 2. Peerless (D) argues that it had a compelling justification for delaying the vote, that *Blasius* does not apply because Proposal 2 did not involve the election of directors, that the adjournment did not prohibit anyone from voting, and that the proposal ultimately succeeded because more votes were cast, indicating that the measure was the shareholders' true will. However, this position is defeated by Peerless's (D) own admission that it contacted only shareholders it thought would cast votes in favor of the proposal. Finally, Peerless (D) contends that the low vote totals for Proposal 2 justified delaying the tally. However, as long as a quorum is present, there are enough votes present to cast a valid vote. Summary judgment denied.

Analysis:

As part of the court's analysis, the judge considers the fact that the earlier vote on the merger was allowed to gain approval on fewer votes than were cast for Proposal 2 on the first day of the shareholder meeting. However, not every effort by a board of directors will be perceived as violating the board's duty to its shareholders. For example, in *In re MONY Group, Inc. Shareholder Litigation*, 853 A.2d 661 (Del. Ch. 2004), the court upheld the board's decision to postpone a shareholder vote on a merger following a determination that additional information needed to be added to the proxies to provide the shareholders with a sufficient basis for their vote.

■ CASE VOCABULARY

CONTINUED MEETING: A meeting that will be or has been resumed after a recess (or a so-called adjournment, which may last for several days but is still technically a recess, since it does not end the meeting). A continued meeting is technically not an "adjourned meeting," and an "adjourned meeting" may also mean a meeting that has adjourned, so the term "continued meeting" is preferable. Also loosely termed adjourned meeting.

QUORUM: The minimum number of members (usually a majority of all the members) who must be present for a deliberative assembly to legally transact business.

Ringling Bros.–Barnum & Bailey Combined Shows v. Ringling

(Corporation) v. *(Stockholder)*

29 Del.Ch. 610, 53 A.2d 441 (Del. 1947)

STOCKHOLDERS MAY MAKE BINDING AGREEMENTS ON HOW TO VOTE THEIR STOCK

■ **INSTANT FACTS** Edith Ringling (P) agreed to vote her stock in agreement with Haley (D), but then refused to do so.

■ **BLACK LETTER RULE** A shareholder may agree with another shareholder to vote his or her stock in a particular way.

■ PROCEDURAL BASIS

On appeal from a Court of Chancery order in favor of the plaintiff.

■ FACTS

Edith Ringling (P) and Haley (D), who owned an equal number of shares of stock in Ringling Bros.–Barnum & Bailey Combined Shows (Ringling Bros.) (D), agreed to consult with each other before exercising their voting rights and to act jointly when voting. Their agreement also provided that they would submit any disagreement to Loos for arbitration and that his decision would be binding. Ringling (P) and Haley (D) voted in accordance with their agreement for several years and were consistently able to elect five of the seven directors on the Ringling Bros. board. The third shareholder, North, owned more stock than Ringling (P) or Haley (D) owned individually, but not enough to elect more than two directors on his own. In 1946, Ringling (P) and Haley (D) agreed on four of the five directors to be elected, but they did not agree on the fifth. Haley's (D) husband, who was acting as Haley's (D) proxy, stated that he would move to adjourn the shareholders' meeting for sixty days to allow Haley (D) and Ringling (P) to come to an agreement. However, at the meeting, Haley's (D) husband refused to move to adjourn because of something Ringling (P) had done. Ringling (P) demanded Loos to arbitrate the dispute, and Loos determined that Haley (D) and Ringling (P) should vote their stock in favor of a sixty-day adjournment. Haley's (D) husband and North both refused to vote for the adjournment. The board's chairman ruled that Haley's (D) stock could not be voted against Loos' direction and declared the meeting adjourned. Despite the chairman's ruling, the meeting continued over Ringling's (P) protests. Loos directed Ringling (P) to cast her votes to elect herself, her son, and Dunn, who had served on the board previously. Ringling (P) complied. Loos directed Haley (D) to cast her votes for herself, her husband, and Dunn. Haley's (D) husband refused, and divided Haley's (D) votes between Haley (D) and her husband. North cast his votes for himself, and for two others, Griffin and Woods. The chairman ruled that the five candidates proposed by Loos, along with North and Woods, were elected to the board. Ringling (P) brought an action to review the election. The Vice Chancellor determined that the arbitration agreement had the effect of appointing Loos as Haley's (D) proxy for purposes of casting a vote, and ordered a new election.

■ ISSUE

Is an agreement between shareholders to vote their stock in a particular way valid?

■ DECISION AND RATIONALE

(Judge Undisclosed) Yes. A shareholder may agree with another shareholder to vote his or her stock in a particular way. The agreement between Haley (D) and Ringling (P) was not unlawful or contrary to public policy, nor did it take unlawful advantage of North, the remaining shareholder. The agreement did nothing more than set out the manner in which each party agreed to vote her shares and require an arbitrator to decide how the shares should be voted. However, the agreement did not contain a grant of authority in the arbitrator to exercise either party's voting rights. Neither shareholder delegated voting rights to any other party. Nor does the agreement contain a provision allowing the arbitrator to force either party to vote according to his direction. The parties were bound only to each other. Haley's (D) failure to vote according to the agreement was a breach of contract, so her votes should not be counted. There was no defect in the voting of North's shares, so his vote against adjournment means that the meeting could proceed, and the six directors for whom Ringling (P) and North voted are elected as directors. Affirmed as modified

Analysis:

Specific performance may have been appropriate here, because it would be difficult, if not impossible, to measure the monetary damages caused by Haley's (D) breach of contract. Specific performance would have put Haley (D) and her husband on the board of directors, rather than ordering a new election (as the Vice Chancellor did). Facts not contained in the opinion hint that Ringling (P) may not necessarily have wanted Haley (D) or her husband on the board. Haley (D) and Ringling (P) made their agreement to keep North from taking control of the corporation, and it served its purpose for many years, with Robert Ringling, Ringling's (P) son, in charge of the corporation. Robert hired Haley's (D) husband to manage the Ringling Bros. (D) circus, and, in that capacity, Haley's (D) husband was prosecuted for the deaths of over one hundred people in a circus tent fire in Hartford, Connecticut. After Haley's (D) husband was released from jail, he and his wife switched their corporate allegiance to North and worked to take control of the company from Ringling (P).

■ CASE VOCABULARY

CHANCELLOR: A judge serving on a court of chancery.

CUMULATIVE VOTING: A system for electing corporate directors whereby a shareholder may multiply his or her number of shares by the number of open directorships and cast the total for a single candidate or a select few candidates.

SPECIFIC PERFORMANCE: A court-ordered remedy that requires precise fulfillment of a legal or contractual obligation when monetary damages are inappropriate or inadequate, as when the sale of real estate or a rare article is involved. Specific performance is an equitable remedy that lies within the court's discretion to award whenever the common-law remedy is insufficient, either because damages would be inadequate or because the damages could not possibly be established.

VICE CHANCELLOR: A judge appointed to act for a chancellor, especially in a chancery court.

McQuade v. Stoneham

(Treasurer/Magistrate) v. *(President)*
263 N.Y. 323, 189 N.E. 234 (1934)

SHAREHOLDER AGREEMENTS MAY NOT RESTRICT A BOARD'S AUTHORITY

■ **INSTANT FACTS** McQuade (P), who was employed as corporate treasurer pursuant to a shareholder's agreement, was discharged.

■ **BLACK LETTER RULE** A shareholder agreement may not control a board of directors' exercise of judgment.

■ PROCEDURAL BASIS

On appeal from orders awarding damages for wrongful discharge and denying specific performance.

■ FACTS

Stoneham (D) owned the majority of stock in the National Exhibition Company. McQuade (P), a city magistrate, purchased some stock in the company. As a part of the stock purchase, Stoneham (D) and McQuade (P) entered into an agreement that provided that the parties would use their "best endeavors" to elect Stoneham (D) and McQuade (P) to the board of directors and to employ McQuade (P) as the corporation's treasurer. After several years, McQuade was replaced as treasurer and voted off the board of directors. Stoneham (D) acquiesced in McQuade's (P) removal and did not try to ensure that McQuade (P) continued on the board or was employed as treasurer. McQuade (P) was not removed for any misfeasance or malfeasance, but because he antagonized Stoneham (D). McQuade (P) sought specific performance of the agreement to employ him as treasurer. The lower court denied McQuade's (P) request but awarded him damages for wrongful discharge.

■ ISSUE

Is a shareholder agreement that controls a board of director's authority enforceable?

■ DECISION AND RATIONALE

(Pound, C.J.) No. Shareholder agreements may not control a board of directors' exercise of judgment. Directors have the discretion to act in any way that is not unlawful or contrary to public policy. Shareholders may combine to elect directors but may not limit the board's authority to manage the corporation. Although this type of agreement is common, especially in closely held corporations, the director's duty is to the corporation, not other officers. The courts should not pass judgment on the motives behind a board's lawful actions. Also, McQuade (P) was a city magistrate, and the law does not allow magistrates to engage in outside employment. Therefore, performance of the shareholders' agreement constitutes a statutory violation. Reversed and complaint dismissed.

CONCURRING OPINION

(Lehman, J.) The majority is correct in ordering the complaint dismissed because the contract violated the prohibition against magistrates' outside employment, but the agreement did not restrict the board's power. The only limitation imposed was on the persons who could be hired as officers, which does not interfere with the board's authority. Directors do not have unfettered discretion in matters relating to corporate governance and are subject to election and removal by the shareholders.

Analysis:

While directors owe their loyalty to the corporation and, by extension, to the shareholders, the shareholders need not exhibit loyalty to anyone. In many closely-held corporations, the line between shareholder and director can be elusive. Close corporations frequently make ownership of stock in the corporation a qualification for election as a director. The challenge for such corporations and their legal counsel lies in ensuring that the parties appreciate the distinction and that they follow the formalities dictated by shareholders' and directors' distinct roles.

■ CASE VOCABULARY

CLOSE CORPORATION: A corporation whose stock is not freely traded and is held by only a few shareholders (often within the same family). The requirements and privileges of close corporations vary by jurisdiction.

MAGISTRATE: A judicial officer with strictly limited authority, often on the local level and often restricted to criminal cases.

WRONGFUL DISCHARGE: A discharge for reasons that are illegal or violate public policy.

Clark v. Dodge

(Treasurer/General Manager) v. (Majority Shareholder)
269 N.Y. 410, 199 N.E. 641 (1936)

SHAREHOLDER AGREEMENTS REGARDING OFFICERS' EMPLOYMENT MAY BE ENFORCEABLE

■ **INSTANT FACTS** Clark (P), who was employed as treasurer and general manager of a corporation pursuant to a shareholder's agreement, was discharged.

■ **BLACK LETTER RULE** A shareholder agreement regarding employment of certain individuals as officers is enforceable if the directors are the sole shareholders.

■ **PROCEDURAL BASIS**

Appeal from an order dismissing the complaint.

■ **FACTS**

Clark (P) owned stock in and was employed by two pharmaceutical companies. Dodge (D) owned the remaining stock in the two companies. Dodge (D) and Clark (P) agreed that Clark (P) would remain in control of the business as long as he remained faithful and competent to manage the business. The agreement provided that Clark (P) would continue to be a director of both corporations, would be employed as the treasurer and manager of the corporations, and would receive one-quarter of the net income of the corporations, either as salary or as dividends. The agreement also provided that no other officer or employee would be paid an unreasonable salary, and that Clark (P) would disclose the formulae of the corporations' medicines to Dodge's (D) son and bequeath his stock to Dodge's (D) wife and children if Clark (P) had no surviving issue. Clark (P) brought suit and alleged a breach of contract by Dodge (D). Clark (P) alleged that Dodge (D) did not use his controlling interest in the company to continue Clark's (P) employment, and that Dodge (D) prevented Clark (P) from receiving his share of the profits by employing incompetent people at inflated salaries. The Appellate Division dismissed the complaint.

■ **ISSUE**

Is a shareholder agreement to continue the employment of certain individuals as officers enforceable if the directors are the sole shareholders?

■ **DECISION AND RATIONALE**

(Crouch, J.) Yes. A shareholder agreement regarding employment of certain individuals as officers is enforceable if the directors are the sole shareholders. The only directors whose discretion was impinged upon were also the corporations' sole shareholders. No outside shareholders' rights were affected by the agreement. Any invasion of the directors' powers was so slight as to be negligible. The agreement's terms were either beneficial to the corporation or did no harm. The statements in *McQuade v. Stoneham*, 263 N.Y. 323, 189 N.E. 234 (1934), to the contrary were largely dicta, and the holding in that case should be confined to the facts of that case. Reversed.

Analysis:

The court's opinion recognizes the realities under which many, if not most, close corporations operate. Although there is a legal distinction between directors and shareholders, it is not always readily made in a business's day-to-day operations. Shareholder protection does not loom large if all of the shareholders are being protected only from themselves. As a practical matter, strict adherence to corporate formalities is not demanded if no one other than the parties to the agreement will feel any impact from enforcing the agreement.

■ CASE VOCABULARY

OBITER DICTUM: [Latin "something said in passing"] A judicial comment made during the course of delivering a judicial opinion, but one that is unnecessary to the decision in the case and therefore not precedential (although it may be considered persuasive).

Galler v. Galler

(Widow) v. *(Survivors)*

32 Ill.2d 16, 203 N.E.2d 577 (1964)

SHAREHOLDER AGREEMENTS RELATING TO THE MANAGEMENT OF A CLOSE CORPORATION MAY BE ENFORCED

■ **INSTANT FACTS** Isadore Galler (D) entered into a shareholders' agreement with his brother, Benjamin, and later refused to abide by the agreement.

■ **BLACK LETTER RULE** Shareholder agreements that relate to the management of a close corporation will be upheld, even if the agreements violate corporate norms.

■ **PROCEDURAL BASIS**

On appeal from the appellate court's order finding the agreement void.

■ **FACTS**

Benjamin and Isadore (D) Galler were brothers who each owned one-half of the stock of Galler Drug Company, a wholesale drug company. In order to protect their respective families, they entered into a shareholder agreement to assure the families equal control of the corporation upon either brother's death. The agreement provided that the board of directors would consist of four members and that the shareholders would vote Isadore (D), Isadore's wife, Rose (D), Benjamin, and Benjamin's wife, Emma (P), as directors. The agreement also provided that they would declare a certain annual dividend and that Isadore's (D) and Benjamin's salary would continue for five years after their deaths, payable to their widows. Isadore (D), Rose (D), and their son, Aaron (D) decided not to honor the agreement, but did not disclose their intention to Emma (P) or Benjamin. Isadore (D), Rose (D), and Aaron (D) tried to destroy the executed copies of the agreement. Benjamin transferred his shares to a trust, with Emma (P) as trustee. The trust endorsed the stock certificates and turned them over to Emma (P). Isadore (D), Rose (D), and Aaron (D) sought to have her abandon the agreement. Although Emma (P) refused, she agreed to allow Aaron (D) to serve as president of the corporation for one year. During that year, Emma (P) attempted to discuss business matters with the defendants, but they refused. After Benjamin's death, Emma (P) demanded that the shareholders carry out the agreement's terms, but the defendants refused. Aaron (D) offered to modify the agreement, but Emma (P) would not agree. The appellate court voided the entire agreement as contrary to the public policy, holding that the "undue duration, stated purpose and substantial disregard of the provisions of the Corporation Act outweigh any considerations which might call for divisibility. . . ."

■ **ISSUE**

May a court uphold a shareholder agreement that relates to the management of a close corporation, even if the agreement violates corporate norms?

■ **DECISION AND RATIONALE**

Yes. Shareholder agreements that relate to the management of a close corporation will be upheld, even if the agreements violate corporate norms. The controlling factors are an absence of a minority shareholder that objects to the agreement and a lack of public detriment. There are significant differences between a close corporation, which is a corporation in which a few individuals or families hold the stock (that is rarely, if ever, traded), and a large, publicly traded corporation. The shareholders in a close corporation often have a considerable investment tied up in the corporation and do not have the option of selling their shares if they are dissatisfied with the way the corporation is being run. A detailed shareholder agreement, such as the one at issue here, is often the only way of protecting all shareholders' interests in a close corporation. A close corporation's shareholders are often also the directors and officers, so it may be impossible to obtain an independent board judgment concerning corporate policy that is free from personal motives. The state's public policy has increasingly upheld shareholder agreements, particularly in cases in which no shareholders object to the agreements. Although this agreement was of an indefinite duration, there is no requirement that a shareholder agreement must have a definite duration. The agreement here is a voting control arrangement that does not divorce voting rights from stock ownership, not a voting trust. The agreement does not have an unlawful purpose, and the salary-continuation promise does not violate the rights of shareholders not party to the agreement because all shareholders are party to the agreement. Reversed and remanded.

Analysis:

Attorneys often advise clients starting a business that a corporation can be relatively complicated to run and that the failure to adhere to corporate governance norms can result in the loss of one of a corporation's biggest advantages—freedom from personal liability for business debts and obligations. After this case, it is fair to ask if any corporate norms apply to close corporations. The court focuses its attention on shareholders' rights, and mentions only briefly the lack of harm to the public. However, the court does not address the risk that corporate governance could become too lax, blurring the distinction between a corporate entity and its owners.

■ CASE VOCABULARY

VOTING TRUST: A trust used to hold shares of voting stock in a closely held corporation, usually transferred from a parent to a child, and empowering the trustee to exercise the right to vote. The trust acts as custodian of the shares but is not a stockholder.

Ramos v. Estrada

(Former President) v. *(Defecting Shareholders)*

8 Cal.App.4th 1070, 10 Cal.Rptr.2d 833 (1992)

A COURT MAY ENFORCE SHAREHOLDER VOTING AGREEMENTS EVEN IN CORPORATIONS THAT ARE NOT CLOSE CORPORATIONS

NO, WE CAN'T MAKE AGREEMENTS ON HOW TO VOTE ONCE WE'RE ELECTED, BUT WE CAN AGREE ON WHOM TO ELECT

■ **INSTANT FACTS** Estrada (D) did not vote her stock in accordance with a shareholders' agreement, and Ramos (P) brought suit for breach of contract.

■ **BLACK LETTER RULE** Voting agreements between two or more shareholders of a corporation are enforceable, even if the corporation does not qualify as a close corporation.

■ PROCEDURAL BASIS

Appeal from a judgment that Estrada (D) materially breached the contract.

■ FACTS

Estrada (D) and her husband were shareholders of Broadcast Corp., which was also known as "Broadcast Group." Broadcast Group combined with another corporation, Ventura 41, to form Television, Inc., and the shareholders of Broadcast Group and Ventura 41 each received stock in Television, Inc. Estrada (D) and the other Broadcast Group shareholders agreed to vote all of their Television, Inc. shares in a manner agreed upon by all of them and to restrict transfer of their shares. They agreed that failure to adhere to the agreement constituted an election by the shareholder to sell his or her shares to the other shareholders and that the buy/sell provision of the agreement would be specifically enforceable. At a special directors' meeting, Estrada (D) did not vote with the other former shareholders of Broadcast Group, but voted with the former Ventura 41 shareholders. The Broadcast Group held another meeting to decide how to vote for directors. Estrada (D) did not attend this meeting and sent a letter that declared the shareholders' agreement null and void. Ramos (P) and other Broadcast Group shareholders sued Estrada for breach of contract, and Estrada (D) claimed that the agreement was an expired proxy agreement that she revoked. The court found that Estrada (D) was in material breach of the contract. The court ordered Estrada's (D) shares sold.

■ ISSUE

Is a voting agreement between or among a corporation's shareholders enforceable?

■ DECISION AND RATIONALE

Yes. Voting agreements between two or more shareholders of a corporation are enforceable, even if the corporation does not qualify as a close corporation. The statute that permits shareholder agreements in close corporations does not make the agreements unlawful in other corporations. This agreement is valid, enforceable, and supported by consideration. It is not a proxy agreement, because the votes were to be cast by the shareholders, not by someone acting on their behalf. The agreement was not unconscionable, because Estrada (D) was an experienced businessperson, able to review the documents and discuss them with counsel. Affirmed.

Analysis:

The statute the Court cites, Cal. Corp. Code § 702(a), was amended in 1997 to apply to shareholders in all corporations, not just close corporations. It is likely that the only reason Television, Inc. did not qualify as a close corporation was that the articles of incorporation failed to include the words "[t]his corporation is a close corporation," which could have been added by amendment. *See,* Cal. Corp. Code § 158(a). The court does not delve into policy reasons for upholding the shareholders' agreement, focusing instead on the fact that it found no reason *not* to uphold it.

■ CASE VOCABULARY

PROXY: One who is authorized to act as a substitute for another; especially, in corporate law, a person who is authorized to vote another's stock shares.

Wilkes v. Springside Nursing Home, Inc.

(Terminated Shareholder) v. *(Employer)*

370 Mass. 842, 353 N.E.2d 657 (1976)

A CLOSE CORPORATION'S SHAREHOLDERS NEED A LEGITIMATE BUSINESS PURPOSE TO TERMINATE ANOTHER SHAREHOLDER'S EMPLOYMENT

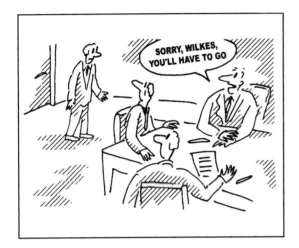

■ **INSTANT FACTS** Wilkes (P), who formed a real estate investment business with three other men who shared equally in the business, created disharmony and was fired when he struck a particularly hard bargain with one of the other shareholders in the sale of some corporate property.

■ **BLACK LETTER RULE** Majority shareholders acting to "freeze out" a minority shareholder by terminating his employment without a valid business purpose have breached their duty to act as fiduciaries.

■ PROCEDURAL BASIS

On appeal following the entry of judgment in favor of the majority shareholders.

■ FACTS

Wilkes (P), a roofer by trade, had a reputation for making profitable real estate transactions. He obtained an option on a building previously used as a hospital, and Riche (D), Quinn (D) and Pipkin joined him in making the purchase. The four men decided to use the property to operate a nursing home. Wilkes' (P) attorney advised him to incorporate the venture to limit personal liability, so the men formed Springside Nursing Home (D). Each shareholder invested $1000 in exchange for ten shares. The shareholders understood that each of them would serve as a director and participate in the company's management. Each investor expected to receive equal payments from the company as operations permitted for fulfilling similar responsibilities. The four men performed relatively equal work. Riche (D) served as president, Wilkes (P) as treasurer, and Quinn (D) as clerk; each man was also a director. The following year, funds became available for each man to draw regular payments, and they each began receiving $35 per week with periodic increases to $100 a week in 1955. Pipkin sold his shares to a new holder, Connor (D), who was the president of a local bank. Connor (D) served as director and received a weekly stipend for providing financial advice. Several years later, a portion of Springside's (D) real estate was sold to Quinn (D) to be used as a rest home. Wilkes (P) forced Quinn (D) to pay a higher price than Quinn (D) had expected for the property. As a result of the sale, Quinn (D) and Wilkes (P) developed hostilities that affected Springside's (D) operations. Despite the breakdown in the relationship between the shareholders, Wilkes (P) continued to act professionally and fulfill his company responsibilities, but he eventually gave notice that he wanted an appraisal of his shares so he could sell them. The following month, the board met to set salaries of its officers and employees. Quinn (D) received a substantial increase, but Riche (D) and Connor (D) continued receiving $100. Wilkes (P) received nothing. At the annual shareholders meeting that followed, the other shareholders failed to reelect Wilkes (P) as officer or director and told him his services as an employee were no longer wanted. Wilkes (P) filed this action claiming the others breached their fiduciary duty by terminating his employment.

■ ISSUE

In a close corporation, in which each shareholder was employed and paid a salary by the company and served as a director, does the board breach its fiduciary duty if it terminates one of the shareholder's employment?

■ DECISION AND RATIONALE

(Hennessey, J.) Yes. *Donahue v. Rodd Electrotype Co. of New England, Inc.*, 328 N.E.2d 505 (1975), provides that stockholders in close corporations have a fiduciary duty of "utmost good faith and loyalty" to each other. In discharging this duty, shareholders may not act "out of avarice, expediency or self interest." In close corporations, the majority shareholders are frequently in a position to freeze out the minority shareholders, whether by demanding them to sell their interest for less than a fair price or depriving the shareholder of employment in the company. Secure employment is a motivating factor for many shareholders to make a serious investment in a close corporation, and a salary may be the shareholder's only return on his investment, so termination effectively frustrates the incentive for the investment. Expanding *Donahue's* good faith standard would eventually erode all limits on legitimate action to operate a business effectively. As a result, if a minority shareholder brings an action alleging a breach of the duty of good faith, the court must analyze the majority's actions to see whether they further a legitimate purpose and whether the majority could accomplish the same goal without injuring the minority shareholders. Here, the majority has no business purpose for terminating Wilkes (P) and does not offer evidence that he was guilty of misconduct. At a minimum, Wilkes' (P) termination is contrary to Springside's (D) long-standing tradition of securing a directorship and employment for each shareholder. With no salary from the company, the board eliminates any possible return on Wilkes' (P) investment. Quinn, Riche and Connor have breached their fiduciary duty, giving rise to money damages. Reversed and remanded.

Analysis:

Wilkes (P) was not obligated to deal fairly with Quinn (D) when he sold the real estate for Quinn's (D) other company to build a rest home because he was not dealing with Quinn (D) as a fellow shareholder. In that context, Quinn (D) was an outsider. Since Quinn (D) was not in a position to demand justice for what he considered a bad bargain, he and the others took out their hostilities by forcing Wilkes (P) from the business.

■ CASE VOCABULARY

FREEZE–OUT: The process, usually in a closely held corporation, by which the majority shareholders or the board of directors oppresses minority shareholders in an effort to compel them to liquidate their investment on terms favorable to the controlling shareholders.

Ingle v. Glamore Motor Sales, Inc.

(Shareholder) v. *(Issuing Corporation)*

73 N.Y.2d 183, 538 N.Y.S.2d 771, 535 N.E.2d 1311 (1989)

SHARE OWNERSHIP IS NOT A GUARANTEE OF CONTINUED EMPLOYMENT ABSENT AN AGREEMENT PROVIDING LIFETIME EMPLOYMENT

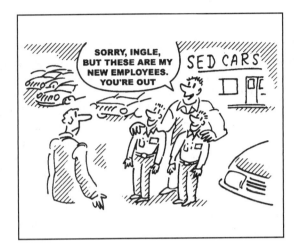

■ **INSTANT FACTS** Ingle (P) was a sales manager at and a shareholder of Glamore Motor Sales, Inc., (D), and when the company terminated his employment, his shares were bought back under a shareholders' agreement.

■ **BLACK LETTER RULE** If a shareholders' agreement provides for the right to repurchase shares upon the termination of a shareholder's employment with the issuing company, the employment is treated as employment at will and the shareholder has no claim for damages upon termination.

■ **PROCEDURAL BASIS**

On appeal from an appellate court decision, affirming the trial court's decision in favor of the remaining shareholders and the issuing company.

■ **FACTS**

Ingle (P) tried unsuccessfully to purchase stock in Glamore Motor Sales, Inc. (Glamore Motor) (D) from James Glamore (D), and was hired as a sales manager without an employment contract. Several months later, Glamore (D) and Ingle (P) entered a written shareholder agreement that provided for Ingle (P) to buy twenty-two of Glamore's shares with a five-year option to purchase an additional eighteen shares. Pursuant to the agreement, Ingle (P) would serve as the corporation's secretary and director, but Glamore (D) would be able to repurchase all of Ingle's (P) shares if Ingle (P) was no longer employed by Glamore Motor (D) for any reason. Ingle (P) purchased the additional eighteen shares, and the parties updated their Agreement. Twenty years later, Glamore (D) and his two sons purchased sixty additional shares that Glamore Motors (D) issued. The four shareholders entered into a new agreement that restated Glamore's (D) option to buy back Ingle's (P) shares for thirty days after termination of Ingle's (P) employment. Shortly thereafter, the company held a special board meeting and terminated Ingle's (P) employment. Glamore (D) notified Ingle (P) that he was exercising his right to repurchase his shares and paid him $96,000 for the shares. Ingle (P) filed suit. The lower courts found that Ingle (P) did not provide evidence to support the existence of an employment contract making his employment other than that of an at-will employee.

■ **ISSUE**

If a shareholder has agreed to a shareholder agreement's terms providing for repurchase of his shares upon termination for any reason, does the shareholder have the right to damages for breach of fiduciary duty if his employment is terminated other than for cause?

■ **DECISION AND RATIONALE**

(Bellacosa, J.) No. As a minority shareholder, Ingle (P) argues that, even in the absence of a written agreement, his employment should be protected by the fiduciary duty owed him as a minority shareholder and that his employment status was protected from termination other than for cause under that duty of loyalty and good faith. Previously, courts have found no implied duty of good faith and fair dealing in employment at-will relationships. Ingle (P) does not claim that the shareholders' agreement's terms are unfair or that the price he received is insufficient. Instead, he relies on *Fedner v. Prescott*, which holds that partners must deal with each other in the employment context with loyalty and food faith. However, that holding does not apply to employment in the corporate context. Fiduciary obligations accrue within the corporate context only in stockholder matters. Equity cannot be used to provide a different result where the principles governing the relationship are clear. Affirmed.

DISSENT

(Hancock, J.) The majority treats the plaintiff's complaint as simply constituting an employment claim. This disregards the fact that it is also an unfair squeeze-out claim. The majority bases their result on the phrase, "for any reason," to support its decision. The purpose behind the agreement was to protect Glamore (D) if Ingle (P) chose to leave his employment. New York law has recognized the need to protect minority shareholders from the majority's unrestrained actions. The law also recognizes that if a shareholder reasonably expects his participation in a corporation's ownership to give rise to an employment claim, any attempts to defeat those expectations should be prohibited. Relating a cash investment in a corporation to an at-will hiring is inappropriate and unfair. Unlike an employee in a large corporation, a minority shareholder has invested personal wealth in the business based on the expectation of employment.

Analysis:

Ingle (P) did not start his career at Glamore Motor (D) as a shareholder. He was hired as a sales manager and had to earn his right to buy into the company. The right to purchase stock was contingent on his signing a shareholders' agreement that protected the company by allowing it to buy Ingles' (P) shares if he left his job. In *Wilkes v. Springside Nursing Home, Inc.*, 370 Mass. 842, 353 N.E.2d 657 (1976), the court acknowledged that the lure to invest in a small business is frequently not the payment of dividends, as with public-company stock, but rather the promise of guaranteed employment. Glamore Motor (D) was a family-owned business. Although Glamore (D) was willing to give Ingle (P) the right to participate as a shareholder as long as he was affiliated with the company, he wanted the right to eliminate non-family members from the business when they left the company. While Ingles (P) may have been afforded more protection without the agreement, the Glamores (D) probably would not have transferred the shares to Ingles (P) without it.

■ CASE VOCABULARY

SQUEEZE–OUT: An action taken in an attempt to eliminate or reduce a minority interest in a corporation.

Sugarman v. Sugarman

(Minority Shareholders) v. *(Majority Shareholder)*

797 F.2d 3 (1st Cir. 1986)

A MAJORITY SHAREHOLDER'S ACTION IS EVALUATED AGAINST HIS FIDUCIARY DUTIES AND MAY BE VIEWED AS A FREEZE–OUT

■ **INSTANT FACTS** Descendants of a corporation's original founders filed a claim for breach of fiduciary duty after the majority shareholder exercised his position to direct profits to himself and his father rather than pay dividends or employ other family members, resulting in a freeze-out.

■ **BLACK LETTER RULE** If a controlling shareholder uses corporate assets for his own personal benefit, an offer to purchase minority shareholders' stock at an inadequate price will be viewed as part of a plan to freeze-out the minority shareholders.

■ **PROCEDURAL BASIS**

On appeal from entry of District Court's judgment in favor of the minority shareholders.

■ **FACTS**

Four brothers formed Sugarman Brothers, a partnership, to sell paper products. In 1918, three of the brothers, Joseph, Samuel and Myer Sugarman, continued to own in equal portions and manage the business. The business grew over the years. Leonard (D), Myer (Leonard's (D) father), and Hyman (the plaintiff's father) were all officers and directors in the company, but as family members retired or died, one branch of the family gained a majority interest and managed the business. The plaintiffs, Jon, James and Marjorie (P) (all Hyman's children) owned 21.78 percent of the stock. Leonard Sugarman (D), the son of Myer who died in 1983, owned sixty-one percent of the stock and served as president and chairman of the board. The company employed various family members from time to time. James (P) never tried to gain employment. Marjorie (P) sought employment but was turned down. The company employed John (P) for a time, but discharged him. The plaintiffs brought this suit seeking a derivative recovery against Leonard (D), arguing that Leonard (D) had abused his position as fiduciary both to the company and to the plaintiffs. The plaintiffs argued that Leonard (D) took excessive salaries and bonuses in order to deprive them of dividends. The plaintiffs also sought to be compensated for Leonard's (D) freeze-out of their shareholder positions through his denial of employment, acceptance of excessive compensation and refusal to pay dividends. At trial, the court found that Leonard (D) had paid his father salary and pension benefits that were not given to Hyman and had offered to buy Jon's (P) and Marjorie's (P) stock at greatly reduced prices. The court also found that Leonard (D) had received, in bad faith, excessive compensation amounting to more than $1 million, as part of an attempt to freeze out the others, and that he had improperly had the company pay his legal fees and other defense costs. The trial court awarded each shareholder their pro rata share of the improper payments.

■ **ISSUE**

May a majority shareholder's denial of employment to the minority shareholders, failure to pay dividends and acceptance of unreasonable compensation be viewed as part of a scheme to freeze-out the minority shareholders and force them to accept a less-than-adequate payment for their shares?

■ DECISION AND RATIONALE

(Coffin, J.) Yes. Shareholders must fulfill, as fiduciaries, a duty to act with the "utmost good faith and loyalty" and refrain from acting out of "avarice, expediency or self interest." In *Wilkes v. Springside Nursing Home*, the court found that three directors had acted to freeze-out a fourth director when they removed him from the company's payroll without a legitimate business excuse and offered to buy his shares at well below their value. A complaining shareholder's claims must be sufficiently supported in fact. First, a minority shareholder must allege that excessive compensation has been paid and that the excessive compensation is part of an attempt to freeze out the minority shareholders. Second, simply offering an inadequate price for shares proves nothing because the stockholder can bring an action for damages. The ingredients for a freeze-out of minority interest are present here. Leonard's (D) actions were taken to ensure the plaintiffs received no financial benefits. He paid no dividends and denied the plaintiffs employment within the company. Leonard's (D) payments to his father exceeded the payments made to any of the others. He continued to receive regular compensation for years after he ceased bringing value to the company. Judgment relating to interest and attorneys' fees vacated and remanded; remainder of judgment affirmed.

Analysis:

Freezing out a minority shareholder, in the absence of a shareholders' agreement or other contract is a tort that allows a greater measure of damages than a breach of contract. As a tort, however, claims for breach of fiduciary duty can be subject to shorter statute of limitations periods, requiring a shareholder to act quickly to recover. Often, as in *Sugarman*, the abuses arise in the context of family-owned businesses where there is pressure to refrain from bringing a lawsuit. In other cases, if the shareholders are not related, one shareholder may abuse his or her position by favoring family members.

■ CASE VOCABULARY

REDEEM: Verb form of "redemption." The reacquisition of a security by the issuer. Redemption usually refers to the repurchase of a bond before maturity, but it may also refer to the repurchase of stock and mutual-fund shares.

Smith v. Atlantic Props., Inc.

(Shareholder) v. *(Property Owner)*

12 Mass. App. Ct. 201, 422 N.E.2d 798 (1981)

A MINORITY SHAREHOLDER MAY ACT IN A MANNER THAT BREACHES HIS FIDUCIARY DUTY TO THE OTHER SHAREHOLDERS

YOU'RE JUST SAYING NO BECAUSE YOU'RE RICHER THAN US!

■ **INSTANT FACTS** Wolfson (D), who owned part of a corporation that purchased property for investment, blocked dividend payments to other shareholders, leading to substantial IRS penalties and limiting the others' returns from their investments.

■ **BLACK LETTER RULE** A minority shareholder may abuse his position by using measures designed to safeguard his position in a manner that fails to take into consideration his duty to act in the "utmost good faith and loyalty" toward the company and his fellow shareholders.

■ **PROCEDURAL BASIS**

On appeal from numerous post-trial motions, following the trial court's judgment in favor of the plaintiffs.

■ **FACTS**

Wolfson (D) agreed to buy land in Norwood for $350,000, with a cash payment of $50,000 and the balance covered by a mortgage loan of $300,000. He mentioned the deal to three other men, Smith (P), Zimble (P) and Burke (P), who each bought one-fourth of the deal for $12,500. Smith (P), an attorney, formed Atlantic Properties, Inc. (D) and prepared articles and bylaws. Both documents contained a provision that "no election, appointment or resolution by the Stockholders and no election, appointment, resolution, purchase, sale, lease, contract, contribution, compensation, proceeding or act by the Board of Directors or by any officer or officers shall be valid or binding upon the corporation until effected, passed, approved or ratified by an affirmative vote of 80% of the capital stock." The provision allowed any shareholder to stand in the way of any proposal made by the others. Atlantic (D) purchased the property and then sold part of it, retaining approximately twenty-eight acres containing twenty old brick and wood structures that required expensive and constant repair. Atlantic (D) started to turn a profit, paid the mortgage and successfully avoided accumulating any long-term debt. The company paid the investors salaries during two years and declared dividends only twice. Because the company's profits were not distributed, Atlantic (D) held $172,000 in cash in 1961. The other shareholders grew angry with Wolfson (D), who wanted to devote all of Atlantic's earnings to property repairs and improvements, while the others wanted to receive dividends. The others warned Wolfson (D) that failing to declare dividends could expose the company to IRS penalties. While the others agreed to some improvements, they demanded the remainder be distributed. The IRS eventually caught up with Atlantic (D) and imposed penalties more than once for undistributed dividends. The shareholders eventually filed this suit against Atlantic (D), seeking a court order for dividends, for Wolfson's (D) removal as director, and for Wolfson's (D) reimbursement of the IRS penalties. The trial judge ordered Wolfson (D) to reimburse Atlantic (D) for the penalties and interest and ordered the directors to declare a reasonable dividend then and as appropriate in the future. Wolfson (D) and Atlantic (D) unsuccessfully moved for a new trial and then appealed. The plaintiffs also appealed a denial of their motion for attorneys' fees against Wolfson (D).

■ ISSUE

Does a minority shareholder breach his fiduciary duty to fellow shareholders by relying on a provision in the corporate charter and bylaws that allows him to thwart any action desired by the majority shareholders?

■ DECISION AND RATIONALE

(J.) Yes. Under *Donahue*, shareholders in a close corporation must deal with each other as fiduciaries based on the similarities between a close corporation and a partnership. In *Donahue*, the court recognized that majority shareholders might need protection from a minority shareholder. However, here, the provision requiring the approval of all actions by eighty percent of the shares, had the effect in a company of four equal shareholders of granting each shareholder the right to veto any legitimate action. Wolfson (D) personally requested that provision to prevent the others from "ganging up" against him. Although Wolfson (D) had a right to protect himself, his actions went beyond reason, exposing the company to IRS penalties, interest and other charges. Wolfson (D) also refused to take any action to minimize the recurrence of IRS involvement. Whatever his motives for refusing to vote in favor of dividends, his actions were not consistent with the required "utmost good faith and loyalty." Affirmed.

Analysis:

This case provides a look at the fiduciary duty concept from the majority's point of view. While courts typically deal with the majority's abusive behavior toward the minority, the proliferation of shareholder agreements and other devices aimed at protecting the minority, the minority can also abuse terms intended to protect it. The broad, sweeping protections afforded shareholders in a close corporation are held to protect the business and each individual, regardless of how the power struggle occurs. Even two shareholders with equal power can find themselves in need of protection and rescue from stubborn shareholders. *See, e.g., Hollis v. Hill*, 232 F.3d 460 (5th Cir. 2000).

■ CASE VOCABULARY

DIVIDENDS: A portion of a company's earnings or profits distributed pro rata to its shareholders, usually in the form of cash or additional shares.

Jordan v. Duff & Phelps, Inc.

(Former Employee) v. *(Closely–Held Securities Firm)*

815 F.2d 429 (7th Cir. 1987)

A FORMER EMPLOYEE MAY RECOVER DAMAGES FOR INCREASED STOCK VALUE AFTER SELLING STOCK BACK TO A CLOSELY–HELD CORPORATION

■ **INSTANT FACTS** Jordan (P), an employee of and stockholder in Duff & Phelps, Inc. (D), left the closely-held company and cashed in his stock according to his stockholder agreement; a pending sale of the defendant firm would have made his stock far more valuable.

■ **BLACK LETTER RULE** If a closely-held company withholds from an employee-stockholder material information about possible increases in stock value in breach of its fiduciary duty, the employee-stockholder may be entitled to damages if he or she can show that the nondisclosure caused the employee-stockholder to act to his or her financial detriment.

■ **PROCEDURAL BASIS**

Appeal from a grant of summary judgment for Duff & Phelps (D).

■ **FACTS**

Jordan (P) was a long-term employee and stockholder of Duff & Phelps (D), a closely held securities analysis and consulting firm. After seeking a transfer to a regional office from the Chicago headquarters for personal reasons (which Duff & Phelps (D) denied), Jordan (P) accepted a position at a rival firm in November 1983. Unbeknownst to Jordan (P) and immediately prior to his resignation, Duff & Phelps' (D) board resolved to sell the firm, although nothing had been formalized by the time Jordan (P) resigned. Under Jordan's (P) stockholder agreement, he was required to sell his stock in Duff & Phelps (D) back to the company upon termination of his employment. The parties would determine the stock price by using the adjusted book value of the stocks on the December 31 that "coincides with, or immediately precedes, the date of termination. . . ." This provision had been enforced uniformly except with regard to one former employee, Franchik, who was allowed by board resolution to retain her stock for five years. Jordan (P) maintained his employment through the end of 1983 in order to receive the December 31, 1983, value of his shares rather than the 1982 value. Duff & Phelps (D) paid him $23,225 for his stock. Prior to cashing his check, on January 10, 1984, Jordan (P) heard of a merger between Duff & Phelps (D) and Security Pacific, the terms of which would have yielded approximately $452,000 and other remuneration to Jordan (P) if his shares had been involved in the transaction. Jordan (P) refused to cash his check and demanded the return of his stock, which request Duff & Phelps (D) refused. Jordan (P) filed suit for damages. In March 1984, the government objected to the Duff & Phelps (D) and Security Pacific merger, and the transaction collapsed in January 1985. Duff & Phelps (D) moved to dismiss Jordan's (P) suit, and Jordan (P) responded by amending his complaint to request rescission rather than damages. Duff & Phelps (D) continued to seek a purchaser, but, finding none, the firm's management formed an "Employee Stock Ownership Trust," borrowed capital, and acquired Duff & Phelps (D) through a new entity, Duff Research, Inc., in December 1985. Employees and stockholders at that time (including Franchik) received substantial rewards; Jordan (P) argued that his shares would have been worth $497,000 at acquisition had he still held them.

■ ISSUE

Does a corporation owe a duty to notify an employee-stockholder leaving the corporation of potential actions that may substantially increase the value of the employee-stockholder's shares in the corporation?

■ DECISION AND RATIONALE

(Easterbrook, Cir. J.) Yes. Close corporations buying back their own stock must disclose all information that is material under *TSC Industries, Inc. v. Northway, Inc.*, 426 U.S. 438, 449 (1976) (materiality exists if there is a "substantial likelihood that, under all the circumstances, the omitted fact would have assumed actual significance in the deliberations of the reasonable shareholder"). While individuals are free to conduct transactions in accordance with private information that may be to their advantage, Duff & Phelps (D), as a closely held corporation, was bound by a fiduciary duty to disclose material facts to its stockholders. Section 10(b) of the Securities and Exchange Act and SEC Rule 10b–5 require a party to a securities transaction to provide all necessary material disclosures to avoid fraud. These provisions cannot be abrogated by contract, and in any event, there is no explicit employment contract in question here, as Jordan (P) was an at-will employee. The stockholder agreement did not remove a duty to inform; in fact, Duff & Phelps' (D) course of dealing was to inform departing employees of the likely value on the next December 31 so employees could determine how to schedule their termination to take best advantage of their stock, as Jordan (P) did. The stockholder agreement did fix the price of the stock at book value, but it did not set terms for the date an employee would depart. Duff & Phelps relies on cases that establish a fixed date for valuation depending on the manner of an employee's departure, but Jordan's (P) stockholder agreement allowed him to make a choice regarding his departure date. The dissent believes that this fact is irrelevant because Duff & Phelps (D) could have terminated employee-at-will Jordan (P) at any time. However, at-will employment does not imply an absolute right to terminate an employee; for instance, state law limits the valid reasons for termination. At-will employment is therefore a type of contractual relationship, and a "term implied into every written contract, and therefore, we suppose, every unwritten one, is that neither party will try to take opportunistic advantage of the other." If Duff & Phelps (D) had terminated Jordan (P) and gloatingly advised him of the stock price advantage he was missing as a result (as the dissent suggests the defendant could have done without penalty), that would have been a breach of an implied pledge to avoid opportunistic conduct. Whether the defendant's omissions here rise to intent to defraud under Rule 10b–5 in light of the materiality of the information and the timing of Jordan's resignation is for the jury. However, rescission is not an available remedy; as the lower court held, stock ownership is predicated on employment with Duff & Phelps (D), notwithstanding the exception extended to Franchik. Damages are therefore the only option open to Jordan (P). The lower court held there were no damages since the Security Pacific transaction did not close, but if there was a securities violation in the failure to disclose the possible transaction, then damages are available if Jordan (P) can show causation. To receive damages, he must show that if he had known of the potential deal with Security Pacific he would have chosen to stay with Duff & Phelps (D), and would further have remained until the Duff Research sale in 1985. That question is also for the jury. Reversed and remanded.

DISSENT:

(Posner, J.) A corporation owes no duty to an employee who is bound to sell his shares to the corporation by a stockholder agreement's clear terms. The agreement conferred no right to receive such information, and Duff & Phelps (D) did not make an undertaking or assume a duty to disclose information regarding the possible future trajectory of a departing employee's stock. There is no implicit duty in the fiduciary relationship between a closely held corporation and its stockholders because a fiduciary relationship does not require disclosure of material information to stockholders. The agreement's terms are plain, entitling Jordan (P) to what he received, and the defendant bore no responsibility to advise Jordan (P) of information from which he had no right to benefit. The stockholder agreement essentially gave Duff & Phelps (D) an option to buy back shares at will at a set or determinable price. The absence of an employment agreement is irrelevant.

Analysis:

This case underlines the important distinctions between obligations to stockholders of publicly traded companies versus closely held entities like Duff & Phelps (D). The court holds that the defendant's failure to provide material information about the possible future value of Jordan's (P) stock raises the possibility of damages in the six figures. The same "material information" could be the subject of an insider trading case were the defendant traded publicly. What policy rationale underpins the difference? Why might the court be so eager to reach a good result for Jordan (P)?

■ CASE VOCABULARY

FIDUCIARY: One who owes another the duties of good faith, trust, confidence, and candor.

FIDUCIARY RELATIONSHIP: A relationship in which one person is under a duty to act for the benefit of the other on matters within the scope of the relationship.

RESCISSION: A party's unilateral unmaking of a contract for a legally sufficient reason, such as the other party's material breach.

SECURITIES EXCHANGE ACT OF 1934: The federal law regulating the public trading of securities. This law provides for the registration and supervision of securities exchanges and brokers, and regulates proxy solicitations. The Act also established the Securities Exchange Commission.

Alaska Plastics, Inc. v. Coppock

(Issuing Company) v. *(Selling Shareholder)*

621 P.2d 270 (Alaska 1980)

A SHAREHOLDER MAY NOT REQUIRE A COMPANY TO PURCHASE ITS STOCK FOR FAIR VALUE IF THE COMPANY HAS NOT DONE SO FOR OTHERS

■ **INSTANT FACTS** Muir (P) received half of her husband's shares in Alaska Plastics, Inc. (D) in a divorce; the company offered to buy her shares at a price Muir (P) believed to be too low.

■ **BLACK LETTER RULE** A shareholder may require a corporation to repurchase its own shares upon the company's breach of fiduciary duty, but the remedy should be less than liquidation, if possible, and a fair price may be less than the appraised value.

■ **PROCEDURAL BASIS**

On appeal from the trial judge's finding that the corporation was obligated to buy the minority shareholder's stock at fair value.

■ **FACTS**

Stefano (D), Gillam (D) and Crow (D) formed Alaska Plastics (D), which manufactured foam insulation. Each of the men owned 300 shares of stock. In 1970, Crow (D) obtained a divorce and gave 150 shares to Muir (P), his ex-wife. Stefano (D), Gilliam (D) and Crow (D) were officers and directors of the company, and Muir (P) was not always notified of the annual meetings. One of the meetings was held in Seattle and Gilliam (D) and Stefano (D) brought their wives at company expense, even though there was no business purpose for doing so. The three men each received a $3000 directors' fee annually, but they never authorized dividend payments. Gilliam (D) also received a $30,000 salary as the general manager. Muir (P) received no money from the corporation. At the 1974 board meeting, Muir (P) was offered $15,000 for her shares. She retained an attorney, who demanded to see the corporation's books and records and estimated the shares had a value between $23,000 and $40,000. Later that year, the board authorized the company's purchase of Broadwater Industries, which it renamed "Valley Plastics" without consulting Muir (P). At the 1975 shareholders' meeting, Muir (P) offered her shares to the corporation for $40,000. The company offered her $20,000, but Muir (P) rejected the offer. Shortly thereafter, a fire forced the company to shift all operations to Valley Plastics, and Alaska Plastics (D) effectively became no more than a holding company for Valley Plastics. The next year, Stefano (D) offered to buy Muir's (P) shares for $20,000, but Muir (P) again refused. Muir (P) sued, seeking to have Alaska Plastics (D) purchase her shares. The trial judge entered judgment against the three other shareholders (D) and Alaska Plastics (D) for $52,314 (representing the shares' value), Muir's (P) attorneys' fees, interest and costs. Both sides appealed.

■ **ISSUE**

In the absence of a prior agreement for repurchase or a change in corporate structure, does a minority shareholder in a close corporation have the right to demand the company purchase its shares at fair value?

■ **DECISION AND RATIONALE**

(Judge Undisclosed) No. In a publicly traded company, a shareholder can usually sell his or her stock when desired. In a close corporation, there is no ready market for the shares, and majority shareholders can often "squeeze out" minority shareholders at low prices. A forced purchase can occur upon an event stated in the articles of incorporation, on involuntary dissolution, at merger or upon other structural changes as provided by statutory appraisal rights, or as ordered by court upon finding a breach of fiduciary duty. In this case, neither the articles nor the bylaws contained any provision addressing repurchase of Muir's shares. Under Alaska law, a shareholder may liquidate a corporation on a showing of illegal, oppressive or fraudulent actions. Liquidation is an extreme remedy, and there is no guarantee that Muir (P) would receive more than she would have received as fair value for her shares. If possible, courts should award alternative remedies. Even if Muir (P) can provide proof of an "illegal, oppressive or fraudulent" activity, she must seek a less drastic remedy. A statutory appraisal is available only following a fundamental corporate change, such as a merger or consolidation, so it is not appropriate here. Forcing the company to purchase its own shares is appropriate where one group of shareholders in a close corporation is allowed to receive benefits that the others are not. This inability to discriminate arises from the fiduciary duty shareholders in a close corporation owe to each other. However, the appraisal remedy provided by the trial court is not the appropriate remedy here. At trial, the court told the jury that once Alaska Plastics (D) made an offer to buy Muir's (P) shares, it was obligated to buy them at a fair price, regardless of their original offer. However, no case law supports a specific performance award if a shareholder has rejected an offer. Muir (P) argues that she should have been able to derive the same benefits from her shares as the other shareholders, but none of the other shareholders sold their shares to the company. However, the other shareholders received directors' fees, and one shareholder received a salary. If the corporation paid money for something other than services, the payments could have been dividends. Muir (P) must establish that the defendants' actions do not deserve protection under the business judgment rule. Muir's (P) complaint makes no allegations that the actions were unreasonable. While Muir (P) alleged that she did not receive the dividends given to other shareholders, that is a personal claim, not a derivative claim. Remanded.

Analysis:

The court did not have enough evidence to determine whether the directors' fees and salary represented fair value for services rendered or were disguised dividends. Minority shareholders frequently find a corporation will avoid distributing dividends to all shareholders in favor of payments to those in control. These disguised dividends may take the form of bonuses, high salaries, excessive expense reimbursement and other employee benefits. In addition to fact that the minority shareholders do not receive these benefits, siphoning off the company's earnings to pay for these perks may make the company appear not as valuable on paper.

■ CASE VOCABULARY

CLOSE CORPORATION: A corporation whose stock is not freely traded and is held by only a few shareholders (often within the same family). The requirements and privileges of close corporations vary by jurisdiction. Also termed closely held corporation; closed corporation.

Pedro v. Pedro

(Shareholder) v. *(Forced–Out Shareholder)*

489 N.W.2d 798 (Minn. Ct. App. 1992)

A SHAREHOLDER MAY OBTAIN VALUE FOR SHARES IN EXCESS OF THAT PROVIDED IN A VALID STOCK REDEMPTION AGREEMENT

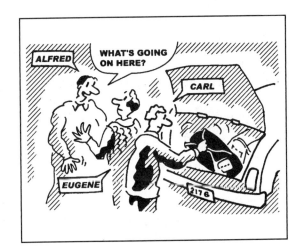

■ **INSTANT FACTS** Members of a family-run business terminated one of the shareholder's employment when he refused to ignore a substantial accounting discrepancy.

■ **BLACK LETTER RULE** A shareholder-employee of a closely held corporation, who was fired by other shareholders in a breach of fiduciary duty, is entitled to damages equal to the total of the difference between his stock's fair value and any lesser amount required by a stock retirement agreement, in addition to the damages arising from his loss of life-time employment.

■ PROCEDURAL BASIS

On appeal following a remand in which the trial court awarded damages for breach of fiduciary duty, wrongful termination and attorneys' fees.

■ FACTS

Three brothers, Alfred (P), Carl (D) and Eugene (D) Pedro, each owned a one-third interest in The Pedro Companies (TPC) (D), a luggage manufacturer and retailer. Carl (D) and Eugene (D) worked at TPC (D) for more than fifty years. Alfred (P) worked for TPC (D) for forty-five years and was fired. While employed, each brother received the same compensation amount and had an equal vote on business matters. In 1968, the brothers executed a Stock Retirement Agreement in anticipation of their father's retirement. The agreement addressed payments to be made at death, on retirement and upon buyout of each of the shareholders. When the brothers' father died, the agreement governed the repurchase of his shares. The brothers' relationship deteriorated when Alfred (P) discovered an accounting error of more than $300,000. Although some of the money was eventually found, much of it remained missing and unexplained. Alfred (P) wanted a financial investigation. An accountant hired to locate the money failed to do so. The other brothers told Alfred (P) to cooperate with them and forget the missing money or be fired. Rather than drop the matter, Alfred hired a second accountant to investigate the missing funds. The other brothers fired Alfred (P) and told workers at TPC (D) that he had had a nervous breakdown. At trial, Alfred (P) was awarded $766,582.23 for his one-third ownership, $563,417.67 for the difference between the value of his shares under the agreement and their true value, and more than $250,000 for termination of his lifetime employment. The trial judge also awarded him attorneys' fees and prejudgment interest after determining that his brothers' actions were "arbitrary, vexatious and otherwise not in good faith."

■ ISSUE

If a shareholder-employee is terminated under conditions that suggest a breach of fiduciary duty, is the shareholder-employee entitled to receive compensation for his shares in excess of that provided in a stock redemption agreement as well as damages for the loss of lifetime employment?

■ DECISION AND RATIONALE

(Norton, J.) Yes. The relationship between shareholders in a close corporation is that of fiduciaries. The trial court found sufficient evidence to conclude that the Alfred's brothers (D) did not deal with Alfred (P) "openly, honestly and fairly." The defendants never offered to repurchase Alfred's (P) shares under the agreement. Instead, they threatened Alfred (P) with termination for looking into financial discrepancies and humiliated him by telling others at TPC (D) that he had suffered a nervous breakdown. The defendants argue there was no breach of fiduciary duty since none of the actions harmed the company financially. There is, however, more to a claim of breached fiduciary duty than a decrease in the company's value. Alfred (P) deserved the compensation awarded by the trial court. The value of Alfred's (P) shares under the agreement represents a forced-out price and not the true value of his shares. Alfred (P) also had a reasonable expectation of lifetime employment. Although the defendants' claim the lower court compensated Alfred (P) twice for the same loss by awarding damages for a breach of fiduciary duty and the lost employment, they are incorrect. Alfred (P) brought his claim of lost employment in his capacity as an employee, whereas he brought his claim for breach of fiduciary duty as a shareholder. Also, because the defendants' actions were "arbitrary, vexatious and otherwise not in good faith," Alfred (P) was entitled to attorneys' fees and interest. Affirmed.

Analysis:

In contrast with Muir in *Alaska Plastics, Inc. v. Coppock*, 621 P.2d 270 (Alaska 1980), Alfred (P) suffered much abuse. While Muir was denied the right to only a few thousand dollars over the course of several years, Alfred (P) was shut out from the operations of his own company, denied the right to investigate the disappearance of hundreds of thousands of dollars, and fired. This court found no impropriety in compensating Alfred (P) both as an employee and as a shareholder of TPC (D). In a close corporation, employment in the business may be one of the shareholder's only financial benefits.

■ CASE VOCABULARY

BUY–SELL AGREEMENT: An arrangement between owners of a business by which the surviving owners agree to purchase the interest of a withdrawing or deceased owner. REDEMPTION: The reacquisition of a security by the issuer. Redemption usually refers to the repurchase of a bond before maturity, but it may also refer to the repurchase of stock and mutual-fund shares. Also termed (in reference to stock) stock redemption; stock repurchase.

Stuparich v. Harbor Furniture Mfg., Inc.

(Unhappy Minority Shareholder) v. (Issuing Corporation)
83 Cal.App.4th 1268, 100 Cal.Rptr.2d 313 (2000)

MINORITY OWNERS ARE NOT GRANTED JUDICIAL DISSOLUTION WITHOUT EVIDENCE OF PREFER-
ENTIAL TREATMENT OF MAJORITY SHAREHOLDERS

■ **INSTANT FACTS** Stuparich (P) and Tuttleton (P), minority shareholders in Harbor Furniture Mfg., Inc. (D), received regular dividends, but wanted to be bought out because they were not on good terms with the other shareholders and their family members.

■ **BLACK LETTER RULE** A court will not order dissolution of a close corporation if the plaintiffs fail to show the dissolution was reasonably necessary to protect their rights.

■ **PROCEDURAL BASIS**

On appeal following the entry of summary judgment in favor of the defendants.

■ **FACTS**

Stuparich (P) and Tuttleton (P) were minority shareholders of Harbor Furniture (D), which their grandfather, Malcolm Tuttleton, founded in 1929. The company purchased land as an investment and later developed the land into a mobile home park, which it continues to operate. Malcolm, Jr. (D), the plaintiffs' brother, worked with his father in the business for years. Malcolm, Sr. made his son the company CEO in 1982 and paid him a salary and bonuses. Malcolm, Jr.'s wife, Jocelle (D), worked as Harbor Furniture's (D) office manager. Their son, Brent (D), worked as a salesman and was paid a base salary plus commissions. Although the plaintiffs attended board meetings, they did not participated in the business operations. The plaintiffs obtained their shares as gifts and inheritance. Malcolm, Sr., sold his shares to Malcolm, Jr. (D) in 1996, giving Malcolm, Jr. controlling interest in the company. The plaintiffs characterized the sale as "clandestine." The plaintiffs became frustrated with the company and stopped attending meetings. They received regular dividends, but Malcolm, Jr. (D) refused to buy them out. The plaintiffs filed an action seeking involuntary dissolution of Harbor Furniture (D) and damages for fraud, conspiracy and negligence. As a result of this action, the parties exchanged blows, and Tuttleton (P) was injured. The court dismissed all claims but the request for dissolution, and Harbor Furniture (D) moved for summary judgment arguing that dissolution could be avoided because the plaintiffs' could appoint a designate to sit on the board and protect their interests, which were not jeopardized because they continued to receive dividends.

■ **ISSUE**

Is dissolution appropriate if the liquidation is not reasonably necessary to protect a complaining shareholder's rights or interests?

■ **DECISION AND RATIONALE**

(Epstein, J.) No. Although the plaintiffs rely on a California statute allowing for dissolution in close corporations, the remedy is still drastic. *Stumpf v. C.E. Stumpf & Sons*, allowed an involuntary dissolution when a shareholder left the company over a management dispute. The appellate court, acknowledging that a shareholder's right to seek dissolution was not unlimited, justified the remedy because the extreme hostility in the family prevented the shareholder from participating in the business operations. On the other hand, in *Bauer v. Bauer*, minority shareholders in a close corporation sought dissolution, and the appeals court determined that the majority shareholders had abused their discretion and that the minority shareholder had established a competing business. Therefore, dissolution was not required. Here, the issue is whether the remedy of dissolution is necessary to protect the minority shareholders' rights and interests. Malcolm, Jr. (D) is a majority shareholder that can outvote the plaintiffs, but that factor alone does not justify imposing dissolution. The plaintiffs claim that because they have been unable to effectively participate in the business, their sole right and interest is to continue receiving dividends (which the court notes have been substantial). Although the plaintiffs contend the company could make more money with a different structure, there is always the possibility that more money can be made, and decisions affecting a company's operations are protected by the business judgment rule. There is no evidence of bad faith simply because of the hostile relationship between the plaintiffs and their brother. Nothing in the trial record necessitates the remedy of liquidation. No case law supports the plaintiffs' claims that a court must order a corporation to purchase a shareholder's shares to avoid dissolution. Affirmed.

Analysis:

In *Pedro v. Pedro*, 489 N.W.2d 798 (Minn. Ct. App. 1992), the court found a breach of fiduciary duty to the shareholder without finding financial damage to the company. In *Stuparich*, the court appears to reach the opposite conclusion. *Stuparich* holds that because the plaintiffs have been receiving substantial dividends for their shares, they were not injured. In other cases, the courts have focused on protecting the minority shareholders' investments. Here, and perhaps also in *Alaska Plastics, Inc. v. Coppock*, 621 P.2d 270 (Alaska 1980), the court was slower to find injury, perhaps because the minority shareholders paid nothing for their shares. (In *Alaska Plastics*, the minority shareholder received the shares as part of divorce settlement; here, the plaintiffs obtained their shares through gifts and inheritance.) Although the acquisition method should not make a difference, it appears to be an underlying, yet unstated, factor in these cases.

■ CASE VOCABULARY

INVOLUNTARY DISSOLUTION: The termination of a corporation administratively (for failure to file reports or pay taxes), judicially (for abuse of corporate authority, management deadlock, or failure to pay creditors), or through involuntary bankruptcy.

Frandsen v. Jensen–Sundquist Agency, Inc.

(Minority Shareholder) v. *(Closely–Held Corporation)*

802 F.2d 941 (7th Cir. 1986)

MERGERS DO NOT TRIGGER THE RIGHT–OF–FIRST REFUSAL UPON SALE PROVIDED IN A SHARE-HOLDER AGREEMENT

■ **INSTANT FACTS** The majority block of shares in Jensen–Sundquist Agency, Inc. (D) was owned by a group of individuals that entered into a shareholders' agreement providing them with protection in the event of a sale of the corporation's stock, and when the company attempted to transfer its primary asset, one of the shareholders demanded to exercise his right of first refusal.

■ **BLACK LETTER RULE** A minority shareholder's right of first refusal that is triggered by the majority shareholders' sale of their stock does not apply to a transaction in which an acquiring entity purchases the corporation's principal asset, after which the corporation is liquidated.

■ **PROCEDURAL BASIS**

On appeal from the District Court's order granting summary judgment in favor of the defendants.

■ **FACTS**

Jensen owned all of the stock in Jensen–Sundquist Agency, Inc. (the Agency) (D), a holding company. Although the Agency's (D) principal asset was the First Bank of Grantsburg (the Bank), it also owned a small insurance company. In 1975, Jensen sold 52 percent of his Agency shares to family members, who together created a majority bloc. Jensen, a lawyer representing his family, and the Bank signed a shareholder agreement pursuant to which each shareholder promised to offer his or her stock to the minority shareholders, if he or she decided to sell, at the same price offered by any other buyer. This majority bloc agreed not to sell any of their shares to anyone who would not also consider purchasing the other minority shareholders' interests at the same price. If they did not so agree, the selling shareholder would buy the other shareholders' interests. In 1984, the Agency's (D) president negotiated with First Wisconsin Corporation for it to acquire the Bank for $88 per share. Each Agency (D) stockholder was to receive $62 per share, after making allowances for the fact that the insurance company was not included in the deal. The Agency (D) asked each stockholder to waive his rights under the agreement as part of the transaction. All shareholders except Frandsen (P) signed the waiver. Frandsen (P) chose to invoke his rights under the agreement to buy the shares from the other shareholders for $62 per share. To circumvent Frandsen's (P) efforts, the parties restructured the transaction so that the company would be dissolved after the transfer. Frandsen (P) sued to enforce the agreement.

■ **ISSUE**

Does a minority shareholder's right of first refusal that is triggered by the majority shareholders' sale of their stock apply to a transaction in which an acquiring entity purchases the corporation's principal asset, after which the corporation is liquidated?

■ DECISION AND RATIONALE

(Posner, J.) No. If the parties had characterized their sale as the sale of the Bank, rather than mentioning the stock, the shareholders' rights under the agreement would never have been implicated. The buyer was not interested in becoming a member of the Agency (D) holding company. Once the parties complete the transaction, the Agency ceases to exist, as typically occurs in a merger. A merger does not activate rights that are triggered by an offer to buy or sell shares. The majority's intent in negotiating the shareholder agreement is to avoid being in a minority position with a stranger. A right of first refusal allowed the individuals the opportunity to stay within the company on their own terms. It did not insulate them from a sale of the company. Frandsen (P) argues the agreement's terms were nevertheless operative because the Agency sought a waiver of the shareholders' rights under the agreement. Frandsen (P) misconstrues the waiver. A waiver can be used like a quit claim deed, so it does not warrant that the grantor necessarily has an interest to transfer. Further, the law requires a narrow construction of any right of first refusal and recognizes the right only where it is clearly found to exist. Finally, as long as First Wisconsin did not induce the Agency (D) to violate the shareholders' agreement, no tortious interference occurred.

Analysis:

A shareholder agreement is an important tool to ensure that shareholders are not forced to accept strangers into their company and, in some cases, to provide them with certainty regarding the financial compensation they will receive if they need to retire, become disabled or prefer to move on. Although a shareholders' agreement is valuable, nothing obligates the company to structure a transaction so as to give the shareholders the opportunity to take advantage of the agreement's terms. In *Loxterman v. Convenient Food Mart, Inc.*, 1996 WL 432458 (Ohio Ct. App. Aug. 1, 1996), a shareholder similarly complained that a company's sale was purposely structured to avoid interference from the rights guaranteed under his shareholders' agreement. However, the court explicitly noted that simply because the parties have entered into a shareholders' agreement, there is no obligation to structure a transaction to provide the parties with the rights provided by the agreement.

■ CASE VOCABULARY

WAIVER: The voluntary relinquishment or abandonment—express or implied—of a legal right or advantage.

Zetlin v. Hanson Holdings, Inc.

(Majority Shareholder) v. *(Minority Shareholder)*

48 N.Y.2d 684, 421 N.Y.S.2d 877, 397 N.E.2d 387 (1979)

SHAREHOLDERS MAY RECEIVE A PREMIUM ON THE SALE OF THEIR SHARES FOR THE CONTROL REPRESENTED BY THEIR SHARES

■ **INSTANT FACTS** Zetlin (P) owned two percent of Gable Industries when Hanson Holdings, Inc. (D) and Sylvestri (D), which owned a controlling interest in Gable Industries, sold their shares to Flintkote Co. for $15 per share at a time the common stock was trading at $7.38 per share.

■ **BLACK LETTER RULE** In the absence of an allegation that a shareholder is looting corporate assets or has committed fraud or other acts of bad faith, a shareholder may obtain a premium price for the sale of a controlling block of shares.

■ **PROCEDURAL BASIS**

On appeal from a decision by the New York Supreme Court rendering partial summary judgment for the defendants.

■ **FACTS**

Zetlin (P) owned two percent of Gable Industries. Hanson Holdings, Inc. (Hanson) (D) and Sylvestri (D) owned 44.4 percent of the company, which represented controlling interest in the corporation. Hanson (D) and Sylvestri (D) sold their shares to Flintkote Co. for $15 per share, when the other common stock was trading at $7.38 per share. Zetlin (P) sued to obtain a portion of the additional value for himself.

■ **ISSUE**

If controlling shareholders transfer their entire interest in a corporation to a new buyer and receive a price in excess of the market price for their shares, are the selling shareholders obligated to share their premium with the minority shareholders?

■ **DECISION AND RATIONALE**

(Memorandum Opinion) No. Minority shareholders may be protected from abuse and unfair advantage from majority shareholders, but they may not inhibit majority shareholders' financial interests. Since those who invest in a business to acquire a majority interest have typically invested more than those holding a minority position, a premium for the sale of their control represents a return on their greater investment. To hold that a majority stockholder must share this premium with the other shareholders would require that controlling interest to be exchanged only as part of a tender offer. This is contrary to existing law. Affirmed.

Analysis:

A control premium indicates the greater responsibilities a shareholder has in disposing of his shares to a new buyer. In *In re Integrated Resources, Inc.*, 1990 WL 325414 (Bankr. S.D.N.Y. 1990), the court discussed the long history that permits a shareholder to obtain a higher payment for his shares if he or she is able to transfer control over the corporation along with the shares. Because the majority shareholder owes a fiduciary duty to his fellow shareholders, courts have placed a duty on the selling shareholder to ensure that a control premium does not abuse the minority shareholders. Courts have held a controlling shareholder who is offered a higher price for his or her shares, must inquire of the buyer's motives if the premium is excessive, the corporation's assets are financing the payment, the buyers are in a hurry, or the corporate assets are extremely liquid.

■ CASE VOCABULARY

CONTROL PREMIUM: A premium paid for shares carrying the power to control a corporation. The control premium is often computed by comparing the aggregate value of the controlling block of shares with the cost that would be incurred if the shares could be acquired at the going market price per share.

Perlman v. Feldmann

(Minority Shareholder) v. *(Chairman and Majority Shareholder)*

219 F.2d 173 (2d Cir. 1955)

A CONTROL PREMIUM MUST BE SHARED AMONG ALL STOCKHOLDERS IF IT REPRESENTS THE TRANSFER OF A CORPORATE ASSET

BUT WHICH FIDUCIARY DUTY HAS HE VIOLATED?

FIDUCIARY

■ **INSTANT FACTS** Feldmann (D), a majority shareholder in a steel mill business, sold a controlling interest in the mill to a company that required steel in the fabrication of its products, and the minority shareholders brought a derivative action against Feldmann (D) to recover the amounts he received in excess of the shares' market price.

■ **BLACK LETTER RULE** A shareholder with a controlling interest who transfers his or her shares is accountable to the minority shareholders for the amount in excess of the market price if the premium is attributable to the sale of a corporate asset.

■ **PROCEDURAL BASIS**

On appeal from U.S. District Court's order dismissing the defendants' action.

■ **FACTS**

Feldmann (D) was the chairman and majority shareholder of Newport, a mill that produced steel sheets for sale to steel product manufacturers. Wilport Co., an end-user of steel, made an offer to buy Feldmann's (D) shares to assure themselves of a steady supply of steel in times of tight supply. In the sale, Feldmann (D) received a premium attributable to the control represented by his shares. Wilport paid $20 for each share of Newport stock while the market price for the Newport shares was $17.03. The plaintiffs, minority shareholders in Newport, argue that Feldmann (D) received payment for a corporate asset with the sale of his shares because Wilport obtained the ability to direct the corporation's end product to itself.

■ **ISSUE**

If a majority shareholder receives a premium for the sale of shares that is attributable to a corporate asset, must the majority shareholder account for that premium to the other shareholders?

■ **DECISION AND RATIONALE**

(Swan, Cir. J.) Yes. As a director and holder of a control block of corporate shares, Feldmann (D) has a fiduciary duty to the minority shareholders. By siphoning corporate advantages for personal gain in the form of market advantages, a shareholder acts for personal gain and against the company and its shareholders. When Feldmann (D) sold the ability to determine the purchaser of the company's products, he received funds that could have been used to make the company more productive, sacrificing the company's good will. The plaintiffs must be permitted to recover in their own right since providing relief to the corporation would provide a benefit to Wilport. Judgment reversed and action remanded.

■ **DISSENT**

(Swan, Cir. J.) While the majority finds that Feldmann (D) was a fiduciary, they do not say to whom he owed his duty and whether he breached it as a shareholder or as a director. A majority shareholder has the right to get the best price possible when he sells his stock. In the process, he is not acting for the corporation unless he knows the purchaser intends to take an action detrimental to the corporation. In that case, he has a duty not to transfer his shares. There is no evidence here that Feldmann (D) knew or even should have suspected an improper motive. Although Wilport intended to purchase Newport's product for its own use, that is permissible. "The ability to direct product during a time of shortage" is not a corporate asset. Feldmann's (D) only possible error was agreeing to turn board control over to the new owners, but that is an error only if Feldmann (D) believed that the new board members were not well-qualified to serve the company. Finally, if Feldmann (D) took a premium for a corporate asset, he must compensate the corporation, not its shareholders.

Analysis:

This result appears to oppose the holding in *Zetlin v. Hanson Holdings, Inc.* 48 N.Y.2d 684, 421 N.Y.S.2d 877, 397 N.E.2d 387 (1979), in which the court assured that any premium the shareholder received for transferring its control block of shares would be upheld. The distinction between *Perlman* and *Zetlin* rests in the propriety of the acquiring company's motive. The Wilport management did not want simply the ability to run the company and make a profit; they wanted to use the company to further their original business.

■ CASE VOCABULARY

ASSET: An item that is owned and has value.

Essex Universal Corp. v. Yates

(Hopeful Purchaser) v. *(Corporation's President and Chairman)*

305 F.2d 572 (2d Cir. 1962)

A CONTRACT TO SELL A CONTROLLING INTEREST IN A CORPORATION MAY INCLUDE CONTROL OF THE CORPORATION'S BOARD

■ **INSTANT FACTS** Yates (D) agreed to sell a controlling block of shares in Republic Pictures to Essex Universal Corp. (P), and the sale agreement required Yates (D) to deliver a board of directors filled with members nominated by Essex Universal (P).

■ **BLACK LETTER RULE** If the transfer of shares is sufficient to constitute the transfer of a controlling interest, a seller may lawfully agree to assist the buyer in installing a favorable board of directors.

■ **PROCEDURAL BASIS**

On appeal from a summary judgment in favor of the defendant.

■ **FACTS**

Yes. Yates (D) was president and chairman of Republic Pictures. Essex Universal Corp. (P) tried to purchase between 500,000 and 600,000 shares of Republic Pictures stock at $8 per share, $2 over the then-current market price. As a condition to closing, Yates (D) was to deliver the resignations of a majority of Republic's board and ensure that the resigning members were replaced with designates of Essex's (P) choosing. Yates (D) informed Essex (P) that he could deliver 566,223 shares, which amounted to 28.3 percent of the stock, and the parties scheduled the closing. Essex (P) brought bank drafts totaling more than $1 million to the closing. The drafts were payable to Essex's banker, who would endorse them to Yates (D). Yates (D) refused to close the deal, worrying that the change in directors would be held improper. Essex (P) sued Yates (D), demanding transfer of the shares and claiming a loss of $2.7 million due to the stock's appreciation.

■ **ISSUE**

Is a contract that provides for the transfer and control of the board of directors illegal *per se* under New York law?

■ **DECISION AND RATIONALE**

(Lumbard, J.) No. New York laws prohibit the sale of a corporate office, but the parties here contracted for the purchase of a substantial block of Republic stock. By virtue of the transferred shares, the new stockholder could have elected a majority of the board. Therefore, the contract for the stock sale was not the bare sale of an office. (The court presumes that Essex (P) was acquiring a controlling block of shares, even though it acquired only 28.3 percent of the outstanding shares, because in a public company substantially less than fifty-one percent of the outstanding shares will generally confer control.) After the purchase, Essex (P) could have installed its own set of directors, but, because the directors' terms are staggered, it would have had to wait for eighteen months to obtain control of the board. Controlling shareholders may obtain a premium from the sale of a controlling block of stock. The problem here is that the transfer is effective immediately. If courts call into question a shareholder's ability to complete this transaction, many transactions may not occur. Therefore, such a transfer is presumed to be permissible, and anyone challenging it has the burden of proof. Reversed and remanded.

■ CONCURRENCE

(Clark, Cir. J.) Not all contracts transferring control of a board of directors are illegal, but summary judgment seems improper here.

■ CONCURRENCE

(Friendly, Cir. J.) Principles of corporate democracy may be violated by a clause such as this. Although the new shareholder will undoubtedly exercise its ability to install directors of its choosing, the shareholders that elected an existing board have the right to expect that their directors will fulfill their terms in office.

Analysis:

The court permitted the parties to contract to change the board of directors more rapidly than the new majority owner could have accomplished on its own because there was no air of wrong-doing. However, in other cases, courts have come to a different conclusion. In cases in which shareholders had close affiliations with related companies and, as part of the transfer of control in the primary company, the parties agreed to change the board membership of the affiliated corporations, courts have found that a "sale" of the board's power occurred and concluded that the power sale was in addition to the ownership transfer.

■ CASE VOCABULARY

COLLATERAL–AGREEMENT DOCTRINE: The principle that in a dispute concerning a written contract, proof of a second (usually oral) agreement will not be excluded under the parol-evidence rule if the oral agreement is independent of and not inconsistent with the written contract, and if the information in the oral agreement would not ordinarily be expected to be included in the written contract.

PAROL–EVIDENCE RULE: The common-law principle that a writing intended by the parties to be a final embodiment of their agreement cannot be modified by evidence of earlier or contemporaneous agreements that might add to, vary, or contradict the writing.

CHAPTER SEVEN

Mergers, Acquisitions, and Takeovers

Farris v. Glen Alden Corp.

Instant Facts: List Industries, which purchased almost forty percent of the outstanding shares of Glen Alden Corp. (D) and characterized its purchase as an asset purchase rather than a merger, proposed a reorganization whereby List would operate Glen Alden.

Black Letter Rule: If a contemplated transaction's result is the same as a merger, the transaction is a de facto merger, and the target corporation's shareholders have the right to dissent and receive fair value for their shares.

Hariton v. Arco Electronics, Inc.

Instant Facts: Arco Electronics, Inc. (D) and Loral Electronics Corp. (D) negotiated to integrate their companies under a reorganization plan that required Arco (D) to sell its assets to Loral (D) in exchange for shares of Loral (D) stock.

Black Letter Rule: A reorganization plan that requires one corporation to sell its assets to a second corporation in exchange for stock in the second corporation and that calls for the first corporation to liquidate and distribute the second corporation's shares to its stockholders constitutes a permissible de facto merger.

Weinberger v. UOP, Inc.

Instant Facts: Signal Corp. (D), which wanted to acquire UOP, Inc., (D), offered to buy a majority of UOP's (D) shares and then used its nominees on UOP's (D) board to help it obtain more UOP (D) stock.

Black Letter Rule: Minority shareholders in a cash-out merger are entitled to damages based on their shares' fair value, as determined by taking into account all relevant factors (including damages based on rescission), if the merger's approval was obtained on less than full disclosure and the merger's terms were unfair.

Coggins v. New England Patriots Football Club, Inc.

Instant Facts: The original founder of the New England Patriots, wanting to reclaim full ownership of the team, structured a merger requiring other shareholders to exchange their stock for cash, and Coggins (P) challenged the merger.

Black Letter Rule: If a company cannot show that a freeze-out merger served a valid corporate objective beyond advancing the majority shareholder's personal interests, the minority shareholders who were "frozen-out" by the merger are entitled to relief.

Rabkin v. Philip A. Hunt Chemical Corp.

Instant Facts: Shareholders brought an action to enjoin a proposed merger, arguing that the acquiring company, which was already a majority shareholder in the targeted company, purposely timed the transaction to avoid paying the minority shareholders a fair price.

Black Letter Rule: Majority shareholders owe a fiduciary duty to minority shareholders and may not unfairly manipulate the timing of a merger to avoid paying the minority shareholders the price agreed upon as part of an earlier transaction.

Rauch v. RCA Corp.

Instant Facts: Rauch (P), an acquired corporation's shareholder, challenged the propriety of a merger accomplished through the conversion of shares to cash.

Black Letter Rule: Pursuant to Delaware General Corporation law and the independent legal signifi-cance doctrine, a shareholder in a corporation undertaking to convert shares into cash as part of a merger is not entitled to rights provided shareholders under a distinct provision of the corporate law addressing the redemption.

VGS, Inc. v. Castiel

Instant Facts: Limited liability company members fought over the company's direction and distrusted the majority owner's ability to further the company's goals, so the remaining members secretly arranged to merge the company to shut out the majority owner.

Black Letter Rule: Mangers that fail to provide notice to all board members of their intent to hold a meeting or seek consent to a written resolution violate their fiduciary duties to each other, even if they believe that keeping an individual member from voting at the meeting is in the company's best interests.

Cheff v. Mathes

Instant Facts: Stockholders brought a derivative suit against the company's directors after the board authorized a series of expensive actions to ward off an outside shareholder's attempts to take over the company.

Black Letter Rule: If a company's board sincerely believes that buying out a dissident stockholder is necessary to maintain proper business practices, the board is not liable for the decision even if, in hindsight, the decision may not have been the best course.

Unocal Corp. v. Mesa Petroleum Co.

Instant Facts: Mesa Petroleum Co. (P), a minority shareholder, made a hostile tender offer for Unocal's (D) stock and filed a complaint to challenge Unocal's board's decision to affect a self-tender for its own shares because, pursuant to the offer's terms, Mesa (P) could not participate.

Black Letter Rule: A board may use corporate funds to purchase its own shares to remove a threat to corporate policy and may deny the dissident shareholder the right to participate in the self-tender offer provided the actions are motivated by a genuine concern for the company and its shareholders and provided that the proposed defensive measures are not out of balance with the threat's significance.

Revlon, Inc. v. MacAndrews & Forbes Holdings, Inc.

Instant Facts: Bidder for corporation's stock brought an action to enjoin certain defensive actions taken by the target corporation and others.

Black Letter Rule: Delaware law permits agreements to forestall or prohibit hostile forces from acquiring a company, but the methods may not breach a director's fiduciary duty, so that once the sale appears inevitable, the board must work to maximize the company's value to ensure the highest possible price.

Paramount Communications, Inc. v. Time Inc.

Instant Facts: Shortly before a merger between Time Inc. (D) and Warner Communications, Inc., was to be put to a shareholder vote, Paramount Communications (P) launched a take-over effort against Time (D), and when Paramount's efforts were rejected, it filed suit seeking a preliminary injunction to halt the Time–Warner merger.

Black Letter Rule: If a board is pursuing a merger for strategic reasons beyond merely the sale or acquisition of another company's assets, it may decline to entertain a competing bid that may yield a higher short-term gain for its shareholders in favor of a merger that ensures greater long-range gains.

Paramount Communications Inc. v. QVC Network Inc.

Instant Facts: Viacom Inc. (D) and Paramount Communications Inc. (D) formed an alliance even though QVC Network Inc. (P) proposed a more valuable offer.

Black Letter Rule: A board selling its corporation has a duty to obtain the best value for its shareholders and cannot give preference to one of the competing bidders.

ACE Ltd. v. Capital Re Corp.

Instant Facts: A holding company brought an action against a corporation, seeking to enjoin it from terminating a merger agreement.

Black Letter Rule: Board members may not surrender their ability to fulfill a fiduciary duty to their shareholders or make the exercise of their duty contingent on a third party's written endorsement.

Hilton Hotels Corp. v. ITT Corp.

Instant Facts: Hilton Hotels (P), which sought to acquire ITT Corp. (D), sued to obtain an injunction precluding implementation of the target company's comprehensive plan.

Black Letter Rule: A target corporation's attempts to restructure itself in an attempt to preclude an acquiring corporation from obtaining a majority on the board constitutes an impermissible restriction on its shareholders' rights to vote for directors.

CTS Corp. v. Dynamics Corp. of Am.

Instant Facts: Dynamics Corporation of America (P) offered to purchase CTS Corporation (D) and was obligated to fulfill state law requirements in order to obtain majority shareholder status.

Black Letter Rule: State law may impose restrictions affecting a company's ability to acquire control of another without running afoul of federal law or the Commerce Clause.

Farris v. Glen Alden Corp.

(Shareholder) v. *(Coal Company)*

393 Pa. 427, 143 A.2d 25 (1958)

SHAREHOLDERS HAVE DISSENTERS' RIGHTS IN A DE FACTO MERGER THAT IS DISGUISED AS AN ASSET SALE

■ **INSTANT FACTS** List Industries, which purchased almost forty percent of the outstanding shares of Glen Alden Corp. (D) and characterized its purchase as an asset purchase rather than a merger, proposed a reorganization whereby List would operate Glen Alden.

■ **BLACK LETTER RULE** If a contemplated transaction's result is the same as a merger, the transaction is a de facto merger, and the target corporation's shareholders have the right to dissent and receive fair value for their shares.

■ **PROCEDURAL BASIS**

On appeal from the lower court's grant of injunctive relief.

■ **FACTS**

Glen Alden Corp. (D), which was engaged in coal mining and manufacturing air conditioning units and fire-fighting equipment, had been experiencing declining operating revenues. List Industries owned a variety of companies. One of List's subsidiaries purchased 38.5 percent of Glen Alden's (D) stock, giving List the right to place three directors on Glen Alden's (D) board. List and Glen Alden (D) signed a Reorganization Agreement, pursuant to which Glen Alden (D) would acquire all of List's assets, including $8 million in cash. Glen Alden (D) would issue 3,621,703 shares of its List stock, to be distributed to its shareholders, and would assume List's liabilities. Glen Alden (D) would then change its name to List Alden Corporation, and the board of directors of both companies would be combined. Finally, List would be dissolved, leaving List Alden to operate the business of both companies. Glen Alden (D) mailed to its shareholders a meeting notice and proxy statement describing the reorganization and recommending its approval. Farris (P) sought to enjoin the vote and stop the reorganization, contending that the notice failed to state that the meeting's true purpose was to approve a merger, did not inform the shareholders of their right to dissent and obtain their shares' fair value, and omitted required text from the state's corporate law. Farris (P) argued that any approval would be invalid, and that he would suffer irreparable harm if the company completed its reorganization plan. The defendants denied that the action constituted a merger.

■ **ISSUE**

If the result of a transaction between two companies accomplishes the same result as a merger, should the target company's management be required to treat the reorganization as a de facto merger and permit its shareholders the right to dissent and receive fair value for their shares?

■ **DECISION AND RATIONALE**

(Cohen, J.) Yes. Pursuant to § 908 of the Pennsylvania Corporation Law, a shareholder in a company proposing a merger is entitled to receive fair value for his or her shares. Certain transactions, even if not

---

called "mergers," result in the effective merger of two companies. In those cases, a shareholder may receive value for his or her shares upon surrender. If the transaction changes a corporation's nature so significantly that a shareholder may not want to remain, he or she should be permitted to leave without economic harm. Under these terms, List Alden will become a diversified holding company rather than a coal mining business. While former Glen Alden (D) members will continue to operate List Alden, the former directors will be a minority on the new board. The new company will have seven times the debt load of the previous company, so that Farris (P) will effectively suffer a net loss of forty percent. The defendants argue that corporate law modifications preclude the court from treating the transaction as a de facto merger. Under the new statute, dissenters' rights are eliminated from reorganization transactions only in bona fide asset purchases. The defendants also assert that their interpretation is supported by the statute committee's comments. However, regardless of the committee's intentions, the legislature exhibited no such intention, and the statute's language does not support the committee's interpretation. Finally, despite the defendants' claims, the result of this transaction is a merger, not a sale, and the shareholders deserve protection for the resulting change in their investment. Affirmed.

Analysis:

The legislature appears to be trying to help corporations accomplish de facto mergers without having to pay the price in dissenters' rights, but *Glen Alden* refused to cooperate. Other state courts, when asked to apply the same reading of their statutes, declined to follow *Glen Alden*. Determining what constitutes a merger is not always easy. Generally, in a merger, two companies unite to form one company and the other company ceases to exist. However, that also frequently occurs when one company chooses to go out of business and sells its assets to an existing corporation. The distinguishing factor in a merger is that in addition to the sale of assets, the acquiring company also takes responsibility for the dissolving company's liabilities.

■ CASE VOCABULARY

APPRAISAL REMEDY: The statutory right of corporate shareholders who oppose some extraordinary corporate action (such as a merger) to have their shares judicially appraised and to demand that the corporation buy back their shares at the appraised value.

DE FACTO MERGER: A transaction that has the economic effect of a statutory merger but that is cast in the form of an acquisition or sale of assets or voting stock. Although such a transaction does not meet the statutory requirements for a merger, a court will generally treat it as a statutory merger for purposes of the appraisal remedy.

PROXY STATEMENT: An informational document that accompanies a proxy solicitation and explains a proposed action (such as a merger) by the corporation.

Hariton v. Arco Electronics, Inc.

(Shareholder) v. *(Dissolving Corporation)*

188 A.2d 123 (Del. 1963)

CORPORATIONS MAY LEGALLY EFFECT A MERGER USING THE STATUTORY PROVISIONS APPLICABLE TO AN ASSET SALE

■ **INSTANT FACTS** Arco Electronics, Inc. (D) and Loral Electronics Corp. (D) negotiated to integrate their companies under a reorganization plan that required Arco (D) to sell its assets to Loral (D) in exchange for shares of Loral (D) stock.

■ **BLACK LETTER RULE** A reorganization plan that requires one corporation to sell its assets to a second corporation in exchange for stock in the second corporation and that calls for the first corporation to liquidate and distribute the second corporation's shares to its stockholders constitutes a permissible de facto merger.

■ **PROCEDURAL BASIS**

On appeal from the trial court's grant of the defendant's motion for summary judgment and dismissal of the plaintiff's complaint.

■ **FACTS**

Arco Electronics, Inc. (D) and Loral Electronics Corp. (D), which were both engaged in the electronics business, negotiated to combine their companies through a Reorganization Agreement and Plan. The Reorganization Agreement provided that Arco (D) would sell its assets to Loral (D) in exchange for 283,000 shares of Loral (D) stock and that Arco (D) would hold a shareholders' meeting to approve the Reorganization Agreement and then dissolve. Upon dissolution, Arco (D) would distribute the Loral (D) shares to its former shareholders. Hariton (D), an Arco (D) shareholder who did not vote at the meeting, sued to enjoin the Reorganization Agreement, arguing the process was illegal.

■ **ISSUE**

May two corporations agree to reorganize if the result is a de facto merger, using the statutory provisions concerning the sale of assets rather than the provisions governing mergers?

■ **DECISION AND RATIONALE**

(Southerland, J.) Yes. The plaintiff argues that the defendant corporations' plan was designed to effect a merger of Arco (D) into Loral (D). In a statutory merger, the target company's shareholders retain rights in the remaining company, but in this transaction, the former company's shareholders are left owning only a part of a holding company that is removed from the business' day-to-day operations. The plan, which allows the companies to accomplish indirectly what they preferred not to do directly, is permitted under Del. Code Ann. tit. 8, § 271, because the merger statute and the sale-of-assets statute are independent provisions. A corporation's principals may use either statute to accomplish their purpose.

Analysis:

In contrast with the decision in *Farris v. Glen Alden Corp.* 143 A.2d 25 (Pa. 1958), *Hariton* takes the statute at face value and allows the contracting parties to obtain the transaction's benefits without

---

disturbing its label. The doctrine of independent legal significance of corporate acts, which the court used here, was explained in *Winston v. Mandor,* 710 A.2d 835 (Del. Ch. 1997) as protecting a corporation's legal acts from being tested against every possible statutory provision. *Winston* explained that the ''acts of the corporation taken in compliance with the provisions of one section of our General Corporation Law need not be tested against the requirements of another, though the result be the same.''

■ CASE VOCABULARY

AMALGAMATION: The act of combining or uniting; consolidation.

LIQUIDATE: To determine the liabilities and distribute the assets of an entity, especially in bankruptcy or dissolution; to wind up the affairs of a corporation, business, etc.

Weinberger v. UOP, Inc.

(Minority Shareholder) v. *(Target Corporation's Subsidiary)*

457 A.2d 701 (Del. 1983)

SHAREHOLDERS' APPROVAL OF A MERGER IS VOID IF INADEQUATE INFORMATION WAS DIS-
CLOSED TO THE MINORITY SHAREHOLDERS

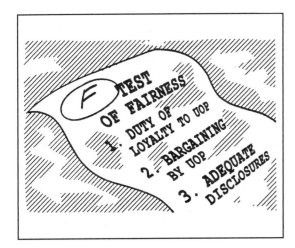

■ **INSTANT FACTS** Signal Corp. (D), which wanted to acquire UOP, Inc., (D), offered to buy a majority of UOP's (D) shares and then used its nominees on UOP's (D) board to help it obtain more UOP (D) stock.

■ **BLACK LETTER RULE** Minority shareholders in a cash-out merger are entitled to damages based on their shares' fair value, as determined by taking into account all relevant factors (including damages based on rescission), if the merger's approval was obtained on less than full disclosure and the merger's terms were unfair.

■ **PROCEDURAL BASIS**

On appeal following a rehearing in the Court of Chancery finding in favor of the majority shareholders.

■ **FACTS**

UOP, Inc. (D) was an industrial company engaged in a number of businesses, including petroleum and chemical services. Signal Corp. (D), which had recently sold a subsidiary and was looking for an investment, identified UOP (D) as a possible target and began negotiations. The parties agreed that UOP (D) would acquire 1.5 million shares of unissued UOP (D) stock at $21 per share. The purchase was also contingent on Signal (D) purchasing 4.3 million shares of UOP (D) stock from the public market at the same price. These transactions would provide UOP (D) with a 50.5 percent ownership in UOP (D). Because UOP's (D) shares sold for $14 per share before the tender offer, the offer was popular. After Signal (D) obtained its shares, it elected six of its representatives to UOP's (D) board. When the president of UOP (D) retired, Signal (D) replaced him with a senior executive from one of its subsidiaries. Signal (D) wanted to obtain more UOP (D) stock and had its directors on the UOP (D) board conduct a feasibility study. The directors concluded that more UOP (D) shares would be a good investment if they were acquired for no more than $24 per share. Signal (D) proposed a cash-out merger to the remaining UOP (D) shareholders at $21 per share. UOP's (D) president supported the proposal. UOP's (D) outside directors and Lehman Brothers conducted a fairness study of the proposal. Their initial reaction was that $20–21 per share was fair, but Lehman Brothers assembled an assessment team to consider the transaction in more depth. Following its due diligence, Lehman again concluded that the $20–21 price was fair. The companies' boards and shareholders approved the merger, but only a little more than half of UOP's minority shareholders voted, with only a slight majority of those stockholders voting in favor of the merger. Weinberger (P) and other UOP (D) minority shareholders sued, challenging the merger's fairness. At trial, the Chancellor ruled that in a challenge to a cash-out merger, a plaintiff must specifically allege fraud, misrepresentation or other misconduct to demonstrate the merger was unfair.

■ **ISSUE**

In a cash-out merger, must a majority shareholder prove that the minority shareholders received all material facts necessary to evaluate a transaction before casting their vote?

■ DECISION AND RATIONALE

(Moore, J.) Yes. In a cash-out merger, if a plaintiff offers some basis to attack the merger as unfair, the majority shareholders bear the burden of showing that the transaction is fair. Also, if a majority of the minority shareholders approve the transaction, the plaintiff must prove the transaction is unfair to the minority. In both cases, the majority must show that the information it provided before the vote disclosed all material facts. The record here does not support a finding that all material information was provided, and withholding information is a breach of fiduciary duty. The merger's terms are not fair. The report Signal (D) authorized fixes the price at a maximum of $24, but the proposed price per share was $21. Having the UOP (D) shareholders accept $21 per share saved Signal (D) $17 million. The report's secrecy is offensive because Signal (D) had two of its directors on UOP's (D) board prepare the report. If the same directors are on both sides of a transaction, the parties must demonstrate utmost good faith and fairness. In deciding "fairness," a court looks to fair dealing and fair price. Fair dealing involves evaluating how the transaction was initiated, structured, negotiated, and disclosed to the directors, and how the directors' and stockholders' approvals were obtained. In evaluating the price, the court must consider the corporation's assets, market value, earnings and future business. Here, there is impropriety in both respects. Part of the duty of fair dealing encompasses a duty of candor. The fact that this feasibility study was conducted by two of the UOP (D) directors installed by Signal (D) is significant. The motivation for the merger came from Signal (D), and it was conducted on Signal's (D) timetable. Although speed does not always demand a finding of unfairness, because of the short time period Crawford, a new director of both companies, never discussed price with Signal (D), except to say he thought the price was fair. UOP's (D) only protection was the Lehman Brothers study, but the UOP (D) shareholders were not told that the Lehman study was rushed and could be flawed. Also, the minority shareholders never knew that, even at $24 per share, Signal (D) considered the stock purchase a good investment. Without all of this information, the shareholders' consent to the merger was meaningless. At trial, the plaintiff offered evidence showing the UOP (D) stock was worth a minimum of $26 per share. The Chancellor rejected the plaintiff's proof in favor of the "Delaware Block" or "weighted average method" that courts have used for decades, but those methods are outdated. A better approach includes proof of value obtained by techniques accepted in the financial community, which is also reflected in statutes that prescribe reaching a decision on value from an evaluation of "all relevant factors." Also, in the future, a merger need not have a valid "business purpose." Reversed and remanded.

Analysis:

Signal (D) failed to see the difference between how it handled its second purchase of UOP (D) stock from how it handled the first installment. While Signal (D) made the first purchase as an outsider, once Signal acquired a sufficient number of shares to represent a majority interest and to inject its own personnel onto the UOP (D) board, Signal (D) directors became fiduciaries to the other board members and owed a duty of care to the other UOP (D) shareholders who were now in the minority. While Signal (D) was given a range of prices that would make the transaction beneficial to them, they began negotiations using the lowest figure and never moved. Although no one would argue that Signal (D) should be forced to lose money on the transaction, it inexcusably decided to save millions at the expense of those to whom it owed a duty of care.

■ CASE VOCABULARY

CASH MERGER: A merger in which shareholders of the target company must accept cash for their shares; also termed "cash-out merger" or "freeze-out merger."

DISCOUNTED CASH FLOW: A method of evaluating a capital investment by comparing its projected income and costs with its current value.

OVERSUBSCRIPTION: A situation in which there are more subscribers to a new issue of securities than there are securities available for purchase.

TENDER OFFER: A public offer to buy a minimum number of shares directly from a corporation's shareholders at a fixed price, usually at a substantial premium over the market price, in an effort to take control of the corporation.

Coggins v. New England Patriots Football Club, Inc.

(Minority Shareholder) v. *(AFL Football Franchise)*

397 Mass. 525, 492 N.E.2d 1112 (1986)

"FROZEN OUT" MINORITY SHAREHOLDERS ARE ENTITLED TO DAMAGES IF THERE IS NO VALID CORPORATE OBJECTIVE FOR A MERGER

■ **INSTANT FACTS** The original founder of the New England Patriots, wanting to reclaim full ownership of the team, structured a merger requiring other shareholders to exchange their stock for cash, and Coggins (P) challenged the merger.

■ **BLACK LETTER RULE** If a company cannot show that a freeze-out merger served a valid corporate objective beyond advancing the majority shareholder's personal interests, the minority shareholders who were "frozen-out" by the merger are entitled to relief.

■ **PROCEDURAL BASIS**

On appeal from the trial court's finding that the plaintiffs were entitled to damages, but not the undoing of the merger.

■ **FACTS**

Sullivan (D) bought an AFL franchise for $25,000, formed the American League Professional Football Team of Boston, Inc., and contributed the franchise to the corporation in exchange for 10,000 shares of its common stock. Nine other investors bought 10,000 shares each, and the corporation offered 120,000 shares of nonvoting stock for sale at $5 per share. Although Sullivan (D) held 23,718 common shares and 5,499 nonvoting shares, he was voted out as president. He decided he would do whatever it took to regain control, and he purchased all of the company's voting shares, renamed the corporation the "New England Patriots Football Club, Inc." (Old Patriots) (D), elected a board favorable to his interests, and reclaimed his position as president. In order to finance his return to power, Sullivan (D) needed to borrow money secured by the company's assets and to eliminate the nonvoting shareholders. To accomplish these objectives, Sullivan (D) set up a new company, New Patriots Football Club, Inc. (New Patriots), intending to merge it with the Old Patriots (D). Pursuant to the merger, Old Patriots' (D) nonvoting stock would be extinguished and its holders would be required to exchange their shares for cash. When Coggins (P), a minority shareholder, learned of the plan, he was upset and voted against the merger. He then brought a class action to avoid the merger. The trial judge approved Coggins' (P) class status but refused to undo the merger, finding that Coggins (P) and others in his class were entitled only to rescission damages.

■ **ISSUE**

If a company cannot show that a freeze-out merger served a valid corporate objective beyond advancing the majority shareholder's personal interests, are the minority shareholders who were "frozen-out" by the merger entitled to relief for rescission?

■ **DECISION AND RATIONALE**

(Liacos, J.) Yes. Ordinarily, if a merger is illegal, the appropriate remedy is undoing the merger. However, this merger has now been in effect for ten years and an orderly rescission is impossible. The court is urged to adopt the approach taken by Delaware courts for reviewing a merger. Delaware initially subscribed to a "business purpose" test, pursuant to which controlling stockholders violate their fiduciary duties by engaging in a merger simply to eliminate a minority shareholder. Delaware abandoned that test in 1983 in favor of a "fairness test," as set out in *Weinberger v. UOP,* 457 A.2d 701 (Del. 1983). The "fairness test," which gives the courts broad discretion to fashion a remedy based on the facts of each case and the minority shareholders' needs, requires that a party on both sides of a transaction must prove the fairness of both the transaction's fair dealing and its fair price. Showing that a merger complies with the relevant statutory provisions does not ensure that the transaction is fair. A controlling shareholder that also serves as a director bears the burden of proving that he has upheld his fiduciary obligations. If the duty is breached, the courts are not limited to awarding dissenting shareholders the remedy of judicial appraisal. The defendants argue that the lower court found the offering price for the nonvoting shares was inadequate, and that its decision that the plaintiffs were entitled to rescission damages was based solely on the inadequate price. However, the trial judge properly considered all of the appropriate factors—the merger's purpose, the disclosures' accuracy, and the price's fairness. A director's first duty is to further the corporation's interest, and a director who benefits from an ownership transfer must show that the transaction furthered legitimate company goals. This merger was solely for Sullivan's (D) personal benefit. Although there is a right to "selfish ownership," that right cannot be achieved at the minority shareholders' expense. A merger's proponents must establish that the corporation pursued the merger for a legitimate business purpose and that it was fair to the minority shareholders. Here, the merger's purpose was to advance Sullivan's (D) personal interests, notwithstanding his claim that the NFL prefers to have its franchises owned by a single shareholder. Absent a corporate purpose, there is no need to consider other factors regarding fairness. Typically, the appropriate remedy for an inappropriate freeze-out merger is rescission. However, Massachusetts' laws permit freeze-out mergers. Also, in the time since the merger, many individuals and businesses have relied on the merger, and their expectations should not be upset. Damages are appropriate, but the damages should not be based on a 1976 appraisal. On remand, the trial judge should receive evidence on the Old Patriots' (D) present value, based on the assumption that the merger did not occur, and each share of stock in Coggins' (P) class should receive its prorated share of the company's *present* assets. The trial judge also dismissed the plaintiff's claim that the merger constituted a waste of corporate assets, but waste may have occurred. If assets were wasted to benefit Sullivan (D), the court, in determining the company's present value on remand, should note the diverted assets and the manner in which they may have been used to benefit the company. Remanded.

Analysis:

Coggins explained that Sullivan's (D) misuse of the corporation to further his own personal goals of solitary ownership may support a claim for corporate waste. The court invited the trial judge to consider on remand whether Sullivan (D) had taken assets from the business that may have been used to increase its value since the merger. In *Cohen v. Mirage Resorts, Inc.,* 62 P.3d 720 (Nev. 2003), the shareholders similarly challenged a wrongful merger, and that court also fashioned broad remedies after finding that a shareholder can obtain remedies beyond injunctions or rescissions. *Cohen* held that once shareholders prove that a merger was wrongfully accomplished, they may receive compensatory and punitive damages and may litigate the value of the merged corporation's stock.

■ CASE VOCABULARY

ALIQUOT: Contained in a larger whole an exact number of times; fractional.

APPRAISAL RIGHT: The statutory right of corporate shareholders who oppose some extraordinary corporate action (such as a merger) to have their shares judicially appraised and to demand that the corporation buy back their shares at the appraised value. Also termed "appraisal remedy."

Rabkin v. Philip A. Hunt Chemical Corp.

(*Shareholders*) v. (*Merging Company*)

498 A.2d 1099 (Del. 1985)

MAJORITY SHAREHOLDERS OWE A FIDUCIARY DUTY THAT GOES BEYOND REFRAINING FROM ILLEGAL ACTIVITY

- **INSTANT FACTS** Shareholders brought an action to enjoin a proposed merger, arguing that the acquiring company, which was already a majority shareholder in the targeted company, purposely timed the transaction to avoid paying the minority shareholders a fair price.

- **BLACK LETTER RULE** Majority shareholders owe a fiduciary duty to minority shareholders and may not unfairly manipulate the timing of a merger to avoid paying the minority shareholders the price agreed upon as part of an earlier transaction.

■ PROCEDURAL BASIS

On appeal from a decision by the Chancery Court denying the plaintiffs' injunction.

■ FACTS

Philip A. Hunt Chemical Corp. (Hunt) (D), a Delaware corporation, merged into Olin Corp. (D), a Virginia corporation, pursuant to a merger agreement recommended by Hunt's (D) board of directors. Before the merger, Olin (D) purchased 63.4 percent of Hunt's (D) common stock from Turner and Newall Industries, Inc. (Turner) at $25 per share. As part of the purchase agreement, Olin (D) agreed with Turner that if Olin (D) bought the remainder of Hunt's (D) stock within a year, Olin (D) would pay the same $25 price per share. A week before the price commitment period expired, Olin's (D) Finance Committee considered purchasing the remaining Hunt (D) shares. The one-year price commitment period expired. Olin (D) offered the remaining shareholders $20 per share—$5 per share less than the price it would have been required to offer if the transaction occurred a month earlier. The fairness opinion supported the $20–per-share price based on the company's earning history and prospects for the coming year. Hunt (D) appointed a committee to study the proposal. The committee recommended to the Hunt (D) board that the $20 price was fair, but not generous. Hunt (D) sought an increase in the price, but Olin (D) refused. Hunt (D) recommended the merger to its shareholders, even though the remaining minority shareholders' approval was not required to approve the merger because Olin (D) owned sufficient Hunt (D) shares to pass the proposal on its own. The proxy statement sent to the minority shareholders made full disclosure, including the existence of the one-year price guarantee that was allowed to expire.

■ ISSUE

Does an acquiring corporation's offer to purchase the remaining minority shares of a target corporation after the expiration of a one-year price guarantee constitute a violation of the acquiring corporation's fiduciary duty to the minority shareholders?

■ DECISION AND RATIONALE

(Moore, J.) Yes. The lower court found that Olin (D) always planned to acquire Hunt's (D) minority shares, but that it wanted to avoid paying the $25 purchase price under the one-year agreement for the remaining shares. The plaintiffs argue that because of the transaction's basic unfairness, they should be entitled to relief that provides them with more than just appraisal rights. Appraisal rights are an inadequate remedy here because they fail to hold the wrongdoers accountable, require the corporation to bear the burden of an appraisal; and do not address the majority shareholder's overreaching and unfairness. The defendants argue that the plaintiffs' claims involve "fair value" claims, so that appraisal is their only remedy. The lower court held that, absent nondisclosure or misrepresentation, *Weinberger v. UOP, Inc.*, 457 A.2d 701 (Del. 1983), provides the plaintiffs with relief in the form of an appraisal. However, *Weinberger* did not limit a shareholder's remedy to an appraisal and specifically allowed the lower court to fashion other relief, especially in light of fraud, misrepresentation, or self-dealing. *Weinberger* did not limit concepts of fair dealing solely to deceit issues. Here, the plaintiffs have a contractual right to be paid $25 per share—a right Olin (D) destroyed by delaying the purchase date. A court must examine a majority shareholder's misconduct carefully. *Weinberger* holds that many of a transaction's characteristics, such as "timing, structure, negotiation and disclosure," impact fairness; as a result, conduct may be inequitable even though it is not illegal. Once Olin (D) obtained the majority interest in Hunt (D), it had a duty to refrain from unfairly manipulating its bargain with the minority shareholders. Reversed and remanded.

Analysis:

Hunt (D) timed its purchase of the remaining Olin (D) shares to avoid paying the higher price to Turner. The facts could have easily worked against Turner. If the price of Olin's (D) shares had skyrocketed just before the one-year option expired, Hunt (D) could have required Turner to sell the Olin (D) shares for what would have then been a bargain price. While it seems that Hunt (D) took advantage of its ability to wait out the one-year price agreement, there is no evidence that it led Turner to believe it would definitely purchase the shares at the premium price. If Hunt (D) had claimed it could not afford to exercise the option during the one-year term without incurring debt or otherwise jeopardizing its financial outlook, the court may not have been justified in finding that Hunt (D) acted inappropriately by purchasing the shares as soon as their financial outlook improved.

■ CASE VOCABULARY

DECEIT: The act of intentionally giving a false impression.

Rauch v. RCA Corp.

(Preferred Shareholder) v. *(Acquired Corporation)*

861 F.2d 29 (2d Cir. 1988)

CONVERTING SHARES TO CASH TO COMPLETE A MERGER DOES NOT CALL A LEGALLY DISTINCT PROCESS INTO QUESTION

■ **INSTANT FACTS** Rauch (P), an acquired corporation's shareholder, challenged the propriety of a merger accomplished through the conversion of shares to cash.

■ **BLACK LETTER RULE** Pursuant to Delaware General Corporation law and the independent legal significance doctrine, a shareholder in a corporation undertaking to convert shares into cash as part of a merger is not entitled to rights provided shareholders under a distinct provision of the corporate law addressing the redemption.

■ **PROCEDURAL BASIS**

On appeal from a dismissal by the United States District Court for failure to state a cause of action.

■ **FACTS**

RCA Corporation (D), General Electric Company (GE) (D), and Gesub (D), GE's (D) wholly owned subsidiary, agreed to a merger. Pursuant to the merger agreement, all common and preferred RCA shares were to be converted into cash. Each share of common stock would receive $66.50, and each share of cumulative preferred stock would receive $40. Rauch (P), who held 250 shares of preferred stock, brought a class action claiming that the merger was a liquidation of RCA (D) and a redemption of the preferred stock. Under RCA's (D) certification of incorporation, the preferred shareholders were entitled to $100 per share. The plaintiff sought an injunction, and the defendants moved to dismiss the complaint. The trial court concluded the merger was a bona fide transaction and dismissed the complaint.

■ **ISSUE**

May a preferred shareholder insist on receiving the rights provided by the statute governing the redemption of preferred shares and the rights provided by the corporation's articles of incorporation if the issuing company seeks to exchange the shares for cash as part of a merger?

■ **DECISION AND RATIONALE**

(Mahoney, J.) No. RCA's (D) Restated Certificate of Incorporation entitles Preferred Stockholders to $100 per share, plus accrued dividends, on redemption. Rauch (P) contends that pursuant to the merger, the preferred shareholders are offered only $40 in contravention of their rights. Delaware Corporation Law permits the exchange of stock for cash as part of a merger or consolidation, and the RCA–GE merger agreement complies with the statute's requirements. Delaware law handles stock redemptions under a different provision, which provides that a corporation may redeem its preferred stock upon the occurrence of a previously specified event. RCA's (D) formation documents do not give the preferred shareholders the right to initiate redemption or provide for redemption upon merger. Under Delaware law, RCA (D) has the right to deal with the plaintiffs' shares as it did. If a company chooses to commence an action under one provision of the law, the action is totally independent of any other statutory provision and cannot be subjected to the validity tests contained in another section. Rauch (P) does not contend that the payment of $40 per share is unfair; rather, she contends that under the RCA (D) contract, she is owed $100 regardless of the transaction's fairness. If Rauch (P) believes that the price is not sufficient, she may bring an action for an appraisal. However, she cannot claim a breach of contract. Affirmed.

Analysis:

The doctrine of independent legal significance was similarly used to support a de facto merger in *Hariton v. Arco Electronics, Inc.*, 188 A.2d 123 (Del. 1963). However, the Pennsylvania courts rejected the doctrine in *Farris v. Glen Alden Corporation*, 393 Pa. 427, 143 A.2d 25 (1958). In subsequent cases, many courts have given deference to the doctrine, noting that shareholders are deemed to know the law when they purchase their shares.

■ CASE VOCABULARY

CONVERSION PRICE: The contractually specified price per share at which a convertible security can be converted into shares of common stock.

CONVERTIBLE STOCK: A security (usually a bond or preferred stock) that may be exchanged by the owner for another security, especially common stock from the same company, and usually at a fixed price on a specified date.

VGS, Inc. v. Castiel

(Post–Merger Company) v. (Shut–Out Manager)

2000 WL 1277372 (Del. Ch. Aug. 31, 2000)

BOARD MEMBERS CANNOT WITHHOLD NOTICE OF A MEETING FROM A DIRECTOR IN ORDER TO ASSURE A RESOLUTION'S PASSAGE

■ **INSTANT FACTS** Limited liability company members fought over the company's direction and distrusted the majority owner's ability to further the company's goals, so the remaining members secretly arranged to merge the company to shut out the majority owner.

■ **BLACK LETTER RULE** Mangers that fail to provide notice to all board members of their intent to hold a meeting or seek consent to a written resolution violate their fiduciary duties to each other, even if they believe that keeping an individual member from voting at the meeting is in the company's best interests.

■ **PROCEDURAL BASIS**

On trial in the Court of Chancery.

■ **FACTS**

Castiel (D) formed a limited liability company, Virtual Geosatellite LLC (the LLC) to pursue a license from the FCC to operate a satellite system. The LLC's original member was Virtual Geosatellite Holdings, Inc. (Holdings) (D). Ellipso, Inc. (Ellipso) (D) and Sahagen Satellite Technology Group LLC (Sahagen Satellite) were the second and third members of the LLC. Castiel (D) controlled Holdings and Ellipso; Sahagen, a successful venture capitalist, controlled Sahagen Satellite. Pursuant to the LLC's operating agreement, Holdings would receive almost two-thirds of the total equity in the LLC, Sahagen Satellite would receive 25 percent, and Ellipso would receive the remaining 11.5 percent. A three-person Board of Managers ran the LLC. Castiel's (D) interest allowed him to appoint two of the three individuals to the board, and two votes were sufficient to block any course of action. Castiel (D) occupied one of the positions, and he named Quinn to the other seat. Sahagen placed himself in the third seat. Castiel (D) and Sahagen began fighting, and Sahagen made repeated offers to Castiel (D) to buy his interest. Sahagen quietly convinced Quinn that they had to remove Castiel (D) for the LLC to prosper. Quinn and Sahagen authorized, by written consent, a merger of the LLC into a new Delaware corporation, VGS, Inc. (P). Following the merger, they extinguished the LLC and vested ownership of the LLC's assets with VGS (P). They did not name Castiel (D) to VGS's (P) board. Sahagen gave VGS (P) a promissory note for $10 million in exchange for two million shares of its preferred stock. VGS (P) issued 1,269,200 common shares to Holdings, 230,800 common shares to Ellipso, and 500,000 common shares to Sahagen Satellite. The transaction dropped the percentage of cumulative shares owned by Holdings and Ellipso from 75 percent in the LLC to 37.5 percent in the new company, while Sahagen and Sahagen Satellite increased their holdings significantly. As this case was brought before the court, VGS (P) was both a plaintiff and a counterclaim defendant; Quinn, Sahagen and the LLC were additional counterclaim defendants; and Holdings (D) and Ellipso (D) were defendants and counterclaim plaintiffs.

■ ISSUE

Is it permissible under either Delaware statutes or the business judgment rule to fail to give a board member notice of a meeting or the opportunity to vote on a written consent in order to ensure passage of a resolution?

■ DECISION AND RATIONALE

(Steele, J.) No. Sahagen and Quinn did not notify Castiel (D) of the merger because Castiel (D) would have removed Quinn from the board and substituted a new, Castiel-friendly manager. The LLC's operating agreement did not state whether Board of Managers' actions needed to be unanimous, or whether a majority would rule. Sahagen and Quinn contend that logic dictates that the majority rule should apply, but Castiel (D) argues that unanimous agreement is required. The LLC agreement provides that any increase in the number of managers on the board must preserve Sahagen's representation on the Board. If unanimity of the Board were required to carry an action, maintaining Sahagen's proportional presence on the Board would be unnecessary because his one vote would give him veto power. The LLC agreement also provides that Sahagen must consent to any merger, consolidation or reorganization, and that the LLC may be dissolved by a vote of two-thirds of the LLC's owners. If unanimity were required, these statements would be unnecessary. Also, it would be unusual to require only a two-thirds vote of the members to dissolve the LLC but to require the managers to take regular actions only upon a unanimous vote. The Delaware LLC act allows managers to act without a meeting if a written consent sets forth the action to be taken, and if the consent is signed by the managers having at least the minimum number of votes necessary to authorize the action at a meeting. Although the LLC Act does not require Castiel (D) to receive notice, the absence of a statutory requirement does not shield Sahagen and Quinn's actions from disapproval. Sahagen and Quinn prevented Castiel (D) from exercising his legal right as an owner, and the legislature never intended the statutory provisions to be used to further corporate conspiracies. Sahagen and Quinn owe a duty of loyalty to the LLC, its investors and Castiel (D), their fellow manager. Sahagen and Quinn's duty to provide Castiel (D) with notice exists even if they believe he will act against the LLC's best interests. Whether Castiel (D) was suited to lead the company is not an excuse for taking secret actions. Nor is Sahagen's and Quinn's breach of loyalty protected by the business judgment rule. Although a simple majority of the LLC's managers could approve a merger, they cannot obtain the approval through deceit. Merger rescinded.

Analysis:

The notice here was so defective as to void the transaction, but other cases involving defective meeting notice have caused the business transacted at those meetings to be voidable, not void. For example, in *Lofland v. DiSabatino*, 17 Del. J. Corp. L. 638, 1991 WL 138505 (Del. Ch. July 25, 1991), a group of dissatisfied shareholders held a meeting to get rid of a management team. The meeting notice contained all necessary information about the meeting except its time and place. *Lofland* held that the lack of notice was simply a mistake and not intended to prevent certain shareholders from casting their votes.

■ CASE VOCABULARY

RESCIND: To make void; to repeal or annul.

Cheff v. Mathes

(*Director*) v. (*Shareholder*)

41 Del.Ch. 494, 199 A.2d 548 (1964)

A BOARD MAY STOP SHAREHOLDERS' EFFORTS TO CHANGE THE COMPANY'S CHARACTER

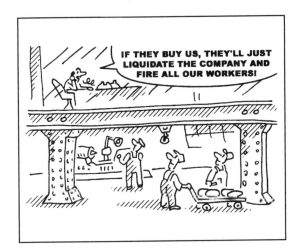

IF THEY BUY US, THEY'LL JUST LIQUIDATE THE COMPANY AND FIRE ALL OUR WORKERS!

■ **INSTANT FACTS** Stockholders brought a derivative suit against the company's directors after the board authorized a series of expensive actions to ward off an outside shareholder's attempts to take over the company.

■ **BLACK LETTER RULE** If a company's board sincerely believes that buying out a dissident stockholder is necessary to maintain proper business practices, the board is not liable for the decision even if, in hindsight, the decision may not have been the best course.

■ **PROCEDURAL BASIS**

On appeal from an order requiring the directors to account for any loss.

■ **FACTS**

The board of Holland Furnace Co. (D) consisted of seven members. Most board members also held stock in the corporation, and some of the members were also shareholders in Hazelbank United Interest (Hazelbank), an investment group used to finance a portion of Holland's (D) transactions. The Holland (D) board attributed some of its success to its direct employment of a sales force. Although sales had declined recently, the company reorganized in response to the slowdown, and its stock price increased. Holland's (D) CEO, Cheff (D), met with Maremont, president of Maremont Automotive Products (Maremont Automotive) (D), to discuss a merger. Cheff (D) declined to pursue the transaction in view of the companies' differing sales practices. A month later, Maremont informed Holland (D) that he had acquired 55,000 shares of Holland (D) stock. Holland (D) checked into Maremont's background, and found that Maremont had participated in a number of corporate liquidations and was not highly regarded. Maremont's ownership in Holland (D) grew to 100,000 shares, and he demanded to become a member of Holland's (D) board, but his request was denied. Maremont's interest in Holland (D) made Holland's employees uneasy, and twenty-five key employees left. Holland (D) and Cheff (D) both started purchasing Holland stock, causing the shares' price to increase. Maremont offered to sell his shares to Holland (D), but the company delayed and Maremont withdrew his offer. Maremont Automotive (D) offered to purchase Hazelbank. Although the Holland (D) members on Hazelbank's board opposed the offer, the remaining directors seemed to favor it, but the matter was set aside. Holland's (D) legal counsel met with Maremont to arrange a purchase of Maremont Automotive's (D) shares of Holland (D) stock. Holland's board authorized the purchase at a price exceeding the shares' market price. Cheff (P) and others brought a derivative suit against Holland (D), its directors and Maremont Automotive (D), claiming that the Holland's (D) dealing in its own stock was undertaken solely to allow the incumbent directors to retain control of the company. At trial, the court found that Maremont posed no threat to Holland (D), that Holland's board's actions were motivated by its desire to retain control of the company, and that Holland's directors must account for any loss. The directors appealed.

■ ISSUE

May a board trade its own stock to frustrate an outside investor's efforts to liquidate the company or change its character to the detriment of the company and its shareholders, if the directors acted on their belief that the outside investor had a reputation for ruining targeted companies?

■ DECISION AND RATIONALE

(Carey, J.) Yes. Delaware statutes give corporations the right to trade in their own stock. The shareholders here argue not that the company's actions were illegal, but that its motives were improper. Courts do not permit a board to use corporate funds merely to further the board's desire to stay in power. However, if the directors sincerely believe that buying out a dissident shareholder is necessary to maintain proper business practices, a court will respect the board's decision, even if the decision may be questionable in retrospect. The burden of proof generally initially lies with the plaintiffs as the board is presumed to have acted in good faith, but if the board members are also shareholders, they have a conflict of interest that requires them to show that the stock purchase was motivated by the corporation's best interests. The plaintiffs argue that Holland's purchase of its shares was unfair because Holland paid more than market price for them, deeming the increase in price a reasonable "control premium." The ultimate concern is whether the board had a reasonable basis for believing that Maremont's takeover posed a danger to Holland's (D) effective corporate policy. If the Holland (D) board engaged in a reasonable investigation, any honest mistake in judgment does not support a finding of blame. The Chancellor found no evidence that Maremont intended to liquidate the company, but Holland's (D) board feared liquidation and worried that Maremont would destroy the sales policies that the board considered vital to its continued success. Substantial evidence supports a finding that Maremont posed a threat to Holland's (D) continued profitability. Reversed and remanded with instruction to enter judgment for the defendants.

Analysis:

Although a company may act in response to a threat from outside raiders to destroy a company, courts require more than bare allegations to support the board's actions. In *Schilling v. Belcher*, 582 F.2d 995 (5th Cir. 1978), the directors tried to hide behind the *Cheff* holding to justify their efforts to thwart a takeover attempt. In *Schilling*, the company bought shares of its own stock to save the company from the bidder's "ruinous" actions. The court distinguished *Shilling* from *Cheff* because the *Schilling* directors did not articulate the basis for their belief that the ownership change would ruin the company.

■ CASE VOCABULARY

BUY–SELL OFFER: A share-transfer restriction that commits the shareholder to sell, and the corporation or other shareholders to buy, the shareholder's shares at a fixed price when a specified event occurs.

CONTROL PREMIUM: A premium paid for shares carrying the power to control a corporation.

Unocal Corp. v. Mesa Petroleum Co.

(Targeted Corporation) v. *(Take–Over Bidder)*

493 A.2d 946 (Del. 1985)

A SELF–TENDER OFFER MAY DISALLOW A TAKE–OVER BIDDER'S PARTICIPATION

■ **INSTANT FACTS** Mesa Petroleum Co. (P), a minority shareholder, made a hostile tender offer for Unocal's (D) stock and filed a complaint to challenge Unocal's board's decision to affect a self-tender for its own shares because, pursuant to the offer's terms, Mesa (P) could not participate.

■ **BLACK LETTER RULE** A board may use corporate funds to purchase its own shares to remove a threat to corporate policy and may deny the dissident shareholder the right to participate in the self-tender offer provided the actions are motivated by a genuine concern for the company and its shareholders and provided that the proposed defensive measures are not out of balance with the threat's significance.

■ **PROCEDURAL BASIS**

On appeal by the defendant from the lower court's grant of a preliminary injunction.

■ **FACTS**

Mesa Petroleum Co. (P) owned thirteen percent of Unocal Corp. (D) stock. Mesa (P) made a two-tier offer to buy approximately thirty-seven percent of Unocal's (D) outstanding stock at $54 per share. The remaining shares would be eliminated under an exchange of stock for junk bonds worth much less than $54. Thirteen of Unocal's board members met to consider the offer. Goldman Sachs reported that the proposal was inadequate and explained defensive strategies available to the board to thwart the take-over, including a self-tender offer under which Unocal (D) would purchase its own shares at a cost of $6.1 to $6.5 billion. Notwithstanding the debt it would create, the company would remain viable. The board rejected Mesa's proposal. Two days later, the Unocal (D) board reconvened and decided to make an offer for Unocal's (D) shares at $72 per share. The resolution stated that if Mesa (P) obtained 64 million shares (the Purchase Condition), Unocal (D) would buy the remaining forty-nine percent of the shares in the market in exchange for debt securities. The board's resolution prohibited Mesa (P) from tendering any of its Unocal (D) shares under the exchange. Mesa (P) brought suit challenging the Purchase Condition. In response to the suit, Goldman Sachs advised the board to waive the Mesa (P) restriction for 50 million shares and suggested that the directors should tender their own shares in a vote of confidence. The board revisited Mesa's (P) exclusion from the plan and reaffirmed its belief that the exclusion was valid because it protected shareholders from receiving junk bonds for their stock and ensured that company assets would not be used to fund Mesa's (P) inadequate proposal. Mesa (P) challenged its exclusion from the self-tender offer and sought a temporary restraining order. The Chancellor issued the temporary restraining order subject to Unocal (D) including Mesa (P) in the self-tender offer.

■ **ISSUE**

Is a company's purchase of its own shares in an effort to remove a take-over threat protected by the business judgment rule if the purchase is reasonable in relation to the threat posed and is supported by a thorough evaluation of the takeover bid?

■ DECISION AND RATIONALE

(Moore, J.) Yes. Mesa (P) argues that Unocal (D) breached a fiduciary duty by preventing Mesa (P) from participating in the self-tender offer, insisting that Unocal (D) cannot hide behind the business judgment rule in extending the self-tender offer because the directors could benefit from the self-tender offer but other shareholders could not. Unocal (D) argues that it owes no duty of fairness to Mesa (P) because its offer was coercive. Unocal's (D) board decided to exclude Mesa (P) in good faith, on an informed basis, and in the exercise of due care. Therefore, it is entitled to protection by the business judgment rule. The board's authority to act in these situations comes from at least three sources: its inherent power to manage the corporation's business; its statutory power to trade in its own stock; and its fundamental duty to protect the company and its stockholders. The business judgment rule protects a board's decision to thwart a takeover if the decision has a rational business purpose. The board must determine that the offer is in the best interests of the company and its shareholders. The directors must show they have a reasonable belief, based on good faith and a reasonable investigation, that the takeover poses a danger to corporate policy and that they are acting in the stockholders' best interests, not solely to keep their offices. The Unocal (D) board concluded that Mesa's (P) offer was inadequate and grossly unfair to the minority shareholders. The board's distrust of Mesa (P) was reinforced by Mesa's (P) reputation as a corporate raider. Unocal's (D) efforts to defeat Mesa (P) would be impaired if Mesa (P) were permitted to participate in the self-tender offer. Based on this evidence, the board's actions were reasonably related to the threats posed. Reversed and preliminary injunction vacated.

Analysis:

The directors sought protection under the business judgment rule, believing that simply because their decisions were related to business, the rule would apply. However, the court emphasized that the board could not benefit from the presumption that it had acted properly unless the board acted reasonably. Also relevant is *Grobow v. Perot*, 539 A.2d 180 (Del. 1988), in which the court found that the plaintiff's complaints did not include claims of fraud, bad faith, or self-dealing. *Grobow* held that in the absence of proper pleading to establish the plaintiff's case, the court would not consider the claim.

■ CASE VOCABULARY

GREENMAIL: The act or practice of buying enough stock in a company to threaten a hostile takeover and then selling the stock back to the corporation at an inflated price; the money paid for stock in the corporation's buyback; a shareholder's act of filing or threatening to file a derivative action and then seeking a disproportionate settlement.

JUNK BOND: A high-risk, high-yield subordinated bond issued by a company with a credit rating below investment grade.

TWO–TIER OFFER: A two-step technique by which a bidder tries to acquire a target corporation, the first step involving a cash tender offer and the second usually a merger in which the target company's remaining shareholders receive securities from the bidder.

Revlon, Inc. v. MacAndrews & Forbes Holdings, Inc.

(*Targeted Company*) v. (*Controlling Stockholder of Acquiring Company*)

506 A.2d 173 (Del. 1985)

THE BOARD OF AN ACQUIRED COMPANY MUST MAXIMIZE THE COMPANY'S VALUE FOR THE BENEFIT OF ITS SHAREHOLDERS

■ **INSTANT FACTS** Bidder for corporation's stock brought an action to enjoin certain defensive actions taken by the target corporation and others.

■ **BLACK LETTER RULE** Delaware law permits agreements to forestall or prohibit hostile forces from acquiring a company, but the methods may not breach a director's fiduciary duty, so that once the sale appears inevitable, the board must work to maximize the company's value to ensure the highest possible price.

■ **PROCEDURAL BASIS**

On appeal from a decision granting the defendants a preliminary injunction.

■ **FACTS**

Pantry Pride, Inc. wanted to acquire Revlon, Inc. (D). Perelman, chairman and CEO of Pantry Pride, met with Bergerac (D), the CEO and chairman at Revlon (D), to discuss an acquisition at a price of $40–50 per share. Bergerac (D) deemed the price inadequate and refused to negotiate further, demanding that Pantry Pride provide Revlon (D) a standstill agreement as a prerequisite to further negotiations so that Pantry Pride would need Revlon's (D) permission before pursuing any acquisition. Revlon's (D) investment banker advised the board that the $45 offer price was inadequate and cautioned that Pantry Pride would attempt to acquire Revlon (D) with junk bonds and then break up the company, returning Pantry Pride a substantial profit. Revlon's (D) special counsel recommended two defensive measures— a self-tender offer for up to five million shares and a Note Purchase Rights Plan (NPRP) containing a poison pill that allowed each Revlon (D) shareholder to exchange a share of stock for a $65 note bearing twelve percent interest. The poison pill would kick in whenever someone acquired twenty percent of Revlon's (D) shares. A hostile bidder was not able to participate in the NPRP, and if the twenty-percent trigger point was not reached, Revlon (D) could redeem the notes for ten cents each. Pantry Pride offered $47.50 per share common and $26.67 per share preferred, and the board rejected the offer. Revlon (D) started their self-tender offer. Pantry Pride made a revised offer and three subsequent bids which eventually topped at $56.25 a share. In the meantime, Revlon (D) approved a leveraged buyout with Forstmann Little & Co. (D), pursuant to which shareholders would receive $56 per share in cash and management would receive stock in the new company through their golden parachutes. Revlon (D) agreed to redeem the notes under the NPRP and waive the preconditions to Forstmann's (D) future borrowing. Revlon's (D) subdivisions would be sold to American Home Products and their cosmetic and fragrance division would be sold to Adler & Shaykin. This deal upset the shareholders. Revlon's (D) stock prices fell, and Pantry Pride continued bidding. The Board approved Forstmann's (D) offer because the price was higher, the note-holders were protected, and Forstmann (D) had financing. MacAndrews & Forbes Holding, Inc. (P), Pantry Pride's controlling stockholder, filed an action challenging the terms of the Forstmann (D) deal. The trial court enjoined the Forstmann (D) transaction, finding that Revlon's (D) directors had breached their duty of loyalty by making conces-sions out of concern for the noteholders rather than concern for maximizing the share prices for Revlon's (D) stockholders.

■ ISSUE

In the face of active bidding for a company where the sale of the company appears unavoidable, may the target company's board continue to thwart take over attempts instead of ensuring a maximum sales price for its stockholders' shares?

■ DECISION AND RATIONALE

(Moore, J.) No. The business judgment rule protects a company's board's defensive actions to a take-over only if the board observes principles of care, loyalty and independence in reaching its decisions. Actions taken by a board in defense of a take-over bid are presumed to be motivated by self-interest. The board has the burden of proving it was motivated by a belief that the takeover posed a threat to the company's welfare and that its response was proportional to the threat posed. While the Revlon (D) board had the authority to enact the poison-pill measure, the questions of whether the measure was reasonable and what motivated it remain. Revlon (D) claims that Pantry Pride's $45 per share offering price was inadequate and that it adopted the poison pill to protect Revlon (D) from hostile takeover while retaining its ability to continue evaluating better offers. Although the NPRP was reasonable when it was adopted, it is rendered moot by the agreement between Revlon (D) and Forstmann (D). A board's steps must be strictly scrutinized to ensure no fiduciary duty was breached. Revlon's (D) self-tender offer for ten million of its own shares was permissible as long as Pantry Pride's offer was inadequate. However, when the offer reached $53, the price was fair and Revlon's (D) breakup was inevitable. Once it was clear that Pantry Pride's efforts would be successful and that Revlon (D) would be broken up, the board must make every effort to maximize the price per share. Instead, the board provided concessions to Forstmann (D) at their shareholders' expense. None of the board's actions were illegal, but legality is not a defense to a breach of fiduciary duty. Revlon (D) gave Forstmann (D) preferential treatment, not to increase bidding, but to put an end to it. Affirmed.

Analysis:

This case has become a cornerstone of the law regarding a court's evaluation of a board's response to take-over offers, and it has been cited thousands of times. While courts have subsequently found that *Revlon* does not create any new fiduciary duties between the board and its shareholders, it allows the court to dig deeper into the process a board uses to evaluate offers and make its recommendations to its shareholders. Notwithstanding the fact that the court will view the board's actions with greater scrutiny under *Revlon*, plaintiffs cannot use the holding to avoid bringing a well-pleaded case. The court will not investigate the board's motives without good reason.

■ CASE VOCABULARY

LEVERAGED BUYOUT: The purchase of a publicly held corporation's outstanding stock by its management or outside investors, financed mainly with funds borrowed from investment bankers or brokers and usually secured by the corporation's assets.

POISON PILL: A corporation's defense against an unwanted takeover bid whereby shareholders are granted the right to acquire equity or debt securities at a favorable price to increase the bidder's acquisition costs.

STANDSTILL AGREEMENT: Any agreement to refrain from taking further action; especially, an agree-ment by which a party agrees to refrain from further attempts to take over a corporation (as by making no tender offer) for a specified period, or by which financial institutions agree not to call bonds or loans when due.

WHITE KNIGHT: A person or corporation that rescues the target of an unfriendly corporate takeover, especially by acquiring a controlling interest in the target corporation or by making a competing tender offer.

Paramount Communications, Inc. v. Time Inc.

(Hostile Bidder) v. (Targeted Corporation)

571 A.2d 1140 (Del. 1989)

IF A MERGER IS MORE THAN AN ASSET SALE, A BOARD MAY DECLINE A COMPETING BID THAT MAY YIELD A BETTER PRICE

■ **INSTANT FACTS** Shortly before a merger between Time Inc. (D) and Warner Communications, Inc., was to be put to a shareholder vote, Paramount Communications (P) launched a takeover effort against Time (D), and when Paramount's efforts were rejected, it filed suit seeking a preliminary injunction to halt the Time–Warner merger.

■ **BLACK LETTER RULE** If a board is pursuing a merger for strategic reasons beyond merely the sale or acquisition of another company's assets, it may decline to entertain a competing bid that may yield a higher short-term gain for its shareholders in favor of a merger that ensures greater long-range gains.

■ **PROCEDURAL BASIS**

On appeal by the plaintiffs, following a denial of the plaintiffs' motion for preliminary injunction.

■ **FACTS**

Time Inc. (D), which had recently expanded into pay television programming and acquired a cable television franchise, began exploring further expansion into the entertainment industry. In 1987, Nicholas, Time's (D) CEO, met with Ross, Warner's CEO, to discuss a joint venture creating a worldwide cable network. Time's (D) board members strongly recommended the venture and, a year later, approved a plan to expand with Warner as long as Time (D) retained control of the resulting entity so it could remain true to its journalistic commitments. Time's (D) board deemed Warner the premier candidate and discussed the venture's structure. Time (D) preferred an all-cash acquisition, but Warner wanted a stock-for-stock exchange and Time (D) eventually agreed. Following the stock exchange, Warner stockholders would own approximately sixty-two percent of the new company. Both boards approved the merger. Time (D) obtained confidence letters from lenders, pursuant to which they agreed not to finance any transactions that would interfere with the merger. Before the final vote, Paramount (P) offered to purchase all of Time's (D) shares for $175 per share, provided Time (D) broke off negotiations with Warner, Paramount obtained certain cable franchises, and the parties obtained a judicial determination that the transaction would not violate the Delaware Anti–Takeover Statute. Time's (D) board discussed the offer but declined to negotiate with Paramount (P). Time (D) restructured its deal with Warner, providing for the purchase of fifty-one percent of Warner's stock at $70 per share, with the remaining shares to be obtained later. Time (D) also agreed to allocate $9 billion to Warner's goodwill. Paramount (P) increased its offer to $200 per share, and Time (D) again rejected it, believing that Paramount's (P) culture was not a good fit. Paramount (P) filed suit, arguing that the Time–Warner agreement was an effective sale of Time (D), requiring its board to maximize short-term shareholder value.

■ ISSUE

If a second merger proposal presents a higher per-share price than the transaction being pursued by the company's board, is the board obligated by its fiduciary duty to pursue the second proposal to maximize benefits to its shareholders?

■ DECISION AND RATIONALE

(Horsey, J.) No. Time (D) did not put itself up for sale by entering into the agreement with Warner. While Time's (D) directors stated the market might see the transaction as a sale, that comment is not conclusive. Nor does the fact that Time's (D) original shareholders are in a minority position in the new venture establish the existence of a sale. Paramount (P) argues that by making their company takeover-proof, Time's (D) directors committed the same error as the directors in *Revlon, Inc. v. MacAndrews & Forbes Holdings, Inc.*, 506 A.2d 173 (Del. 1985), by failing to maximize the share price for its stockholders. Paramount (P) also contends that the Chancellor erred in finding that Time's (D) board could properly view Paramount's (P) takeover a threat to Time's policies and that Time (D) could not have made a fully reasoned investigation at the time of their offer because it rejected the offer so quickly. Paramount (P) misreads the law. The *Revlon* considerations are relevant only if evidence shows that the contemplated transactions will result in the company's break-up. The board anticipated Time's (D) continued existence, and *Revlon* does not apply if a transaction simply has some characteristics in common with a sale. A court's must determine whether sufficient evidence exists to find that the Time–Warner agreement was made in the proper exercise of business judgment. Paramount (P) would have drastically changed the targeted company, and Time's (D) board concluded that the Paramount (P) offer was not simply inadequate in value, but that their proposal did not present a strategic business combination. Also, because Paramount's (P) offer came at the eleventh hour, the board viewed it as an effort to confuse Time's (D) board and its shareholders. Allegations that the board failed to conduct a proper investigation are moot because Time (D) conducted an investigation *before* it began negotiating with Warner. Therefore, the board's decision to reject Paramount's (P) advances was made in good faith. Directors are not obligated to take a better short-term offer for their shareholders if to do so would harm long-range plans. Affirmed.

Analysis:

The non-sale aspects of this transaction are important. Unlike the unavoidable result in *Revlon*, where the company would have been broken up and sold in parts, the evidence establishes that throughout its negotiations with Warner, Time's (D) board took special care to ensure that after any merger, Time would retain its reputation and the integrity of its journalistic publications. The result here echoes many of the considerations addressed in *Cheff v. Mathes*, 199 A.2d 548 (Del. 1964), in which the board was concerned that if the outsider was successful, the business as it was known in the market would cease to exist.

■ CASE VOCABULARY

NO–SHOP PROVISION: A stipulation prohibiting one or more parties to a commercial contract from pursuing or entering into a more favorable agreement with a third party.

Paramount Communications Inc. v. QVC Network Inc.

(Targeted Company) v. *(Take–Over Bidder)*

637 A.2d 34 (Del. 1994)

IN A CORPORATE SALE, A BOARD MUST OPTIMIZE THE PRICE FOR ITS SHAREHOLDERS AND TREAT COMPETING BIDDERS EQUALLY

■ **INSTANT FACTS** Viacom Inc. (D) and Paramount Communications Inc. (D) formed an alliance even though QVC Network Inc. (P) proposed a more valuable offer.

■ **BLACK LETTER RULE** A board selling its corporation has a duty to obtain the best value for its shareholders and cannot give preference to one of the competing bidders.

■ **PROCEDURAL BASIS**

On appeal following the entry of an order granting a preliminary injunction enjoining the alliance between Viacom (D) and Paramount (D).

■ **FACTS**

Viacom (D) and Paramount (D) formed an alliance to thwart an unsolicited tender offer by QVC (P). QVC (P) made an unsolicited offer to acquire Paramount (D). Paramount (D) renewed its efforts to merge with Viacom, but the discussions stalled on price. Paramount (D) subsequently learned of QVC's (P) interest in Paramount (D) and informed QVC (P) that Paramount (D) was not for sale. Viacom's (D) stocks' price increased, which QVC claims was due to Viacom's (D) primary stockowner trading his own shares. Viacom (D) and Paramount (D) resumed negotiations, and the parties performed due diligence assisted by financial advisors, Smith Barney and Lazard Freres, respectively. Paramount unanimously approved the merger that would convert Paramount (D) stock into Viacom (D) shares and Paramount (D) exempted the transaction from its poison pill provisions. The agreement contained provisions to ward off advances from other interested buyers by imposing a no-shop provision, which prohibited Paramount (D) from discussing competing bids, provided that Viacom (D) would receive a $100–million termination fee if the companies' merger was cancelled, and granted Viacom (D) a Stock Option Agreement that allowed Viacom (D) to purchase 23,699,000 shares of Paramount's stock at $69.14 if a triggering event occured. Also, Viacom (D) could pay for the stock with subordinated debt and force Paramount (D) to compensate it for any difference between the stock's price and the put price. The merger was announced, but QVC (P) persisted. Paramount (D) told QVC (P) that the merger agreement prevented it from merger discussions with others absent certain conditions and asked QVC (P) to provide proof of financing. QVC (P) complied and presented a two-tiered tender offer, pursuant to which fifty-one percent of the shares would be purchased at $80, with the remaining shares participating in a stock-for-stock exchange. The offer was contingent on Paramount (D) canceling its stock option agreement with Viacom (D), which was at the time worth over $200 million. Viacom (D) realized that the QVC (P) deal was a better offer and tried to negotiate a new deal with Paramount (D). Viacom (D) and Paramount (D) reached a new agreement that was not much better than the original Viacom (D) agreement. The terms governing competing bids were unchanged. Viacom (D) and QVC (P) launched their tender offers, but QVC (P) was unable to get Paramount (D) to engage in realistic negotiations. At the next Paramount (D) board meeting the board rejected the QVC (P) proposal because it contained too many conditions and because the board believed that the Viacom (D) merger was the better deal. QVC (P) sought to have the court enjoin the Viacom (D) merger, and the court issued the injunction.

■ ISSUE

Is a board that agrees to the sale of a corporation or the transfer of control obligated to obtain the best price for the shares?

■ DECISION AND RATIONALE

(Veasey, J.) Yes. The law recognizes that managing a company's affairs is normally protected by the business judgment rule. However, a court must closely scrutinize the board's conduct if the transaction being considered results in a sale of the corporation or if the actions are designed to defend a threat to corporate control. In this case, the transaction will create a new majority shareholder and is effectively a grant of control to the purchaser. Therefore, the stockholders should be paid for the loss of control. If a board decides to resist an acquisition, the decision must be well informed, but if *control* is for sale, the board must insist on obtaining the best value for its stockholders. Deciding the best value may include more than simply the price, so the transaction must be analyzed as a whole, with any non-cash component quantified. A court must review a board's action with enhanced scrutiny any time there is a diminution of voting power, the sale of a control premium, or an action to impede a stockholder's voting rights. Only after the decision passes this enhanced scrutiny will the business judgment rule protect the board's decision. The court's enhanced scrutiny must include a review of both the directors' decision-making process, including an examination of the information used by the board, and the reasonableness of the directors' action in light of the circumstances. The directors have the burden of proving that they were adequately informed and acted reasonably. Paramount (D) argues that the fiduciary obligations and enhanced judicial scrutiny are not invoked in a merger case that does not break-up the corporation, but this argument is based on an erroneous reading of the law. There is no reason to limit *Revlon* to cases involving a break-up of the company. If a corporation participates in a transaction that leads to a change in corporate control or a break-up of the corporate entity, the directors' obligation is to seek the best value for the stockholders. Here, the Viacom–Paramount transaction will shift control of Paramount (D) from the public stockholders to Viacom (D). Once Paramount (D) directors decide to sell control of the company, they must determine that all material aspects of the Paramount–Viacom transaction are in the Paramount (D) stockholders' best interests. Paramount (D) contends it was precluded by contract with Viacom (D) from negotiating with QVC (P), but contract provisions that are inconsistent with a director's duties are invalid. Paramount's (D) directors decided to sell, and they had an obligation to continue their search for the best value reasonably available to the stockholders and to evaluate both the QVC (P) tender offer and the Paramount–Viacom transaction to determine which offer was best. Paramount (D) did not properly consider the consequences of the defensive measures demanded by Viacom (D), and QVC's (P) interest gave the Paramount (D) board a bargaining tool to obtain a higher price from Viacom (D). When the Paramount (D) directors considered QVC's (P) tender offer, they missed an opportunity to eliminate the restrictions they had imposed on themselves. As the process progressed, the Paramount (D) directors chose to remain paralyzed in their assessment of the QVC (P) offer, staying blind to the better offer. Affirmed and remanded.

Analysis:

Paramount (D) insisted so strongly on the transaction it had reached with Viacom (D) that it refused to believe that a better deal may exist for the company and its shareholders. Perhaps Paramount (D) was still haunted by the result of its claim against Time Inc., presented five years earlier in *Paramount Communications, Inc. v. Time Incorporated*, 571 A.2d 1140 (Del. 1989). In the Time-merger matter, Paramount (D) was the unsuccessful, hostile bidder. Now Paramount (D) had found a merger target, Viacom (D), and it did not want to let go. Unlike Paramount (D) urged the Time directors to do, Paramount (D) refused to consider price and long-term debt. Paramount (D) could not justify that the merger represented a chance for the company to improve its long-range market objectives.

■ CASE VOCABULARY

TENDER OFFER: A public offer to buy a minimum number of shares directly from a corporation's shareholders at a fixed price, usually at a substantial premium over the market price, in an effort to take control of the corporation.

ACE Ltd. v. Capital Re Corp.

(Bidder) v. *(Targeted Corporation)*

747 A.2d 95 (Del. Ch. 1999)

A BOARD OF DIRECTORS MAY NOT AGREE TO LIMIT THEIR ABILITY TO FULFILL THEIR FIDUCIARY DUTIES TO THEIR SHAREHOLDERS

WELL, IT SOUNDS GOOD TO ME--A BERMUDA-BASED COMPANY MEANS WE COULD MEET IN A WARM, SUNNY, CORPORATE-TAX-FREE ENVIRONMENT.

■ **INSTANT FACTS** A holding company brought an action against a corporation, seeking to enjoin it from terminating a merger agreement.

■ **BLACK LETTER RULE** Board members may not surrender their ability to fulfill a fiduciary duty to their shareholders or make the exercise of their duty contingent on a third party's written endorsement.

■ **PROCEDURAL BASIS**

On motion for a temporary restraining order.

■ **FACTS**

Capital Re Corp. (D) was a reinsurance company, and ACE (P) was a Cayman Islands holding company that engaged in insurance and reinsurance through its subsidiaries. Capital Re (D), which needed a capital infusion, exchanged 12.3 percent of its stock for $75 million from ACE (P). Even with the infusion, Moody's downgraded Capital Re's (D) rating from AAA to AA2. In order to avoid further downgrades, Capital Re (D) and ACE (P) agreed to a merger pursuant to which Capital Re (D) shareholders would obtain .6 of a share in the new company for each Capital Re (D) share. Capital Re (D) signed the merger agreement, knowing ACE (P) held only 12.3 percent of Capital Re's (D) shares, but that it had agreements with other shareholders for about 33.5 percent of Capital Re's (D) shares. Under these agreements, the 33.5–percent shareholders were obligated to support the merger, provided the Capital Re (D) board did not terminate it. Through the agreements, ACE (P) controlled slightly less than half of Capital Re's (D) shares and needed few additional votes to effect the merger. Capital Re (D) was virtually locked into the merger even if a better offer came along. ACE (P) wanted the strongest commitment possible from Capital Re (D), given the investment ACE (P) had in Capital Re (D) and the strategic opportunity the merger presented. Capital Re (D) knew it needed to protect its shareholders. In exchange for Capital Re's (D) freedom to walk away from the merger, the agreement contained a "no talk" provision, which prohibited Capital Re (D) from actively seeking merger inquiries from others, and a provision that prohibited Capital Re (D) from responding to an unsolicited offer without a belief, based on outside advice, that the proposal was likely to result in a better offer. ACE (P) was to receive notice of any other offer. Capital Re (D) could terminate the merger if it had not breached the merger agreement and if its board authorized a binding written agreement that was superior to the merger agreement, provided ACE (P) failed to respond in five days with a proposal at least as good as the new offer, and Capital Re (D) paid ACE (P) a $25–million termination fee. After the merger announcement, the price of ACE's (P) shares fell. The day before the scheduled merger vote, Capital Re (D) received a better offer from XL Capital Ltd. to purchase the company. At an emergency board meeting, outside counsel told the board that if it considered the XL Capital offer to be a superior proposal, the board must consider the offer to fulfill its fiduciary obligations to shareholders. The board decided it must investigate XL's offer. As a result of their discussions, XL raised its bid to $13 per share. At the following board meeting, the board concluded that the XL Capital offer was preferable to the ACE

(P) merger, so Capital Re (D) sent the required notice to ACE (P) of the superior offer and of its intention to terminate the merger unless ACE (P) increased its offer in five days. ACE (P) increased its offer, but its increase was met by another increase by XL. Capital Re (D) sent a new notice of intent to cancel to ACE. Instead of matching that offer, ACE sought an injunction to stop Capital Re (D) from terminating its agreement.

■ ISSUE

May parties agree to terms in an agreement limiting the board's ability to fulfill its fiduciary duties to its shareholders to investigate better offers?

■ DECISION AND RATIONALE

No. ACE (P) argues that Capital Re (D) violated the merger agreement by discussing a merger with XL Capital without the required written notice and that the appropriate remedy is an injunction against terminating the merger. ACE (P) needs to prevent the cancellation in order to bind the 33.5–percent shareholders to their obligation to vote in favor of the ACE–Capital Re merger. Capital Re (D) contends that determining whether the board's fiduciary obligations compel them to explore another company's offer is left to its own good faith. A board must make its own decisions. Although the merger agreement's terms are not absolutely clear, the better reading is one that leaves the board's fiduciary duty decisions to the board. Here, the board knew that failing to investigate the XL Capital offer would subject its shareholders to a merger with ACE (P) despite a drastic decrease in ACE's value. ACE (P) claims it bargained for the protections stated in the merger agreement and contends it has the right to insist on the written notice. However, if parties contract for provisions that exceed a party's authority, the law will not automatically enforce the contract. A court must examine the party's knowledge and whether the promise will affect public policy considerations. If the other party has reason to know the promise can be performed only on shaky ground, the court will not enforce it and will grant damages. In this case, Delaware law gives deference to the stockholders' interests, regardless of contracts that purport to disable the board. The court should evaluate three questions in considering whether to enforce the contract provision. First, did the acquirer know of the breach of fiduciary duty? Second, has the transaction been consummated? And, finally, does the board's violation touch on especially significant policy considerations? Here, ACE (P) had to know that the contract provision was questionable because ACE's (P) contract rights cannot take precedence over the rights of Capital Re's (D) shareholders, who would be harmed by literal enforcement of the contract provision. The second question also cuts against ACE (P). The merger has not occurred, so the court need not undo the transaction. Finally, the importance of the public policies at stake here demands a disregard for ACE's (P) strict interpretation of its contract provision. A board's fiduciary duties to shareholders are superior to third party suitors' rights. Therefore, ACE (P) is not likely to be able to convince a court on final hearing that Capital Re (D) breached a valid contractual provision by entering into discussions with XL Capital. Motion denied.

Analysis:

In the merger craze that occurred in the 1980's, many companies believed that if they were not involved in merger negotiations, the company was in trouble. Once ACE (P) had Capital Re's (D) stock tied up, it did not want to risk losing the deal, especially because the agreement gave ACE (P) the opportunity to expand into markets previously closed to it. Under the Restatement (Second) of Contracts § 193, a fiduciary obligation cannot be eliminated by agreement with a third party, especially if a shareholder is relying heavily on that fiduciary duty to protect its interests. Although a board has broad discretion in deciding how to respond to a threat, it cannot lock itself into responses without examining whether the proposal is actually a threat.

■ CASE VOCABULARY

TRO: Abbreviation for "temporary restraining order"; a court order preserving the status quo until a litigant's application for a preliminary or permanent injunction can be heard.

Hilton Hotels Corp. v. ITT Corp.

(Acquiring Company) v. *(Targeted Company)*

978 F.Supp. 1342 (D. Nev. 1997)

A TARGETED COMPANY MAY NOT RESTRUCTURE ITSELF TO FRUSTRATE A TAKEOVER

■ **INSTANT FACTS** Hilton Hotels (P), which sought to acquire ITT Corp. (D), sued to obtain an injunction precluding implementation of the target company's comprehensive plan.

■ **BLACK LETTER RULE** A target corporation's attempts to restructure itself in an attempt to preclude an acquiring corporation from obtaining a majority on the board constitutes an impermissible restriction on its shareholders' rights to vote for directors.

■ **PROCEDURAL BASIS**

On a motion for an injunction.

■ **FACTS**

Hilton Hotels Corp. (P) proposed a $55 per share tender offer for ITT's (D) stock and announced a plan to engage in a proxy contest at ITT's (D) next annual meeting. ITT (D) rejected Hilton's (P) offer, sold some of its non-core assets, and held off its annual meeting. Hilton (P) filed a motion to compel the meeting. The court determined that under Nevada law, ITT (D) had eighteen months from the last meeting to schedule the next meeting. ITT (D) announced a Comprehensive Plan to split ITT (D) into three entities: ITT Destinations, which would include the hotel and gaming business and hold 93 percent of the company's assets; ITT Educational Services, which would consist of the current technical schools; and ITT's European Yellow Pages Division, which would remain with the current ITT (D) as ITT World Directories. Although members of ITT's current board would run ITT Destinations, the memberships would be staggered so that a third of the directors would be elected each year for a three-year term. Eighty percent of the company's shareholders were required to approve any measures repealing this provision. The Comprehensive Plan also contained a poison-pill provision creating a $1.4 billion tax liability for Hilton (P) upon its successful acquisition of ITT Destinations. ITT (D) tried to implement the plan without shareholder approval. Notwithstanding the plan, Hilton (P) amended its tender offer to $70 per share, but ITT (D) rejected the offer. Hilton (P) then brought an action asking the court to enjoin ITT (D) from implementing the Comprehensive Plan, to hold that the ITT (D) board had breached its fiduciary duties to ITT (D) and its shareholders, and to bar ITT (D) from implementing the plan without shareholder approval.

■ **ISSUE**

In the face of an attempted hostile takeover, may a targeted corporation eliminate its shareholders' rights to elect a board of directors?

■ **DECISION AND RATIONALE**

(Pro, J.) No. Hilton (P) must show irreparable injury and must actually succeed on the merits of its claims to justify an injunction. A tender offer coupled with a proxy fight puts the board in a tough position. Poison pills can frustrate many hostile takeovers, but proxy fights are an effective means to circumvent them. Nevada case law does not address the issue, but Delaware case law can provide

---

guidance. Under Delaware law, any defensive reaction to a takeover bid must be evaluated in terms of the board's overall response, the measure's justification, and the results. Shareholders need to be assured free exercise of their voting rights, and any measure that disenfranchises the shareholders is strongly suspect and can be upheld only upon compelling justification. Adoption of a plan like the one proposed here is not generally subjected to a shareholder vote. However, this plan allows the board to adopt measures that will affect the shareholders' rights to vote for the board's members. Therefore, it must be enjoined. Although Nevada law allows a board to resist changes in control, the powers granted to the board under the plan cannot be reconciled with those rights. A company's shareholders' rights to vote for the board limits the board's powers, so a board must have a compelling justification for limiting those rights. ITT (D) argues that its plan is better for its shareholders than the Hilton (P) offer, but "better" is not the issue. The defendant must prove that Hilton's (P) offer threatens corporate policy, and ITT (D) has failed to establish such a threat. Also, there is no proof that ITT's (D) board conducted a good faith and reasonable investigation and although an inadequate price may present a threat, ITT (D) has not demonstrated resulting harm to the company. Furthermore, even if Hilton's (P) offer is a threat, ITT's (D) response must be reasonable. Although a corporation may adopt a classified board structure, it cannot adopt the measure simply to prohibit shareholders from engaging in a proxy contest. Here, the timing of the Comprehensive Plan with the staggered board is suspect. The ITT (D) directors approving the plan are the same ones who would fill the positions on the ITT Destinations board. There is no justification for not seeking shareholder approval of the plan. By classifying the board, the shareholders are prevented from electing a majority of the directors at their next meeting. Finally, ITT (D) did not seek an opinion from the IRS on the effect of their split, and proper business practice requires tax issues to be investigated before embarking on a venture. The primary purpose for ITT's (D) adoption of the Comprehensive Plan is to impede the shareholders' right to vote for directors. Motion for permanent injunctive relief issued.

Analysis:

ITT's (D) reaction to Hilton's bid is similar to Paramount's reaction in *Paramount Communications Inc. v. QVC Network Inc.*, 637 A.2d 34 (Del. 1994). Without fully examining the QVC bid, Paramount rejected it as inferior to its agreement with Viacom. ITT's (D) reaction here was also extreme. ITT (D) failed to make their decision in a manner that would protect it by the business judgment rule. Also, the court noted that ITT's (D) plan seemed to adopt some of Hilton's plan's features, serving as more evidence that Hilton's proposal had some merit that ITT (D) simply chose to overlook.

■ CASE VOCABULARY

PERMANENT INJUNCTION: An injunction granted after a final hearing on the merits. Despite its name, a permanent injunction does not necessarily last forever.

CTS Corp. v. Dynamics Corp. of Am.

(Targeted Corporation) v. *(Buyer)*
481 U.S. 69, 107 S.Ct. 1637, 95 L.Ed.2d 67 (1987)

STATE LAW MAY RESTRICT THE GRANT OF CONTROL OF A CORPORATION

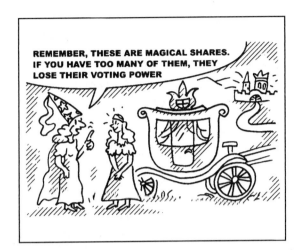

REMEMBER, THESE ARE MAGICAL SHARES. IF YOU HAVE TOO MANY OF THEM, THEY LOSE THEIR VOTING POWER

■ **INSTANT FACTS** Dynamics Corporation of America (P) offered to purchase CTS Corporation (D) and was obligated to fulfill state law requirements in order to obtain majority shareholder status.

■ **BLACK LETTER RULE** State law may impose restrictions affecting a company's ability to acquire control of another without running afoul of federal law or the Commerce Clause.

■ **PROCEDURAL BASIS**

On certification to the U.S. Supreme Court from a finding that the Indiana Business Corporation Law violated the Commerce Clause.

■ **FACTS**

The revised Indiana Business Corporation Law included a chapter on Control Share Acquisitions that applied to any issuing public Indiana domestic corporations, including existing corporations, unless the corporation's board specifically amends its articles or bylaws to opt out of the provision. Under the act, an "issuing public corporation" is a corporation with 100 or more shareholders that has "its principal place of business, its principal office, or substantial assets" located in Indiana and that has either (a) more than ten percent of its shareholders residing in Indiana; (b) more than ten percent of its shares owned by Indiana residents; or (c) 10,000 shareholders residing in Indiana. The act focuses on "control shares," which are shares acquired when the holder has control of 20 percent, 33 1/3 percent, or 50 percent of the shares. The control shares' holder is not necessarily allowed to obtain the corresponding percentage of votes; he or she will be limited to as much voting power as the other shareholders allow. The statute's effect is to subject control of the corporation to the disinterested shareholders' approval. If the shareholders withhold majority rights, the shareholder that acquired the shares can ask the corporation to redeem its shares. Dynamics (P) owned 9.6 percent of the common stock of CTS (D), an Indiana corporation. Dynamics (P) announced a tender offer for one million CTS (D) shares, bringing Dynamics' (P) ownership of CTS (D) to 27.5 percent. The CTS (D) board determined that CTS (P) would comply with the act's provisions, and Dynamics (P) sought a legal determination that the Act was preempted by the William Act and constituted a violation of the Commerce Clause. The District Court held that the Williams Act pre-empted the Indiana Act and granted Dynamics' (P) motion for declaratory relief. A week later, the court issued an opinion agreeing that the act violated the Commerce Clause by posing a substantial interference with interstate commerce. The court of appeals agreed with the trial court's decision.

■ **ISSUE**

May state law impose restrictions affecting a company's ability to acquire control of another without running afoul of federal law or the Commerce Clause?

■ **DECISION AND RATIONALE**

(Powell, J.) Yes. In deciding whether a state statute is pre-empted by a federal statute, a court will generally find pre-emption only if adhering to both sets of regulations creates a physical impossibility or if the state impedes a Congressional purpose. In this case, a company may comply with both the Williams Act and the Indiana Act, so a court must determine whether the Indiana law frustrates the federal law's purpose. The Williams Act was passed in response to the increase in hostile take-overs. It requires an offeror to file a disclosure statement about any tender offer, establishes rules concerning the duration of the offer and the withdrawal of tenders, and requires that an offeror pay the same price for all shares purchased within the offer. Indiana's act is not similar to the Williams Act or the Illinois statute examined in *Edgar v. MITE Corp.,* 457 U.S. 624 (1982). In *MITE*, the Illinois statute sought to overturn the balance struck by the Williams Act, installing the state's restrictions on tender offers in contradiction with the Williams Act's provisions. Based on *MITE*, the Indiana Act passes muster. The Indiana statute protects independent shareholders, placing investors, often at a disadvantage in takeovers, on equal footing. When faced with a tender offer, many shareholders make an early tender, not necessarily believing the acquisition to be the best action, but to avoid having to take a lesser position after the first phase of a takeover. The Indiana law allows shareholders to act as a group and reject an offer in the corporation's best interests. The Court of Appeals rationalized that the Indiana act will lead to delays in the purchase of shares for as long as fifty days, which is the outside time for seeking a shareholders' vote on the rights. Arguably, this conflicts with the twenty-day waiting period imposed by the SEC. However, the Indiana act does not demand a fifty-day delay, and a purchaser may buy shares as soon as the federal law permits. If the buyer is concerned about not having voting rights, the tender offer can be made conditional. The Williams Act is designed to prevent only unreasonable delays, and, under the Indiana act, the longest delay is fifty days, which is not unreasonable. The Court of Appeals also considered that the Indiana act may violate the Commerce Clause. However, the Indiana law treats in-state and out-of-state concerns equally, and the act regulates only those corporations subject to its rules. Every state regulates corporate governance and allows some transactions while prohibiting others. In transactions such as mergers, the variations from state to state are vast, and some states make it easy for companies to merge, while others make it more difficult. Although the difficult laws may inhibit mergers, they are not illegal. Indiana's Control Share Acquisitions act does not conflict with the William's Act's provisions or purposes. Although the act may affect interstate commerce, the interference is justified by the state's interests in protecting shareholders. Reversed.

■ CONCURRENCE IN PART

(Scalia, J.) As long as a state's laws affect only its own corporations and do not discriminate against out-of-state interests, they should survive this Court's scrutiny under the Commerce Clause, regardless of their ultimate effect. Although the law may not be completely wise, it is not unconstitutional.

■ DISSENT

(White, J.) The majority's decision will foreclose some tender offers for stock in Indiana corporations. The law undermines the Williams Act's policy by preventing minority shareholders from acting in their best interests by selling their stock and burdens interstate corporate ownership, especially if other states adopt similar provisions. The Commerce Clause intended to prevent this type of interference.

Analysis:

The Williams Act was Congress's attempt to deal with the growing number of tender offers being made for unsuspecting shareholders' companies. Although a state that has provided the charter for a corporation's operations should also be able to regulate how that company deals with its shareholders, the Court here is faced with objections from outsiders who contend that once the corporation is interacting with businesses from other states, those seeking to acquire an interest are faced with surprises. One of the factors that likely influenced the outcome of this decision is the fact that there is no reliance problem under the Indiana act. Companies that formed under Indiana law before the act had the chance to opt out of the provision, and companies that were formed after the act could have incorporated in a different jurisdiction.

■ CASE VOCABULARY

WILLIAMS ACT: A federal statute, enacted in 1968, that amended the Securities Exchange Act of 1934 by requiring investors who own more than five percent of a company's stock to furnish certain information to the SEC and to comply with certain requirements when making a tender offer.

CHAPTER EIGHT

Corporate Debt

Sharon Steel Corp. v. Chase Manhattan Bank, N.A.

Instant Facts: UV Industries (UV) issued bonds to raise corporate capital and then decided to liquidate operations, selling each of its three divisions in separate sales with the final buyer, Sharon Steel Corporation (Sharon Steel) (P), assuming responsibility for the bonds.

Black Letter Rule: Boilerplate successor obligor clauses that do not permit assignment of public debt to another party in the course of a liquidation unless "all or substantially all" of the company's assets are transferred to a single purchaser prevent a purchasing corporation that acquires only fifty-one percent of the liquidating debtor's assets in the last of a series of sales from becoming the issuer's successor obligor.

Metropolitan Life Ins. Co. v. RJR Nabisco, Inc.

Instant Facts: Metropolitan Life Insurance Co. (P) brought an action against RJR Nabisco, Inc. (Nabisco) (D) to recover the loss in value of the Nabisco bonds the plaintiff held following the KKR group's leveraged buyout of Nabisco (D).

Black Letter Rule: A bond indenture does not contain an implied covenant restricting any action that might subject the bondholder's investment to an increased risk of nonpayment.

Katz v. Oak Indus., Inc.

Instant Facts: Bondholder sought to enjoin the consummation of an exchange offer and consent solicitation made by a corporation to long-term debt holders.

Black Letter Rule: An offer to exchange debentures does not violate an offeror's duty of good faith and fair dealing if it is not coercive and does not violate the indenture's obligations regarding redemption.

Morgan Stanley & Co. v. Archer Daniels Midland Co.

Instant Facts: Archer Daniels Midland Co. (D) sought to redeem $125 million in debentures, and Morgan Stanley & Co. (P) sought a preliminary injunction against the proposed redemption.

Black Letter Rule: Using the funding obtained with proceeds of common stock issued by a bond issuer is a lawful means of redeeming outstanding debentures, notwithstanding the fact that the debtor corporation had also obtained funding that was prohibited from being used to effect a redemption.

Sharon Steel Corp. v. Chase Manhattan Bank, N.A.

(Successor Company) v. *(Bond Trustee)*

691 F.2d 1039 (2d Cir. 1982)

BUYER IN A PIECEMEAL SALE OF A CORPORATION IS NOT A SUCCESSOR CORPORATION

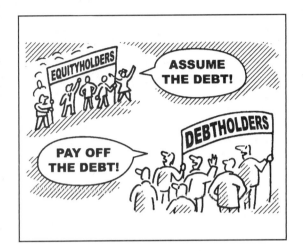

■ **INSTANT FACTS** UV Industries (UV) issued bonds to raise corporate capital and then decided to liquidate operations, selling each of its three divisions in separate sales with the final buyer, Sharon Steel Corporation (Sharon Steel) (P), assuming responsibility for the bonds.

■ **BLACK LETTER RULE** Boilerplate successor obligor clauses that do not permit assignment of public debt to another party in the course of a liquidation unless "all or substantially all" of the company's assets are transferred to a single purchaser prevent a purchasing corporation that acquires only fifty-one percent of the liquidating debtor's assets in the last of a series of sales from becoming the issuer's successor obligor.

■ PROCEDURAL BASIS

On appeal from the trial court's grant of a directed verdict and summary judgment in favor of the trustees.

■ FACTS

UV Industries (UV) issued debentures that paid interest at below-market rates over time. Because of the low rates, the bonds were sold on the market for less than their value at maturity. UV decided to liquidate its operations and to distribute the proceeds to its stockholders. UV conducted its business as three entities: Federal Pacific Electric Company (Federal Pacific), which produced sixty percent of UV's revenues; a second business involving oil and gas properties, which generated only two percent of UV's revenues; and Mueller Brass Company, which provided thirty-eight percent of UV's revenue. UV also held cash and other liquid assets. As part of the liquidation, UV sold Federal Pacific to Reliance Electric Company for $345 million in cash and distributed a portion of the proceeds to UV stockholders. Several months later, the oil and gas division was sold to Tenneco for $135 million in cash. UV's remaining assets were the Mueller Brass mining properties and $300 million in cash, which was subject to the debenture holders' claims of approximately $123 million. Sharon Steel (P) bought UV's remaining assets, including the cash, paying UV $107 million in cash and assuming responsibility for all of UV's outstanding obligations, including its responsibilities on the subordinated debentures now selling at below-market. Neither Sharon Steel (P) nor UV could repurchase the subordinated debentures on the market because once the bondholders knew of their efforts, they would demand a higher price. If Sharon Steel (P) had to pay off the bondholders before maturity, it would be short of cash and would have to borrow replacement funds at a higher market rate. The indentures, which contained a provision concerning consolidation of the company, allowed UV to merge or consolidate with another company or sell its assets without objection from the bondholders, but the surviving company was required to observe all conditions under which the bonds were issued. Also, the surviving corporation was required to pay all principal and interest. Sharon Steel (P) brought an action against the indenture trustees (D) seeking to have them execute supplemental indentures to allow Sharon Steel (P) to assume the liquidating debtor corporation's obligations under indentures.

■ ISSUE

Is a purchasing company deemed to have purchased substantially all of an issuing company's assets if the purchasing company buys only half the issuing company's assets as part of the last in a series of sales disposing of portions of the company's assets?

■ DECISION AND RATIONALE

(Winter, J.) No. At trial, Sharon Steel (P) argued that the judge should have submitted to the jury all issues concerning the meaning of the successor obligor clauses. However, bonds all contain "boiler-plate" language concerning successor obligations, and those provisions are viewed differently from language that is designed to reflect specific circumstances involved in the offering. A uniform interpretation of boilerplate provisions comes from basic contract law and presents a question of law, not fact. A bondholder is generally not protected against the issuer's actions unless he or she brings an action based on the contract terms governing the indenture. Sharon Steel (P) argues that the successor language in the bonds permits it to assume UV's responsibilities on the bonds. Sharon Steel (P) bought all UV-owned assets, including the proceeds of the previous sales (because it purchased UV's cash). The indenture trustee (D) argues that Sharon Steel (P) could not have purchased all that UV owned because some UV's assets had been sold in earlier transactions. Under Sharon Steel's (P) argument, UV could be deemed still to own all it sold Sharon Steel (P) because UV received the proceeds from that sale. Taken to the next step, if UV still owned what it sold to Sharon Steel (P), this suit is unnecessary because no event triggered the successor clauses. Sharon Steel (P) contends that the purpose of the successor obligor clause is to allow the issuing corporation the freedom to merge or sell assts, not to protect the lenders. The trustees (D) contend the purpose is to protect lenders by assuring continuity of ownership. Under the rules of construction, if conflicting interpretations are offered that may protect both parties, the court must apply the interpretation that does the least injury to both sides. The trustees' (D) interpretation is most appropriate. Sharon Steel's (P) interpretation would permit an issuing corporation to engage in piecemeal dispositions of its assets to the minimum level allowed by the indenture. At that point, the issuer could then engage in a sale of "substantially all" of its remaining assets. The result would be a substitution of a new debtor through a sale that may simply be a "cash-for-cash sale." Affirmed.

Analysis:

Boilerplate language can be important. It may seem that boilerplate terms have no purpose other than to make the contract appear complete, and the parties, perhaps even the parties' attorneys, may include the language out of tradition or habit. However, the terms and conditions contained in boilerplate may be significant. As Sharon Steel discovered, it can even result in greater obligations being imposed.

■ CASE VOCABULARY

BOILERPLATE: Ready-made or all-purpose language that will fit in a variety of documents; fixed or standardized contractual language that the proposing party views as relatively nonnegotiable.

BOND: A long-term, interest-bearing instrument issued by a corporation or governmental entity, usually to provide for a particular financial need; especially, such an instrument in which the debt is secured by a lien on the issuer's property.

CORPORATE INDENTURE: A document containing the terms and conditions governing the issuance of debt securities, such as bonds or debentures.

DEBENTURES: A debt secured only by the debtor's earning power, not by a lien on any specific asset.

INDENTURE TRUSTEE: A trustee named in a trust indenture and charged with holding legal title to the trust property; a trustee under an indenture.

Metropolitan Life Ins. Co. v. RJR Nabisco, Inc.

(*Bond Holders*) v. (*Bonds Issuer*)

716 F.Supp. 1504 (S.D.N.Y. 1989)

BONDHOLDERS MAY NOT USE IMPLIED COVENANTS TO ENLARGE THEIR RIGHTS AGAINST A BOND ISSUER

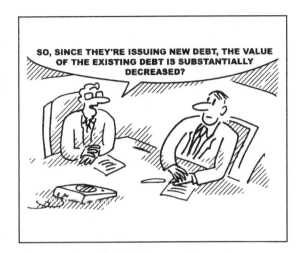

■ **INSTANT FACTS** Metropolitan Life Insurance Co. (P) brought an action against RJR Nabisco, Inc. (Nabisco) (D) to recover the loss in value of the Nabisco bonds the plaintiff held following the KKR group's leveraged buyout of Nabisco (D).

■ **BLACK LETTER RULE** A bond indenture does not contain an implied covenant restricting any action that might subject the bondholder's investment to an increased risk of nonpayment.

■ **PROCEDURAL BASIS**

On a motion by the plaintiff bondholders for summary judgment based the issuer's breach an implied covenant of good faith and fair dealing.

■ **FACTS**

RJR Nabisco (Nabisco) (D) was the target of a leveraged buyout (LBO), causing a bidding war for its stock. Nabisco's (D) directors appointed a committee to investigate the LBO offers and make a recommendation. Metropolitan Life Insurance Co. (Metropolitan Life) (P) complained that Nabisco's (D) actions in succumbing to the LBO impaired the value of the bonds it purchased, causing it to suffer millions of dollars in losses. Throughout the time Nabisco (D) was being pursued in the LBO, Metropolitan Life (P) assured its bondholders that Nabisco's (D) board wanted to maintain Nabisco's (D) preferred credit rating, but Nabisco's (D) credit rating suffered. Metropolitan Life (P) asked the court to find that the indenture contains an implied covenant of good faith and fair dealing, that the covenant was breached, and that Nabisco (D) must redeem its bonds. Metropolitan Life (P), with assets worth more than $88 billion, alleged it held more than $340 million in Nabisco's bonds which it purchased in six separate offerings. Jefferson–Pilot Life Insurance Co. (Jefferson–Pilot) (P), another plaintiff, held more than $9 million in bonds from three separate Nabisco (D) offerings. The plaintiffs could have sold their bonds at any time before the Nabisco (D) buyout.

■ **ISSUE**

Does an issuer whose bond value is impaired breach of an implied covenant of good faith by engaging in a leveraged buyout?

■ **DECISION AND RATIONALE**

(Walker, J.) No. The indenture governing the bonds permits Nabisco (D) to engage in mergers and assume other debts. The parties knew the indenture's terms at the time Nabisco (D) sold the bonds. Imposing additional terms on the indenture through implied covenants would create a burden that was not part of the parties' bargain. Even though indentures are not often the result of face-to-face negotiations between the buyer and the seller, underwriters typically consider the buyer's needs and concerns when negotiating the agreement. The agreement controlling these bonds contains no restriction on company debt. Article Three of the indenture provides for payment of interest and principal and contains a negative pledge against mortgages and other liens. Article Five addresses the procedures to remedy defaults and restricts bondholders from bringing suit on the indentures without a demand by twenty-five percent of the bondholders. Article Ten concerns consolidations, mergers and conveyances and provides that Nabisco (D) may consolidate, merge or sell its assets, provided the resulting entity is a U.S. corporation that agrees to assume Nabisco's (D) debt and not to default under the bonds. Although those bond provisions appear to discourage leveraged buyouts, they were renegotiated before the LBO. Metropolitan Life (P), which was concerned with the buyout trend and expressed concern over its effect on bond values, considered either insisting on more restrictive covenants in the bonds or exiting the market. It even drafted a proposed model indenture with a covenant against stockholder profits designed to injure bondholders' positions, but the proposal never went beyond discussion stages. Metropolitan Life (P) and Jefferson–Pilot (P) cannot claim to be ignorant of the market risks. When the plaintiffs purchased Nabisco's (D) bonds they assumed that Nabisco (D) would work to obtain a high credit rating, had the ability to pay interest on its bonds, and promised to attempt to retain their high credit rating. The plaintiffs cannot violate the parole evidence rule by contending that Nabisco executives' speeches formed part of their agreement to invest. The bonds addressed merger possibilities, but did not prohibit mergers. The plaintiffs argue in favor of finding an implied duty of good faith. However, when boilerplate language is used and relied upon by the entire market, the court cannot ignore the terms and imply the existence of a duty not to frustrate the purpose of the debtholders' contracts. Also, implied covenants cannot provide the plaintiffs with any rights that would be inconsistent with the contract's express conditions. The plaintiffs argue that the court can imply the protections they need from the terms contained in the contract, but, if that were true, the investors would not need new terms and conditions or face having to exit the market. The plaintiffs' remaining claims argue unjust enrichment, frustration of purpose, breach of fiduciary duty and unconscionability. Each of those claims must fail. Order issued.

Analysis:

Metropolitan Life does not allow a bond issuer to act with impunity and destroy an investor's rights. If the bond contract contained a provision holding executive salaries to less than $100,000 per year, the plaintiffs would be justified in suing to stop the issuer from paying higher salaries. Here, the bondholders wanted the court to prohibit Nabisco (D) from participating in the LBO even if their indenture granted them the power to do so. The court refused to provide the investors with a right that the contract clearly withheld from them.

■ CASE VOCABULARY

LEVERAGED BUYOUT: The purchase of a publicly held corporation's outstanding stock by its management or outside investors, financed mainly with funds borrowed from investment bankers or brokers and usually secured by the corporation's assets.

PROSPECTUS: A printed document that describes the main features of an enterprise (especially a corporation's business) and that is distributed to prospective buyers or investors; especially, a written description of a securities offering.

Katz v. Oak Indus., Inc.

(Bondholder) v. *(Bond Issuer)*

508 A.2d 873 (Del. Ch. 1986)

AN EXCHANGE OFFER DOES NOT OFFEND NOTIONS OF GOOD FAITH IF THE EXCHANGE IS VOLUNTARY AND NOT UNILATERALLY IMPOSED

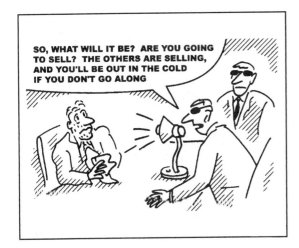

SO, WHAT WILL IT BE? ARE YOU GOING TO SELL? THE OTHERS ARE SELLING, AND YOU'LL BE OUT IN THE COLD IF YOU DON'T GO ALONG

■ **INSTANT FACTS** Bondholder sought to enjoin the consummation of an exchange offer and consent solicitation made by a corporation to long-term debt holders.

■ **BLACK LETTER RULE** An offer to exchange debentures does not violate an offeror's duty of good faith and fair dealing if it is not coercive and does not violate the indenture's obligations regarding redemption.

■ **PROCEDURAL BASIS**

Action by the plaintiff for preliminary injunction.

■ **FACTS**

Oak Industries, Inc. (Oak) (D) operated several affiliated companies and foreign subsidiaries engaged in manufacturing and marketing communication equipment and components. Oak (D), which was in financial trouble, terminated its unrelated operations, procured a buyer (Allied–Signal) for its materials segment, and was seeking a buyer for its communications business. The Oak (D) board attempted to buy time for the company to regain profitability. Oak (D) had $230 million in corporate bonds outstanding that it tried to exchange for notes, common stock, and warrants. Oak (D) was successful in retiring approximately $180 million of the $230 million, reducing some of the company's cash drain. However, those transactions did not resolve Oak's (D) problems, so Oak (D) began negotiating with Allied–Signal. Oak (D) and Allied–Signal entered into an Acquisition Agreement selling Oak's (D) materials segment for $160 million in cash and a Stock Purchase Agreement, pursuant to which Allied–Signal would buy ten million shares of Oak's stock. As a precondition to Allied–Signal's obligations under the Stock Purchase Agreement, Oak (D) was required to retire at least eighty-five percent of Oak's (D) bond obligations. Katz (P), who owned long-term bonds issued by Oak (D), brought a class action to stop Oak (D) from exchanging long-term debt for stock under an exchange offer and consent solicitation. Oak (D) provided its bondholders with two exchange offers based on the interest rate attached to their bond. The exchange offers were conditioned on Oak (D) having a minimum number of notes tendered and a minimum amount of each class of debt securities tendered. Also, the exchange offer required the bondholder's acceptance of proposed amendments to the indentures. In order to qualify for the exchange offer, the bondholder was required to consent to the modification of the bond's contract terms. The required modifications effectively removed financial covenants from the indenture and had the potential to adversely affect the bondholders who did not tender their bonds. Without the appropriate amendments to the indentures, Allied–Signal could not proceed with its purchase of Oak (D).

■ **ISSUE**

Does a voluntary proposed bond exchange constitute a violation of the issuer's duty of good faith and fair dealing by presenting unlawful coercion, provide the bond issuer with an impermissible method to vote its debt or violate the indenture's redemption obligations?

■ DECISION AND RATIONALE

(Allen, J.) No. The plaintiff complains that the Exchange Offer benefits Oak's (D) common stockholders at the expense of the bondholders. A company's board of directors is obligated to maximize its stockholders' long-range interests, even if it is at the expense of others. In corporate restructurings, bondholders are often asked to bear a greater risk of loss. However, a court cannot afford protection against this risk absent relevant legislation or provisions in the indenture. The plaintiff also contends the exchange offer is coercive, but coercion is a matter of degree. Some coercion is clearly harmful, while other coercion is not. The question is whether Oak's the degree of coercion present in its exchange offer has breached its obligation to act in good faith. To answer this question, a court must analyze whether, at the time the parties negotiated the initial contract, the drafters would have proscribed the proposed action as a breach of the implied duty of good faith. Nothing in the indenture provides bondholders with the ability to veto modifications to the indenture or prohibits Oak (D) from providing an inducement to the bondholders to obtain their consent to changes. Katz (P) states that the indenture prohibits Oak (D) from voting debt securities it holds in its treasury and contends that by conditioning its offer to retire debt on the debtholders' consent to changes in the indenture, Oak (D) has effectively ensured the outcome of the vote. In reality, the bondholders have similar interests, including the desire to maximize the return on their investment. Therefore, while Oak (D) has fashioned the exchange so as to encourage consent to the indenture's amendment, it has not breach an implied duty of good faith. Katz (P) also contends that Oak's (D) efforts to get its bondholders to tender their instruments in exchange for a price that is less than its redemption price is a breach of good faith. However, the redemption is not mandatory and the debtor cannot act unilaterally. Whether the price is attractive is a function of the market and cannot be characterized as an effort by Oak (D) to subvert its obligations under the indentures. Injunction denied.

Analysis:

Katz depends on boilerplate language to reach its result. The plaintiffs claim that the boilerplate language is unclear because of the lack of any evidence as to the negotiations that occurred when drafting it. *Kaiser Aluminum Corp. v. Matheson*, 681 A.2d 392 (Del. 1996), notes that a court usually relies on extrinsic evidence to determine a party's intent and, in the case of boilerplate language, extrinsic evidence is not very helpful. Furthermore, early debenture negotiations often take place between the issuer and the underwriter, and the ultimate purchaser does not even participate in the process.

■ CASE VOCABULARY

EXCHANGE OFFER: A takeover attempt in which the bidder corporation offers to exchange some of its securities for a specified number of the target corporation's voting stocks.

TENDER OFFER: A public offer to buy a minimum number of stocks directly from a corporation's stockholders at a fixed price, usually at a substantial premium over the market price, in an effort to take control of the corporation.

Morgan Stanley & Co. v. Archer Daniels Midland Co.

(Debenture Holder) v. *(Debenture Issuer)*

570 F.Supp. 1529 (S.D.N.Y. 1983)

EARLY REDEMPTION IS PERMITTED IF THE ISSUER CAN IDENTIFY A PERMISSIBLE FUND FROM WHICH TO REDEEM THE BONDS

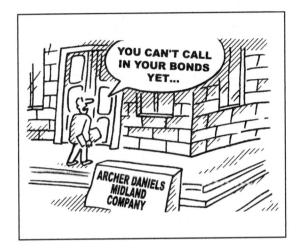

■ **INSTANT FACTS** Archer Daniels Midland Co. (D) sought to redeem $125 million in debentures, and Morgan Stanley & Co. (P) sought a preliminary injunction against the proposed redemption.

■ **BLACK LETTER RULE** Using the funding obtained with proceeds of common stock issued by a bond issuer is a lawful means of redeeming outstanding debentures, notwithstanding the fact that the debtor corporation had also obtained funding that was prohibited from being used to effect a redemption.

■ **PROCEDURAL BASIS**

On motion for summary judgment by debenture issuer.

■ **FACTS**

Archer Daniels Midland Co. (ADM) (D) sought to redeem $125 million in debentures. Morgan Stanley & Co. (Morgan Stanley) (P) brought an action under federal and state securities and business laws and sought a preliminary injunction against the proposed redemption, claiming that it was prohibited by the indenture and violated securities laws. The debentures, which were to be protected by a sinking fund, would pay sixteen percent and would mature in May 2011. Pursuant to the indenture, the debentures could be redeemed on a minimum of thirty and a maximum of sixty days' notice at the company's election. The original contract provided that upon redemption, the company must pay all accrued interest and the premium set forth in the contract. The provision contained certain redemption restrictions based on incurring debt at lower interest rates or in anticipation of funds from certain transactions. ADM (D) raised money on two occasions at effective rates less than the debenture rate and raised capital through two stock offerings. In anticipation of the high interest payments, Morgan Stanley (P) paid $1252.50 for each $1000 note for more than $15 million of the debentures, and $1200 for each $1000 face amount for another $500,000 of debentures. The day following Morgan Stanley's (P) second purchase, ADM (D) announced it was calling the debentures, paying for them from the sinking fund infused with the capital it received in its common stock offering. Before ADM's (D) call, the debentures were trading in excess of the call price. The plaintiff claimed that the call violates the terms of the indenture agreement's call provisions and violated the Trust Indenture Act of 1939. The plaintiffs also alleged that ADM (D) violated the indenture agreement by using proceeds of financing acquired at a rate less than that of the debentures, and that the fact ADM (D) raised sufficient funds to redeem the debentures through its common stock issue was an irrelevant juggling of funds.

■ **ISSUE**

When redeeming debentures at a time during which the redemptions are subject to a covenant prohibiting them from being funded by an exchange for lower-cost debt, may the redemption proceed if

---

the borrower has obtained lower-cost debt but has also obtained funds from other, non-prohibited sources?

■ DECISION AND RATIONALE

(Sand, J.) Yes. Morgan Stanley (P) asks the court to bar redemption at any period during which the issuer has borrowed funds at a rate lower than that prescribed by the redemption provision. ADM (D) contends that redemption should be permitted if the company can point to a permitted source for the funding. The redemption language is boilerplate, and the defendant contends it had no fraudulent plan to call the obligations at the time the debentures were issued. The financing plan was designed to give the issuer financing flexibility. The indentures are subject to New York contract law. *Franklin Life Ins. Co. v. Commonwealth Edison Co.*, 451 F. Supp. 602 (S.D. Ill. 1978), interpreted similar language to allow early redemption when the redemption proceeds came from a common stock offering. In *Franklin*, the prospectus noted that the money raised was intended to provide the company with interim construction financing, the total cost of which would require raising additional capital. The additional capital was subsequently raised at rates below that promised under the debenture agreement. Commonwealth Edison then announced it would be redeeming the preferred stock with proceeds obtained from its common stock offering. Franklin brought suit, making the same allegations as Morgan Stanley (P) does here. The district court rejected Franklin's claims, finding that the stock offering proceeds were being used to finance the redemption and that any lower-cost borrowing was not relevant. The court focused on the fact that the source of the redemption funds was the stock offering. The plaintiff here asks the court to reject this "source" rule, contending that the court should reexamine the contract provisions and give them a new meaning. However, no other plain meaning can be reached. Because the language is boilerplate, it is difficult to justify imposing any ambiguities against the drafter. Also, both parties had access to sophisticated counsel who could ask for clarifications in the contract. Morgan Stanley (P) knew the uncertainties involved with early redemption when it purchased the debentures. Even though *Franklin* was decided under Illinois law, it is the sole existing precedent and the parties could have predicted it would affect any subsequent decision on the same issue. Given the paramount importance of uniform interpretation of boilerplate language, the court should follow *Franklin*. Summary judgment granted.

Analysis:

Problems dealing with early redemption appear to be common in the bond market. Corporations use a variety of techniques to get around early redemption when current interest rates make it favorable to escape from high-interest obligation bonds. Several methods corporations have used are described in James E. Spiotto, *Early Redemption and Leveraged Buyouts*, 304 Prac. L. Inst. 511 (Jan. 11, 1988). When corporations have financial obligations that have turned into financial suicide, companies may even engage in deliberate actions leading to a default. Once default has been established, the issuers are *required* to redeem under the default provisions, and it is not important where the issuer obtained the funds or how much they paid for them.

■ CASE VOCABULARY

CALL: To redeem (a bond) before maturity.

REDEMPTION: The reacquisition of a security by the issuer. Redemption usually refers to the repurchase of a bond before maturity, but it may also refer to the repurchase of stock and mutual-fund stocks.

SINKING FUND: A fund consisting of regular deposits that are accumulated with interest to pay off a long-term corporate or public debt.

SINKING FUND DEBENTURE: A debenture that is secured by periodic payments into a fund established to retire long-term debt.